Narrating the Holocaust

Narrating the Holocaust

ANDREA REITER

Translated by PATRICK CAMILLER

CONTINUUM

London and New York

in association with the European Jewish Publication Society

Continuum
Wellington House, 125 Strand, London WC2R 0BB
370 Lexington Avenue, New York, NY 10017–6503

The European Jewish Publication Society
PO Box 19948
London N3 3ZJ

First published 2000

Originally published in German as *"Auf daß sie entsteigen der Dunkelheit": Die
literarische Bewältigung von KZ-Erfahrung* © Löcker Verlag, Vienna, 1995.
This translation © Patrick Camiller 2000
Epilogue © Andrea Reiter 2000

British Library Cataloguing-in-Publication Data
A catalogue record for this book is available from the British Library.

ISBN 0–8264–4736–8 (hardback)
   0–8264–4737–6 (paperback)

Library of Congress Cataloging-in-Publication Data
Reiter, Andrea Ilse Maria, 1957–
   ["Auf dass sie entsteigen der Dunkelheit". English]
   Narrating the Holocaust / by Andrea Reiter; translated by Patrick
   Camiller.
      p. cm.
   Includes bibliographical references (p.).
   ISBN 0-8264-4736-8 — ISBN 0-8264-4737-6 (pbk.)
   1. Literature, Modern—20th century—History and criticism.
2. Holocaust, Jewish (1939–1945) in literature. 3. Holocaust, Jewish
(1939–1945)—Psychological aspects. 4. Concentration camps in
literature. I. Title.

PN56.H55 R4513 2000
809'.93358—dc21   00-022678

Typeset by York House Typographic Ltd, London
Printed and bound in Great Britain by Biddles Ltd, Guildford and King's
Lynn

Contents

Acknowledgements

The present work is intended as an analysis of survival strategies as they manifest themselves in written texts. Interviews have therefore not been used as a research instrument. I did, however, have informal conversations as well as correspondence with a number of Austrian survivors or their descendants – for example, Frau Mali Fritz, Herr Kurt Langbein, Herr Dr Viktor Matejka and Herr Gerhard Heilig – and I should like to thank them here for their willingness to pass on information. I also owe a debt of gratitude to Herr Herbert Exenberger of the Documentary Archive of the Austrian Resistance for his ever-prompt supply of material, to Professors Karlheinz Rossbacher and Karl Müller for their constructive criticism, and to the Österreichische Forschungsgemeinschaft for its financial support. For the translation grant, thanks are due to the Austrian government, the Austrian Cultural Institute in London and the European Jewish Publication Society (EJPS). Last but not least, I should like to thank John Mountford for looking over the translation.

Andrea Reiter

Note for the Reader

Most of the source references are given in the text itself. The names of authors of primary sources are shown in bold.

For Bill

Gegen Vergessen

Ich will mich erinnern	I want to remember
daß ich nicht vergessen will	that I want not to forget
denn ich will ich sein	for I want to be I
Ich will mich erinnern	And I want to remember
daß ich vergessen will	that I want to forget
denn ich will nicht zuviel leiden	for I want not to suffer too much
Ich will mich erinnern	I want to remember
daß ich nicht vergessen will	that I want not to forget
daß ich vergessen will	that I want to forget
denn ich will mich kennen	for I want to know myself
Denn ich kann nicht denken	For I cannot think
ohne mich zu erinnern	without remembering
denn ich kann nicht wollen	for I cannot want
ohne mich zu erinnern	without remembering
denn ich kann nicht lieben	for I cannot love
denn ich kann nicht hoffen	for I cannot hope
denn ich kann nicht vergessen	for I cannot forget
ohne mich zu erinnern	without remembering
Ich will mich erinnern	I want to remember
an alles was man vergißt	all that one forgets
denn ich kann nicht retten	for I cannot save
ohne mich zu erinnern	without remembering
auch mich nicht und nicht meine Kinder	not myself and not my children
Ich will mich erinnern	I want to remember
an die Vergangenheit und an die Zukunft	the past and the future
und ich will mich erinnern	and I want to remember
wie bald ich vergessen muß	how soon I must forget
und ich will mich erinnern	and I want to remember
wie bald ich vergessen sein werde	how soon I shall be forgotten

Erich Fried

Introduction

What is the justification for a literary study to occupy itself with texts which, for good reason, have not mainly been classified as 'literary'? Should these not rather be entrusted to historians who can gauge their objective importance in the light of the facts contained within them, or perhaps to the champions of 'history from below' whose attention will be caught by the subjective importance of the texts?

At a time when attempts are being made to derive new significance from the 'compensatory function' of the human sciences (Odo Marquard, 1988), some encouragement may be found in the thoroughly existential (that is, life-prolonging or life-securing) quality of literature, even when the circumstances that produced the literature were horrific in the extreme. Least of all in these texts, where individual fates conjure up a whole epoch in a way that is likely to get under the reader's skin, should the act of narration itself be underestimated. And yet, it would be wrong to limit ourselves to a perspective of compensation. For the testimony of former prisoners of Nazi concentration camps has a quite distinctive quality that holds up even in terms of the literary canon; it represents an attempt to compensate in literature for a life that has been degraded or taken away. Only in this sense is there some justification for speaking here of compensation.

From the point of view of the study of history, the testimony largely consists of primary memories of events expressed in language. The fact that participants and reporters are one and the same places their accounts in a metahistorical perspective (Koselleck, 8/1989: 658–60). The questions of when, by whom, and from what viewpoint the story is being told – questions which, so to

1

speak, determine historiography 'from the outside' – become of central significance in the textual analysis characteristic of literary studies (cf. Stanzel, 1985). But do they have a crucial influence upon the process of linguistic expression itself, whose conditions and possibilities are a topic of critical discussion in the present work?

Which linguistic devices, which genres, do the survivors rely upon to communicate their experiences? How does literature in the broadest sense, and language and genre more narrowly, become a means of coming to terms with life? The greatest debt of these former camp inmates, we may say, is to a tradition of discourse about the authorial self that stretches back to the Middle Ages. From its mystical antecedents onwards, the autobiographical genre has changed time and again to take account of the most recent experience of life. This does, however, considerably limit the representation of reality. Formal literary traditions threaten to annul the individuality and the specificity of experiences such as those in concentration camps. The same is true of language: on the one hand, it is possible to communicate only in language and with its help; on the other hand, language stores meanings that modify what is being stated. Since 'change in language occurs more slowly than the ... consequences of events' (Koselleck, 8/1989: 668), the capacity of language to represent reality simultaneously limits its authenticity. If it is accepted that language grounds and structures thought and therefore perception, this awareness also has repercussions on experience itself. In the end, it would seem that authentic experience is overlaid with conventional (that is, linguistic) patterns. As we shall see, this may to some extent be demonstrated in the metaphorical language employed by survivors. Thus, in our analysis of the linguistic patterns that ordinary people – ordinary people, in particular – bring to the literary field to communicate their memories, a critique of experience will always be implied.

One would assume that literary theory would be interested in texts such as the personal recollections of former camp inmates, especially when its special concern is with questions of literary production or the relationship between fact and fiction. Surprisingly, however, this is not at all the case.[1] A glance at the last quarter of a century shows that the literary study of authentic first-hand accounts has by no means kept pace with the generally increased attention of historians to the Nazi period, which began with the opening of the archives in the 1960s and the lifting of taboos as one generation succeeded another. The most extensive research in this field has always been in the United States, where a series of monographs and articles have been published since the mid-1970s, mainly by specialists in English literature or Jewish studies. One of the first to take up the theme was Lawrence Langer, in *The Holocaust and the Literary Imagination* (1975), *The Age of Atrocity: Death in Modern Literature* (1978), *Versions of Survival: The Holocaust and the Human Spirit* (1982) and *Holocaust Testimonies: The Ruins of Memory* (1991). Although Langer's publications set the standard until very recently and largely determined the questions being asked in American research, they have one obvious weakness. Since Langer measures the text against what actually happened, he overlooks the epistemological consequences of expressing something in writing (Koselleck, 8/1989: 669f.), namely, that the linguistic form of the story takes priority over the event itself. For this reason his approach keeps tending towards moralistic criticism of the survivors. As his most recent book shows, his research is also marked by the deeply pessimistic view that survivors – and *a fortiori* those who read their accounts – cannot learn anything even from the most terrible experiences, so devoid was the Holocaust of all meaning. Any attempt to deny this, even by survivors, Langer treats as ideologically suspect. For he does not think that what happened can lead survivors to discover any deeper truths; the meaninglessness of the death camps extends to written testimony about them.

> How is it possible, without violating the complex and contradictory truths of Auschwitz and the other death camps, to create out of such uncompromising material a literature celebrating the growth of the human spirit? ... Heroic defiance, growing into tragic insight, needs a vision of moral order to nourish it, and this is precisely what the Holocaust universe lacks. (Langer, 1982: 85)

Langer appears not to notice that, although earlier persecutions of the Jews (not least those recorded in the Bible) did not reach the level of those in Nazi Germany, his conclusion should, to be consistent, also apply to them in some degree.

Except in one of his most recent books, *Holocaust Testimonies* (1991), where he confines himself to analysis of documentary material (taped interviews with survivors), Langer does not draw a sharp dividing line between the testimony of victims and other texts about the annihilation of the Jews. Nor does he distinguish between the millions of Jews who were sent directly to the gas chambers as they arrived in the camps, and those who had some slender chance of survival, if only as slave labourers forced to work under degrading conditions. For the former, any question of meaning is certainly beside the point – or anyway would be extremely difficult to answer – but this does not at all mean that it was not posed for the latter group. Since Langer cannot, however, accept the will to survive as a legitimate factor in survival, it is difficult for him to see the force of this distinction.

Langer mainly illustrates his criticisms by reference to the work of Bruno Bettelheim and Viktor Frankl. He accuses them of using linguistic devices from the sphere of 'normal' life to interpret a meaningless death as meaningful, whereas the idealization of human dignity no longer had any relevance in face of the naked struggle for survival. Whatever truth there may be in this criticism – especially in the case of Bettelheim, who was released from Buchenwald in 1939 and had no direct experience of a death camp – Langer appears not to realize that attitudes such as Frankl's or Bettelheim's may have played a contributory, if not ultimately decisive, role in their survival as individuals. Only their (later) generalization to the whole camp population is questionable. Many first-hand accounts show that, although survival chances may have been crucially affected by such factors as the period of arrival in the camp, they also depended upon the person's physical and psychological constitution and, often enough, on sheer good luck. Langer fails to take into account that survival was ultimately not a mass but an individual phenomenon, and therefore different in each instance. Traditional models could to a certain extent provide a basis for hopes of survival.

For Terence Des Pres, whose book *The Survivor: An Anatomy of Life in the Death Camps* (1976) is approvingly mentioned by Langer in contrast to the recollections of former inmates, the individual plays an incomparably greater role in survival. He is thus able to recognize individually compensatory modes of behaviour and to grasp them as 'experience of growth and purification' (*ibid.*: 20). Des Pres also accepts that survival involved preservation of the individual's humanity – which is important, because the internees thereby actively countered the wholesale dehumanization that was the explicit purpose of detention in the camps – and that the will to survive was directly bound up with the idea of bearing witness.

In 1978 Alvin Rosenfeld and Irving Greenberg published *Confronting the Holocaust: The Impact of Elie Wiesel*, which included, as well as their own introductory pieces, contributions by Sidra Ezrahi and Elie Wiesel, and others. Since the essays largely deal with fictional texts, they are not directly relevant to our investigation – except that Rosenfeld's introduction anticipates some major points in his book that appeared two years later, *A Double Dying: Reflections on Holocaust Literature* (1980). He is one of the most forceful critics of the Auschwitz metaphor: '*There are no metaphors for Auschwitz, just as Auschwitz is not a metaphor for anything else*' (*ibid.*: 19; emphasis in the original). In the English-speaking countries, it was in fact quite late – following the Vietnam experience or the anti-racism debate – that Auschwitz first became a metaphor for Judaeocide. Originally, 'Buchenwald' had served this function in the United States, and 'Belsen' in Britain. In Germany, on the other hand, 'Auschwitz' had stood for the Nazi murder of the Jews and hence for all the other camps at least since the publication of Theodor W. Adorno's *Minima Moralia* in 1951, which had theorized it as 'a caesura or irredeemable break in the history of civilization'.[2] In the late 1960s, the students in revolt took up 'Auschwitz' as an argument against their parents' generation.[3] Only in recent years – in his polemic against the unification of the two German states – has Günter Grass taken the position that the former unitary state was the 'precondition of Auschwitz'.[4] Hence, in Grass's view, Auschwitz stands metonymically for the horrors of a German past that is forever catching up with the present.

In 1984 David Roskies's *Against the Apocalypse: Responses to Catastrophe in Modern Jewish Culture* introduced a paradigm shift in American studies on the literature of the Holocaust. In relating this literature to apocalyptic and other archetypes in the Jewish tradition, he broke with his predecessors' ban on metaphor and cleared the path for detailed linguistic investigation; criticism of the survivors made way for criticism of the texts. Roskies shows how the Holocaust, as the latest and most deadly persecution of the Jews, requires the development of new archetypes – or has

itself become an archetype. This contradicts the previous con-
sensus in US Holocaust research that any symbolic or
metaphorical analysis falls short of the experience of Auschwitz
and should therefore be considered inadmissible. Roskies is much
closer to Des Pres's view that, in an extreme situation, anything at
all can become a symbol; that, in the shadow of the gas chambers,
metaphors lost their status as images and stood for nothing other
than themselves (Des Pres, 1976: 67f.).

James Young's more recent contribution on the subject, *Writing
and Rewriting the Holocaust: Narrative and the Consequence of
Interpretation* (1988), is indebted to Roskies and others, but also to
Barbara Foley's essay 'Fact, Fiction, Fascism: Testimony and
Mimesis' (1982), which offers a critique of the genre. Foley
classifies the Holocaust literature into four groups: personal recollections, realist novels, non-realist novels and pseudo-factual
accounts. She argues that the latter is the most appropriate
medium for Holocaust material, both because it avoids con-
demnatory moralizing and because it opens up the concrete
historical situation to the reader's imagination, without diminishing the significance of what actually happened.

Young has a broader understanding of the portrayal of the
Holocaust. Alongside linguistic analysis, he is also motivated by
post-structuralist concerns with stone monuments as texts.
Museums and memorials, which in Europe, Israel and more
recently the United States maintain the memory of the Judaeocide, suggest the idea of the *Gesamtkunstwerk* as alone capable of
conveying the horrific events at once comprehensively and
comprehensibly.

While drawing upon new theories in the field of history, Young
engages more than his older colleagues with the specificity of the
text. His attention is directed at the distinctive quality or factual-
ness of memory. This partly overlaps with the research interests of
the present book, although here a wide range of survivor testimony will highlight the further step from memory to
representation.

Of the works produced on the subject in Israel, in particular one
should mention Sidra DeKoven Ezrahi's *By Words Alone: The
Holocaust in Literature* (1980). For DeKoven, as for Roskies, the
aim is to set Holocaust literature in the perspective of Jewish
responses to catastrophe. But whereas Roskies limits himself to

the documented testimony of East European Jews, DeKoven widens her base to include Yiddish, Hebrew and European literature of the Holocaust.

Israeli studies share with American ones a focus on the texts of Jewish survivors, either neglecting or only briefly touching upon material produced by political and other victims of persecution. This selectiveness has its effect on the textual interpretation. For, whatever the analyst's point of view, he or she usually discusses the personal testimony as a sacred text (in the sense of the Bible) and interprets the suffering and death of the Jews in the camps as a directly religious event. To this end, researchers adopt Hebrew expressions such as *sho'ah* or *churban*, considering them more appropriate than the Greek term *holocaust* for the distinctively Jewish suffering. Although this now widely accepted Greek expression lacks something in clarity of focus, and may even be misleading, the suggested substitutes introduce a general meaning which, as we have seen, many researchers rightly or wrongly do not wish to accept.

A special place should be accorded to Claude Lanzmann's film *Shoah*. The title already establishes the programme: Lanzmann does not want his work – in the manner of the Hollywood film *Holocaust*, for example – to bring the story of the persecution and murder of the Jews into everyone's living room, to recall and situate it as a past occurrence. Rather, *Shoah* is a work of art which attempts to create a 'counter-myth' – that is, to 'call to mind' the Holocaust there and then, or rather here and now, in and through the words of survivors (cf. Lanzmann, 1996: 12). One might well criticize Lanzmann for the ways in which he obtained information, or for his restriction of the Shoah to the death camps, but he does succeed in presenting a more extensive picture than the methods of literary studies allow.

In German-speaking Europe, no major studies were published on the theme until the late 1980s. There are three worth mentioning, all of them academic works such as dissertations or postdoctoral theses. In order of publication, they are: Michael Moll, *Lyrik in einer entmenschlichten Welt. Interpretationsversuche zu deutschsprachigen Gedichten aus nationalsozialistischen Gefängnissen, Ghettos und KZ's* (1988) ('Lyric Poetry in a Dehumanized World: Interpretations of German-language Verse from Nazi Prisons, Ghettos and Concentration Camps'); Birgit Kröhle, *Geschichte und Geschichten. Die literarische Verarbeitung von Auschwitz-Erlebnissen* (1989) ('History and Stories: The Literary Treatment of Auschwitz Experiences'); and Helmut Peitsch, *Deutschlands Gedächtnis an seine dunkelste Zeit. Zur Funktion der Autobiographik in den Westzonen Deutschlands und den Westsektoren von Berlin 1945 bis 1949* (1990) ('Remembering Germany in Its Darkest Period: On the Function of Autobiographical Writing in the Western Zones of Germany and the Western Sectors of Berlin, 1945 to 1949'). As the descriptive titles indicate, these works deal either with a particular genre (lyric poetry, autobiography), or with a particular period (1945–49), or with a particular aspect of interpretation (the fictional treatment of historical events). They were preceded by a few essays, such as Adorno's 'Erziehung nach Auschwitz' (1966) ('Education after Auschwitz'), Reinhard Baumgart's 'Unmenschlichkeit beschreiben' (1966) ('Depicting Inhumanity'), and Martin Walser's 'Unser Auschwitz' (1968) ('Our Auschwitz').

Undoubtedly one of the most thought-provoking contributions to the field is *The Order of Terror: The Concentration Camp*, a work reminiscent of Michel Foucault, first published in German in 1993 by the sociologist Wolfgang Sofsky. This book, which has its origins in a postdoctoral thesis, interprets the 'phenomenon' of the concentration camp in terms of the theorem of absolute power. This basis and precondition of the terror differentiated it from all previous forms of repression:

> Absolute power goes on a rampage whenever it so desires. It does not wish to limit freedom, but to destroy it. It does not seek to guide action, but to demolish it. It drains human beings, depleting them by labour both useful and senseless. It sets economic goals from which it then breaks free. It liberates itself from ideological convictions, after first having organized camp society in accordance with its ideological model of social classes. Even killing, the final reference point of all power, is not sufficient. Absolute power transforms the universal structures of human relatedness to the world: space and time, social relations, the connection with work, the relation to the self. It seizes on various elements and methods of traditional forms of power, combining and intensifying them, while casting off their instrumentality. In this way, it becomes a form of power of a distinctive, singular kind. (Sofsky, 1997: 18)

Sofsky's thesis casts an illuminating light upon Hannah Arendt's dictum about the banality of evil: that modern organizational structures can dispense with out-and-out villains. The interweaving of central command and extensive vertical delegation that even put pressure on the designated victims to play along; the specific tie-up of standardization and deregulation; above all, the ideologically and often also geographically defined distance between perpetrators and victims: it was these which enabled the concentration camp to operate as a well-run business. On the other hand, the camp regime of terror – precisely because it had not been planned and ordered in its finer detail – left plenty of scope for collective or individual excesses. Indeed, personal initiative was built into the calculus of the dissemination of terror.

With the help of the theorem of absolute power, it becomes possible for the first time to explain certain aspects of the concentration camp in their interconnection. Thus absolute power instrumentalizes space and time, overdetermines the social structures of the interned population, strips work of its economic utility, and brings death under its sway through the arbitrary exercise of violence.[5]

What unites most of the research on the literature of the Holocaust, despite the underlying differences of focus and problematic, is the fact that their framework is never exclusively that of literary studies. Accompanying work in history is unavoidable, but so are considerations from the field of psychology. It is precisely the analysis of how experience is related to the testimony of experience – an analysis attempted in the present study – which suggests comparison with the work of the psychotherapist. And the fact that survival itself had something to do with the psychological make-up of individual inmates, is confirmed not least by the testimony of psychologists such as Bruno Bettelheim and Viktor Frankl.

However strong the link between language and the mind, psychologization is to be avoided in literary studies because the text should as far as possible constitute the focus of attention and debate. Problems of genre or fictionality will therefore be addressed here with the help of case studies, while aspects of communicability and the linguistic tradition will be illustrated with a multiplicity of briefer references. The aim is to strike a balance between continuous description of a few selected texts and partial citation of most of the rest.

The research base is some 130 texts that appeared in book form between 1934 and the late 1980s, most of them by authors writing in German. But the testimony of German and Austrian *émigrés* who have published work in English is also considered, and some translations of important testimony in Polish, Italian and French are used to put the conclusions in perspective. The study examines previously published material, as well as unpublished manuscripts in the keeping of the Leo Baeck Institute in New York.

Although, in the past two decades, a number of texts have appeared for the first time or again become available in print, the greater part of the earlier texts in particular can no longer be consulted except in relevant collections such as the Wiener Library in London. In so far as the facts are available, a biographical appendix tries to tackle the problem that most of the authors discussed here are unknown.

Notes

1. Since I completed my research for the German edition of this book, cultural theorists have become interested in these texts. See, for example: Michael Roth, *The Ironist's Cage: Memory, Trauma, and the Construction of History*, New York: Columbia University Press, 1995; Aleida Assmann and Manfred Windisch *et al.* (eds), *Medien des Gedächtnisses: Deutsche Vierteljahresschrift für Literaturwissenschaft und Geistesgeschichte* (special issue, 1998).
2. Quoted in Günter Grass, 'Schreiben nach Auschwitz', *Die Zeit*, 23 February 1990.
3. Gudrun Ensslin, for example, declared to her fellow students: 'You can't talk to them, they're the Auschwitz generation.' Quoted in Karl-Heinz Janszen, 'Die Revolution der '68er I: Die große Wut', *Zeit-Magazin 24*, 5 June 1992, p. 16.
4. Günter Grass, 'Kurze Rede eines vaterlandlosen Gesellen', *Die Zeit*, 9 February 1990.
5. Since the completion of the research for the German edition of this book some important studies on the subject have appeared, for example, Dominick La Capra, *History and Memory after Auschwitz*, Cornell: Cornell University Press, 1998.

1

Communication

He [i.e., generic man] cannot live his life without expressing his life.
(Ernst Cassirer, *An Essay on Man*)

'It is good to tell about things,' said the old man suddenly. 'I survived the camp because I wanted to tell about it. But words are like ships: they go under if the load gets too big.'
('Am Strand von Israel', *profil* 33, 17 August 1987)

All representation – whether in picture, word or sound – is a compromise with chaos.
(Bernard Berenson, *Sehen und Wissen*)

In this study of the literary recollections of former concentration camp prisoners, the main concern is not with the what but with the how of communication, not with the facts as such but with the ways and forms in which the experience is communicated.[1] The reservations about memoirs expressed by Hans Magnus Enzensberger (Enzensberger, 1990) do not apply in this study, where the key question is *how* the respective authors handle the linguistic reworking of their experience in the camps. Our investigation will be concerned to examine, above all, each author's selection of experiences, their mode of ordering in the text, and the form of speech in which they are presented (Peitsch, 1990: 30). The period of composition, and the intended effect, will also be of significance.

An attempt is thus made to gain access to the individual through language – an approach that has parallels to the psycho-analyst's concern to trace the meaning of a communication through symbolic modes of expression (Lorenzer, 1973: 87f.; Gebhardt, J. 1980: 48–57). Although we too are mainly interested

11

in the psychological rather than the logical meaning of the testimony (Peitsch, 1990: 138), the differences with the situation of the analyst are quite evident. In the first place, the survivors themselves seek through the act of writing to gain greater awareness of the conditions and background to their detention. Not only does the literary specialist have to do with things put down in writing, he can assume that the writer's cognitive interest was consonant with his own. He analyses the linguistic structures of the testimony, in order to clarify whether and how, in each case, language assisted survival and a coming to terms with the concentration camp – or, in other words, how the former prisoners ascribed a certain meaning to their experiences by means of the text. While due consideration will be given to sociological and strictly linguistic aspects, our main concern will be with the connection between narrative structure and its function (cf. Peitsch, 1990: 22).

The nature of the experiences of camp inmates makes it difficult for a reader to understand their testimony, since there is no 'stock of communicated anticipations' common to author and recipient, and – more important still – the latter is excluded from 'participation in the [former's] life practice' (Peitsch, 1990: 197). Even if he tries to imagine himself in the same situation, he can never do more than approximate to the author's intended meaning.

The prisoners themselves faced the problem of having to insert into a horizon of meaning a set of experiences that seemed to be completely without meaning. Only in very few cases did survivors articulate this dilemma in writing, but certain conclusions can be drawn from the way in which they handled questions of language and genre. For although the constitution of meaning is subject to the variables of situation and time, genre and language have a potential that may be of help to the individual in the production of meaning.

The premise of the communicability of experience

Even if the firmament above us were made of parchment and the seas were full of ink; even if all trees were feathers and the Earth's inhabitants all writers; and even if they wrote day and night – they would not be capable of describing the greatness and the radiance of the world's creator.

Fifty years separate me from that Pentecost when the young boy recited those opening lines of the long Aramaic poem faithfully handed down from generation to generation, together with an unalterable oral commentary. My memory of that poetry reading always grows lively when I am forced to realize that we will never succeed in explaining the Churban, the Jewish catastrophe of our times, to those who will live on after us.

(Manès Sperber, *Churban oder Die unfaßbare Gewißheit*)

The communicability of lived experience concerns both the level of production and the level of reception. Although experience is always already marked by language (cf. Gadamer, 1989: 383; Habermas, 1984: 94), its communication was a problem for camp inmates that is also reflected in their testimony. The incompatibility between the experience and the affected person's capacity to report it is due to the fact that 'real events do not offer themselves in the form of stories' (White, 1987: 4). The language of experience therefore requires suitable adaptation to intersubjectivity in order to function in the act of communication; it is geared to the recipient in terms of both expressiveness and comprehensibility. In the case of concentration camp survivors, however, there is a further dimension of credibility. Already in the camps, when they had listened to the testimony of fellow-victims, they had realized how difficult it was to understand an experience if they had not lived it themselves. And Jews who managed to escape deportation to a camp could scarcely believe what little they heard in their place of hiding; they protected themselves in this way from total despair, as Inge Deutschkron has convincingly testified (**Deutschkron**, 1978: 129). Later, when the testimony was being written down, the inadequacy of language had to be even more clearly recognized.

The quite exceptional nature of the camp experiences places heavy demands on the expressive powers of language, constantly threatening the survivors' testimony with failure. In their case especially – and certainly more than in that of any 'realist' literature – a text fulfils its potential only through the activity of its readers, who can always protect themselves from the immensity of it all by denying its authenticity and reading it as fiction (cf. Moll, 1988: 96–8). The author is unable to prevent his or her quite literal account from being taken as metaphorical, particularly as the very character of the narrated events encourages a reaction of disbelief on the part of the recipient (cf. Wiesenthal, 1988: 285). For this reason, many survivors later felt themselves belittled and fell silent. The cynical reaction of the post-war world kept Mali Fritz, for example, from reporting on Auschwitz until a very short time ago. How can I present the horrors of my concentration camp detention in a way that makes them credible? How can I make it clear that someone might survive the camp without becoming a collaborator, yet still be marked by it for life? These were the questions with which she wrestled for many years, before she finally found a solution in writing about 'what remained spared to her'. Her family's survival, her luck and good fortune helped her to live through the camp (**Fritz**, 1986: 137–9).[2] Lucie Adelsberger already anticipated, while she was still in a camp, the doubt that would creep into the minds of future readers of her testimony:

> Many [readers] will lay aside such terrible accounts with a feeling of nausea … Others, not wishing to see that the reality in Auschwitz concentration camp exceeded the capacities of the human imagination, will treat the testimony as a propagandistic invention. This is precisely what makes it possible to accept my time in the camp. If such things actually happen in the world, one must see them with one's own eyes – otherwise people will not believe them or else draw away out of a wish for a quiet life. (**Adelsberger**, 1956: 65f)

Adelsberger expresses understanding for this incredulity, recognizes its causes, and even draws from it some meaning for the time she is still spending in the camp. Of course, the satisfaction of (scientific) curiosity can hardly have been the standard reaction of those detained in the camps. Even if psychologists among them, such as Viktor Frankl or Bruno Bettelheim, tried to remain conscious of everything that was happening, in order later to turn it to scientific account, many former prisoners speak of their unwillingness to believe the mass murder and other things that so contradicted their previous experience of life. For such events called into question their moral values and convictions, and hence ultimately their understanding of civilized humanity. Self-protection required new arrivals at Auschwitz to fend off reports of selection parades, gas chambers and crematoria. They trusted instead, like Margareta Glas-Larsson, in the logic of ordinary life: 'I said that all the stories being told were untrue. It could not be true that people were being killed, in a war for which everyone was

needed' (**Glas-Larsson**, 1981: 121). Future deportees had themselves dismissed reports of what was being done in the
concentration camps, because these threatened totally to shatter
their faith in the world (**Begov**, 1983: 14). But this meant that
they were psychologically quite unprepared to cope with the
'admission shock' on arrival (**Frankl**, 1977). If this blindness was
kept up even in the camp, it often led in the end to despair at
reality. Filip Müller, who was one of the few members of an
Auschwitz *Sonderkommando* to survive, observed this in those
transferred to Auschwitz from the so-called family camp at
Theresienstadt:

> When they were still living in the Family Camp they had heard many
> a tale about these strange rooms [i.e., the gas chambers and cremato-
> ria]; but then, despite much obvious proof, they did not wish to know
> about them. Now they were here themselves and realized, too late,
> that all they had heard was indeed true. (**F. Müller**, 1979: 108)

Fredy Hirsch, who looked after the Theresienstadt children in
Auschwitz, was so desperate when the truth finally dawned on
him that he committed suicide just before they were taken off to
the gas chambers (cf. Adler, 1960: 56). It would appear that self-
deception could serve a protective function only so long as the
prisoner's own life, or that of others in his care, was not in
immediate danger. This is confirmed by the case of Adam Czerniaków, the chairman of the Jewish Council in the Warsaw Ghetto,
who committed suicide in 1942 when the deportations started to
the death camps (cf. Gilbert, 1986: 390). However great the
external resemblance to resignation in the face of evil, there is this
difference that Czerniaków and Hirsch felt compelled to end their
own life when they were instructed to hand over the children in
their care. Unlike Hirsch, Czerniaków may still have had some
capability of resistance – as Tzvetan Todorov points out in
reproach (Todorov, 1993: 254). But the views of historians are
divided about this (Loewy, 1990: 44).

Even when they were enlisted to get rid of the traces of mass
murder, many prisoners refused to believe that it was happening.
It seems reasonable to assume that this reaction was driven by the
will to survive. For Simha Naor it was mixed with feelings of guilt
towards her slaughtered co-religionists: 'I did not want to think
about it,' she writes about the mass murder. 'I did not want to

admit what is now a certainty: that we were shovelling human ashes, that I went on and on shovelling, faster and faster. You got to eat your little titbits, you were even glad to be still alive – for how much longer?' (**Naor**, 1986: 59).

Mali Fritz explains sociologically the unwillingness that she observed in prisoners at the women's camp in Ravensbruck to recognize the fact of mass annihilation. She thinks that this was a result of the family situation from which the girls and women had come. The reality of the camp was too difficult for them to face, because their 'relation to the outside world . . . had in most cases been mediated by their father, brother or husband. Once separated from that reference figure, they felt abandoned and their distress weakened them a great deal' (**Fritz**, 1986: 42).

Survivors, then, see self-protection, guilt feelings and role socialization as the reasons why they were unwilling to face up to the fact of mass annihilation. But it was incomparably more difficult to reach a common understanding about the experiences with people who had not been directly affected by them. If hermeneutic understanding is determined by 'the context in which the understanding subject initially acquired his patterns of interpretation' (Habermas, 1971: 122f.), it is astonishing that any attempt at all is made to communicate an experience such as that of the concentration camps. For survivors – many of whom realized it only when they sat down to write – the special difficulty of communication consisted in the fact that the camp conditions brought about a change in the meanings of concepts and largely annulled the 'intersubjectivity of language' (Apel, 1980: 10). Witnesses such as Antonia Bruha thus find fault with historical accounts of the camps, on the grounds that they do not do justice to the suffering individuals who were actually involved. Academics merely 'see the statistics, and figures do not feel pain' (**Bruha**, 1984: 101).[3]

The consternation of the victims themselves is naturally the greatest language-barrier. Even when they let many years pass before reporting their experiences, the distance can be too small for them. This, as Michael Moll points out, is what makes it difficult for historians to read the texts as documents (Moll, 1988: 87). On the other hand, the cognitive interest of the literary specialist in genuine experience actually presupposes a textual situation of this kind.

Now and again, however, the need to face the camp conditions makes more demands on the authors than they are able to bear. Lina Haag complains: 'It is beyond my power to write all those horrifying things down, although they should be written down so that they are never forgotten' (**Haag**, 1985: 179). Mali Fritz, too, says that she wrestled desperately with language in trying to present her experiences.[4] Isa Vermehren reports similar difficulties, although she does not seem to focus quite so much on herself. More concerned with questions of personal morality, she explains the problem of communication in terms of 'the observer's lazy superficiality, which closed itself off from reality so as not to have to accept the truth contained within it' (**Vermehren**, 1979: 66).

The difficulty of subsequently facing the reality of the camp is reflected with special clarity when it comes to describing painful experiences. Perhaps more than anything else in the camp, it was torture which shattered the prisoners in both body and mind. The memory of physical pain and associated feelings of humiliation make it difficult for those in question to express themselves about it. If they nevertheless bring themselves to testify, they may, like Jean Améry, do so with reservations:

> It would be senseless to try to describe here the pain inflicted on me. Was it 'like a scorching iron in my shoulder' or was it 'like a blunt wooden stake stuck in the back of my head'? – one comparative image would merely stand for another, and in the end we would be pulled around in the hopeless carousel of figurative speech. The pain was what it was. There is nothing more to say about it. Types of feeling are as impossible to compare as they are to describe. They mark the limits of the capacity to communicate in language. Someone who wanted to communicate his physical pain would have to inflict it and thus become a torturer himself. (**Améry**, 1980: 63)

Améry therefore describes only the methods of torture that caused his pain, not the pain itself. Kurt Hiller does the same, for the same reasons (**Hiller**, 1934/35: 17). Both are of the view that there are neither words nor images for the pain they experienced – and indeed, that it would be not only inappropriate but derisory to try to approximate the experience in words.

Other survivors, less self-aware than Améry or Hiller, think that they have to apologize for their linguistic impotence. Images such as 'hell' or 'satanic power' can, in the view of Floris Bakels, do only poor justice to his memories of the camp (**Bakels**, 1977: 79).

Besides, it was hardly demonic monsters who guarded and harried the prisoners, but quite ordinary warders and torturers (cf. Sofsky, 1993: 319). Bernhard Klieger even doubts the usefulness of historical or literary comparisons, although he himself – as we see in the following quotation – does not refrain from employing them:

> With what words should one describe seeing thousands of innocent young creatures dragged into the gas chambers; or seeing SS officers grab babies by the feet and smash their little heads against tree trunks; or seeing mothers stand there unable even to scream at the horror, because their mouth had remained open in mid-scream! Could I describe that? If I could, I would no longer be a man but a god. **(Klieger, 1960: 95)**

The narrating self reflects upon lived experience with the help of a well-known rhetorical device, the trope of unutterability. Klieger, of course, is already describing at the moment when he thinks about how such things can be described. Although he does not explicitly refer to it, he is also following the example of Jeremiah 31:15, which deals with the murder of the servants of Israel on King Herod's orders.

The survivors' testimony also discusses the lack of adequate linguistic means to describe the hunger they suffered and the significance that food generally had for them. Once, when Simha Naor was recovering from typhus in Auschwitz, she received from friends a package with sugar cubes and crispbread. To explain the significance of such a present in the camp, she searches in vain for a comparison in 'normal' life **(Naor, 1986: 131)**.

There are no comparisons from the world outside that could truthfully describe what was experienced in the camps. Although most of the survivors who turned to writing hold this view, they all nevertheless tried to find a language for their memories because they thought it inadmissible to remain silent about them. 'It is not possible to write well, in a literary sense, about Auschwitz,' Adorno agreed, 'yet by abdicating one becomes part of the general regression' (Adorno, 1980: 9). Witnesses therefore had to keep overcoming their resistances in order to tell of things which their persecutors had never intended to be seen in the light of day.

The similarity between the theme of incommunicability in literature about the camps and the more general trope of unutterability is strikingly confirmed by Ernst Wiechert. While affirming that he cannot begin to describe a roll call at Buchenwald, he contradicts himself in the same breath:

> then the whole thing was indeed a picture of the damned appearing phantom-like out of some underworld, or a vision from some hell that no great painter's brush or great etcher's block could ever attain, because no human phantasy and not even the dreams of a genius could ever reach as far as a reality whose like had not been seen for centuries, or indeed perhaps ever. (**Wiechert**, 1984: 81f.)

By the very act of drawing a negative comparison with images from the Christian religion (Hell) and Greek mythology (the Underworld), Wiechert expresses himself metaphorically. He thus relies on the same dialectic that characterizes the trope of unutterability: his statement that something is indescribable is itself a description.

Still, the conviction of most camp survivors that their experiences are beyond linguistic communication should be respected. The fact that 98 per cent of them have never written any testimony already speaks volumes (cf. Langer, 1982: 54).[5] As the above examples show, however, psychological and cognitive reasons must have played a role in this along with failings of language. Even after their release, the former camp inmates still had difficulty in understanding what they had lived through – sometimes they were not even sure about the real reasons for their silence about it.[6] It remains to be seen which experiences the survivors actually set down when, in spite of everything, they decided to put pen to paper.

Disruptive experiences

The testimony of concentration camp survivors differs from any other category of memoir or autobiography in covering not only the same period of time but also essentially the same causes of experience. Our analysis of these texts will be concerned not so much with their experiential content as with the ways in which individuals assess and come to terms (in language) with what they lived through in the camps. The crucial factors will be sought both in the individuals themselves (their constitution and character) and in their socialization (education, occupation, family situation and, by no means least, the precise conditions in their camp). Whereas an assessment of character and socialization has to be based upon indirect references in the texts or on occasional details provided by their author, historical research on the camps is far enough advanced to allow us to form a relatively clear picture of the objective conditions for survival (see, e.g., Broszat, 1984).

Where is it best to start the analysis of people's experiences? Peter Sloterdijk suggests taking the crisis points in the life of the individual (Sloterdijk, 1978: 112ff.). One crisis point was undoubtedly the initial internment in the concentration camp. But the multilayered nature of the camp experience means that a further differentiation needs to be made, giving a number of occasions – what Sloterdijk calls 'disruptive experiences' (Sloterdijk, 1978: 113) – which sharply diverged from the pris-oner's previous experience of life. Most of the survivors had to contend with four especially dramatic events: arrival, release, death and torture. The following sections will analyse how each of these was experienced, or rather, how each was reported in the survivors' testimony.

Arrival

The world of the concentration camp was all the further from the life of the ordinary citizen between 1933 and 1945, the more he or she had been politically and socially integrated. People who had stood out in this respect – and this applied especially to Com-munists – had always had to reckon with the possibility of internment. Bruno Bettelheim underlines the importance of prior experiences, especially with regard to social position and political convictions, in influencing how someone would face the 'primal trauma' of arrival in the camp. He distinguishes four general types of reaction to life in the camp, corresponding to the positions of: the criminal, the political prisoner, the non-political middle class, and the upper classes (Bettelheim, 1979: 56–8). It was the third of these four groups which had the greatest difficulty in finding their feet. They brought with them to the camp neither any relevant experience (like that of criminal and political prisoners), nor feelings of superiority (like those of the upper class) which might have hardened them against the injustice of the camp.

Pre-camp experience had a positive effect on individual sur-vival to the extent that social techniques learned outside could be applied there. Previous conspiratorial activity, among other things, meant that political prisoners started out with relatively the best chances.

Nevertheless, most of the prisoners – not excluding political detainees – experienced the arrival procedure in the camp as especially painful. Scarcely any reports fail to describe it. The loss of all personal possessions, civilian clothes and body hair, together with the violation of physical integrity (including tattooing in the case of Jews at Auschwitz), made new arrivals brutally aware that they had ceased to exist as individuals with a name and an identity. For many, however, their conscious mind resisted adjustment to the situation. The Dutchman Floris Bakels speaks of the radical break with his previous life that this experience meant for him (**Bakels**, 1977: 241). Lucie Begov seems to analyse quite soberly the triggering effect of this 'shock', when she writes: 'We newcomers went to one of the lower levels of extermination; it was a quarantine camp in Section A of the women's camp' at Auschwitz. But she too grew numb at the first sight of a Jewish prisoner there, who made her vividly aware of the scale of the annihilation (**Begov**, 1983: 107f.). Mali Fritz felt a similar paralysis on her arrival at Auschwitz, when she discovered what it meant to have got through the selection on the ramp (**Fritz**, 1986: 13f.). The women, in particular, find powerful metaphors for the suffering they endured as disfiguring clothes were forced upon them and their hair was shaved off. Fania Fénelon gave up her fur coat with a sense of losing the 'last contact with her past'. 'Plucked in my place,' she writes, 'I remained standing where I was amid clothes that had been strewn on the ground around me, like the skin shed by a snake' (**Fénelon**, 1977: 21). Antonia Bruha bewails the loss of identity that went with her undressing: 'Glad as I am to get rid of my dirty clothes, I feel as if I am taking off my own self, as if I am being pushed by force into an alien destiny' (**Bruha**, 1984: 90). As modern interaction theory confirms, clothing and haircuts in ordinary life are the primary attributes through which identity is communicated (Parow, 1973: 105); job and social position are of only secondary importance. It is not surprising, then, that the survivors' testimony is so concerned with physical changes. Not only did Bruha feel robbed of her identity; she also had to recognize in the end that not even a human destiny had been marked down for her (**Bruha**, 1984: 92). The Polish woman Krystyna Zywulska also came to the conclusion that she and her fellow-sufferers 'had been brought to the level of animals within the space of twenty-four hours' (**Zywulska**, 1980: 20). Historians stress that the admission shock was especially strong for women, because it violated their sense of privacy (Matussek and Grigat, 1971: 28). To have to undress among all the other prisoners and in front of the SS felt to them like a form of corporal punishment.[7]

Male prisoners were also shattered by the 'initiation rite'. Precisely because most of them were received by a group of dehumanized inmates, they were shocked at having to become part of a repulsive mass (cf. **Pawlak**, 1979: 47). Even the act of dressing again, as Siegfried Neumann testifies, did not leave them unscathed, since the prison clothing allocated to them finally tore apart their view of the world. 'Many received striped flannel suits; others, including myself, a former field-grey uniform. So now clothing that had once been respected in the world war was worn as convict's dress' (**Neumann**, 1976: 21).

If internees wanted to have the slightest chance of surviving the camp, they could not give way to this experience of shock. While others intuitively adopted the right form of behaviour, the psychologist Viktor Frankl adjusted to the new situation by making a conscious break with his former life (**Frankl**, 1977: 32). For many new arrivals, the admission experience already aroused a spirit of resistance and a belief that they must at least preserve their innermost life. This is how Lucie Adelsberger puts it:

> We were shut away from the outside world, uprooted from our homeland, torn from our family – a mere number, significant only for the camp office. Nothing was left but naked existence – for most not even that much longer – and the thoughts in our breast. Not even the SS could rob us of those, and that is all we managed to save. (**Adelsberger**, 1956: 40)

Adelsberger, being a doctor, has in mind the intellectual capacities to which she resolved to cling in her need for identity, and which she also seems to ascribe to those who were murdered immediately upon arrival in the camp. Primo Levi, on the other hand, talks of a more general feeling of resistance, as the duty of each individual to keep a part of what their earlier existence meant 'behind their [lost] name' (**Levi**, 1987a: 33).

Viktor Frankl treats behaviour on admission as the first of three phases of psychological response, a kind of barometer reading for how the individual would cope with life in the camp (**Frankl**, 1977: 26). Generalizing from observation of himself, he diagnoses an astonishing optimism in the form of a 'pardon mania'. His own testimony can scarcely, however, be considered representative of that of camp inmates in general. Many authors, it is true, report that they clung to a belief that their internment had been a misunderstanding; that this was being cleared up and they would soon be released. But this reaction was mostly limited to members of the Jewish middle classes who had arrived in the camps following the pogrom of November 1938, before the large-scale deportation of Jews began.

First impressions of the camp, as described in the survivors' testimony, are always marked by the same contradiction. Each writer states that he or she reacted with an acute speech difficulty. 'Then for the first time we became aware that our language lacks the words to express this offence, the demolition of a man' (**Levi**, 1987a: 32). Grete Salus describes the same feeling: 'Having been kitted out, we looked at one another – mute, speechless. Now we were a mass of women in rags, with nothing to distinguish one from another' (**Salus**, 1981: 21). Loss of identity is here experienced as loss of speech – which is important because, as is well known, any constitution of meaning takes place through the medium of language. Thus, if the authors perceived their helplessness in the new situation as a kind of desertion by their powers of linguistic expression, they seem in their testimony to have largely overcome that loss. While Fania Fénelon uses the image of 'a snake shedding its skin' to evoke the forced undressing, Bakels mythologizes the experience in the metaphor of a 'baptism of fire' (**Fénelon**, 1977: 21; **Bakels**, 1977: 82). By thus associating it with the 'Pentecost experience', the Christian Bakels later gives it a meaning which is compatible with his identity, and which allows him to attach a certain sense to his detention in general.

Release

Admission into the camp had its extreme counterpart in the experience of being released. For most of the writers in question, this happened only in 1945 through liberation by Allied forces – after a number of years' detention, often in more than one camp. Whereas they had not in their majority been prepared for the initial incarceration, they had naturally been longing for and picturing to themselves this recovery of freedom. It was therefore to be expected that it would have quite a different experiential value for them. On the other hand, most of the inmates had adapted so extensively to the conditions of life in the camp that release was inevitably experienced as another shock, bringing with it a new loss of identity. Usually, it was not that they had internalized the standards of the camp, but – on the contrary – that their categorical removal from life outside the camp had also distanced them from its value norms. Political prisoners, in particular, expected that their experience in the camp would make them well suited to play an important role in the construction of a new society. For certain groups, such as gypsies and homosexuals, liberation entailed only a gradual improvement in their lot, as they were not legally able to claim the status of concentration camp victims (Wiesenthal, 1988: 274). Not only were they deprived of any financial support; they even had to keep quiet about their time in the camp, for fear of renewed marginalization. It is hardly surprising, then, that homosexuals do not figure at all among the authors of literature about the camps – if one excludes a single text published under a pseudonym (**Heger**, 1980).[8] Until recently there was also no testimony on the experience of gypsies in the camps (cf. Wiesenthal, 1988: 273; **Stojka**, 1988).

All former prisoners had to cope with the sudden ending of psychological pressure, the 'total relaxation of inner tension' which, as Frankl puts it in an electrical image, followed the 'mental high tension'. This stood in the way of a swift reintegration into 'normal' life, and in more than a few cases led to fresh torments or even suicide.

It may fairly be assumed that how an individual reacted to the recovery of freedom depended upon the particular circumstances and upon his or her physical and mental constitution at the time. The return to society was also marked by gaps between expectations and the reality actually encountered there.

A distinction should be drawn between releases while the Nazi regime was still in place and the general liberation of 1945. In the late 1930s, the only Jews to be released, apart from a few political prisoners, were those who could lay their hands on an exit visa and undertake to leave the German Reich without delay (cf. **Wenke**, 1980: 174; Broszat, 1984: 80; Pingel, 1978: 94). As such people had usually spent only a short time in a camp, their release did not have such a traumatizing effect as in the case of the general liberation. Besides, they generally needed all their wits about them to arrange their departure from the country, and so it is not really surprising that they do not attach too much importance to the event in their memoirs.

Those imprisoned for criticism of the regime took their release rather differently. They had had to buy their freedom by solemnly undertaking to refrain from any political statements or actions in the future. Wolfgang Langhoff even had to sign up with a German-language theatre in a foreign country, when fortunately the Schauspielhaus in Zurich offered him an appointment (**Langhoff**, 1986: 103). For this group, the end of incarceration was a problem that they tried to tackle through literature. Langhoff, the dynamic young actor, greeted his release as a return to active life:

> I must spend one more night in the old cell. Twelve more hours. Then my wife will be there. Forebodings, desires and temptations rush in on me. It is like the night before your birthday. Tomorrow I shall be born again. Become a human being. No other thought, no other image can be captured and pinned down, no other joy conjured up. Life is roaring inside me, as I lie sleepless and count the hours struck by the Prettin church clock. (**Langhoff**, 1986: 302)

Only the thought of comrades he had to leave behind troubled Langhoff's effusive joy. In the testimony of Ernst Wiechert, however, melancholy almost entirely displaces the happiness of being free again. Unlike Langhoff, he does not promise never to forget his companions in suffering, but rather avows his fateful link with them in a 'mystical union'. Johannes, the main character in his story, had the good fortune to be out and alive:

> but it was as if he was carrying the fate of all those thousands [*sic!*] along with him. No, he had not gone through it 'like a stone'. The blood of all those sufferers had flowed into his blood and made it heavier and darker with all their torments – yet heavier and darker than it already was. He knew that he would never enjoy life again, as much as he had sometimes enjoyed it in his youth or even later. (**Wiechert**, 1984: 148)

Erwin Gostner from Innsbruck, released before time into military service, did not really rejoice at his release either:

> How often had I imagined this moment in my most beautiful dreams. I wanted to give out a yodel that would fill a whole valley. But I went silent with my two companions into the hall. We looked one another in the eye and tightly squeezed hands. (**Gostner**, 1986: 164)

There is something almost trivial about this description of farewell gestures – which shows how emotional the situation still was for Gostner at the moment of writing.

A wider range of responses may be found in the testimony of those who had to await liberation by Allied forces, in many cases having first to suffer the shock of a 'death march' (the name used in histories of the concentration camps for forced evacuations before the advancing enemy). All this often meant that they by no means experienced the hour of their release in the way that they had imagined beforehand; sheer exhaustion was another factor sapping their enthusiasm at the end of servitude. 'The really great joy that I should have felt,' writes Nico Rost in his diary about his release from Dachau on 29 April 1945, 'is not yet there – it does not want to appear yet' (**Rost**, 1983: 244). For Filip Müller, a member of the *Sonderkommando* in Auschwitz, his release was devoid of any drama. He even experienced it as a negative climax:

> This moment, on which all my thoughts and secret wishes had been concentrated for three years, evoked neither gladness nor, for that matter, any other feelings inside me. I let myself drop down from my rafter and crawled on all fours to the door. Outside I struggled along a little further, but then I simply stretched out on woodland ground and fell fast asleep. (**F. Müller**, 1979: 170)

This state of exhaustion, brought on by physical privation and the discharge of mental tension, could last for a long time and take on a pathological character (**Frankl**, 1977: 144). Release apathy also explains the inability of former prisoners to make a rapid adjustment to the new reality. They approached the situation cautiously, with doubts in their mind, 'testing' freedom in small doses as if it were an unfamiliar food. Many authors also use eating metaphors to help them describe their experience:

> Alex and I ran to the camp gate, opened it and walked hesitantly out into the road. We did not say a word to each other; our nerves were tensed up. Is it possible that we are free? Free? After more than three

years' confinement, we are alone in the road without any supervision, without the SS, without soldiers carrying rifles and fixed bayonets. As the camp was a long way from any residential area, there was no one to be seen on the road, and Alex and I went further on out just to savour freedom a little. (**Elias**, 1988: 244)

Lucie Adelsberger makes the comparison explicit: 'We were not capable of fully absorbing freedom in that first moment, any more than our famished bodies immediately wanted to eat' (**Adelsberger**, 1956: 167).

Primo Levi reports other difficulties in adjusting to his newly gained freedom. He was not able to get his oppressors out of his system, so long had he been surrounded by the camp's 'destruction and death' (**Levi**, 1987a: 175). Even when victims were no longer in the camp, they still seemed to be in the power of the SS. Although most were by then too physically weak to escape from the area straightaway, they found it difficult to await the time when they would finally be able to leave the camp behind – which, for various reasons, could take weeks, months or (in the case of displaced persons) even years. Many describe the torment of being forced to wait to be 'taken home', instead of being able to set off at once. This is not at all contradicted by the fact that people like Ella Lingens-Reiner, after a first outing to freedom, returned to the camp as matter of course:

[T]he first time I walked on the sunny road to the little town of Dachau, accompanied by a friend, not in a group, without supervision, there was only one circumstance which astonished me: that this seemed so natural, and that all the same it did not enter my mind to stay outside the camp. In the evening it was just natural to me to go 'home' – to the concentration camp. (**Lingens-Reiner**, 1948: 190)

This sense of belonging to the camp often took a long time to erase. At first they were proud of their concentration camp identity, which distinguished them from those who had collaborated with the Nazis. This was also visible in their camp clothing, which many did not want to give up immediately (cf. **Pawlak**, 1979: 248), or else in the red stripe that political prisoners refused to tear off (cf. **Ch. Müller**, 1981: 216). But it was not only that clothing and tagging symbolized political identity and integrity; the status of an internee had become for them over the years the only possible identity. Karl Röder speaks of a fellow-prisoner who, on being informed of his early release from Dachau, reacted in the following surprising manner:

> He said nothing. His child-like face unmistakably expressed what he was feeling: now the great life is over, and the misery begins. What am I supposed to do outside, in that world where everything is rotten and dying? I would rather stay here with you. He knew for sure that it was only there with us that he could be a spiritual being. Outside the camp things would swallow him up. He did not think of whether his life would be saved. (**Röder**, 1985: 206)

After everything that we learn of Röder from his own testimony, it remains doubtful whether he is not to some extent projecting his own thoughts. Nevertheless, it is interesting that any internee should be able to think in that manner.

Thus, trepidation was the main feeling that the liberated prisoners had as they prepared to face the outside world. The Jews among them feared in 1945 that what they would encounter would be facts of an irreversible kind. During their detention, the resolve to see their family again had been the only thing that kept them going. Now it was possible that their worst fears would be confirmed – fears that they had so far succeeded in suppressing (cf. **Scheuer**, 1983: 101).

Various strategies to overcome this disappointment are documented in the survivors' testimony. Leon Wells, whose whole family had been murdered, subsequently tried to get over the loss by choosing a profession that conformed to his parents' ideas (**Wells**, 1966: 310). In however limited a way, this would allow him to preserve something of his past in the world after the concentration camp.

Other survivors were less enthusiastic about holding on to their pre-camp identity. Children and young people, who had spent important years of their development in a camp, found it difficult to get used to a teacher–pupil relationship or to be resocialized among other classmates or students. The experiences that they brought with them from the camp stood in the way. Evelien van Leeuwen only remembers being hungry in the period after her release (**van Leeuwen**, 1984: 50); the teaching materials seemed trivial to those who had been aged and shaped by years and experience.

Nearly all the accounts of liberation from the camps record – and try to explain – this lack of enthusiasm. Fania Fénelon, for instance, describes how the arrival of American soldiers did not correspond at all to her anticipation of the end of imprisonment:

> We saw them, but did not take it in. We had held out only to live this moment. A hundred times, two hundred times, we had pictured it to ourselves, polished it, touched it up with a thousand details of satisfied revenge, and now suddenly we saw this procession passing through the camp and did not understand that the longed-for moment had finally arrived! They were driving the newly vanquished in front of them. (**Fénelon**, 1977: 304f.)

In these lines is a sadness that nothing in the world has changed, that there are still oppressed and oppressors. What shakes the reader is not so much Fénelon's sympathy for suffering as the illusion, now destroyed, which she had still been able to cherish in a world like Auschwitz.

The accounts which speak of unclouded joy at the hour of liberation remain in a minority. It rings true in the testimony of Charlotte Müller, a Communist who could present her detention in terms of the anti-fascist struggle and see her recovery of freedom as a political victory. The celebrations on 1 May 1945 after liberation by the Red Army looked exactly as 'we had year after year longed for them to be' (**Ch. Müller**, 1981: 217). Joseph Schupack's account is less ideologically coloured: when, forty years later, the Jew from the Polish shtetl looked back to the day of his release from Bergen-Belsen, he remembered only secondarily his sadness at the loss of friends and relatives:

> 15 April 1945. When I think back to the tortures of the ghetto, the sufferings of Majdanek, the fear of Auschwitz, the hunger at Dora Lager and Bergen-Belsen, it was on that day that the world began again for me and my kind. The joy was immense; there were only laughing and crying faces. One would have had to be made of stone not to be carried away by those feelings, however unpleasant everything was around us. (**Schupack**, 1984: 194)

For many survivors, the joy was mingled with thoughts of revenge – or even a blind destructive rage, as in the case of Kitty Hart (**Hart**, 1961: 152ff.). Remarkably, however, there are few examples of these understandable reactions, and in later years they were rationalized and downplayed by those concerned. Victims felt ashamed of such feelings (cf. **Wenke**, 1980: 158).[9] Without necessarily being aware of it, the former prisoners were afraid that in giving way to vengeance they might come to resemble their oppressors (cf. Todorov, 1993: 264). Jean Améry, however, at least temporarily looked beyond moral categories and argued that physical force was the only way for (Jewish) prisoners to regain their dignity, embracing resentment despite Nietzsche's definition of it as a personalized form of revenge (**Améry**, 1980).

Many former internees set about recovering their psychological equilibrium in a pragmatic fashion. Mali Fritz and Hermine Jursa, for example, set off on foot together to make their way back from Ravensbrück to Vienna. This helped them to escape the post-camp depression which, as we have seen, often affected people as they waited to be 'taken home'; and the slow overcoming of distance enabled them to get used again to the idea of being free and responsible for their own lives. But they were not able to decide the struggle for survival all by themselves; their very assurance that in the end nothing would happen to them led them to extreme efforts (**Fritz and Jursa**, 1983: 26).

Even these extreme efforts did not enable them fully to shake off the memory of the camp:

> This lack of echo [in the area through which they were passing] causes Auschwitz to come back to mind; it is always there behind me, alongside me. I therefore keep running on, in order to escape that endless scream and whimper. I talk myself into believing that this march back will draw a veil over everything behind me and hold back all the horrors. (**Fritz and Jursa**, 1983: 52)

Fritz and Jursa took the effort of this march upon themselves, in the hope that the experience of physical distance would also make the psychological distance from the camp grow all the faster. But this happened only to a limited extent.

The prisoners freed themselves at different tempos, and with varying effectiveness, from the experiences through which they had just lived. Inability to reintegrate is known to psychology as the 'survivor syndrome' (Niederland, 1980). Survivors complain of a loss of trust in other people, and of an exaggerated emphasis on life's basic needs (**Elias**, 1988: 252f.). Even language becomes strange to them. They no longer 'know the gestures and words of normal life' (**Fénelon**, 1977: 307). Concepts, after the camp, turn out to be no longer the same as before. Thus Lucie Begov reported that 'the concept of "illness" – temporarily – lost all its terrors, when she first met curing, helping doctors again after her release, and saw the first chemist's shops with shelves full of medicines' (**Begov**, 1983: 186). A biological comparison occurred to the Viennese journalist Rudolf Kalmár, when he thought of the experiences that distinguished former concentration camp prisoners from the rest of the population: 'The people in the last chapter lived for seven years under different stars from ours. Seven years is a long time – enough, so they say, for the whole substance of the body to be replaced' (**Kalmár**, 1988: 202). Or at another point: 'We trotted, like animals at the rear of a cart, past people whom we had once resembled when we still belonged to them' (**Kalmár**, 1988: 204). The experience of detention in the camp had had an effect similar to that of biological change: 'It is said that we grew apart from one another,' writes Kalmár. 'There is something deeply tragic in this outcome, which stretches the seven-year curse of barbed wire far beyond the hour that blew it up' (**Kalmár**, 1988: 203). Marianne Krasovec puts the same idea into a direct image: 'You cannot erase from life what has happened. It just keeps running after you' (**Berger, Holzinger** et al., 1987: 48).

The victims became aware of their mental disturbance in the form of embitterment and disappointment after their release (cf. **Frankl**, 1977: 146). This was triggered not only by incompatibility between the strategies they had used to survive in the camp (e.g., changed ethical notions and values) and resocialization into the world outside, but also by the lack of understanding which that world displayed towards them. Experiences which tend to contradict this – the case of Ella Lingens-Reiner, for example, who made allowances for the fact that the journalists pouring into the camp were honestly seeking to understand the atrocities committed there (**Lingens-Reiner**, 1948: 194) – simply confirm the sad rule. The remark, 'It couldn't have been all that bad if you are still here' – which Mali Fritz heard from a doctor – is symptomatic of the lack of sensitivity towards survivors. Fritz bitterly remarks: 'Obviously I would have had to have been through the gas chambers and the chimney to be allowed as a witness' (**Fritz**, 1986: 136f.). Often, too, the victims had to avoid being branded as criminals because of their time in the camp (**Elias**, 1988: 250). The renascent political Right, such as the Association of Independents (VdU) founded in Austria in 1949, could once again permit itself publicly to discredit former concentration camp prisoners. Disappointment with the world in which they lived was therefore quite widespread among survivors. They had expected that 'everyone would reverently fall silent in the face of so much pain, so much unimaginable suffering' (**Salus**, 1981: 53), and they must have found it incredible when people around them protested that they had known nothing about the camps and the extermination especially of Jews (cf. **Elias**, 1988: 250). It is hardly surprising, then, that many survivors complained of a diminishing courage to face life.[10] Not even the occupation authorities did them proper justice. The Germans among them, especially – as Isa Vermehren found out – encountered a blanket rejection which equated them with their oppressors. Her own shock at such behaviour was expressed in a paradoxical wish to return to the camp, 'where it had been possible to feel innocent [*sic!*] in the hands of the guilty' (**Vermehren**, 1979: 176).

Many Jewish victims countered the sense of exclusion and later discrimination by reaffirming their Jewishness, if they had not already done so in the camp. Loss of their families made those remaining draw closer together: All the surviving Jews, writes Leon Wells:

> without prior consultation or suggestion, used the same word to recognize one another: *amchu* (your people). When you met a Jew, you simply said *'amchu'* and everybody answered in the same way. Then you drew close, embraced and kissed each other, asked about each other's origin and name and where you had been hiding yourself away. (**Wells**, 1966: 274)

This awareness of a common destiny expressed itself in spontaneous acts of mutual aid, as well as in marriages between survivors. This had a lot to do with the fact that they understood each other without having to engage in painful conversations; former companions in suffering did not have to explain to each other a sudden attack of pain or peculiarity of behaviour. Jean Améry sublimates the group feeling among victims by redefining positively what psychologists call their 'differentness' or 'distortedness' – defining it, that is, 'as a morally and historically higher form of human existence than healthy straightness' (**Améry**, 1980: 110). In this way, he puts a new interpretation on the sense of group exclusion which he and all other survivors were seen as having in the 1960s. A little over ten years before his death by suicide, he refused to accept a way of 'coming to terms with the past' that tried to get victims to integrate into post-war society. What he said about the historical and moral superiority of the former concentration camp prisoners was designed to help the rehabilitation of their personal integrity. He would have had no sympathy for Bruno Bettelheim's criticism that the survivors displayed antisocial behaviour after their release (cf. **Bettelheim**, 1961: 251).

The intellectually elaborate strategy of demarcation from the surrounding world contrasted with a more practical orientation. Many survivors, if they were released in time, immediately reported for duty in the struggle against the Third Reich (e.g., **Wells**, 1966: 265). This gave their existence an immediate meaning in which they could find new strength. Others threw themselves into their work, whatever it might be, trying to make up as quickly as possible for lost time. We have, for instance, two writers who provide the best illustration of this. Gerty Spies wrote: 'By day ... I plunged into activity with all the strength of an existence that had been given me anew. I continued to write. My life had a new purpose' (**Spies**, 1984: 156). Peter Edel called the feeling he had at work:

> a special kind of joy: to have demands put on one not just as an observer but as a participant in the building of a new culture [in the former Soviet zone of occupation]; to be needed by people with similar views; to be greeted as an able comrade-in-arms; to catch up with so much that he had not read, not learnt, not acquired as knowledge – learning with learners. (**Edel**, 1979: II, 367)

This sense of being needed for meaningful work did correspond to what former prisoners had wished and imagined for the time after their release. Not surprisingly, then, survivors who were granted this experience found it easier than others, at least for a time, to settle into 'normality'. As soon as something needed to be done, it completely engrossed them and left them with little time to think about their past.

In addition to political convictions and artistic activity, religious faith also offered a possible meaning which helped survivors come to terms with what they had been through. Christians often saw their release as part of a divine plan of salvation, and this made it easier for them to get over the initial shock. Isa Vermehren describes her experience of release in connection with a religious service:

What a momentous and deeply binding hour – to receive benediction and peace as children! The grace abounding from that first hour left the glow of silent worship for a long time in many hearts, until even that restraint dissolved in pure and warm-hearted joy – 'Heinrich, the carriage is breaking apart' – 'No, sir . . . ' Now the last iron band came away, and hearts breathed a deep sigh of relief in freedom never before felt. (**Vermehren**, 1979: 158)

Vermehren's joy and relief are here expressed in two images from quite different fields. On the one hand, she plays on the divine childlikeness which the believer freely assumes, as opposed to the infantile regression that Bettelheim observed in the camp (Bettelheim, 1979). In this spirit, she is able to interpret her release as a divine intervention. But it also means release from the mental suffering against which she had armoured herself, as the Frog King's servant Heinrich had done in the Grimm Brothers' fairy tale. In this image, Vermehren concentrates the vulnerability against which prisoners in the camps tried to be forearmed. Even after they had regained their freedom, many of them still needed this protection, and the failure of reintegration can often be traced back to a premature relinquishment of it.

The depiction of release, as of the initial entry into the camp, posed a problem that had to be overcome by literary means in the authors' testimony. The former prisoners do not write with only their own experience in mind, but treat it as also representative of the experience of others who are unable or unwilling to report what they lived through. This significance is most apparent in the choice of vocabulary. The metaphors which the authors use to describe their release express the idea that what is happening is different and new. Elias speaks of a 'fairy tale' (**Elias**, 1988: 248), and Liesel Pintus evocatively employs a 'fresh sheet of paper' to recount her release from Theresienstadt (**Pintus**, 1947: 22). The latter image is one of those metaphors for a fresh start with which numerous survivors hailed their longed-for freedom. The priest Leonhard Steinwender used for this the image of a 'second inaugural mass' (**Steinwender**, 1946: 132), obviously a rather personal mode of expression. Much more frequent is the metaphor of birth. One variant of this, surprisingly common in the survivors' testimony, is the image of a 'rebirth' borrowed from Eastern religions (e.g., **Langhoff**, 1986; **Elias**, 1988: 273), but the same idea is present in the Christian message of the Resurrection.

Rudolf Kalmár, for instance, describes 'a rare feeling of appearing among those still alive as a man resurrected' (**Kalmár**, 1988: 201).

Of course, a closer look at the reality of survival after the camp makes this euphoria rather questionable. Guilt feelings (Lifton and Olson, 1974: 116f.), mental and physical suffering (Niederland, 1980; Leiser, 1982), frequent cases of suicide: these long-term effects of detention in the camps show that to survive the Holocaust was no guarantee at all of rebirth (Lifton and Olson, 1974: 137). 'Leben nach dem Überleben' ('Life after Survival'), as in the title of a psychological study of long-term damage suffered by former camp inmates, did not begin in a vacuum but was always marked by 'life before'. It was not only numbers that were tattooed on Jewish prisoners in Auschwitz; the experience of the camp was tattooed on them in a much broader sense.[11] The birth imagery thus reveals itself more as wishful thinking than as picturing of the objective situation. The same is true of a further variety of 'new beginning' metaphors, which centre on recovery from a dangerous illness. Josef Schupack felt himself to be a convalescent when, after liberation, he was sent for treatment to the former SS barracks at Bergen-Belsen (**Schupack**, 1984: 204). In fact, a majority of prisoners needed some medical care after their release from the camps, although recovery was by no means assured. Many died of the effects of undernourishment, infectious disease or simple debilitation.

Death

Whether prisoners found themselves in a 'detachment' where the heavy workload and Kapo harassment made death a frequent occurrence (as in the cynical motto 'Annihilation through Work'), or whether they had a relatively safe position in the prisoners' 'sick bay' or in the death-files department of the camp office, there was not a moment when death was absent from their thoughts. Soon after arrival, especially at Auschwitz, they learnt to fear the so-called selections. They had to get used to the sight of public executions and became familiar with the machinery of killing. But the camp administration and the conditions prevailing there forced them to suppress their emotions in the face of death. Officially, they were not supposed to know what happened at the selections, or even that there were gas chambers in the camp. An individualized relationship to death would have called into question the absolute power of the oppressors, which reached a climax in their control over life and death (cf. Sofsky, 1997). Nevertheless, the prisoners had to work out some way of relating to the ubiquity of death which would make it possible for them to go on living. The SS, in its own way, equated the living with the dead in the camp, by referring to both alike as 'figures' (**Wells**, 1966: 231).

The 'normal' reaction of prisoners to death was one of habituation. Hanna Lévy-Hass tersely notes in her diary: 'Complete indifference to death and the dead' (**Lévy-Hass**, 1979: 57). Ruth Elias was hardly surprised that she had to help make coffins in Theresienstadt, when the cabinet-makers could no longer keep pace with death (**Elias**, 1988: 116). The very use of coffins, far from common in the camps, allowed a certain link to be preserved with civilian burial rites, which, as is well known, are part of the process of coping with loss.

Such details confront us all the more intensely with the ubiquity of death in the survivors' testimony. Even death changed its aspect there: 'I used to think that death was full of dignity,' writes Zacheusz Pawlak. 'I was wrong. Here, under these conditions, it had none of its dignity and gravity. It was a terrible death, full of shame and humiliation' (**Pawlak**, 1979: 55). Quite apart from the fact that a burial ceremony was not allowed, it was hardly possible for prisoners to mourn their dead. 'When life no longer counts for anything, respect for the dead also goes by the board' (**Adelsberger**, 1956: 54). This is Lucie Adelsberger's explanation for the irreverent way in which the dead were treated in the camp. As a doctor working in the Auschwitz 'sick bay', she experienced several times a day how the dead were cleared away without further ado. Viktor Frankl describes one such scene:

> I eventually pulled myself together and instructed the 'orderly' to take the corpse out of the shack (an earth hut). Once he had braced himself, he grabbed the body by the legs, pulled it down the narrow gangway between the two rows of boards (on which fifty people lay with fever), and dragged it over the bumpy ground to the door of the hut. There were two steps which led up and out into the open – always a problem for us, weakened as we were by chronic hunger: ... First he hauled himself up there, and then the corpse; its feet, then its trunk,

and finally – with an eerie clattering – its skull bumped over the pair of steps. (**Frankl**, 1977: 43f.)

The forced lack of sentimentality in dealing with death went hand in hand with the knowledge that every individual was replaceable. Käthe Starke describes how, because of the deportations from Theresienstadt to Auschwitz, she rose in the briefest time from library assistant to chief librarian; 'a meteoric career typical of Theresienstadt', she comments ironically (**Starke**, 1975: 151). Simon Laks and René Coudy relate how the Auschwitz prisoners' orchestra, in rehearsing the pieces to be performed, already built into its calculations the expected death of certain of its members (**Adler** *et al.*, 1984: 188).

The SS selection principle was also based upon this idea of dispensability, which Adorno considered to be the logical outcome of historical development: 'even in his formal freedom, the individual is as fungible and replaceable as he will be under the liquidators' boots'. Consequently, it was not the individual who was killed in the camps but a 'specimen' (Adorno, 1988: 362). Superficially, the SS eliminated the weaker prisoners, but in fact the numbers were mainly decided by a pre-established percentage figure. This led to such grotesque scenes as the one reported by Ella Lingens-Reiner, in which an SS man found himself protecting a Jewish woman (**Lingens-Reiner**, 1948: 81f.). But it also placed upon camp doctors a responsibility for which they were by no means prepared. 'It was neither just nor fair,' writes Lingens-Reiner, 'that some women stayed alive only because they had certain contacts, while the others were left to die. And yet it was better to have saved a few than none' (**Lingens-Reiner**, 1948: 79).

Individual prisoners were prey to feelings of guilt at the way in which their destiny interlocked with that of their fellow-sufferers. Mali Fritz wondered:

Who could say of themselves afterwards that they managed to keep out of the mire? If it hadn't been me, it would have been someone else – there would still have been sixty 'to be taken away'. It would be cynical to conclude that one could get out of being killed, and equally cynical to claim that one's escape was due to oneself alone. (**Fritz**, 1986: 102)

Since Kitty Hart, as a member of the so-called Canada Detachment, had access to extra food, she was surprisingly able to recover from a serious deficiency disease. Indirectly she therefore profited from the mass murder in Auschwitz. 'Was it not grotesque to see my own life saved – at least for the moment – at the very place where millions lost theirs?' (**Adler**, *et al.*, 1984: 84).

If the selection was 'a general organizational schema by which "superfluous" human beings were sorted out from workers and liquidated' (Sofsky, 1997: 241), the way in which they were marked down for the gas chambers was still governed by arbitrariness and chance. The prisoners thus had no way of 'preparing' for it, nor any opportunity to derive any meaning from it for themselves. 'The administrative murder of millions made of death a thing one had never before had to fear in that way. There was no longer any chance that death would enter the living experience of individuals as somehow congruent with the course of their lives' (Adorno, 1988: 362 – translation modified).

Although survivors deny that death had any dignity in the camp, many of them acknowledge its power to release. Compared with the harassment to which Jewish prisoners were especially subject,[12] death often appeared the lesser evil (e.g., **Schupack**, 1984: 170). In this, too, the experience of the camp left its mark.

> I used to think of death as a struggle in which the body tries to hang on to departing life. Here [in Mauthausen], there is no struggle; death comes in a last drawing of breath. Like expiring candles, one after another fall to the ground. Here death is truly a release. (**Gostner**, 1986: 137)

Death loses all its terror for those who seek it as a release; the lack of a will to live is thus adorned with a religious significance. Yet there were few cases of suicide in the camps (Langbein, 1980a: 144–9).[13] 'Closer to death,' writes Des Pres, 'survivors are rooted more urgently in life than most of us' (Des Pres, 1976: 21). But many did lose the courage to face life and simply let themselves go: they no longer made an effort to obtain extra food, became visibly run down, and eventually fell victim as so-called 'Musulmans' in an SS selection.

Belief among Christian prisoners in a better afterlife encouraged a certain fatalism, as the Catholic priest Pater Lenz realized from conversations in the camp: 'Nowhere else in life can we die as easily and as well as here,' he sums up this attitude. 'Hopeless affliction made farewells easy. It was a release – up towards God' (**Lenz**, 1956: 160).

Prisoners in the camp developed a quite distinctive relationship to death, determined by its constant proximity. This is how Lucie Adelsberger puts it:

> We lived not only spatially but mentally in the shadow of the chimney. It was the alpha and the omega of all conversation. It was already spread on dried bread at breakfast and served up as dessert at every mealtime. Death was as close and familiar to us as a landscape into which one grows through life. (**Adelsberger**, 1956: 58)

Leon Wells, too, sees the association between death and feeding: not only as a matter for conversation in the camp, however, but also in the shape of actual corpses that he and his fellows 'received every morning with breakfast' (**Wells**, 1966: 178). As a member of the *Sonderkommando* at the Janowska camp in Lvov, Wells had to burn the bodies of murdered Jews – an experience that does not lend itself to metaphors. The relationship between eating and death – which may seem macabre to anyone who has not passed through the school of the camps – occurs in other reports, too, in a rather unmetaphorical manner. Thus, prisoners' officials sometimes tried for a while to hush up a victim's death, in order to have an extra food ration for themselves; or prisoners working in the sick bay would pounce on the soup of someone who had just died. Erwin Gostner tells of a chief cook estimating the number of those killed at a delousing session; he no longer had to distribute portions to them (**Gostner**, 1986: 157). Many survivors even report cases of cannibalism in the camp.

Prisoners describe death as a daily companion with which they conversed (**Bruha**, 1984: 31–3), or call it their 'most loyal fellow-resident' (**Lévy-Hass**, 1979: 48). Others stress that, in the camp, the living and the dead were not really distinguished from each other (**Fritz**, 1986: 100). Life and death were no longer two different forms of being – as Terence Des Pres suggests (Des Pres, 1976: 8). Michael Moll persuasively attributes this to the fact that 'there was no longer a clear cultural division between life and death', since the 'aesthetic ritualization' of death customary outside was lacking inside the camp (Moll, 1988: 111). Moll makes this point in connection with Jean Améry's account of the intellectual's experience of Auschwitz (**Améry**, 1980: 40). In this way, the inmates displayed their resistance to a form of death that meant no more than a 'passing into the raw material of nature' (Moll, 1988: 109).

The above examples show how prisoners in the concentration camps conducted themselves in relation to the idea of death, if we can put it like that. But how did they react when they stood face to face with those marked down for death? How did they behave when they themselves were in that situation? Members of the *Sonderkommando* at Auschwitz, who were forced to assist in the genocide of the Jews, had to ask themselves this question several times a day. They knew that the people they helped undress, or whose hair they cut, were not only going straight to their death but would vanish without trace in the ensuing cremation. Understandably, therefore, any contact with the victims was strictly forbidden. In Filip Müller's account of *Sonderkommando* work, which is representative of the few such testimonies to have come down to us, he wrestled with himself over whether there was any point in breaking the rules and informing the victims of what lay ahead. Only when he had to take some fellow-countrymen to the gas chamber did he finally crack. He tried to become one of the group himself, but then desisted when the victims pleaded with him, as the only witness, to live on and testify to their murder (**F. Müller**, 1979: 110). Krystyna Zywulska came across one 'transport' waiting to be sent to its death, and what especially depressed her was the contrast between the 'picnic' atmosphere of the men as they ate and their unknowing closeness to death (**Zywulska**, 1980: 198f.). Tadeusz Borowski suffered from the fact that the only possible sympathy he could show for the death candidates was to lie to them (**Borowski**, 1982: 116). Joseph Drexel, another survivor, describes how he found the strength to go on living when he faced the body of someone who had been tortured to death. Later he mystified this experience by making it sound like Christ's passion:

> As I became engrossed with all my soul in this stranger's martyrdom and fraternally exalted his terrible death with the few powers I possess, as I carried out this unspoken task of sitting in wake, there grew in me the strength to endure any torture and humiliation as a light burden and to make myself invulnerable to the ruses of death. (**Drexel**, 1980: 85)

Käthe Starke documents a special kind of death at Theresienstadt. Since the camp did not have a gas chamber of its own, deportations were organized to Auschwitz or other extermination camps. In the autumn months of 1943, this still affected only the sick and the elderly:

> Between the Magdeburg [prisoners' quarters were named after German towns] and myself, a flat cart was rolling forward very slowly in the mud of the main street, tugged jerkily along in the usual way. Its load was not bucketfuls of food, nor was it dead bodies – at least, they were not dead yet. It was frail little old women with pointed noses, carrying some paltry piece of luggage. Their dangling legs bumped now and then against the wheels. The men walked alongside, as in a funeral procession. With bowed heads, they awkwardly held their mothers' hands as they bore the still-living to the grave. (**Starke**, 1975: 84)

A little later, younger prisoners were also 'given a place on the transport', as the Theresienstadt jargon put it. And similar scenes were acted out:

> In the Hamburg, women and children started to gather in the passageways to take their leave of husbands and fathers, but then a wooden partition was erected that closed off the corridors. The pitiless hammer blows echoed through the large buildings, as if innumerable coffins were being nailed down. (**Starke**, 1975: 145)

This time, too, Starke followed the 'procession':

> Again we went on a last walk through black streets slippery from the rain. The dead accompanied us on their own two feet, and with considered self-control performed the final movements for their own annihilation. (**Starke**, 1975: 149)

The similarity between deportation and burial may have occurred to Käthe Starke only after her release from the camp, but it is quite possible that she already glimpsed it at the time. Unlike those Jews who were taken straight from their homes to the unloading platform in Auschwitz, the victims at Theresienstadt already had enough experience of the camps to know that deportation meant a big change in their lives, if not a journey to extinction.

As to the way in which people faced their own imminent death, we must for obvious reasons rely almost exclusively on third-party accounts. A number of witnesses describe, for example, the execution of Mala Zimetbaum, the 'camp runner' of Birkenau, after she had attempted to escape together with a Polish prisoner.

In a heroic gesture, she cut her arteries right beneath the gallows, in order to forestall her murderers. Such events not only stunned prisoners who were forced to stand there and watch, but gave them the strength to go on living as a demonstration of resistance. Taking their role of witness as a kind of personal legacy, they were clearly moved by the sang-froid with which many of those marked down for death assumed their fate. Often they were dismayed at the thought that they would never themselves be capable of behaving in such a fashion (e.g. **Pawlak**, 1979: 31).

It was not easy for survivors to put into words the murder of their former companions in suffering. One feels that the terms are lacking. Many tried to make up for this with the help of metaphors: they called the mass murder 'the end of the world', or compared it to the operation of a factory (**Zywulska**, 1980: 195, 210). One spoke of the 'sacred flame' (**Berger**, 1987: 187), and Fred Wander talks of an *Ernte* or 'reaping' (**Wander**, 1985: 66). It is uncertain whether he knew of, and deliberately chose, the cover name used by the SS for the mass shooting of the Majdanek Jews on 3 November 1943 (**Pawlak**, 1979: 134–47).

Mali Fritz describes how people in prison first 'went rigid' – that is, cast off any emotion – and then faded away (**Fritz**, 1986: 20). Rudolf Kalmár finds a similar image for the slow dying of patients in the sick bay: 'Their days did not come to an end like the life of a man who has exhausted himself in work or the daily struggle for existence; they gradually drained away, like the wax of a candle in the wind' (**Kalmár**, 1988: 138). Thus, both Fritz and Kalmár borrow from nature to speak of the 'passing' of their comrades.

In all these metaphors one is immediately struck by their incompatibility with the matter to be expressed – whether they evoke a religious context or suggest an inevitable conformity to natural law. The lack of aggression in images such as 'passing' or 'draining away' also sharply contrasts with the brutal methods of killing in the camp. Yet this metaphorical shortfall may be seen as reflecting the wish of former prisoners to keep at least linguistic sovereignty over the violent ending of life. It is debatable how effective this is, but in any event it draws some of the sting from what they lived through. If, following Harald Weinrich, we understand metaphor as an 'aspect of our interpretation of the world' (quoted in Stoffer-Heibel, 1981: 100), then the emphasis shifts from the discrepancy between metaphor and experience-to-be-conveyed to the image as mirroring the consciousness of the experiencing subject. The hypothetical character of the metaphorical statement makes it more bearable for the witness to recall the horrors through which he or she lived.

The terse, seemingly detached account of what happened serves the same purpose:

> Now and again, the corpse-burning ran into some hitch. On 'heavy' days with high import figures, the capacity of the ovens was not enough. Then the corpses were burnt in front of the crematorium, in deep trenches specially dug for the purpose. If gas had to be saved because of a shortage, victims were cremated in a merely stunned state. (**Begov**, 1983: 93)

Even Begov, however, from whose testimony this quotation is taken, does not entirely forego metaphorical expression, as her use of economic jargon such as 'import figures' and 'capacity' demonstrates. But her description affects a cool detachment, which in another context might well bring a judgement of cold-heartedness down upon her. Her language here comes quite close to that of the murderers, who, in the spirit of instrumental reason (Horkheimer, 1985: 31), viewed their victims purely as objects to be used. In this passage from Begov's testimony, however, the effect is to underline the horror of the genocide, by depicting 'authentically' (that is, from the killers' point of view) the efficiency of the annihilation machine or the problems that a temporary malfunction might pose for the camp administration.

Zacheusz Pawlak's description of the corpse removal is also intended to shock through clarity of detail. It is as if he can master the enormity of what he saw only by describing it as accurately as possible.

> After the prisoner's number had been written with an indelible pencil on his moistened thorax, after he had been deleted from the block register and lifted down from the plank bed onto the floor beside the lavatory, the sick bay's responsibilities ceased. Shortly afterwards, the *corpse-bearers* arrived with the stretchers. One or two bodies were placed on each of the stretchers and taken outside. As well as handles on either side, the stretchers had wide straps which the bearers placed across the corpse's neck and shoulders to make the carrying easier. Then the corpses were loaded onto the waggon that went past each hut and took them through the camp gate to the crematorium or the pyre. At times the odd-job men had to carry the corpses out of the sick

bay and line them up in front of the gable end of that block. (**Pawlak**, 1979: 101; emphasis in the original)

Pawlak then narrows the focus to one particular victim, who serves as an example in a minutely detailed description of the techniques and equipment of corpse disposal. Repetition of the term 'corpse' gives it the status of a keyword and adds special vividness to the account. The writer thus relies on a device which cannot work in relation to the mass extermination. Simon Wiesenthal confirms this problem in his remarks on the judge's question to Eichmann at his trial (guilty or not guilty?): 'Actually the judge should have asked him the question six million times' (Wiesenthal, 1988: 108). Eschewing clarity of detail, in this context Tadeusz Borowski opts instead for an extremely vague description. All he needs is one short sentence – 'And they all went, the same way' – which he repeats with slight changes at fixed intervals of two pages. He uses this mode of presentation not only because details, such as those which Pawlak remembers seeing, escape him, but because he is unable to depict murder which exceeds all imagination through the separate fates of individual victims. The chorus-like refrain conveys directly in language – one might say – the repetitive and unspectacular character of events, their absolute desolateness, as well as the writer's own personal desolation. More conscious than Pawlak of form, Borowski the poet here borrows from the lyrical repertoire in his use of repetition. It enables him to make a formal strategy serve the statement of content in the most economical way possible (cf. Schulte-Sasse and Werner, 1990: 133).

Torture

Although prisoners who suffered torture in the camp may be found among the survivors, and although scenes of torture were often publicly staged to instil terror, considerably less space is given over to them in the reports than to the experience of death. This may have to do with the fact that victims felt ashamed to write of the abuse to which they had been subjected. Whereas the degrading circumstances of death in the camp entered into the experience mainly of those left behind, the victims of torture who survived had, in addition, to come to terms with their own humiliation. Authors who deal with this in their texts struggle hard to incorporate it into their view of life. They try to get clear in their mind what feelings were triggered in them by the blows – or else they relativize the experience in various ways. Many write about the torture as a measure of their capacity for 'mental' resistance. But in no testimony from the camps does its importance outstrip that of the encounter with death.

For Jean Améry, torture was the central experience not only in his brilliant essay 'Torture' (**Améry**, 1980: 46–72) – which Alfred Andersch goes so far as to say is of greater significance than the experience itself (Andersch, 1972: 229) – but probably also for the whole of his post-camp existence. Even for such an eloquent essayist, however, it was by no means easy to speak of what he had experienced; only in the 1960s was he able to describe it at all. It is clear from the literature he cites that he had all the time been wrestling with the topic, but this did not make it any easier to come to terms with his personal experience. Finally, not least through the encouragement of Helmut Heißenbüttel, he resolved to try to overcome it through writing. It says a lot about the importance of the concentration camp experience in Améry's thinking that it was in the volume *Jenseits von Schuld und Sühne* (which contains both his testimony of the camp and his essay on torture) that he found his own genre, the implacable autobiographical essay.

Améry's interpretation of torture is based on two convictions. 'The limits of my body are the limits of my self', he asserts by way of adapting Wittgenstein's well-known dictum. If the individual can no longer be sure that the person or persons with whom he is in contact will respect these limits, he loses his 'faith in the world' (**Améry**, 1980: 56). The very first blow is enough – not because of its intensity, but because any such violation of boundaries makes that loss irrevocable. Just as one does not believe a liar even when he is speaking the truth, a single experience of a fellow-human as 'anti-human' (**Améry**, 1980: 73) cancels the relationship of trust once and for all. The feeling of being at someone's mercy, with no possibility of outside help, is seared into the mind of the torture victim; once the physical pain has passed, the mental pain is still there. But Améry has no wish to minimize the physical side of torture. Invoking Thomas Mann's claim in *The Magic Mountain* that 'man is all the more bodily, the more hopelessly this body of his is bound up with suffering' (**Améry**, 1980: 64), he stresses that torture reduces people to their 'flesh'. This is the second major theme in his analysis. Both in himself and in other people, he observed that it was not possible for the torture victim to withdraw into a realm of the mind.

In his own case, Améry was suspended a metre or so above the ground, his hands tied behind his back. He describes this as follows:

> During those few minutes, when you are already at your last gasp, with sweat on brow and lips, you are not going to answer any questions. Accomplices? Meeting places? You scarcely hear the words. Your whole life, concentrated in one precise part of the body, the shoulder joint, does not react – for it is completely exhausting itself in the effort. (**Améry**, 1980: 62)

Améry also deals with the mentality of his tormentors. They are sadists in the existential-psychological sense defined by Georges Bataille; their aim is to 'cancel out the world' by abolishing fellow-humanity. Améry interprets torture accordingly as the 'apotheosis of National Socialism' (**Améry**, 1980: 59), seeing it as the refutation of Hannah Arendt's notion of the 'banality of evil'. 'If something happens which stretches us to the limit, we should not use the word banality in relation to it. For at that point there is no longer any abstraction, nor does the power of our imagination even come close to the reality' (**Améry**, 1980: 52). Evidently, Hannah Arendt and Jean Améry are speaking of different things when they say 'evil'. Arendt means the 'desk criminal' Eichmann; Améry means the henchmen of the Nazi regime, who carried out the orders of an Eichmann with their own hands. Améry's criticism of Arendt, then, is not altogether valid. But other examples of torture, though less powerfully drawn, confirm the basic point he is making.

Kurt Hiller, whose testimony on the camps was probably known to the widely read Améry, is one of the few others to stress, as Améry does, the sheer physical pain of torture (**Hiller**, 1934–35: 40). Joseph Drexel, who tried hard enough to subordinate his physical being to his intellect, had to recognize in the end that he had not succeeded (**Drexel**, 1980: 117). Pain is a fact that cannot be negated through a mental effort, and any attempt in that direction remains no more than a half-hearted placebo. Nevertheless, survivors testify that they tried again and again to focus on the concomitants of the pain. Viktor Frankl has a special recollection of the mental pain caused by the blows to his body (**Frankl**, 1977: 45ff.). Simha Naor mainly remembers her rage at those in charge who wantonly inflicted pain on the prisoners. When she arrived in Auschwitz, she did not understand how prisoners could react so calmly to their abuse (**Naor**, 1986: 39–67). Gerhart Seger was so startled by his tormentors' hate that this took his mind off the physical pain (**Seger**, 1979: 32).

In these and similar ways, most of the authors play down the physical aspect. Without realizing it, they thereby refute Bruno Bettelheim and others who detect in the prisoners' reaction to abuse a 'regression to childlike behaviour' (Bettelheim, 1979: 76–7). A child experiences the authoritarian, punitive parent entirely as someone who inflicts pain; whereas an adult has a broader view that allows him or her to abstract from this and to react in a variety of ways. In the camps, Bettelheim argues, the prisoner lost that capacity and again displayed childlike modes of behaviour, essentially involving submission to the abusers. But the above examples show that this is a wrong judgement about the reaction of people interned in the camps. The testimony of Mali Fritz (**Fritz**, 1986: 42) or Joseph Schupack (**Schupack**, 1984: 152f.), for instance, suggests that their fellow-prisoners played down the pain and were able to offset the abuse with their feelings of anger. Both consoled themselves that death through gas or hunger would have been worse than 'mere' abuse.

Admission and release, death and torture, were therefore key experiences in the prisoner's life in the camp, because they were matters directly affecting physical survival and objectively impelling certain types of action. Since the camp drastically limited the individual's capacity for physical action, it set up a pressure to switch to mental action. Such substitute activity was of the 'coping' kind; it delineated a learning process whose aim was to fit the prisoner into life in the camp and, after release, into 'normal' life. As the scope for action was greater in the freedom of the outside world, the pressure to integrate could more easily be replaced there by a suitable physical activity (such as work). Moreover, it was objectively open to survivors to sublimate their need for action in writing, although there were subjective resistances to this. Jorge Semprún displayed this ambivalence in an interview that he gave to *Die Zeit*: 'I was clear in myself that for me writing meant writing about the camp. But I was unable to write about the camp, for I would have had to prolong that death.' He therefore turned instead to politics, which embodied the future for him (Raddatz, 1989; Semprún, 1994). Only anger at 'the amateurish, confused and clumsy narratives told about Mauthausen by comrades in the Party' finally induced him in 1962 to say what he felt about his experience of Buchenwald (cf. Löffler, 1992).

Notes

1. Truth content, which is of supreme importance for the historian (Atteslander, 1975: 65–9), therefore has only a secondary place in the present study.
2. Mali Fritz reaffirmed this to me in a letter of 16 January 1989.
3. At conferences where aspects of the Judaeocide are discussed, survivors in the audience repeatedly object that the actual victims are passed over too perfunctorily.
4. She told me this in a personal letter dated 16 January 1989.
5. By 1960, roughly six thousand books had been published in thirty languages. A further ten to twenty thousand unpublished reports and diaries are to be found in specialist archives in Israel, America and Europe (Friedman, 1960: 11–16).
6. In an interview, given years after his account of Buchenwald, Jorge Semprún said that he was now writing a book about 'the connection between my silence and my writing' (Löffler, 1992; see also **Semprún**, 1994).
7. Though important in relation to the admission shock, gender differences do not seem to have been a significant factor in how people faced the experience of the camp in general (cf. Matussek and Grigat, 1971: 233).
8. A book review of 1991 suggests that academic research on the Nazi persecution of homosexuals still leaves a lot to be desired (Hans-Georg Stümke, ' "Endlösung" oder "Umziehung"? zu Burkhard Jellonnek, *Homosexuelle unter dem Hakenkreuz. Die Verfolgung von Homosexuellen im Dritten Reich*, Paderborn: Ferdinand Schönigh 1990'; Richard Plant, *Rosa Winkel. Der Krieg der Nazis gegen die Homosexuellen*, Frankfurt/Main: Campus 1991', *Die Zeit* 29 March 1991).
9. Already in the title of his testimony, *Recht, nicht Rache* ('Right, not Revenge'), Simon Wiesenthal indicated how he wanted his persecution by the Nazi criminals to be viewed.
10. Women seem to have had an even harder time of it than men after their release. Karin Berger, for example, observed in her interviews with survivors that 'only very few women . . . went onto the offensive against personal or public attacks. Most of them withdrew into silence' (**Berger**, 1987: 311).
11. Peter Sloterdijk concerns himself with a definition of beginning and birth in relation to literature. That there is actually no beginning for him is expressed in the image of 'tattooed life', by which he means that all literary expression has a prior stamp in the life of its creator (Sloterdijk, 1987: 1988).
12. The conditions for Jews in the camp were considerably worse than those of other prisoners, and did not improve over time (cf. Pingel, 1978: 92f.).

13. Elsewhere Langbein makes a direct link between the low suicide rate and cultural activity in the camp (Langbein, 1980a: 157). But this should also be understood in the sense that cultural activity already presupposed a certain 'standard of living', which itself reduced the danger of suicide. The sanctions for an unsuccessful act of suicide also seem to have deterred prisoners (Sofsky, 1997: 57–8, referring to Bruno Bettelheim's *The Informed Heart*, pp. 150–1). In the Soviet Gulag, too, there were few cases of suicide (Caroline Moorhead, 'Out of the Darkness', *Independent Magazine*, 26 January 1991).

2
Genre

There are various opinions about what literature is, but one thing it certainly represents is the collective memory of human beings. It is the storehouse, the most extensive collection of things lived and thought, a special stock of experience of the world. Everything is saved and transcended within it; all that has been endured and acquired, sought and lamented over the millennia has found expression in it.

(Siegfried Lenz)

Genres embody standardized conventions of meaning (Stierle, 1975: 51). The reader associates with them a certain number of expectations, whose fulfilment guides the construction of meaning.[1] But genres are not only aids to orientation; they are chiefly a means for the author to organize what he or she has to say.[2]

The genre of the concentration camp report should be placed among autobiographical forms. It has been well documented in the secondary literature how the form of narrative commentary, which served to articulate the self-consciousness of the bourgeoisie in the eighteenth and nineteenth centuries (cf. Neumann, 1970: 32), developed into the authorial autobiography of the twentieth century, with its characteristic 'reflections on existence' (cf. Picard, 1978).[3] But since literary theory has taken Goethe's *Dichtung und Wahrheit* as the yardstick in its mainly evaluative discussions of autobiography, it provides a poor theoretical foundation for an analysis of the concentration camp literature.

A genre is also a kind of model for coming to terms with things, which displays its effectiveness through adaptation to a concrete situation. As the works discussed by Rudolf Picard show, a transformation of the structural pattern formulated in language becomes necessary when a change occurs in people's awareness of life and the world. Unusual experiences not directly related to an existing pattern, such as those of concentration camp prisoners, will therefore lead one to expect the authorial models to be radically different in a way that matches the novelty of the experience. This claim should be tested with reference to a number of examples.

Meaning is not, however, manifested only in the structural pattern; it is directly conveyed by content patterns in which the experience of generations is compressed. This is the basis for Peter Bichsel's view that literature is 'repetition'. 'The histories of this world,' he argues, 'are written in the Bible, in the Hasidic tales, in Homer' (Bichsel, 1982: 68). Certain Jungian categories have gained entry to literary theory, too, especially in the study of myths; and thematic history and the demonstration of archetypes have become legitimate areas of research.[4] What Bichsel has in mind, however, are not these rather particular traditions, but the self-contained literary work as a paradigm for representation in a text.[5] He thus understands archetypes in Northrop Frye's sense of 'associative clusters', which identify literature as one of the techniques of civilization (Frye, 1957: 124ff.). For an analysis of the concentration camp reports, this heuristic approach does seem promising, because archetypal patterns such as the image of apocalypse are actually quite widely used, even in everyday life, as a means of communicating unusual experiences and events (cf. Baigent *et al.*, 1987). The imaginative force of the Apocalypse, according to Frye, encompasses the whole of (animate) nature, which would not otherwise be accessible to us; it is therefore itself a legitimate category in literary criticism (Frye, 1964: 141–50). A glance at contemporary literature (Grimm *et al.*, 1986: 8–10) confirms that the archetypal image of the Apocalypse is by no means a thing of the past, even if it nowadays appears in secular guise. But the concentration camp report, by contrast, takes over the biblical image in its original form, as first shaped in the Book of Ezekiel and revived in John's Book of Revelation. For them, there is an 'afterwards'. The common illusion that a better world would follow annihilation meant that a rude awakening lay in store for many prisoners after their release from the camp. But, of course, that is another story.

The texts that we shall now consider are all examples of autobiographical writing in the form of letters, journals and testimony which meet the criterion of an 'explicitly individual interest in understanding' (Ott, 1968: 227).

It is possible to speak of *correspondence*, in the ordinary sense of the term, only for the early period in the history of the camps – between 1933 and 1934.[6] At that time, the (mostly political) prisoners still had other ways of keeping in touch with their family – for example, they might be visited by close relatives or even, in exceptional circumstances, be granted home leave (**Wandel**, 1946) – but their written communications with the outside world were subject to strict censorship. Nevertheless, letters then obviously had a different significance from that which they would soon have in camps run along the lines of Dachau, with their much stricter rules on frequency and length (Broszat, 1984: 46ff.). Relatives were supposed to receive information about little other than the prisoner's continued existence, perhaps on printed forms with fifteen lines that he or she could 'fill in' at intervals between two weeks and three months (Simon, 1973; Mozdzan, 1982). Similar restrictions applied to letters from relatives. Moreover, the camp administration used the withholding of 'epistolary contact' as a means of disciplining prisoners, usually as collective punishment for a breach of regulations, while the SS often arbitrarily held back an incoming letter after notifying the relevant prisoner of its arrival.

The minor importance that individuals attached to letters may be seen in the fact that the available testimony does no more than mention their existence and hardly ever directly quotes from them. With a few exceptions from the early years – one being the letters to his wife sent in 1933 from the Kislau camp by Ludwig Marum, a Reichstag deputy in the Weimar Republic (**Marum**, 1988) – the camp correspondence which has survived scarcely merits publication.[7] Family correspondence was unlikely to be among the objects that prisoners took out with them after liberation: not only because of the lack of space and chaotic living conditions inside the camp, but also because they were expressly forbidden to keep any but the most recent letter. Erich Schweinburg reports how one fellow-prisoner, on being informed of his surprising release from Dachau, destroyed his secret store of letters so as not to jeopardize his return to freedom (**Schweinburg**, 1988: 159f.).

The letter had a different meaning when it was chosen as the (artificially stylized) form for a survivor's testimony. Lina Haag reported on life in the camp to her husband, who had been released from Mauthausen for military service at the front, and in this way subsequently to the reading public (**Haag**, 1985).[8] With the help of this quasi-dialogic method, the author was able both to secure her own immediate past and to renew her bond with her husband. Although, for the time being, she could not actually send what she wrote, it somehow gave her the strength to bear waiting for her husband's return; she wrote so as not to 'scream' (**Haag**, 1985: 12, 130f., 144f.; cf. Peitsch, 1990: 158). Two further aspects are significant in Haag's use of the letter form. First, it reaches into the past, serving to clarify how her experience fits into a higher 'meaning of life'. The passages concerned are the ones that most clearly subvert the author's choice of the letter form – especially where she reports words spoken by her husband or things that must already be known to him because he himself experienced them. Second, however, the letter form is convincing where it allows a productive anticipation of the future, communicating Lina Haag's hopes and desires to her husband. Nor should one underestimate the opportunity that it offered her to write about her past experience: this dimension must have made it easier for former prisoners to cross the barrier to writing when they suddenly found themselves in an authorial role. But in Haag's case, there was the additional factor that she began writing her testimony in 1944 (hence 'illegally') and could not count on its being published in the near future. She therefore needed her husband as an interim presence to whom it could be addressed.

Another of the autobiographical forms is the *journal*. Given what has already been said, it is hardly surprising that any kind of written record was generally forbidden in the camps, sometimes on pain of death. Although this ban was enforced with varying severity from camp to camp – and was even absent in the case of Theresienstadt – prisoners had little prospect of being able to smuggle a journal out (cf. **Edel**, 1979; **Gross**, 1946). Nevertheless, it is clear from the testimony published that a number of prisoners did write. Many tried in this way to regain the identity damaged by the conditions of detention. But since the likelihood of surviving the camp must have seemed rather small, the main reason for keeping a journal was probably to inform posterity of their own and their fellow-captives' existence (cf. Foley, 1982: 336). In so far as the camp journal deviated from the genre in general, it bore more likeness to a report or testimony. This is also apparent in the fact that entries often did not occur daily, but were separated by intervals of days or weeks. Many prisoners – Primo Levi, for instance – did not begin to keep a journal until shortly before their liberation.

Along with the fear of discovery, another obstacle was the difficulty in obtaining writing materials. Prisoners used their imagination to the utmost to lay hands on the necessary paper. Nico Rost recalls writing on the reverse side of fever charts from the Auschwitz infirmary. He could count on the help of several comrades.

> The hunt for writing-paper became a real sport for me, and I would ask anyone I remotely suspected of being able to supply me with some.
>
> The whole office was already involved in this game, and they dragged along everything possible – old newspapers or wrapping paper from packages received, even paper meant for more mundane purposes ...
>
> Here I am 'the crazy Dutchman who devours books and gobbles up paper'! (**Rost**, 1983: 34)

Fania Fénelon managed to save one possession from a 'bed check' at the block in Auschwitz containing the girls' orchestra. It was a notebook which would accompany her throughout her time at the camp, and to which she developed a very personal relationship. 'After just a couple of days it had become indispensable to me. I grew fond of it as a close friend; my hand liked it, stroked it, as the silky-soft fur of a comforting kitten, or a warm, trusted, beloved skin' (**Fénelon**, 1977: 162).

It was also difficult for prisoners to obtain a pen or pencil, and they often made do with a surrogate such as the lead from a tube of toothpaste (**Haag**, 1985: 51). Imagination came into play here, as we can see from Corrie ten Boom's account of how she hid her pencil in her hair (**ten Boom**, 1954: 11).

When journal writers were in a less exposed situation, the periodic act of writing could, even in the concentration camp, take on the function of resistance against the life imposed upon them. In the ideal case, they could try to use writing to defend their private autonomy, to distance themselves from the mass of prisoners.[9] The camp forced people more than ever before into a 'community' that was, of course, quite different from a 'purely ideological community', but even in this extreme situation, a regular journal could help them escape into a 'hidden life of their own' (Hocke, 1963: 189f.). It also served a cognitive function, in that prisoners thereby attempted to overcome their enforced passivity and to become clear in their own minds about what was happening to them.

Journals were usually started in a period of personal or social-political crisis (Hocke, 1963: 26). Between 1933 and 1945, the political climate in Germany provided the occasion for a large number of personal records (Breloer, 1984), so it is hardly surprising that even the unfavourable conditions of a concentration camp did not drastically dampen the will to self-expression. Writing was a form of compensatory action. Pressure to counter dehumanization induced by the reality of the camp – pressure which could sometimes trigger a wanton 'flight into a higher spiritual realm of education and beauty' (Hocke, 1963: 187) – lay behind many decisions to keep a journal (cf. Weiss-Laqueur, 1971), including those people who had never written before yet wanted to put their thoughts on paper.[10]

After 1945 the journal form began to acquire another function, not infrequently serving as an 'entry ticket to the political life of occupied Germany' (Peitsch, 1990: 232). The importance that could attach to this justificatory writing is apparent not least in the fact that some 'journals' came into being retrospectively, even if their authors very rarely admitted this (cf. Peitsch, 1990: 233).

What can make letters so interesting – whether or not they were originally intended for publication – is the use made to reflect on personal experience of the camp. The author's knowledge relates only to the past up to the moment of writing; he or she must therefore always judge what has happened in that limited state of knowledge, without the overview that retrospection would afford. This feature of the letter is shared by the journal; writers of each can only speculate about the future development of their situation. In the case of the journal, however, the author usually has even less temporal distance, so that his or her assessment of past experience – or speculation about its feared or hoped-for sequel – takes place on the basis of smaller 'portions' of incremental knowledge. One would have thought that the journal would therefore provide especially good material for the study of how interpretive meaning in the camp was gradually developed and modified through writing. But that is not so. The production of meaning already begins with the experience itself, but it remains partial and provisional for the rest of that period of life. Only from a position subsequent to the event can the individual ascribe to it a certain meaning within a whole. That many survivors were aware of this defect, is suggested by the example of Karl Adolf Gross. When he was preparing his journal for publication, he divided it into chapters and gave to each a short, synoptic title that created after the event an air of suspense and purposefulness, even a touch of adventure. Through these additions, Gross's text acquires a certain proximity to a work of fiction – rather as chapter headings were customary for a while in the eighteenth-century novel, for example (cf. Stanzel, 1985: 58f.) – and this impression is reinforced by the publication of the Dachau journal together with some of the verse he composed there, in the form of the trilogy: *Zweitausend Tage Dachau* [Two Thousand Days of Dachau], *Fünf Minuten vor Zwölf* [Five Minutes to Twelve] and *Sterne in der Nacht* [Stars in the Night].

It is mainly in the *report*, however, that the attribution of meaning takes place. This form makes it possible to endow experiences with a definitive time structure marked by a beginning, a middle and an end (cf. Kermode, 1967; Brooks, 1974; White, 1987), as well as making them subject to the principles of selection and evaluation (cf. Atteslander, 1975: 71). Both of these characteristics involve aspects of interpretation, which give the form of testimony an affinity to fictional representation.[11] Temporal structuring and selection read a certain meaning into experience – which is undoubtedly the reason why the report is the form in which personal experience of the camps is most often cast. It is akin to what many writers on literature have defined as genuine autobiography or memoirs. Two of the most illuminating approaches to the question are those of Bernd Neumann (1970) and Peter Sloterdijk (1978). Neumann seeks to distinguish autobiography and memoirs according to both a content criterion and an ensuing temporal criterion. Autobiography, he concludes, is that form with whose help the ' "self-directed" bourgeois individual' represents himself or herself; whereas memoirs are the preferred form of the ' "tradition-directed" feudal individual'

(Neumann, 1970: 176f.). Since Neumann sees the development of personality as the central focus of autobiography, and the practical testing of the author in public life as the central focus of memoirs, he is able to treat the two forms as temporally sequential. To put it rather schematically, one might say that for Neumann memoirs begin where autobiography leaves off, with the completed formation of individual identity and the entry into working life; or that autobiography comes into play again when the individual's role in public life ends with retirement. However, apart from the fact that Neumann develops his theory of autobiography by reference to eighteenth-century and nineteenth-century society, his ideal typology is itself also susceptible to criticism. For it is really not an adequate tool for the analysis of texts from the concentration camps, since most of these neither deal (as in autobiography) with the genesis of the individual, nor present the individual as bearer of a social role, as what Neumann calls a 'man or woman of action' (Neumann, 1970: 10f.).[12] Rather, the reports from the camps concern themselves with an identity which, precisely because of what is described, has lost its self-assuredness. They depict people whose hands are tied, who do not take any far-reaching decisions of their own, and who can take active responsibility for their lives only in the most exceptional situations (cf. Langer, 1982: 74f.–94).[13] These texts differ from autobiography in that, instead of objectifying the self, they present concrete experience with the surrounding world: that is, in the camp. The developmental pattern of traditional autobiography proves to be of little use here (cf. Foley, 1982: 338); it would seem more appropriate (within Neumann's terminological framework) to speak of 'anti-autobiographies' or 'anti-memoirs'. But since such a negative definition would not be very fruitful, other criteria must be sought for the autobiographical character of the concentration camp testimonies.

What these texts crystallize is an attempt to master an exceptional threat to the personality and life of the individual – that is, to give it some sense and thereby lay the basis for a meaningful further existence. Hence, we need a definition of autobiographical writing which focuses upon an exemplary coming to terms, or failure to come to terms, with experience. Peter Sloterdijk's heuristic categories of 'proto-political experience' and 'dialectical learning' are meant to serve this purpose (Sloterdijk, 1978:

112–23). As we have seen, self-reflection is sparked off by 'dis-ruptive experiences' which, being incapable of integration into the customary interpretative framework, necessitate at least a partial revision of the individual's picture of the world. This occurs in a process of dialectical learning, 'when the subject is constantly faced with the causes and forces of the shaping of knowledge' (Sloterdijk, 1978: 116f.). In reporting on this learning process, the individual becomes aware that what it depicts is his or her political subjectification, so that some of the disruptive experiences may be said to acquire a 'proto-political' or pre-political quality. In the concentration camp texts, of course, the term 'political' must be understood in a very broad sense, not simply that of party politics, and care must also be taken with the use of the concept of learning.[14] Nevertheless, this approach centred on experiential history and critique does afford some insight into the personality-related process of coming to terms with life in and after the camp – a process which did not happen automatically, but depended upon the individual's circumstances and experiences before internment. It was these which provided the interpretive pattern for any attempt to gain some bearings in the chaos of camp life. Thus, coping always has something to do with remembering.[15] Since events in the camp only very rarely tallied with previous experience of life, the individual was compelled either to deploy that experience in rough-and-ready forms, or to modify it accordingly, or to switch right over to interpretive patterns from other fields (usually mediated through reading).

The Hasidic tale as explanatory model: Fred Wander, Der siebente Brunnen

> The secret of redemption is remembrance.
>
> (Jewish saying)

In comparison with other testimonies, Fred Wander published his with considerable delay: *Der siebente Brunnen* (The Seventh Foun-tain) appeared only in 1971. Although Wander does not speak in this work of the reasons for the 25-year gap between his release from Buchenwald and the written record of his experiences, it may be assumed that he had been struggling to find the appropriate form. Wander confirmed this impression in an interview that he gave when his 'tale' was published. Before he was able to tell the story, he said, he had had to 'come to terms' with the material (cf. Trampe, 1971). When he, as an acculturated and assimilated Jew[16] (Strauss and Hoffmann, 1985: 9–27), opted for a specifically Jewish type of narrative, he did this with the clear aim of incorporating his own fate into the broader framework of Jewish (especially East European Jewish) history.[17]

Wander's text describes three historical levels: the most encompassing – the one that provides the general framework – is that of the Second World War; the second takes in Buchenwald and Auschwitz and their outlying camps; the third is the fate of the Jews, especially the East European Jews. In this way, Wander integrates his own destiny into the general history of the Hitler regime and the Judaeocide.[18] The 'transcendence' of his personal experience in the destiny of the group to which he felt he belonged not only provided him with a formal model but also enabled him to participate in the structure of meaning which the group created for itself. The very title of the work already expresses this duality. 'Der siebente Brunnen' is taken from the poem 'Die sieben Brunnenkränze' by the sixteenth-century Kabbalist from Prague Rabbi Jehuda Loew.[19] Wander's chapter of the same name deals with the pleasure that the East European Jews took in telling tales – indeed their compulsion to do so. By taking the title of his 'tale' from Loew's poem, he adopted an interpretive model for his experiences in the concentration camps: for Rabbi Loew had used 'the water of purity' as a symbol for cleansing and purification. Mendel Teichmann, a fellow victim in the camps, conveyed this theme to Wander as the explanation for their captivity:

> The curse upon us is like the water from the seventh fountain. How did the great Rabbi Loew put it? The seventh fountain will wash away what you have accumulated: the golden candlesticks, the house and your children. You will be left naked, just as you came from your mother's womb. And the pure water of the seventh fountain will cleanse you, and you will become transparent; the fountain itself, ready for future generations, so that they emerge from the darkness with pure and clear eyes, their heart utterly light. (**Wander**, 1985: 51)

That which remained ambivalent in Rabbi Loew's text becomes explicitly positive in Wander's subsequent narrative. Man is purified in the concentration camp, so that he can contribute in turn to the purification of coming generations. Wander thus combines two themes that are often found in testimony from the camps. On the one hand, the authors seek, by exposing the experience of inhumanity, to prevent its repetition in the future – that is one of the reasons why they record what they have lived through. On the other hand, they use the image of purgatory as an explanatory framework, alluding to Dante's descriptions of Hell and Purgatory. Even academic texts such as the article by Dr Lucie Adelsberger, herself an Auschwitz survivor, have recourse to this image (Adelsberger, 1947: 124f.).

Only at first sight does the metaphor seem inappropriate to the Judaeocide of the recent past. The Jewish conception of guilt and its erasure can actually be made compatible with it. For sin in the Jewish religion differs in two main ways from sin in Christianity: first, people are already punished for it in this world (not just in an afterlife, as in Christianity);[20] and second, it affects not so much the individual as the entire people.

Wander's understanding of purification appears influenced by Christianity in that he interprets it as an individual process. It emerges from his 'Letter to Primo Levi' that he conceives of a personal coming to terms with experience as opposed to a 'political coming to terms with the past': only the surviving victims can effect this personal coping (Wander, 1982: 23).

Symbolic use of the fountain may also be found in the lyric verse of Nelly Sachs, where it is invoked both as preserver of past utopias and as mirror of that which should not be forgotten – and hence as a connecting link between past and present.[21]

Wander's narrative form is rooted in the tradition of Hasidism, a popular Jewish movement of the eighteenth century which was directed against rabbinical Judaism and its claims that access to God was confined to scholars and their interpretation of the Scriptures. Hasidism was founded by Israel ben Elieser (1700–60), also known as Baal schem tow, which means more or less 'spokesman' of the people (cf. Buber, 1984: 31). The new doctrine, which encouraged devotees to rejoice in everyday life and the world as it is, overcame the division between the sacred and the profane (Buber, 1984: 18f.). It is with and in the active life – and no longer the Talmud – that the Hasid communicates with God. Right from the beginning, the spread of Hasidism was assured by the texts upon which the movement was based. These were written not in the Hebrew of rabbinical Judaism, but in the language of the people, in Yiddish. Thus, for the first time women had the possibility of taking an active part in religious affairs (cf. Eliach, 1985: 12–17; Roskies, 1984: 133f.).

Literature in the language of the people also promoted the art of narrative. It is therefore no accident that narrative played a central role in Hasidism.[22] Martin Buber, who rediscovered and renewed Hasidism, saw in the 'narrative word' a guarantee of the continuity which 'carries what has happened over to future generations'. In fact, he thought that 'narrative is itself a happening; it has the solemnity of a sacred action' (Buber, 1984: 5). Jaffa Eliach, Buber's 'spiritual granddaughter', today sees the Hasidic tale as embodying the power 'to restore order and to renew the severed contact between fellow-humans, between heaven and earth' (Eliach, 1985: 16). The Hasidic tale re-establishes connections where they have been lost, in both a 'diachronic' and a 'synchronic' sense. As it binds grandparents to grandchildren in the sequence of generations, so it promotes cohesion within generations. And it is in times of crisis that this narrative form unfolds in all its power.

For Buber, however, the Hasidic tale not only brings something about; 'the holy essence is produced within it', in an ontological sense (Buber, 1984: 5f.). This accounts for the spiritual power that it gives the Hasidim in situations of distress. In his *Tales of the Hasidim*, Buber explained the threefold function of the Hasidic tale. In the form of legend, it documents the mythical life of the Zaddikim, the 'Saints', and thus passes on knowledge at once historical and religious. Second, in its words, it preserves the advice of the Zaddik. And finally, it testifies to the persecution and repression of the Jewish people in eighteenth-century and nineteenth-century Ukraine, thereby making a major contribution to Jewish history.

An example of the multifunctionality of the Hasidic tale, which has become widely known through the musical *Fiddler on the Roof*, is Sholom Aleichem's tale of the milkman Tevye. The problematic marriage wishes of his daughters gain a further dimension of meaning from the historical background of persecution. Perchik, whom Tevye's second daughter Hodl follows into Siberian exile, embodies the figure of the Jewish revolutionary. Shava, the third daughter, runs away with the 'goy' Shvedka and is accordingly disowned by her father. Only when all the Jews are driven from the village does she find her way back to the family.

In the beginnings of Judaism, historiography and testimony about persecution already overlapped with each other. What made these early writings instructive for generations of readers, and what still makes them so readable today, is the fact that they impart not so much facts as the meaning of events (cf. Roskies, 1984: 35). The Talmud, begun in Babylonian captivity, is in the end nothing other than a written record of expulsion and repression.[23] Only in the eighteenth century, when the Jews began to assimilate more and more to the host nations, did the Bible lose its power of historical integration (cf. Kochan, 1977: 59–68).

Not by chance was it precisely at this time that the Hasidic legends arose in Eastern Europe, taking up and continuing under the impact of the pogroms the older historiographical tradition. It is legitimate to read even the reports about the latest and most devastating case of persecution – the mass murder of the Jews under the Third Reich – as a new form of writing about the repression of the Jewish people. Jaffa Eliach, for instance, calls her collection 'Hasidic Tales from the Twentieth Century' (Eliach, 1985: 14). It contains the stories which Hasidim survivors told her in Brooklyn, New York in the late 1970s and early 1990s (Eliach, 1985: 7). In the concentration camp reports one can also find references to this model of explanation: Primo Levi, for instance, speaks of a 'new Bible' in connection with the written reports on the Judaeocide (**Levi**, 1987a: 72).

Fred Wander's text takes over both the narrative tradition of the Hasidic tale and its historiographical character. He calls his book simply a 'tale', although in many respects it is more like the 'legends' that grew up around the Zaddik, who, as Martin Buber puts it, 'made it easier for his Hasidim to gain direct access to God' (Buber, 1984: 21).[24] This legend-like character of Wander's 'tale' is expressed in the fact that he pictures many of his fellow camp-inmates in the role of a Zaddik. Special mention should be made here of Mendel Teichmann, who, quite in the didactic manner of the Maggid (cf. Buber, 1984: 36), as the Zaddik is also known, passed on the Hasidic narrative tradition to Fred Wander. He introduced his disciples to the art of storytelling, not systematically but with the help of a tale whose meaning Wander himself 'discovered only much later' (**Wander**, 1985: 8). In his more recent book, *Hotel Baalbek* (1991), we can still detect the influence of Teichmann's teaching.

As in the tales of the Hasidim (cf. Eliach, 1985: 19), one should not too quickly categorize Wander's work as fiction. By describing the particular fates of his companions in suffering – sometimes in their own words – Wander brings the unbelievable to life for those who read him. It is the reporting of the individual's torments which allows us to grasp, if at all, the meaning of the mass murder of a whole ethnic group. Thus, contrary to the view of Reinhard Baumgart (Baumgart, 1966: 28), an individualized account cannot be excluded in a field such as the Holocaust. Indeed, it is only in concrete instances of suffering that the genocide loses its abstractness. The task of art, argues Günther Anders most appositely, is to 'narrow the focus, so that we are not entirely excluded from a truth by its incomprehensible enormity' (Anders, 1985: 203).

Fred Wander concentrates on the narrative act itself, convinced of its ability to prolong, though not ultimately to preserve, life. He learnt this from Hasidic Jews in the camp, 'who have been persecuted for centuries and therefore live in the Word' (**Wander**, 1985: 46). As storytelling, for many Jews in the eighteenth century, offered the only possibility of leaving the ghetto or shtetl, so the power of the storyteller's imagination – in accordance with Brecht's motto that 'imagination is the only truth' (cited by Eliach, 1985: 19) – was of benefit to many interned in the Lager.[25] When Leon Feinberg, for example, told his travellers' tales, he carried his listeners to each of the places in which he stopped. Wander recalls:

> Lying in the hut in the pitch dark, without ever having been to Odessa, Granada, Riga, Lvov or Kursk, I got to know the smell of those old towns from shaky individual words, melancholic confessions, declarations of love evoking a particular place, a suburban street, a small back garden with a pear tree, a moss-covered garden step, a little house. (**Wander**, 1985: 90)

But Wander does not only mention exotic places that prisoners exchanged for a while with the concentration camp. Family, home and Jewish festivities also remained alive within the sufferer's imagination. 'The word had magical powers,' writes Wander in describing a kind of Hasidic *locus amoenus*.[26] 'It conjured up a richly laid Sabbath table, the charm of a Jewish *maedl*, the fragrance of

sweet Palestinian wine and currant cakes, a beautiful lost world'
(**Wander**, 1985: 8).[27] In the Lager, then, storytelling had a compensatory function similar to that which it had in the East
European shtetl; it helped Wander's fellow-captives to reassure
themselves about everything they had to give up in the camp: their
individuality, their self-esteem, even nourishment for their body.

Storytelling was also bound up in other ways with survival. For
without someone to listen, thoughts of revenge – a powerful, if not
the principal, motive to continue the fight for life – could not
acquire their full force. Wander's fellow-captives had to speak
about their cares and wishes, had to keep reassuring themselves
that they were still alive. 'His eyes blazed as he said it. A vast
weariness and a great will vied with each other inside him'
(**Wander**, 1985: 30). This is how Wander describes a fellow-
prisoner who had let his friends in on his ambition to survive. But
Pépé too, a 'political', looked to words to sustain himself: 'His
cascading words were not poetry like the speech of Mendel
Teichmann; they were the Revolution' (**Wander**, 1985: 78). In
Wander's memory, then, speech and storytelling did not display
their power only among the Hasidim who escaped into the ideal
world of their occupational activity or their tranquil family life.
Other internees transported themselves and their listeners into a
future of vengeance and political overthrow. In both cases, language (at least temporarily) took the prisoners out of the camp
routine and made their lot a little easier.[28]

Wander's interest in the Hasidic storytelling tradition is not
only theoretical; it is also apparent in the content of his work.
Whether a fellow-captive in mortal anguish is seeking refuge in a
Hasidic wise saying – 'When the body suffers, the soul should
laugh! That is what Baal-Schem taught us' (**Wander**, 1985: 105)
– or whether someone is quoting the storyteller Mendel Teichmann as an authority, Wander points up the same Hasidic trust in
the word of the Maggid. In the situation of the concentration
camp, a special meaning attaches even to the words of the
prophets. Where a physical expression of sympathy was not
permitted under the watch of the SS, a quotation had to take its
place.

> He [an old Jew 'with the face of a magus'] sees a lost Jewish child
> crying. He nods in a friendly way, wanting to caress him. But instead
> he quotes Jeremiah: *If you will only remain in this land, then I will build*

you up and not pull you down; I will plant you, and not pluck you up; for
I am sorry for the disaster that I have brought upon you. Do not be afraid
of the king of Babylon, as you have been; do not be afraid of him, for I am
with you, to save you and to rescue you from his hand. (**Wander**, 1985:
71; emphasis in the original)

Precisely because the (hi)story of the Jews is a (hi)story of
persecution, it is suited to give comfort in situations of crisis. The
attitude of the Jewish people to history is, as is well known,
fundamentally different from that of other peoples. Through
centuries of living in the diaspora, a certain kind of Jewish self-
protection developed not only in close family ties but also in a
strong sense of historical continuity.[29] A person's life and actions
are attributed with lasting significance for their descendants.
Although tradition may also be experienced as a burden – a theme
treated, for example, in Kafka's 'Investigations of a Dog' – Wander's Hasidic Jews are capable of living, or rather surviving, with
the 'wisdom of their fathers' (**Wander**, 1985: 108). His fellow-
captives have the 'cunning' of survival, 'which has grown out of
centuries of persecution' (**Wander**, 1985: 110), and yet they still
fall victim to the Nazi machinery of death. By these means,
Wander modestly presents his very personal case for the prosecu-
tion against the mass murderers.

The shocking climax of Wander's 'story' is his report of the
death of a young fellow-prisoner. Tadeusz Moll, thrown completely unprepared from a sheltered existence into the horror of
the concentration camp, dies as a result of his naive carelessness.
The archetypal theme of martyrdom no longer fits the meaninglessness of death in the Lager (cf. Roskies, 1984: 217),[30] also
because individual death – as Terence Des Pres notes – simply
helped a further victory of evil. Under the innocuous title 'What
Does the Forest Remind You Of?', Wander turns to a mode of
representation which impressionistically associates feelings and
memories from life before the camp, from his internment in
France, and then from Buchenwald.

What does FOREST remind you of, o sleeper? . . . Forest smells, forest
sights, the peace in the thick of a copse, the rustling leaves above, the
majestic nodding of the treetops in the wind – for all time, the forest
odour will be mixed with the smell of burning, and with the image of
poison-white clouds of smoke on the naked bodies of the dead of
Crawinkel. But also the memory of hot childhood afternoons at the

foot of the Kahlenberg in Vienna, weary and drunk with colour and light, ... and in the distance, agreeably tiring too, a scrap of conversation beneath the scorching sun, the laughter of farm girls and reapers in the fields, a suppressed cry of pleasure. The world is still unscathed. A deep harmony lies over the steaming earth ... Forest vision, never again will I drink your unalloyed delight. Forest, you who change everything to your ends of peace and silence, you who store rain and suckle streams, who convert life into decay and decay into life, emptiness and plenitude, microscopic life and eternity in a dew-drop, you will not make me forget this image: a platform in the middle of the Thuringian forest raised above six sturdy young trees, musicians blaring, tootling, banging on drums: young men, lovely sons full of tender care for their mothers, young know-alls, deft scalers of walls and fences, playing with danger, denying a hierarchy of deadly prohibitions, barbed wire, watch-towers and graves, searchers after God – and among them, Tadeusz Moll! (THE GALLOWS TOO, the wide gallows of good juicy oak in the muster yard, a right-angled excision from the green spruce forest of Crawinkel, THE GALLOWS TOO HAD SIX HOOKS. What kind of a joker had thought of that? Wait a moment, the soldiers whispered, until the number is made up. How many posts does the structure have?) (**Wander**, 1985: 112–14).

Anna Seghers describes a similar situation in her novel *Das siebte Kreuz*: there, too, the hooks on the gallows slowly fill up with recaptured escapees. And since no text known to me other than Wander's situates the incident in one of Buchenwald's outlying camps, it cannot be excluded that he is here partly drawing upon Seghers's account. Another indication of this is the similarity between the titles of the two works. For although Wander's title is itself partly a quotation and emphasizes an aspect missing in Seghers, the congruence is nevertheless quite striking.

The experience of the camp violently breaks into the romantic image of the forest (cf. Busse, 1982: 18), marked by childhood memories and the encounter with nature. The idyllic picture is completely displaced by the confrontation with death, so that romantic themes such as the interconnectedness of all things (cf. Blankenagel, 1968: 334) take on a (surreal) meaning of their own (cf. Ott, 1968: 371).[31] The gallows replace the forest, and the moon 'hangs behind clouds'. But Fred Wander writes in his imagination of Tadeusz Moll's thoughts: 'He loves the spruce trunks and the beams of light; he loves the air, the cold, the solitary moon – for all this is life' (**Wander**, 1985: 120). The pseudo-romantic thematization here serves to bring closer the experience of a death that has lost all meaning.

At the moment of the camp's liberation, Wander diverges for the first time from reporting about fellow-captives and focuses directly upon his own experience. This section also differs from the rest of the text in its choice of images and explanatory models, turning away from the symbolic world of Hasidism towards much older archetypes in the Jewish apocalyptic literature.[32] On the SS withdrawal from Buchenwald, which he survived in the children's hut,[33] Wander comments: 'The walls of Jericho had fallen, but Joschko and his brothers had not heard the trumpet' (**Wander**, 1985: 139).[34] The children – especially a Joschko distantly related to the biblical Joseph, who watched over his brothers and 'at ten years of age [already] functioned as father and tribal elder' (**Wander**, 1985: 140) – became for Wander symbols of a new beginning that would at the same time be a continuation of the lost (or thought-to-be-lost) world. At that moment he grasped the true connection between dying and living on:

> In my enchantment ... I looked once at the children, then again at the old man next to me, and was amazed. I was amazed at the extravagant splendour of nature: a handsome old stranger without a name, a wise man with regular features, a well-shaped white beard and a nose as if carved from ivory. He lay spread out on his back, not like someone dead but like a statue (eyes and mouth firmly shut), a portrait of the perfection of man: now grown old, his life complete, thrown down without protest and without a superfluous word. When had he come? What had brought him to the children's hut? He smiled in death, as if giving an answer to my question. He was the only dead man in all those years whom I saw smiling.[35] He had passed on the baton to Joschko and his brothers; he had dropped it and they, without knowing, had picked it up and carried it forward. (**Wander**, 1985: 141f.).

This optimistic conclusion or outlook of the 'story' shows that, for Fred Wander, writing became what David Roskies calls an 'act of faith' (Roskies, 1984: 198ff.). To come to terms with the Judaeo-cide, the surviving Jews had to give up a retrospective-historiographical attitude in favour of a prophetic one. This counted as an existential necessity for those survivors who took up the pen. Only an orientation to the future allowed them to come anywhere near to coping with the violent death of their family and fellow-victims. By including the dead in their prophetic vision, they gave their death a meaning which it would not otherwise have had. This elucidatory hypothesis, however, is unthinkable without the assumption of a distinctively Jewish identity, which assured the individual of a place in the community (cf. DeKoven, 1980: 95).

As in the Hasidic tales, Wander's concern is not with the communication of factual truths but with authentic narration as an act of survival. This authenticity essentially resides in the atmosphere created in the text. Deictic openings such as 'This is the story of Tadeusz Moll' (**Wander**, 1985: 97), or the answering of one question with another (**Wander**, 1985: 137), which is considered a Jewish particularity, conjures up the milieu of the shtetl as well as the tacit Jewish self-criticism of the narrator. 'Jargon' terms such as *nebbich* ('tough!'), *Jiden* ('yiddishers') or *Chawer* ('pal') also contribute to the atmosphere, as does the characteristic style of the verbal report: 'because the just are rich already' (**Wander**, 1985: 91), or 'Nu, I've been waiting patiently' (**Wander**. 1985: 22). Wander even quotes whole passages in Yiddish, when he wants to stress the emotional character of a situation. This applies, for instance, to a baseless act of abuse committed by an SS guard: '*Far wos schlogt er Jiden? Wos macht asa alte Mann? Far wos sitzt er nit in der Hejm un trinkt Kawe?*' ('Why is he hitting Jews? What's that old man doing here? Why isn't he home drinking coffee?') (**Wander**, 1985: 24). When the prisoners think of their own home, Wander himself uses the familiar idiom in his report: '*Kinderlach, hot Modche Rabinowicz geriefen, ojfgeregt, schier nit vin Sinnen, as mir welln mir sejn in der Hejm, werd Maminju bentschen Lecht, un der Tate werd brechen die Chaleh*' ('Children – Modche Rabinowicz called out excitedly, almost out of his mind – when we're back home, Mother will bless the candles and Father will break the challah') (**Wander**, 1985: 26).

The argument that a radically new form was used to communicate the experience of the death camps is not supported by analysis of Fred Wander's text. Rather, he turns back to a very traditional form, and must thus accept that the highly abnormal events will be presented in a way that gives them a high degree of comparability. By recording his experiences as a Hasidic tale, he also takes

over the interpretative model from the tradition of Jewish persecution. The novel element in his account is what he does with the
rediscovered form. At a surface level, the use of Hasidic legend in
an autobiographical setting already represents a break with tradition, since its character was in the broadest sense biographical.
But the internal structure also contains elements incompatible
with the Hasidic narrative tradition – above all, the crucial
juxtaposition of different segments of memory in the account of
the meaningless death of Tadeusz Moll. The qualitative change is
in keeping with the situation that confronted Jews in the Nazi
period. Whereas, up to and including the nineteenth century,
pogroms mainly flared up in response to the otherness of the Jews
and their relative unwillingness to assimilate, anti-Semitism in the
Third Reich denied Jews the right to exist, simply because they
had been born Jewish (cf. Silbermann, 1981: 13–26).

If one compares Wander's formal changes with those which
Hans Rudolf Picard noted in French autobiography of the same
period, the great traditionalism of the concentration camp report
fairly leaps to one's eyes.[36] This may be explained by the fact that,
for authors like Wander, the main point is not to depict their
feelings as authentically as possible, but to paint an objective
picture of the time they spent in the camps. With some exceptions
such as Wander's text, the concentration camp reports are mainly
characterized by the similarity of experiences. This is not surprising, given Himmler's drive to make the camps as uniform as
possible in construction, management and administration (cf.
Broszat, 1984: 46). With regard to the reports, therefore, it must
be assumed that their conceptual figures and their forms of
articulation carry a collective stamp (cf. Osterland, 1973: 413).

The travel report as explanatory model:
Albert Drach, Unsentimentale Reise

Albert Drach's 'Report', as the sub-title calls his memories of
escape from the Nazis, falls into three parts of uneven length,
corresponding to the periods of time they describe. Each of these
three parts, and periods, has its distinctive content. Drach was a
23-year-old lawyer when he left his native Vienna and set off for
France, having lost his profession and status, as well as any
illusions about the new regime, soon after the Nazis marched into

Austria in 1938. The first-person narrator, Peter Kucku, tells of this experience, but only in retrospect.[37] His direct account begins with his recent internment in a French holding camp. From Nice, where he has previously been staying, he is deported together with other Jews after the German occupation of France to the Rives Altes camp; this brings Part One to an end. Drach's experience of the camp does not last long. He manages to escape onward deportation to a German death camp in Poland by taking a very positive line with his French guards. This sets the tone for the other parts of his report. Whether in transport trains or in camps, Peter Kucku does not quietly put up with things. Although he lays himself open to both the anger of his captors and the anxious criticism of those who share his fate, he owes it to this assertive conduct that he is released along with a few others from the holding camp. What distinguishes this picaresque impudence (cf. Manthey, 1988) and makes the reader easily overlook the seriousness of the situation, is the native cunning on which it is based. Kucku – who, unlike his companions in the train compartment, can produce no valid reason for possible dispensation from internment – knows how to convince the French authorities that two 'Aryan' grandparents on his mother's side mean that he should not be placed at the mercy of the German Reich. The fact that these were actually forebears of his father's first wife and his own step-sister certainly causes him occasional pangs of conscience, but this does not prevent him from sticking with them through thick and thin. A second, similar manipulation of his family connections is used when it comes to the question of religious affiliation. When his mother got him a new certificate of domicile in 1939, the Nazi authorities in Austria had endorsed it with the initials 'I.K.G.' for 'Israelitische Kultusgemeinde' (Israelite Religious Community). With French officials, however, Kucku passes this off as 'Im Katholischen Glauben' (In the Catholic Faith). For the authenticated translation that he needs in order to be issued with a certificate stating him to be non-Jewish, he eventually succeeds in having this abbreviation interpreted as 'Cathol. rel.'.

Part Two of Drach's report covers the period of ceaseless wandering between the French and Italian authorities to protect himself from the German occupiers and to obtain a residence permit. After discovering the unhelpfulness of 'friends' of people he met in detention, he finds friends of his own who also come up with most peculiar ways of offering assistance. His ever provisional salvation is mainly due to chance acquaintances, especially women with a dubious background. Thus a strange baroness – who only enlists him to talk her nymphomaniac daughter out of going into a convent – puts him in touch with acquaintances in the little village of Caminflour in the mountains above Nice, where he is in the end given a surprisingly cordial welcome. This is not the end of his persecution, however. For financial difficulties and denunciations to the Germans (who eventually take control of the village) keep driving him into desperate courses of action, which chance and good luck help him to survive. But this belongs to the third part of the report.

In Caminflour, Kucku meets a number of other eccentric figures, such as the tubercular poet Lebleu, who admires the Germans and receives Kucku tumultuously in his home as a 'kindred' spirit. A colonel, a retired colonial official, several Jews in hiding, an Anglo-French widow, Mrs Withorse, and her three children complete the list of outside people living in the village. This third part of the report also includes the never more than latent relationship between the narrator and Sibylle, the daughter of Mrs Withorse, known as Darling, who keeps up his will to survive. All members of the group into which Kucku is received are the sort of people who know how to get by in life. They have no occupation, and live on income whose sources are never quite clear. The Lebleus take Kucku as a lodger for two thousand francs a month. When his money begins to run out, and the Lebleus' old mother dies (having basically provided for the family out of her pension), Kucku supplies them with mushrooms or other things obtained from the local peasants by barter.

The liberation of France by American troops finds Kucku still in Caminflour. Something that he then does purely out of an instinct for self-preservation makes him the village hero of the hour; he is even offered, but declines, the office of mayor. He makes contact again with friends in Nice, who have all been marked in various ways by the German occupation.

In his report, Drach puts his faith in the literary tradition of the travel novel. The archetypal situation of the journey permits an organization of memory, both formally and in respect of content (cf. Possin, 1972). But Drach does not stop at the general programme that this involves; the very title of the book refers to a most particular model, namely, Laurence Sterne's *Sentimental Journey through France and Italy by Mr Yorick*. This novel, first published in 1768, had quite a strong impact in the eighteenth century, which was not limited to the British Isles (cf. Michelsen, 1962). It was the stress on the author's individual consciousness (cf. Possin, 1972, 19), as opposed to the representation of empirical reality, which aroused such admiration and encouraged others to emulate it. The highly subjective travel impressions, which attach greater meaning to a chance encounter with a typical person from the area than to the observation of famous works of architecture, are interwoven with erotic experiences in a way that has fired the enthusiasm of generations of readers. Albert Drach uses the well-tested model, but – as the title indicates – he turns it into its opposite. The experience of travel gives him only limited self-knowledge, and no self-fulfilment at all. The reason for it is no longer voluntary.

Two factors account for the unsentimentality of Drach's travels: one is their involuntary character; the other is the death which his persecutors intend to be the conclusion. It is only for a relatively short time, during the preliminaries to deportation to Germany, that physical elimination seems to Drach an inescapable reality. Yet the continual necessity of avoiding capture has a deadening effect upon him. Although the prospects of physical survival increase with the length of the 'journey' (**Drach**, 1992: 282), Kucku-Drach loses more and more of his humanity. Thoughts of other captives, who did not have the good fortune to be set free on the eve of deportation to Germany, begin to torment the narrator. He must remain on his guard, as Dr Honigmann whispers to him, because survival is still not assured. Dreams of friends from his youth, encountered in unexpected and peculiar surroundings, suddenly come true in disturbing ways (**Drach**, 1992: 176, 186, 275–6).

Sterne's account mainly concerned France. Because of illness, he was only able to complete two of his planned four volumes, and the journey to Italy promised in the title is lacking. Nor is the existing text really a travel report in the popular sense of the term. The French topography between Calais and Lyons is simply the catalyst for Yorick's 'sentimental' experiences. Mr Yorick, the country parson who is a thin disguise for the author, meets people who are all from marginal groups in society; they arouse his sympathy, just as the numerous women arouse his spontaneous love. These two feelings, then, dominate the work. The humorous element is introduced by Yorick's servant, a man of unaffected peasant cunning.

The differences from Sterne's novel are more obvious than the similarities. Kucku-Drach is forced into his journey out of Austria, and its purpose is not pleasure but escape from the Nazis. The escalating measures against Jews in his homeland, and finally the occupation of France by the Germans, turn the journey more and more into a flight. Looking back, Drach describes it as follows:

> I was chased from my profession and my country, I had been in foreign countries without means or connections and was driven from place to place, arrested repeatedly, saw people die next to me, and was taken unconscious to a central camp, from which they intended to send me for annihilation. (**Drach**, 1992: 189).[38]

In fleeing from Austria, he leaves behind his old mother, who already looks on their parting as final. Kucku attempts to snatch her from the machinery of annihilation, but he fails. And in one of the retrospective sections of his report, the narrator thinks he can see a link between his escape and his mother's death:

> Then I murdered my mother by deserting her, and I fled alone. Then I went to the woman with whom my mother didn't want me to sleep, and I abstained up to the day of departure but not on that day, although I had a feeling that my mother would die the next year if I let myself go. I ... won't see that woman any more, nor my mother. (**Drach**, 1992: 178)

In the end, a merciful death following a difficult operation saved her from deportation to a death camp in Poland. But Kucku feels that he symbolically murders her a second time, when he appropriates the 'Aryan' ancestors of his step-sister's mother and even has this officially registered through a certified translation of the documents.

Although Kucku does not simply yield to his fate, he cannot determine when and how his journey is interrupted. Even after his lucky escape from the transport to Poland, it is others who fix his route and its stopping places. He says without illusions:

> As I arrived in Nice, it became clear to me that only one leg of my journey was over and that I couldn't know when it would continue. It would have to be resumed some day, maybe without my having

anything to do with it, probably against my will, certainly without my being able to prevent it unless I preferred to perish on the spot. For the time being anyway I had arrived at the destination. (**Drach**, 1992: 89)

The journey to the French transit camp, and thus the report as a whole, begins with Kucku's awakening from a state of unconsciousness. At the last moment, he attempts to escape the involuntary 'journey', by drinking enough alcohol on an empty stomach to induce an attack of biliary colic. The effects first appear, however, only after the doctor in charge has passed him and his fellow-deportees as fit to travel. The involuntary character of the journey's beginning is described as follows in an introductory passage:

> The curtains are drawn tightly. After a jolt I am in motion without stirring. They are carrying me along mechanically. I am at full speed. I don't know where we are going. I am not making my way to anywhere, am lying down too. Nobody has asked my destination. I don't remember buying a ticket … I didn't choose my travelling companions. (**Drach**, 1992: 5)

Unconsciousness and involuntariness also dominate the rest of Kucku's journey. Whereas Mr Yorick planned his 'sentimental journey' and willed it into shape, Kucku has almost no influence over the course of his.

Although Kucku's unsentimental journey invokes by contradistinction Mr Yorick's sentimental one, some similarities can be discerned between the two. Both lead through France and Italy, although Sterne's hero is motivated by curiosity about land and people, and Drach's by the search for protection from annihilation. Both first-person narrators experience a series of erotic adventures. But whereas the parson Yorick can give himself up to these in a 'sentimental' spirit, such an attitude is denied Kucku by the 'unsentimentality' of the situation in which he finds himself. Women do offer themselves to him, but he holds himself back. His balance-sheet is full of regrets:

> I wanted Ilse before she was gassed; it didn't happen. I wanted Jeanne Varien after my return. I have missed every opportunity. I was in love with Darling Withorse, flirted with Veronica, and I almost possessed the handsome gendarme's ugly wife right before her husband's eyes. (**Drach**, 1992: 245)

Kucku's relationship with Darling Withorse is contradictory. At barely seventeen years of age, her sexual knowledge seems to be extraordinarily developed, but Kucku can only infer this from the way in which she behaves with other men. She remains rather cool towards him, publicly exposes him once as a Jew, and throws herself at the newly arriving American soldiers. When she finally shows more than a flirtatious interest in him, this conflicts with the 'unsentimental' character of his journey. Not only does her affection hold out to him the prospect of becoming a 'different person'; it would bring his unsentimental journey to an end (**Drach**, 1992: 339f.), that is, he would die.

Although such a stroke of good fortune is ultimately denied him – an unsentimental journey can never end on a sentimental note – Kucku does know moments of happiness in the course of his flight.

> I have no calendar and would have to look at my permit to see when I may have arrived and when it was extended, or I would have to ask to know today's date. But to me that seems like a betrayal of this hour, which is rather a minute of eternity. And from my bed I see the stars rise outside the window and beyond the balcony, which only the neighbour and his family use, and this way I gain the impression that not the balcony in front of the window but the sidereal bodies in their vastly remote altitude most definitely belong to me somehow, and maybe that is even too much for an unsentimental journey. (**Drach**, 1992: 204)

It is the feeling of unity with nature which, on a few rare occasions, transports the narrator into an ecstatic state. The memory of such moments leads Kucku, even after the German withdrawal from France, to make his way back to Caminflour.

Kucku lays claim not only to such moments of sentimentality, but also to 'sentimental memories' (**Drach**, 1992: 133) and dreams: 'I pretend to myself that dreams are still permitted even on an unsentimental journey' (**Drach**, 1992: 326). His concession to dreams recalls testimony such as that of Fred Wander, for whom daydreams were a means for prisoners to overcome their situation in the camp. But he too thought that sentimentality, especially when shown, was inappropriate to the situation, because it weakened the capacity for resistance. Kucku-Drach recognizes this, but without giving it much consideration. 'I would like to stop crying, because I am very much ashamed of myself, because I don't do that otherwise, and because no sentimentality is permitted on this unsentimental journey' (**Drach**, 1992: 153). The description of the 'unsentimental journey' here replaces analysis of the described situation and justification of the narrator's conduct.

But the epithet 'unsentimental' not only stands in contrast to Mr Yorick's journey; it also modifies a series of convictions and habits of 'normal' life. When the narrator speaks of the threat of annihilation, for example, his attitude to life as such changes:

> I wonder whether something inside me changed. I believe it did. The difference is that I no longer take life so seriously, since I know that the laws protecting it have been suspended. I'll still have to take everybody's life seriously. What is different is how one acts in the face of death, and how one acts when one believes that death is somewhere else. The difference is the objective certainty that we are on an unsentimental journey, and that nobody knows when or how it will one day end, or where it is leading. (**Drach**, 1992: 87)

Inevitably this different attitude to life brings a change in values. Kucku is no longer ashamed of being invited to dinner by a woman (**Drach**, 1992: 94), and generally refrains from showing women the customary attentions. The symbols regulating relations between the sexes lose their meaning, and indeed their legitimacy, because of the unsentimentality of the journey (**Drach**, 1992: 194). Nevertheless, reflexes persist which have a constricting effect upon sexual permissiveness (**Drach**, 1992: 77). Of course, this is bound up with the special situation in which the narrator finds himself. At one point Kucku rationalizes his sexual abstinence as a result of his internment in Rives Altes. Even before his life became 'completely transcendental', he had already died. In sexual intercourse he can do no more than pass on his death. 'I am not allowed to love, and that is why all my efforts in that direction fail. At most it would be the activity of an incubus' (**Drach**, 1992: 206). This image from the fund of medieval superstition simultaneously refers to his pursuers, whose methods of persecuting the Jews are patently linked to those current in the Middle Ages.

The narrator further observes that 'unsentimentality' has become a feature of the surrounding world and of the behaviour of his contemporaries. Unable to depend on anyone, he is thrown back upon his own resources (**Drach**, 1992: 177). Partly out of self-protection he forgets the ones left behind in Rives Altes, as soon as he regains his own liberty. He notes with regret:

> I no longer think of how closely united I felt with those Polish Jews who danced the horah in the camp in the face of impending annihilation. I also forget the beauty of the landscape, although in the camp I still admired the sun rising over a not very attractive region. You forget a lot on an unsentimental journey. (**Drach**, 1992: 152)

Significantly, it is only when he is himself out of danger that he first thinks of the fate of his deported companions. Dr Honigmann, a fellow-passenger on the transport train, 'speaks' repeatedly to him and reminds him that, despite his physical survival, he carries death inside himself. After the strain of the daily struggle for survival has abated, feelings of guilt towards the murdered ones begin to appear. What Drach poetically expresses in Dr Honigmann's voice is known to psychologists as the survivor syndrome (Niederland, 1980).

At certain points Drach's report follows his English model, but he reinterprets the material in accordance with his completely different starting-point. This may be seen in the theme of vanity or futility, which is of crucial importance in Sterne's novel (cf. Possin, 1972: 171). Whereas Mr Yorick's overpowerful imagination prevents him from reaching his destination, the political conditions facing Kucku mean that the wish for a destination does not even arise. He has to put all his strength into surviving the journey. The theme of futility takes shape in Drach's unfulfilled and unfulfillable sexual life.

A further parallel between the two works is the picaresque element due to the main characters. Both Mr Yorick and Peter Kucku are men on the move, albeit for different reasons. They both employ ruses to make their way through life. But it is reserved for Drach's hero to do this out of existential necessity. Whereas Yorick, still fully in the tradition of the classical picaresque novel, holds a mirror to the various layers of society, Kucku encounters people who have been marked by fascism.

The names of the two protagonists already play a role in characterizing them. While Yorick is derived from Hamlet's court jester (cf. Possin, 1972: 172), Drach gives his narrator a name which not only triggers certain associations but which, missing the final phoneme, gives rise to various speculations.[39] Kucku leaves his fellow-travellers in doubt about the origin of his name. He himself uses it as a peg on which to hang his philosophy.

> 'Krone's my name.' After this introduction, which the manufacturer has directed at me, he waits for more.
>
> 'Peter Kucku', I say, to comply with his wish.
>
> 'How's that?' He doesn't believe my name. I wait. 'Something's missing.'
>
> 'You mean the final "ck". It doesn't belong to it anymore. We are all incomplete.'
>
> 'But for that to be expressed in your name . . . ,' he shakes his head doubtfully. 'I'd sooner believe that one of your relatives comes from France; that's roughly how those birds are called there.'
>
> 'It's possible,' I say. 'Those birds get around a lot and deposit their offspring everywhere. As far as I'm concerned, I do believe I'm a German-speaking cuckoo rather than a French one, for I feel I still lack something to be a Kuckuck!' (**Drach**, 1992: 17)

Other reports also use the metaphor of the journey, though not as such a consistent leitmotif, to interpret their experience of the Nazi death machine. A few titles are enough to make this clear. Isa Vermehren calls her reminiscences of the camps *Reise durch den letzten Akt* (Journey through the Last Act), Erich Schweinburg calls his *Eine weite Reise* (A Long Journey), and Jorge Semprún chooses the title *Le grand voyage*. Vermehren seems to understand the term 'journey' in a purely 'spiritual' sense; her report on Ravensbrück does not record any movement, not even that of the transport arriving in the camp. In Schweinburg, on the other hand, the 'journey' to Dachau plays a major role. Even before he enters the camp, events in the train give a good idea of what is awaiting him. The sadistic tormenting of the prisoners by the transport guards – which reaches a climax in the murder of film producer Nikolaus Deutsch – make it obvious that his life no longer counts for anything. Schweinburg's report ends with a further journey. After his release from Dachau, he emigrates to England – so that his 'long journey' has taken him from Vienna via Dachau to the British Isles. Finally, Jorge Semprún makes his deportation to Buchenwald the focus of his report, inserting along the way various presentiments of the camp itself.

In other texts, the theme of the journey plays a role that rests upon the well-known fact that most of the deportations took place by rail. The German railways worked out regular schedules for this purpose: journeys were calculated at 'group travel' rates, and the price paid by the deportees themselves (cf. Hilberg, 1981). Behind the innocuous veil of this heuristics of organizing lay a journey which haunted survivors until long after their liberation. Schweinburg himself had the dubious privilege of travelling in a passenger coach and being personally harassed; later transports of Jews were in overcrowded cattle trucks and often dragged on for several days. Bruno **Bettelheim** (1961) and Primo **Levi** (1987a) are just two of the authors to have described such a journey.

Whereas former captives recall with dread their deportation to the first camp, they often experienced the journey from one camp to another, or their evacuation, as a pleasant 'trip'. Simha Naor even remembers looking forward to one (**Naor**, 1986: 111). For although prisoners feared any change in their existence as a source of danger, they still hoped that any departure from a camp would bring an improvement in their situation. The prospect of catching a glimpse of 'normal' life *en route* also gave them a lift. Those interned in Auschwitz, in particular, took their departure as a good omen to which they clung in their desperate struggle for survival (see, e.g., **Adelsberger**, 1956: 153).

Just as Fred Wander does not take over the Hasidic narrative tradition without adapting it to his subject matter, Albert Drach is also productive in the use he makes of his model. Although the theme of the journey does, of course, suggest itself in the special conditions of his flight from the Nazi thugs, Drach's starting-point is quite different from Sterne's and requires the model to undergo modification. Yet, as in the case of Wander and of other concentration camp survivors, the adjustments he makes for his expressive needs are not as radical as one might have expected. In terms of reception theory, then, both Wander's and Drach's texts evoke 'a certain horizon of expectations on the part of their readers, marked by conventions of genre, style or form', but they only nullify it to a small degree (cf. Jauss, 1974: 176).

In comparison with these two authors, who already had some experience as writers when they came to compose their report, the overwhelming majority of those who set down their testimony did not engage in any challenging of traditional literary forms. Their story is usually told chronologically, sometimes also with a thematic structure. As 'oral history', it thus tends to revive the bourgeois tradition of family chronicles, of memoirs and reports intended for succeeding generations (cf. Mattenklott, 1992: 176). Many point out in a preface that their intention is to write not an 'artistic' account but a plain and sober record of what they lived through. Wanting to make a personal contribution to the documentary history, they take the report as their formal model and use it with varying degrees of success. The emphasis on factual accuracy is meant to exclude the ways in which they have been affected in their own personal existence. This certainly proves successful as far as the form of their testimony is concerned, but less so in relation to their choice of vocabulary. As we shall see, there develops that 'distortion of truth by the act of contemplation' which Roy Pascal defined as a 'necessary condition of autobiography' (Pascal, 1960: 72).

What distinguishes Wander's and Drach's texts from most others is their courageous plunge into the existential-subjective dimension of their experience. One factor that bars them, however, from a consistently existential-reflective mode of narration – the mode that Picard finds in contemporary autobiographies of writers – is doubtless the very subject matter, the time they spent in camps or in flight from the Nazis. In order to make us understand these experiences, they involve themselves in compromises. The dualism of 'narrative structure and response to "real events"' (Kronsbein, 1984: 65), which is a characteristic feature of autobiography, is almost cancelled in the concentration camp report through an over-emphasis upon the factual. The exceptional position of Drach's and Wander's texts within the genre may thus be ascribed to their efforts to maintain the balance typical of autobiography.

Notes

1. According to H.R. Jauss, a literary work predisposes the recipient through 'open and disguised signals, familiar markers or implicit pointers to a quite definite mode of reception' (Jauss, 1974: 175). The form of the first-person narrative constitutes one such complex. The reader therefore feels cheated if, for example, the first-person narrator suddenly dies – as in Erich Maria Remarque's *All Quiet on the Western Front*. It had been taken on trust that, however horrific the hero's experiences – in this case, the wartime experiences of Paul Bäumer – he must have survived them in order to tell the tale. Franz Stanzel may technically define the continuation of the narrative by another narrator as the replacement of an internal by an external

perspective (Stanzel, 1985: 290), but this does not make the act of reporting any easier to swallow.

2. Cf. Heinz Hillmann (Hillmann, 1977: 161), who sees in literary genres 'action-structured patterns of interpretation accumulated over generations, which the writer uses to organize his own problems and to control his own patterns, and which are thus reorganized in this process of application'.

3. See the informative research report in Kronsbein (1984).

4. Edward Timms, for instance, in his study of the work of Karl Kraus, convincingly shows that he used apocalyptic symbolism in his critique of the world around him (Timms, 1986). (I owe this reference to Karlheinz Rossbacher.)

5. In Hebrew literature the poetry of lamentation is one such paradigm, to which later authors turned when they tried to represent the Holocaust (Dekoven, 1980: 100f.).

6. On the history of the camps, see here and elsewhere Broszat (1984: 9–133).

7. Even the surviving letters of Viktor Matejka from Dachau, which average two to four pages in length and deal with various cultural topics (Klamper, 1981: 310–26), have not yet appeared in print.

8. Else A. Behrend-Rosenfeld also used the form of imaginary correspondence to tell how she survived. See *Ich stand nicht allein. Erlebnisse einer Jüdin in Deutschland 1933–1944*, Hamburg (1949). For a detailed discussion of this report on several camps, see Peitsch (1990: 165–71).

9. This function was also served by lyric poetry composed in the camp (Moll, 1988: 67).

10. The journal was also used by Jews in hiding as a means to keep sane. The most famous example are the diaries of the Romance linguist Victor Klemperer, in which he recorded the gradual Nazification of the German language (**Klemperer**, 1995).

11. The eye-witness report will be more closely distinguished from fictional texts about the camps in Chapter 4, 'The Narrative of Lived Reality'.

12. People who played a role in politics or culture, either before or after their internment in a camp, often use the form of autobiography (or memoirs, in Neumann's definition) to report on their development after their exclusion from public life. In this, the experience of the camp forms only one part, which is inserted into the interpretation of their whole life e.g. **Matejka** (1983), **Maleta** (1981), **Engelmann** (1983).

13. This situation changed towards the end of the war, at least for those political prisoners who, by dint of their long period of detention, had achieved some existential minimum and therefore a certain 'negative' freedom of action. German political prisoners, for example, could refuse to visit the brothels allocated to them and thereby express an attitude of resistance (cf. Pingel, 1978: 166).

14. Michael Moll does not believe in the possibility of 'constructive learning in Auschwitz' (Moll, 1988: 225). At another point, however, he admits that the prisoners' survival could well depend on whether, and to what extent, they adapted to the camp situation (see also Pingel, 1978: 156f.). Charlotte Delbo, a Frenchwoman who was in Auschwitz, describes everything she learnt there as 'useless knowledge', which completely estranged survivors from the world (Charlotte Delbo, *Trilogie. Auschwitz und danach*, Frankfurt am Main: Stroemfeld/Roter Stern (1990), quoted in Judith Klein: 'Am Rande des Nichts', *Die Zeit*, 23 November 1990).

15. Arnold Gehlen, referring to Aristotle, stresses the organic connection between experience (*Erfahrung*) and remembrance (*Erinnerung*) (Gehlen, 1936: 27f.). Manfred Bierwisch, from a psychological point of view, stresses the connection between language and memory (Bierwisch, 1979). And Jürgen Gebhardt defines cognition as 'a dimension of the world of consciousness and experience from which the structural patterns of symbolic forms have taken shape' (J. Gebhardt, 1980: 48).

16. Fred Wander grew up in an already assimilated family. His parents were religious, but not orthodox, and they did not bring Wander up to be religious (cf. Renoldner, 1987: 6).

17. Wander's maternal grandfather had made him familiar with the tales of the Hasidim, and passed on the Yiddish language to him (cf. Renoldner, 1983: 6).

18. In his essay 'The Holocaust: Some Reflections a Generation Later', Bruno Bettelheim criticizes the expressions 'Holocaust' and 'genocide' as 'technological' and therefore inhuman; they were not appropriate to the feelings aroused by the enormity of the event (Bettelheim, 1978: 102f.). As we see, however, he had difficulty in finding an alternative term, and himself used 'Holocaust' in the title of his essay.

19. On the person and life of Rabbi Loew, see Bokser (1954); Thieberger (1955).

20. For example, Jewish legends trace the destruction of the temple in Jerusalem back to the sinful life of King Solomon, especially to his marriage with the (non-Jewish) daughter of the Egyptian pharaoh (cf. Ginzberg, 1967: IV/128f.; VI/278–281).

21. See Anton Thuswaldner: 'Nelly Sachs', in *Kritisches Lexikon zur deutschsprachigen Gegenwartsliteratur*, p. 3.

22. Sholom Aleichem's transformation of the Cartesian 'Cogito ergo sum' into 'I speak, therefore I am' even attached an existential meaning to Yiddish narrative (cf. Roskies, 1984: 163).

23. Lionel Kochan points out that the account was a way 'to make sense of the catastrophe in terms of human guilt and thus salvage even that catastrophe as part of the continuing schema of redemption' (Kochan, 1977: 10).

24. Buber's distinction between tale and legend is itself not always consistent.

25. On the critical, future-oriented function of phantasy, see H. Marcuse (1956: Chapter 7).

26. Wander's almost programmatic conception of the meditative life of the Hasidim is confirmed by his 'Letter to Primo Levi', in which he praises Levi's novel *Pausing for Breath*: 'It reads as the story of an adventure – the great adventure of recovered life and the magic of existence, mirrored in the smallest things which are nevertheless priceless, unmeasurable in terms of gold' (Wander, 1982: 23).

27. It is well known that food plays an eminently important role in the Jewish home, in close association with the figure of the mother. Other internees also tried to cling on to this (cf. 'Life after Death Camps', *Guardian*, 1 May 1989).

28. Michael Moll confirms that this was generally true of artistic production and reception in the camps, whose function he sees as 'the preservation of life' or 'existential defiance of the slavedrivers, aimed at preventing complete mental and physical collapse' (Moll, 1988: 218).

29. George Steiner emphasizes this point: 'The Jew has his anchorage not in place but

in time, in his highly developed sense of history as personal context. Six thousand years of self-awareness are a homeland' (Steiner, 1967: 175).

30. Shaul Esh speaks of a paradigm shift in Jewish eschatology. In the case of the Nazi murder of the Jews, justification of death (*Kiddush ha-shem*) removed the justification of life (*Kiddush ha-hajjim*). 'The Jews of Eastern Europe felt in fact that victory over the enemy lay in their continued existence, for the enemy desired their extinction' (Esch, 1962: 106f.).

31. See also Karlheinz Rossbacher's analysis of Bernt Jentzsch's 'In stärkerem Maße' (Rossbacher, 1977: 40). In the line 'Tattoo-drummer, forest, green landsknecht', Rossbacher argues, 'the metaphors identifying forest with tattoo-drummer and landsknecht, with the step of marching columns in camouflage, develop into the forest grave as the site of violent death'.

32. On these archetypes, see Roskies (1984), especially Chapter 2, 'The Liturgy of Destruction', pp. 15–52.

33. Right at the end, the SS ordered all the Jews to form up to be taken out of the camp. Of those who obeyed, hardly any lived to see freedom (cf. Kogon, 1985: 356–62).

34. See The Book of Joshua, 6:5: 'as soon as you hear the trumpet . . . the wall of the city will fall down flat, and all the people shall charge straight ahead'.

35. The smile of the dead at the hour of liberation seems to be a topos of the concentration camp texts. The same theme may be found, for example, in Edgar Kupfer-Koberwitz's account of the liberation of Dachau: 'He must have seen something beautiful – he still had a smile on his face. And I have taken this smile with me. Among the thousands who died, there was one who smiled' (**Kupfer-Koberwitz**, 1960: 263).

36. This is true not only of the concentration camp prose (cf. Rosenfeld, 1978: 6; Braham, 1983: 107 – both quoted in Moll, 1988: 273), but also of the lyrical verse. Michael Moll, however, treats the prisoners' preference for the sonnet form as a sign of 'their conscious wish to pursue poetry as art' (Moll, 1988: 62). As for prose, the traditional forms of testimony and autobiography were meant to redeem a truth claim for which art counted as deception.

    Apart from concentration camp survivors, other groups such as former Communists have taken their formal orientation from classical autobiography.

37. The period prior to *Unsentimentale Reise* is the theme of Drach's book Z. Z. *Das ist die Zwischenzeit*.

38. The translation of Drach's novel has been slightly modified here and in other extracts [*trans. note*].

39. In this paragraph, the English reader should bear in mind that the German word for cuckoo repeats the letters 'ck' at the end: *Kuckuck*. The French word, however ('*coucou*'), like the English, omits this final sound. The name of Drach's hero – Peter Kucku, which obviously sounds like the French word – plays upon this linguistic difference [*trans. note*].

3
Coming to terms with experience through language

A language, as the product of historical and social factors, plays a crucial role in the construction of meaning. The knowledge and experiences of a community, stored and compressed in language over generations, provide both the structures and the semantic potential within which the socialization of individuals takes place. Thus, language facilitates communication by establishing which units bear meaning, but it thereby also limits the individuality of what is expressed.[1] As 'the objective element that cannot be circumvented', it stands 'between the author's feelings and the printed pages' (Schlösser, 1992: 419). This is bound up with the fact that language not only has a creative function (cf. Zimmermann, 1978: 247), but is itself a conservative and conserving force. The speaker is most likely to be aware of the relatively static (rigid) character of language when he or she tries to do justice to an unusual experience. The fact that only some 2 per cent of concentration camp survivors have so far written (most of them very reluctantly) about their experiences – a figure not so small, of course, in comparison with groups such as painters or sculptors – cannot be explained, *pace* Hans Keilson (Keilson, 1984), simply by referring to the oft-quoted seventh proposition of Wittgenstein's *Tractatus*: 'What we cannot speak about we must pass over in silence'; for it is also clearly rooted in the victims' fear of remembering and having to relive events. It was to be expected that, when survivors did try to grasp in words what they themselves often said they could not speak about, they should have needed to find a special language for this task. In common with those

84

German and Austrian writers who called for a new beginning in language after 1945,[2] they needed to take quite new paths in their literary testimony. And to some extent this demand was given practical effect, especially in the case of poetry.[3]

Only a minority of those who later managed to express themselves in writing about the camps did so in the form of verse, although at the time that was often the only possibility of grasping in literature what they were living through. These poems, with a highly traditional form and a content usually concerned with everyday life in the camps, will not be analysed here.[4] Indeed, Ilse Aichinger's prose might serve us better as a yardstick. Her attempt to come to terms with her experience of National Socialism, in her novel *Die größere Hoffnung* (1948), or with her knowledge of the concentration camps, in her short story *Herodes* (1965), is so impressive precisely because she is at pains to use a 'new' language in keeping with her subject. It would be not only 'unfair' but out of place to measure the texts of survivors by the prose of a writer as distinguished as Aichinger;[5] nor is that the intention of the present study. Reference to her work is meant only to highlight the fact that it is possible for writers to develop a mode of expression corresponding to new experiences.

In the literary analysis of texts such as reports from the concentration camps, the question of their evaluation inevitably comes up again and again. The importance of their content is not in question, and each from its subjective point of view certainly helps to make the term Holocaust more vivid and intelligible for others of the same or later generations. As literature, however, these texts are not reducible to their communicative function.

The problem is more complex with regard to form. The discussion of genre has already brought out the weak impetus to originality, even among survivors who were accomplished writers. The overwhelming majority of the testimony takes over a structural model without adapting it in any way.

According to the conventional division of literature into the great and the slight, the concentration camp reports seem to fall outside the framework, excluded from the former by their form and from the latter by their content. In traditional theories of autobiography, moreover, they have been thought of as not measuring up to the artistic standard set by works such as Goethe's *Dichtung und Wahrheit*. So should a literary analysis of these texts rather forego any value judgement? A positivist current, especially prominent in the United States, would argue precisely that. For Northrop Frye, the purpose of analysis is to subject not only problematic texts but literature in general to purely objective criteria (Frye, 1957), offering explanation and helping the reader to achieve better understanding. Frye's approach has often been criticized, however, and may be considered today as superseded. Of the approaches that have taken its place, the one centred on ideological critique has rightly argued that subjective evaluation needs to be combined with understanding; and that literary theorists would do better to make this clear both to themselves and to a wider public (cf. Schulte-Sasse, 1976: especially 181–3). What does this imply for the testimony of concentration camp survivors? While the importance of its content has to be recognized, the forms used to convey that content need to be critically examined. In other words, an attempt must be made to analyse the ways in which the terrifying and the unutterable are narrated. Highly traditionalist attitudes to form should thus be judged in terms of how they are determined by the content. The Marxist (and especially Brechtian) requirement that new realities can be adequately conveyed only in new forms cannot apply to the concentration camp literature. Indeed, a form that tried to match the radical novelty of its object would have hindered rather than facilitated communication.

Camp jargon

The use of language to come to terms with the experience of the camps is most apparent, and frequently documented, in the individual semantic shifts that led to a so-called camp jargon. This fostered a group consciousness, which even helped to overcome language barriers among prisoners from different countries. The camp, then, represented a special case of a situation described by Max Weber: not only did conscious 'opposition to third parties' create a bond among members of the same linguistic community (Weber, 1964), but a common language developed that sealed prisoners off from the enemy. Victor Klemperer, persecuted by the Nazis on racist grounds, documented the language of inhumanity in his *Lingua Tertii Imperii. LTI* (1946), and a number of survivors from the camps have tried to do the same – even producing a veritable lexicon, the *Auschwitz Wörterbuch* (Oschlies, 1986). The camp jargon is an expression of the prisoners' need not so much to come up with new concepts for their experience, as to endow words from 'normal' usage with meanings specific to the camp. Here 'there were almost no words to designate feelings'; it was a skewed 'language of naming and calling, threat and warning, order and demand' (Sofsky, 1997: 157).

'Musulmans' is one widespread expression peculiar to the camps: it designated those living dead who gave up the struggle for existence and let all the rigours of the camp wash over and bury them. The origin of the term is not altogether clear. Hermann Langbein reports that he first came across it in Auschwitz, and that 'musulman' was only later used in other camps. He also thinks that this term – which applied to female prisoners, too – arose from the bent body posture that distantly reminded people of a praying Arab (Langbein, 1980a: 111–28, especially 113f.).

Other jargon terms, such as *Kassiber* [secret message] and 'to sing', were derived from thieves' cant and probably found their way into the camp through people with some experience of prison life. The verb 'to organize' [*organisieren*] was also taken over, with the special meaning of obtaining goods 'in ways not completely on the level'.[6] But in the camps it largely lost its negative connotation, as Viktor Matejka testifies with regard to the obtaining of books for the camp library in Dachau:

> The SS were at all times past masters of 'organization'. *Organisieren* was the New High German term for stealing. The SS stole human beings. Wherever it went on its triumphal march through Europe and beyond, it stole and it 'organized'; it was a model of stealing, organizing and killing. Nothing was safe from the SS. It is not surprising that such a model also affected the camp inmates – not as a repellant, but in such a way that they tried to humanize theft in so far as that was at all possible. Necessity tempts people into doing things, and the cunning needed for mental and physical self-preservation does not stop at 'organizing'. (**Matejka**, 1983: 93)

To the extent that internees became familiar with the language of the camps, they adapted their living or their surviving to the new situation. That this did not happen overnight emerges, for example, from Lucie Begov's testimony: 'Then we heard the word "organizing" for the first time in its everyday meaning usual in the camp, and I and probably all of us saw in it an as yet unknown possibility of helping ourselves to something' (**Begov**, 1983: 155). Only with time was Begov forced to accept how much the activity denoted by this term was not only overturning her moral ideas but also marking the finality of her existence in Auschwitz. For she found herself on the way to becoming like the oppressors themselves. The richest source of 'organizing' in Auschwitz was the so-called 'Canada' (cf. Heubner, 1979: 16–21), the storehouse where the deportees' personal effects were kept. Benedikt Kautsky suspects that the term was coined by Polish prisoners, and that it alluded to 'the fabulous ideas they had once associated with emigration to that much-prized land' (**Kautsky**, 1946: 95). In the 'Canada', a prisoners' detachment sorted the wares and packed them for shipment to the 'Reich'. Although the work was much sought-after, it caused the Jewish prisoners, in particular, pangs of conscience that they only slowly (and never entirely) overcame.

The frequent transfers from one camp to another favoured the spread of a uniform terminology. But although certain expressions were understood in all camps, the prisoners in Theresienstadt, for instance, used the verb *'schleusen'* [literally, 'to pass through a lock' and, by extension, 'to smuggle'] instead of *'organisieren'*. Ruth Elias still recalls its second (indeed original) meaning, as applied to the process whereby deportees newly arriving in the camp tried to salvage a few bits and pieces from the luggage that was immediately taken away from them (**Elias**, 1988: 99f.). The term then seems to have been extended from this 'smuggling' activity to other forms of unauthorized appropriation.

Whereas internees mainly attached new meanings to words they had brought with them to the camp, their oppressors reserved for themselves the actual coining of new terms – in most cases, euphemisms of the kind that characterized the Nazi use of language in general (cf. Berning, 1964). This was felt especially acutely in the names of many work detachments. Begov, to take a typical example, refers to *'Außendienst'* [that is, 'service outside the camp'] as in effect 'death service', because of the exceptionally harsh conditions that it involved (**Begov**, 1983: 232). 'The names of all these detachments,' she says elsewhere, 'did not suggest the horrors lying behind them' (**Begov**, 1983: 93). The term 'bunker', which denoted the camp's 'prison within a prison', was used for similarly euphemistic effect. Max Abraham calls the bunker 'a burial chamber'. When he left it, he felt 'for the first time a kind of "relief" ' (**Abraham**, 1934: 19) – and the fact that he could experience in this way the rigours of camp life accurately defines the sense of the term 'bunker'. It is in the comparison between bunker and camp that the meaning of the bunker-torture for Abraham becomes evident. What prisoners literally came to feel in their skin is known in structural semantics as hyponymy (cf. Lyons, 1972), that is, the inclusion of one term in another term. The more general concept 'camp' includes the more specific concept 'bunker', in so far as it denotes the prison within the camp yet becomes gradually distinct from it.

This selection of expressions reported in the testimony from the camps may suffice for our present purposes. One characteristic of camp life that survivors treat as especially important is the collective process of wrestling with language. More interesting, however, appears to be the individual act of coming to grips with it, as we shall see in the following section.

Talking about the camps

An awareness of language is not at all a general feature of the survivors' testimony, and even the few accomplished writers among them seldom reflect on their understanding of language. The painful confrontation with the Nazis' use of euphemism ought to have put them on their guard, but former internees also sometimes use Nazi jargon in their reports without giving it any thought. This shows the extent to which they internalized the terminology along with the way of life into which they were forced. Primo Levi was one of the few who recognized this danger (e.g. **Levi**, 1987a: 129). Joel König also displays a certain sensitivity to language when he remarks in hindsight:

> It was not the first time that we had used such expressions as 'surviving the war' or 'saving one's life'. We had already spoken like that in December 1939, when we had been working on the land; they had meant more or less the same as 'reaching Palestine' or 'getting out of Germany': that is, becoming human again, not a pariah. Now the word 'survive' had a new and deadly serious ring for us. (**König**, 1983: 166)

For Jews like König who were hiding in Berlin, the deportations and the rumours of genocide gave a new meaning to certain words. Inge Deutschkron testifies to the fact that this did not involve only abstract concepts. When Jews in Berlin began to be deported from their homes in furniture vans, this means of transport became the 'terror of Berlin Jews' (**Deutschkron**, 1978: 101).

Inmates of the camps soon became aware that many expressions from normal life had changed their meaning behind the barbed wire. 'With the pulverization of bodies and dwelling places,' writes Peter Weiss, 'the values associated with them were also pulverized' (P. Weiss, 1968: 184). Traditional terms were no longer appropriate for the living conditions to which prisoners were subjected:

> Just as our hunger is not that feeling of missing a meal, so our way of being cold has need of a new word. We say 'hunger', we say 'tiredness', 'fear', 'pain', we say 'winter' and they are different things. They are free words, created and used by free men who lived in comfort and suffering in their homes. (**Levi**, 1987a: 129)

This experience leads Fania Fénelon to argue for the coining of new terms, 'not yet used or hackneyed' (**Fénelon**, 1977), although she clearly does not succeed in doing this in her own report. Mali Fritz, who had a more realistic view of the linguistic capabilities of prisoners in the camps, felt an irresistible desire 'simply to transfer to this hell various designations and conditions from the world "outside"'. She thought that prisoners tried in this way 'to cover up, or at least to draw a veil over' the conditions in which they lived (**Fritz**, 1986: 108f.). The terms, then, contain a clear element of reassurance; their familiar ring serves to deaden the fear and insecurity, to salvage some part of the 'normality' of life before the camp. This fits in with Karl Röder's unargued (but often confirmed) conjecture that prisoners endeavoured to adapt familiar terms to the new reality they found there (**Röder**, 1985: 170f.). It was with fear, however, that they reacted to the Nazis' ideological monopolization of language to prettify the surrounding reality. The conceptual unclarity and camouflage undermined their linguistic competence:

> What was really the difference between 'resettlement', 'repatriation' and 'deportation'? Or was there no difference at all? Were they perhaps just different names for the same thing? 'Repatriation' might,

as the meaning of the word suggested, refer only to Jews with foreign citizenship. So there were differences, after all. Officials from the Jewish Community in Berlin employed yet another word: 'emigration'. But what did all these expressions mean? No one gave us a clear answer. (**König**, 1983: 178f.)

Paradoxically, then, language produced the very sense of unfamiliarity and novelty that it is generally designed to overcome.

As well as individual terms, certain styles of speech also took on a new meaning in the context of the concentration camps and the Judaeocide. Albert Drach illustrates this by removing the metaphorical meaning from a familiar expression: 'Agnes with her fair hair and blue eyes comes up to me: "You tell jokes so well. Can't you amuse us to pass the time?" "Unfortunately," Kucku counters, "I can't pass this time"' (**Drach**, 1992: 45). Simha Naor recognizes, self-critically, that she took categories of freedom into the camp and did not directly adapt her language to the conditions there: 'I coughed pitifully, but is there still such a thing as pity?' (**Naor**, 1986: 100). The phenomenon of linguistic 'inertia' (Gadamer, 1989) played more of a role in the camps than in ordinary life; for internees had no way of matching in language the suddenness with which they had to respond to their radically altered situation. But although they were discontented with the terms and expressions, the spoken word continued to hold great power for them. It could 'destroy' them (**Salus**, 1981: 36) as well as give them courage to go on living (cf. **Wenke**, 1980: 188). The situation in the camps contributed to an emotionalization, and hence also an instrumentalization, of terminology (Horkheimer, 1985: 31).

Behind the barbed wire, individual words also had a much greater power to trigger feelings. Whether an expression gave rise to hope or to fear depended on the context in which the prisoners were introduced to it. Once they had a certain experience with it in a camp, they continued to associate it reflexively with that meaning, even when they later encountered it in a different setting: 'What does "trucks as per instructions" mean?' wondered Grete Salus when she arrived in Auschwitz. 'Instructions: that also had an evil ring in Theresienstadt. One had learnt that people who went as per instructions disappeared without trace' (**Salus**, 1981: 16). Salus also reports how certain expectations, based upon terms current in the camp, accompanied their return to Theresienstadt from the Oederan labour camp: 'We reached Leitmeritz and drew closer to Theresienstadt. We were torn out of our apathy, for Theresienstadt – whatever it might look like today – appeared to be our salvation.' But the relief that emanated from the word Theresienstadt for Salus and her fellow-sufferers did not last long: 'They said we would be taken to the Little Fortress. Little Fortress – that was something else – and our joyful mood slackened considerably' (**Salus**, 1981: 82). Theresienstadt, to which Salus had been deported from Prague, was by then associated in her mind with relatively pleasant memories. In comparison with Auschwitz and Oederan, which she got to know later, it seemed almost like paradise. But those interned in Theresienstadt had heard that, in the proximity of the 'ghetto', there was a so-called Little Fortress where political prisoners were ill-treated (see, e.g., **Scholten**, 1988). Not surprisingly, Salus's heart sank when they were told that that was their destination.

One experience in Auschwitz convinced the narrator in Tadeusz Borowski's *This Way to the Gas, Ladies and Gentlemen* that the spoken word had a different kind of magic in the camps. His angry wish for a fellow-prisoner to be selected for the gas chamber, which was promptly translated into reality, elicits the following remark: 'I felt as if I was to blame for the whole theatre. Every word here can mean a destiny. In this cursed Auschwitz, every evil wish has the power to be fulfilled' (**Borowski**, 1983: 103). Borowski is here also lamenting the instrumental character of language, made apparent by the situation in the camps.

Incalculable as language might seem, it was the only relatively secure system of reference for concentration camp inmates. In it was manifested their relationship both to their oppressors and to their fellow-victims. Newcomers soon learnt that survival depended on, among other things, their ability to understand the orders of the SS and to work out their camouflaged meaning. Communication with other prisoners might also become a matter of life and death. Primo Levi sums up the seriousness of the problem in a biblical image: 'One is surrounded by a perpetual Babel, in which everyone shouts orders and threats in languages never heard before' (**Levi**, 1987a: 44). In the diversity of languages in the camps, especially after the beginning of the war, German was the only officially permitted means of communication, and mastery of it was not only an advantage in trying to find a 'good' work assignment (cf. **Berger**, 1987: 123; Pingel, 1978: 101), but also a prerequisite for any personal contact with the guards that might result in better treatment (cf. Todorov, 1993: 197). On the other hand, foreign prisoners often looked with suspicion on their German fellows – for understandable reasons.

As far as we can tell from these various accounts, language had a meaning beyond communication for prisoners in the camps. Whether they distrusted words or uncritically adopted them, whether they drew strength from them or collapsed under their weight, they lived with and in language.

We should now consider what is the relationship in general between language and individual experience. The reciprocal determination of speaking and thinking, expression and experience, may be assured in the philosophy of language. Ernst Cassirer tried to eludicate this in his *Essay on Man* (1944), as it manifests itself in the written text, and Leo Weisgerber's *Grundformen sprachlicher Weltgestaltung* (1963) takes this idea further, without explicitly referring to Cassirer. The significance of these two contributions for the present study makes it necessary to digress for a moment and discuss them in a separate section.

Excursus: Ernst Cassirer and Leo Weisgerber: symbolization of the environment as a means of coming to terms with things through language

> On that which is incommensurate with all experience, one can speak only in euphemisms.
>
> (Adorno, *Noten zur Literatur* II, p. 286)

As literature in general, the concentration camp texts involve a symbolic shaping of the world. Sidra DeKoven Ezrahi conjectures that in the survivors' testimony symbolization serves to impress the narrated event more firmly in the memory, and is therefore an aspect associated with the text's reception (DeKoven, 1980: 219). This seems too one-sided, however. For it can hardly be denied that the nature and the intensity of the camp experience presented special problems of expression even for articulate people with an awareness of language. In other words, symbolization is also – if not primarily – part of the act of production. According to Cassirer, crisis situations produce, more strongly than everyday life, a need to harmonize new experiences with those through which one has already lived (Cassirer, 1944: 46; cf. J. Gebhardt, 1980: 41): that is, to process them mentally in such a way that they can be incorporated into the existing 'world picture', or else modify that picture.[7] A constitutive factor for the integration of the new into the horizon of the familiar is a clear knowledge of the past; it is this which makes it possible for human beings to systematize and organize their experiences. They are helped in this by the objectivizing patterns of language, myth, religion, science and historical discourse (Cassirer, 1944: 62).

Following Wilhelm von Humboldt, Cassirer understands language as product and expression of a 'world view'. It is therefore a means not of photographic reproduction, but of intellectual exploration and fashioning of reality. Children already discover with concepts a certain world, their world (Cassirer, 1944: 120–32). Cassirer has a similarly ontologistic view of art: it too does not reproduce reality, but is a mode of condensation and concretization, and thus an act of production (Cassirer, 1944: 143). Formal elements are an integral part of intuition itself, not superimposed later. Although Cassirer emphasizes the 'immanent' character of the symbolic power of art (Cassirer, 1944: 157), this way of thinking identifies form as an aspect of interpretation directed beyond the work toward its recipients. Similar knowledge is involved in historiography, except that there Man is of interest not as a psychological being but in his relationship to the world. For Cassirer, then, history is not an empirical but a hermeneutical science (Cassirer, 1944: 184).

In sum, Cassirer distinguishes two tendencies in the symbolic exploration of the world: a force of conservation, and a force of renewal (Cassirer, 1944: 226). In this he is at one with Heinz Hillmann's production theory of art, in which there is no longer any question of symbolization and the main focus is on genesis and function. In particular, Hillmann stresses the capacity of language to generate meaning.[8]

In a similar way, Leo Weisgerber speaks of 'linguistic mastery of life' as a 'mental fashioning of "the world" in accordance with human possibilities' (Weisgerber, 1963: 7). The productive character of this process is expressed in Weisgerber's concept of 'wording the world' (Weisgerber, 1963: 8). Following Humboldt, language and understanding-of-the-world are for him as for Cassirer related to each other. 'Everything that the power of language can acquire displays the basic character of the world: building blocks of the lived world that are accessible to human consciousness and in accordance with human possibilities' (Weisgerber, 1963: 27f.). The degree to which language 'contains' the world depends upon the type of experience with which the individual is confronted. The more unusual this is – that is, the less it has already been rendered in language – the more directly does a conflict appear between language and the encounter with the world. In such situations, the individual's use of language documents his or her attempt to come to terms with this conflict.

* * *

One tendency in American writing on the Holocaust holds that the concentration camp experience actualized the realm of the symbolic. 'It is as if amid the smoke of burning bodies the great metaphors of world literature were being "acted out"', writes Terence Des Pres (Des Pres, 1976: 70, 174). In this way the experience itself acquires a 'literary' character of its own. Des Pres's argument rests more upon a critique of perception than upon a critique of communication – which means that he psychologizes the literature of the camps. At the level of the texts, however, what is at stake is not a de-metaphorization of metaphor, but how – or indeed whether – an image can be found that is adequate to the experience.

Superficially, the use of metaphor in witness testimony replaces something real with merely figurative expressions. In this interpretation, which goes back to Aristotle's *Poetics*, metaphor mainly serves a stylistic function. Alongside its ornamental character, however, Aristotle also attributes a potential to constitute meaning – that is, an innovative, cognitive function (cf. Stoffer-Heibel, 1981: 4–7). Whereas the substitution theory of classical rhetoric still has an effect on the modern theory of metaphor,[9] psychological and philosophical theories of language evince new and less formalist approaches to the definition of metaphor (cf. Stoffer-Heibel, 1981: 12–24).

With regard to personal testimony, it is necessary to keep in mind the linguistically creative power of metaphor – and to ask whether and how survivors have made use of it. At least one author, Fred Wander, is aware of the problem of finding a language adequate to a hitherto unheard-of experience, as he shows in his previously mentioned Letter to Primo Levi, where he grants that Levi found this by turning to the language of the Bible (Wander, 1982: 25).

The choice of language for a report already involves a decision that is significant for the evaluation of a survivor's experience itself. In texts written by *émigrés* from Germany, it is striking that they avoid using their mother tongue. Although the better chances of being published abroad are often decisive in this choice,[10] psychological considerations also play a role (cf. Young, 1988: 160). A corpus of unpublished reports from the camps kept by the Leo Baeck Institute in New York demonstrates that certain psychological compulsions resulted from the experience through which the survivors had lived. Many such authors explicitly mention in a kind of preface that, despite the difficulties they still have with the respective foreign language, it is impossible for them to use their mother tongue; like Peter Weiss they hear in it 'only shouts and threats' (P. Weiss, 1968: 186). George Steiner, on the other hand, suspects that German is the only foreign language 'in which any attempt can be made to say something insightful, something responsible about the Shoah' (Steiner, 1987: 197), because it is the one in which both anti-Semitism and warnings against it have been expressed for centuries. For the concentration camp survivors, however, German has been corrupted by the crimes committed against them in that language.[11] The Nazi regime was responsible for 'linguicide' as well as 'genocide', as Alvin Rosenfeld puts it (Rosenfeld, 1978: 115). The German language was murdered through that destruction of a characteristic idiom which heralded and accompanied the extermination of the Jews. Significantly, reports written in other languages mostly keep German for the expressions used by the persecutors: it would be 'ridiculous and contrary to the facts', writes Jean Améry on behalf of many others, 'to have the SS bellow in French' (quoted in Hirschauer, 1989: 125).

The evidently symbolic use of a language[12] in these examples should therefore already be considered as productive of meaning. When the former victims try through their testimony to free themselves from their traumatic past, the adopted foreign language demonstrates that a new life has really begun in the author's consciousness. They seek, as it were, to anticipate the message in the medium. Naturally the reports only hint at the fact that this aim is not always crowned with success, that the past can catch up with the prisoners even years after their release.

Some survivors did make a success of integration. Judith Sternberg-Newman, like many others in various countries of exile, started a family and built a new life for herself in the United States; only then, when her new identity was sufficiently strong for her not to be threatened by memories, did she sit down to write her survivor's report on Auschwitz (**Sternberg-Newman**, 1963). Her report reflects the initial difficulties of her new life (due not least to language), but it also stresses her gratitude to the new homeland that made her fresh start possible. By the time she began to write her testimony, she had already acquired the foreign language as a means of conversation in which she came to grips with her new life. The symbol of her integration into the new society was her passing of the examination for the Registered Nurses' Certificate in 1948.

The option for a foreign language was thus often bound up with the wish for a new identity. At the same time, it was imposed on the *émigrés* by their 'hosts'. Ludwig Marcuse remembers how he once felt uncomfortably conspicuous in his American exile, because he spoke German in public with his writer friends (Marcuse, 1975: 290). This may have been a special case. But exiles newly placed in British internment camps certainly tried hard to demonstrate their loyalty by learning the language of their host country as rapidly as possible (cf. Seyfert, 1984: 68–70).

The coming to terms with experience through symbolic use of language can perhaps best be seen in the process of metaphorization. For in the broadest sense, any narrative of lived events is a metaphorically fashioned account (cf. White, 1987). The above theoretical considerations would thus lead one to expect a high degree of metaphor in the description of experiences such as those of concentration camp prisoners. Whereas criteria are lacking to assess the 'originality' of experiences (cf. Weisgerber, 1963: 29), the quality of the images with whose help they are rendered in language may be measured by reference to traditions and models. The option for or against common metaphors, or the mode of adopting them, not only tells us something about the author's linguistic affinities, but also permits conclusions about his or her linguistic socialization. In this sense, we shall now examine the use of selected narrative strategies such as metaphorization, as well as the special function of humour and irony in the concentration camp reports.

Metaphors in the reports

the compelling objectivity of these photos – the shoes, the spectacles, the hair, the corpses – spurns any dealing in abstractions; it will never be possible to comprehend Auschwitz, even if it is surrounded with explanatory words.

(Günter Grass, *Schreiben nach Auschwitz*)

Recent studies of metaphor that explicitly refer to Wilhelm von Humboldt[13] emphasize its communicative-pragmatic function (e.g., Ingendahl, 1970; Köller, 1975; Stoffer-Heibel, 1981). They facilitate the naming, and therefore the mental grasping, of reality. In the act of rendering something in language by means of metaphor, however, the individual also acquires additional knowledge about reality. The cognitive function of metaphor rests upon this world-discovering, world-creating potential, which enables it 'to speak analogically about matters that are in principle beyond all possible sensory or empirical experience' (Köller, 1975: 259). Thus, since metaphor makes it possible not only to speak in new ways about the known world but also to render new impressions in language (cf. Kaiser, 1951: 126), it must be assumed that the metaphorical process is already part of our encounter with the surrounding reality, without our necessarily being aware of it (cf. Patzig, 1966: 14).[14] This has anyway been established for the linguistic development of young children (cf. Nieraad, 1977: 114–18). Children first use metaphor unconsciously. Only 'in a stage of development when they are capable of conceptual thinking and metalinguistic reflection' (Stoffer-Heibel, 1981: 18) can they consciously form and recognize metaphors.

If linguistic interpretation is already an integral part of experience, then a 'coming to terms with experience through language' may be hypothesized in situations of crisis. The victims rely in their reports on an interpretation of their experiences which goes back to the camps. There is, to be sure, no secure yardstick for this attribution of meaning, but experience and interpretation would seem most likely to coincide in the reports written immediately after liberation. Constant images in later recollections, on the other hand, lead one to suppose a collective rather more than an individual coming to terms with experience. Discourse *in* the camps subsequently determined discourse *about* the camps. It is in this sense that we should understand James Young's view that diaries produced in the camps differ from reports written after liberation only through the manner in which experience is converted into literature (Young, 1987b: 416). The same applies to the judgement of reports written at different points in time. For in the later texts, an author's individual confrontation over a period of years with experiences in the camps finds greater expression in the structuring and overall assessment of events, and thus, for example, in their insertion into an individual life history or a broader historical context.

The highest priority for concentration camp prisoners was to lessen the alien character of their experience. They were helped in this if they could name new things with their existing vocabulary and thus include them in the horizon of the familiar. By naming them, however, they were interpreting them. Manès Sperber considers that the tendency 'to try to interpret everything', though typically Jewish (Sperber, 1979: 20), also marked the spontaneous reaction of non-Jewish prisoners. The effectiveness of their will to survive required them to make the camp reality their own and to diminish that anguish before the unknown of which Søren Kierkegaard already spoke (cf. Köller, 1975: 295f.). Only through 'the supposition of familiarity for the unfamiliar' (Blumenberg, 1979: 11f.) was it even possible for them to rationalize existential angst into ordinary fear. Only through the act of naming, and therefore of metaphorization, could a diffuse, objectless angst be converted into grounded fear and thereby overcome. Most of the angst-producing circumstances in the camp did not, of course, lend themselves to being overcome in this way. It is also an open question how far the 'identity-securing power' of metaphor (Köller, 1975: 296) was suited to restore the self-awareness destroyed by conditions in the camp. The 'sensuous and emotional components' of metaphor (Köller, 1975: 304) do appear, however, to have lastingly eased the survivors' pain of recollection. Not least, it helped them to document their continuing humanity in their accounts of the torments they had to endure.

The authors of the various reports employ metaphor not only to assure themselves of their own existence in the camps, but also to gain access to their readers. They thus consciously effect the fusion of two semantic realms: those of the producer and the receiver of images. This does not call for any really unusual intellectual operation. The role reversal between producer and receiver, such as Mali Fritz carries out when she speaks of the plague of rats in Auschwitz 'as if they were SS hounds' (**Fritz**, 1986: 24), already has its effect. The affective content of the metaphors helps to convey a sensuous image to the reader and thus makes it easier to comprehend what is being described. 'It is only metaphor,' writes James Olney, 'that ... mediates between the internal and the external, between your experience and my experience, between the artist and us' (Olney, 1972: 35). Metaphorization in the camp reports does not undermine the authors' attempts at objectivity, but facilitates description (cf. Young, 1987b: 403–23) and communication with readers who have not even remotely shared the experience.

Any assessment of the linguistic devices in concentration camp reports must take account of the fact that the overwhelming majority were penned by people who had never written anything before, and often never would again. Value criteria commonly used in judging literary works are therefore out of place. For example, a comparison between the use of metaphor in Paul Celan's verse and in the camp reports would be not only unproductive but even improper. As a poet, Celan pursued ends diametrically opposed to those of the authors in question here. Whereas Celan – in his poem 'Todesfuge', for instance – consciously placed oxymoron in the service of articulating that which cannot be imagined (let alone verbally expressed), the former concentration camp prisoners still attempt, even when concepts fail them, to achieve a narrative-reporting style in which the use of metaphor is mainly unconscious. The criterion of quality loses its relevance beside the authenticity of the account – a judgement of Werner Vordtriede about exile literature that applies with greater justification to these texts (Vordtriede, 1968: 558). Terence Des Pres is most persuasive here: 'Extremity makes bad art because events are too obviously "symbolic". ... Their testimony is in no way "literary", and yet everywhere great and terrible metaphors are embedded in events described.' This is bound up with the fact that, in the extreme situation of the concentration camp, metaphor became reality (Des Pres, 1976: 175, 174). A metaphor cannot be judged here in terms of its poetical quality, for a linguistic image that appears awkward may well represent a cognitive achievement and thus be altogether appropriate (DeKoven, 1980: 217).

The following analysis will therefore focus on the function of metaphor in the camp reports – on its origin, its effectiveness in coming to terms with experience, and its role in the production of meaning. Of special importance is the question of when (that is, in the context of which experiences) the authors most frequently turn to imagery. Instead of the common division of metaphors into bold, pale and formulaic, the emphasis will therefore be on their content and the function they are intended to serve.

The metaphors used in the camp reports may be roughly grouped into two functions: either they serve to describe impressions, or they incorporate experience into a horizon of meaning. Of course this is only a heuristic division, since the descriptive function of a metaphor already includes an element of intellectual comprehension. The heuristics is justified by the fact that it permits a certain systematization of analysis.

Formally, the metaphors with a mainly *descriptive function* range from simple 'as' comparisons to extended discursive imagery. In most cases, however, they are fleeting images which enrich the account through a lightning flash of association. Only rarely is an image developed over a longer stretch of text.

One peculiarity of the *ad hoc* metaphor is represented by its almost epigrammatic form in Viktor Matejka. Following as a writer in the footsteps of Karl Kraus, and especially of the *Fackel*[15] (cf. **Matejka**, 1991: 30), Matejka describes his experience with a profusion of sarcasm and self-irony, and comes up with expressions for camp life that are meant to be humorous: for example, 'intensification of unfreedom' or 'Himmler's sanatorium'. Characterizing the SS with a term reminiscent of freemasonry, 'grandmasters of organization' (**Matejka**, 1983: 74, 85, 93), he not only ironically praises their skilful moneymaking out of the ownership of prisoners, but also turns their own weapons against them.[16] Nowhere does Matejka make an effort to describe his experiences with precision. Instead, he delivers cutting remarks that do not take the describability of events as in any way problematic. His description of his own experiences is thus astonishingly brief. His memory appears to have made them contingent, to have stored them together with corresponding keywords.

More extensive imagery is sometimes used by the few accomplished writers who composed concentration camp reports – people like Ernst Wiechert, but also survivors with literary ambitions such as Erich Schweinburg. Only exceptionally do writers belonging to neither of these groups employ metaphor on a large scale. One of these is Grete Salus, who could write:

> Strong body, soldier without morals, a true freebooter. Imperiously demanding its rights, it did not let go so easily and do people the favour of a quick and easy death. Once thrown into battle, it fought relentlessly to the bitter end, with all the weapons at its disposal. **(Salus**, 1981: 23)

Salus notes with mixed feelings her body's capacity to resist. The military metaphors underline the harshness of the struggle for survival, and the body is reduced to its animal level. Elsewhere Salus refuses to accept this, for she is fully aware that intellect and the will to live are essential factors in survival. The fact that Salus here plays off a preconscious, combative body against the conscious mind would appear – if we take seriously her depiction of herself – not so much to characterize her own experience as to be the result of observation of her fellow-prisoners. Imagery swings into action in the conveying of experiences that cannot be directly grasped in language, such as the judgement on a strong body that prevents a quick and easy death. The military metaphors characterize the combative behaviour of a body outside the individual's control.

Salus makes a further extensive use of imagery in describing the shortage of food in Theresienstadt just before the liberation, and the consequences that resulted from it:

> The old people should have had quite different food, but there were thousands of children who had to be saved ... But the tablecloth did not stretch everywhere; some places were always uncovered. One pulled it here and there, calculated and experimented – still it did not suffice. **(Salus**, 1981: 90)

Unlike in the previous image, Salus is here locked into the 'female domain'. According to this understanding of roles, she uses a kitchen metaphor to formulate the iron law of the camp: that priorities should be respected in the division of life's necessities. The image of the tablecloth that is too small characterizes the dilemma as unavoidable and insoluble. But there is no doubt here about the emotional strain that the iron law placed on the prisoners.

Lisa Scheuer also makes metaphorical use of a woman's role: 'We lay like little spoons in a cutlery canteen.' The simile then makes her think of the way her life has changed: 'Where are the times when I owned a canteen for my silver?' (**Scheuer**, 1983: 29). Typically, her life before the camp seems very far off, although only a few months separate her from it. From her distinctively female point of view, a status symbol of the solid middle-class housewife becomes a model for a shortage, and a longing for things lost becomes the expression of the unbearability of reality. The female standpoint apparent in the metaphor is significant, because the SS made no distinction between the sexes as far as work performance and living conditions were concerned. Even the need to have a separate identity from men was not directly present because of the strict segregation of the sexes.[17]

The morning roll-call – which, because of the masses of people in Auschwitz and the speed at which it had to take place, seems to have usually degenerated into chaos – made a powerful impression especially upon female prisoners, who had not previously had any contact with this kind of military institution. Antonia Bruha finds an image for this, however, which has nothing in common with militarist drills: 'Everything seems like the meaningless and purposeless dance of a human throng, moving up and down the camp street like the dance of mad people' (**Bruha**, 1984: 95). The intention behind this metaphor is not at all, as it may appear at first sight, to attach an artistic quality to the experience in question. It is to record the feeling of disquiet, brought in from outside the camp, at the uncoordinated, unmotivated and uncontrollable behaviour of psychologically disturbed people.[18] Contained in this is also a fear of being made the same. Prisoners sometimes suffered the so-called camp madness – a complete psychological breakdown, which could develop into outright insanity. Some survivor reports testify to a special block at Auschwitz-Birkenau for the mentally disturbed, who were periodically taken away and gassed, although this has not been verified by historical research.

However inappropriate it may seem, there are actually metaphors in the concentration camp texts which derive from the sphere of art. Escape into art offered prisoners a welcome opportunity to forget the everyday reality for a while or to overcome their anxiety (cf. Grossmann, 1981). Together with the (limited) writing, we also read of Fine Art. For although the SS eventually came to exploit this for propaganda purposes[19] – in Auschwitz some artists painted for the SS quite officially (cf. **Edel**, 1979/II: 12ff.), and in Dachau a 'museum' was even opened – artistic activity gave prisoners an illusion of liberty and free choice, such as works of the imagination usually impart (H. Marcuse, 1956). The metaphors, however, do not stress the artistic self-understanding of internees, but functionalize the discrepancy between expression and experience so as to increase the expressiveness and vividness of what is depicted.

In this sense, Erich Schweinburg conceives of his time in the camp as stage experience. At first, he sees himself as a mere spectator or witness of the brutality of the SS guards, on the train travelling from Vienna to Munich with Dachau as the final destination.

> This is the stage. On it and through it, I receive an education in becoming tough and growing out of feeling sorry for myself ... On it and through it, the character and destiny of a strange fellow-sufferer bring each other to maturity. (**Schweinburg**, 1988: 59)

It is neither cynicism nor intellectual exhibitionism which induces Schweinburg to compare the transport to a stage that makes him familiar with a way of life hitherto completely alien to him. The theatre, Schiller's 'moral institution', has undergone a peculiar change. For the stage metaphor running through Schweinburg's report is his attempt to come to terms intellectually (in this case, through literary association) with the horror that he observes. Soon, however, he realizes that he is by no means just an observer, but is himself at the centre of the stage. The compulsion to objectify experience is in constant danger of being overwhelmed by its directly personal effects. Precisely when the camp offers the least hope, however, a refuge appears in the shape of language and literature. Language, especially the imagery embedded in it, offers itself to the prisoner as a way of integrating experience into a horizon of meaning and, to a certain extent, of making it objective.

The following group of metaphors concern strategies for coming to terms with experience at an individual and interhuman level. Daydreaming was still available to the individual prisoner as a means of escape: 'While he ['man'] hauled wood and crushed lice, his humiliated soul withdrew into deep and unfamiliar realms' (**Wander**, 1985: 17). Here Wander describes the dual existence of the concentration camp prisoner, who compensated for the forced depersonalization, indeed dehumanization, by turning his thoughts to his 'spiritual existence'. In agreement with other survivors, Wander thinks he can see in this the impetus to survive. His metaphors often evoke the memory of better days. One camp orderly he praises as follows: 'He opened the phlegmona, as Mama divides the fish on the Sabbath' (**Wander**, 1985: 64). With the help of pleasant thoughts about life before the camp – about good food, for example, and above all a caring Jewish mother – Wander tries to cast a soothing light upon the painful deficiency disorders that afflicted prisoners in the camp. But in so doing, he also expresses the childlike trust that they placed in fellow-victims who helped a little to relieve their misery. Wander's tactic of harmonizing the life of suffering in the camp may be seen at work elsewhere: 'Drifts of toxic smoke [from the burning of corpses in Buchenwald] crept sluggishly over the roots of trees and covered the jumble of naked bodies as with balls of cotton-wool' (**Wander**, 1985: 101). The machinery of death, by thus giving the dead a reverence which the camp thugs had withheld from them, could paradoxically even be interpreted as a corrective to the surrounding brutality.

Antonia Bruha experienced the natural elements as a soothing force. They had to replace the lack of tenderness in prison and thus lessen her physical alienation: 'The drops of water ran over the body as if they were living creatures. They not only cleaned, but caressed the prisoner and for a while made a human being of him or her' (**Bruha**, 1984: 38). The exclusion of prisoners from their human surroundings, their loss of all contact with friends, forced them to develop surrogate experiences. Contemplation of Nature, which was beyond the oppressor's control, was a typical reaction that led to romantic ideas about man's connection to the universe. The fondness for romantic imagery, and especially the receptiveness to Nature, will be discussed below in greater detail. As the quotation from Wander's report shows, not only did

Nature escape the dominion of the oppressors, even the chemical reactions unleashed by them showed 'sympathy' with the tormented.

Erich Schweinburg's text – as far as the use of metaphor is concerned – occupies a special position among the concentration camp testimonies. His memories of the camp are expressed almost exclusively in metaphors. Many of them hardly seem appropriate to what he is describing – for example, the statement 'The streak of sky blue thus closed again on his eyes' (**Schweinburg**, 1988: 89), with which he records the closing of the hatch on the cattle truck. It is well known that up to a hundred people might be crammed into these trucks, with at best a little straw and a bucket in the corner for them to relieve themselves. Apart from the intense pressure on space, the air supply was much less than they needed. On SS orders, the tiny hatches had to remain shut for the whole journey. Thus, what Schweinburg stylized in metaphor as a natural process was in reality a merciless instruction issued by the oppressors. Nor is his image capable of conveying the terror after the closing of the hatch plunged the truck into darkness.

Schweinburg's metaphors reveal an intellectual with linguistic ambitions. He both criticizes language in imagery and uses it as imagery. The High German of the SS guards on the journey to the camp 'crunched at the seams like new boots', and on another occasion 'the shoes took on a watery language, in which they appeared to exchange memories of an earlier existence as ducks' (**Schweinburg**, 1988: 63, 150). Schweinburg's fellow-prisoners are, at least in his eyes, as cultivated as himself in literature. They perform 'lesser' work, such as window cleaning, with the greatest precision, but they feel that it is far beneath them. 'He just smiles gloatingly if what he does is praised,' writes Schweinburg about one fellow-captive. 'His whole being – even sitting on the stool – expresses a contempt that is legible even to illiterates as an "up yours" to SS boss Heinrich Himmler' (**Schweinburg**, 1988: 137). With the image: 'Here he is like a dress shirt, still pleated but without the desirable stiffness' (**Schweinburg**, 1988: 137), he describes a prisoner who continues to behave as if he were in fashionable society, while having to rely in every way upon the support of his fellow-prisoners. Schweinburg's metaphors clearly involve an individual attempt to come to terms with events, but now and again they border on the inappropriate. His report shows a special liking for 'humid' metaphors, especially ones constructed around the verb 'to drip'. Insults, words and dangers 'drip', while 'silence trickles', prisoners 'seep' into the corridor, and music falls on them 'like fine rain'. The idea of water is also present in this image: 'The words ... dance on the fountain of my relief, like those light and variously coloured glass spheres or celluloid balls in a shooting gallery' (**Schweinburg**, 1988: 182).

Schweinburg's eloquence on the subject of death can have an irritating effect, especially when he uses extended metaphor not in its cognitive function but for purely ornamental ends. It is a style that sometimes risks descending into the depths of banality. For most of his imagery does not serve the aim of coming to terms with experiences in the camp itself, but has a purely stylistic function in the sense of classical substitution theory. The abundant metaphors, which distinguish *Eine weite Reise* from other reports, should be seen simply as part of a process of reflection.

Images are problematic when they evoke a meaning that does not necessarily relate to the concentration camp. The situation in the camp, experienced as something quite unique, is then in danger of losing its singularity. Consider, for example, how Wolfgang Langhoff describes his first impressions on arriving at Lichtenburg concentration camp: 'The thick walls of Lichtenburg, witness to thousands of sighs and curses, seemed to hold and crush me: a torture chamber of the mind' (**Langhoff**, 1986: 277). Although Langhoff's association is appropriate in that Lichtenburg did serve as a prison before becoming a concentration camp, it blurs the very distinction that this changeover signified. 'Sighs and curses' were certainly uttered there by people who could still trust in a legal order. But since the concentration camp denied any pretence at justice to those who were imprisoned within it, the 'sighs and curses' took a completely different turn there. It is true that the effect of metaphor generally rests upon the multiplicity of meaning that it produces (cf. Stoffer-Heibel, 1981: 99), but it is out of place when it can be interpreted, as in this example, as playing down the novelty of the actual experience. A non-figurative account would have been preferable to a figurative one in this instance.

A second group of linguistic images is employed to speak about the *meaning* of captivity or about a particular situation in the camp. In contrast to more descriptive metaphors, these refer to something transcending the described situation. In many cases, they could only be developed retrospectively, as in Ruth Elias's realization that her family had been given a 'foretaste' of its future in an assembly area prior to its deportation to Theresienstadt (**Elias**, 1988: 79). But when Mali Fritz compares herself as a 'whip detachment' worker with a 'weaver': 'We do not weave, we twine black, sticky rubber strips of all kinds and deadly sorrow; we become black from them' (**Fritz**, 1986: 103), she may perfectly well be assimilating ideas that she already associated with her experience at the time. The image of weavers evokes slave labour, as depicted by Gerhart Hauptmann in his play *The Weavers*, combined with a touch of the mythical. The 'deadly sorrow' that Fritz and others 'wove' into the whips is both her own and that of her comrades who will be beaten with them. The tension in the metaphor results from the ambiguity of the described situation: the observation that they became black from the work refers both to the dirt from the rubber used as raw material, and to a blackness inside themselves. Fritz feels guilty that she actively contributes to the torture of her companions in suffering.

Prisoners found it unendurable when they saw that they played some role in their comrades' death. 'Again there was that gruesome puppet play,' writes Grete Salus about Theresienstadt. 'We did everything ourselves out of inescapable necessity. We even had self-administration, letting old people die of starvation, even putting together transports and sending our own people to their deaths' (**Salus**, 1981: 91). The puppet-play metaphor suggests that the SS in Theresienstadt pulled the strings of the prisoners' so-called self-administration, but this is immediately contradicted by the term 'inescapable necessity' and its implication of a numb belief in destiny. This contradiction is evidence that Salus has seen through the mechanism of power in Theresienstadt yet is unable to give clear linguistic expression to her insight.

Of particular interest are metaphors used by internees to interpret their experience. Bruha keeps to the memory of better times. After she has told a companion of trips to the mountains in her life of freedom, she turns to her situation in captivity:

Now I also have a mountain to climb, and it is by no means easy. For the way has so far led through dark gorges. Isn't it sad to be making this ascent without my husband? No, this mountain trip isn't nice, and it's better if I do it alone. But if I keep going to the end, if I reach the summit high above all cares and woes, I shall no longer be alone, for we will all meet up at the summit of achievement. (**Bruha**, 1984: 58)

The image of the scaler of peaks who leaves all human misery behind is already known in the *völkisch*-tinged *Heimat* literature, where it fits into what is called 'mountain art'. Friedrich Lienhard, one of its programmatic theorists, understood it as a renunciation of social commitment (cf. Rossbacher, 1977: 56–60). Surprisingly, Bruha's imagery takes over this ideological charge, and in this she does not seem alone among the authors of concentration camp reports. Other survivors, too, seem unaware that the cult of the strong personality, given concrete form in the image of the climber exposed on the mountainside, belongs to the discourse of their oppressors. Jochen **Köhler** entitles his interviews with survivors *Klettern in der Großstadt* ['Climbing in the City' (1981)][20] – itself a quotation from the account of Walter Seitz, who had been a member of the resistance group around Ruth Andreas-Friedrich (cf. **Andreas-Friedrich**, 1986). Seitz sees the connection between mountain-climbing and anti-Nazi resistance in the courage to face danger. For both Bruha and Seitz there is a certain background in experience, in that they both climbed mountains in their youth. It is still disturbing, however, that they should have so readily taken up the image. In the *völkisch* mountain novel, too, an ideological charge attaches to the strenuous ascent, the sense of danger and exposure to fate; here too, the breezy summit is associated with a victorious rising above everyday cares (cf. Aufmuth, 1989). And it is well known that the extreme situation in the mountain novel, which served to validate and glorify the strong personality, anticipated the ideological themes of National Socialism. One may therefore at least question the significance of an uncritical adoption of mountain metaphors in the concentration camp reports.

In Erich Schweinburg, by contrast, we find a metaphor unburdened by this literary tradition. Taking the mountain in its 'deep dimension', he compares his situation in the camp to that of someone:

trapped in a mine, who just a short time before had been making his carefree way in the light of familiar objects. So does my despair call out: 'Over here, my friends! I'm still alive – eerie though it is to have all this on top of me. I'm still amazingly free from injury. But I can't tell you how scared I am, how far away from you I feel. Will I ever return to your daylight?' (**Schweinburg**, 1988: 110)

Schweinburg's image does not stem from personal experience, but is probably derived from reports of firedamp accidents. Whereas the mountain-climbing image connotes activity and a desire for self-mastery and personal success, Schweinburg's metaphor is more a cry for help to the outside world. Two completely different views of captivity are involved. As a Jew who had already been interned before the great deportations, Schweinburg naturally hoped that he might be released if a way could be found for him to leave the Reich. The political prisoner Bruha, on the other hand, when she was arrested in October 1941, saw little if any prospect of being released as long as the Nazi regime was in place. Her destiny was: annihilation through work.

One image in Joseph Schupack's text shows that aggressive self-preservation was not the only alternative to hope that assistance would come from friends and relatives outside the camp. He could not see any power, whether coming from outside or within himself, that might assist his survival:

> I felt like someone who has missed both the first and the last train out: the train to death and the train to life. All that was left was to keep my mind on the way ahead and to put myself in the hands of chance. (**Schupack**, 1984: 156f.)

The prisoner did not act according to his own will; only at a spiritual-intellectual level could he preserve some degree of freedom and independence. But Schupack does not seem to have set much store by this. Isa Vermehren even experienced her thoughts as a burden: 'For all the concentrated efforts to shut oneself off, one constantly felt like an aerial under stress, from which even the faintest oscillation of the waves elicited huge sounds' (**Vermehren**, 1979: 23). Thus Vermehren also saw herself in the camp not as active but as a receiver; she simply reacted to what flowed over her. Grete Salus uses a similar image to describe the prisoners' receptiveness to signs of the war's end: 'We listened attentively all the time and registered the downfall in its slightest oscillations' (**Salus**, 1981: 76).

The mountain-climbing metaphor was an optimistic exception in the prisoners' estimation of their own possibilities. Joseph

Drexel, for example, compares their situation in general to a process governed by the laws of nature, a 'slow, perverse hollowing out of man, applied as if in slow motion with the constancy and malice of dripping water, whose purpose was to strip living bodies of all being' (**Drexel**, 1980: 170). In his variations on the German proverb 'A slow drip wears away a stone', Drexel ascribes effective human purpose to the dripping water and thus expresses in metaphor the prisoner's situation as he experienced it. This mingling of physical and mental carries with it a more general meaning for other prisoners and the whole of life in the camp. Although this metaphor, like others already mentioned, was coined by a politically conscious author, Drexel's testimony resembles many others in enlisting images that tend to blur the role of the oppressors. His metaphorical mode of expression thus sharply contrasts with his otherwise clear political vision.

In reflecting on the meaning of their captivity, survivors of the camps also draw their comparative material from clearly demarcated spheres such as *religion*. The overwhelming majority of religious images do not seek to arrive at a global explanation, but are content to remain at the level of particularity. Begov, for example, makes the following use of biblical metaphor: 'Yes, at the twelfth hour, there occurred one of those countless miracles which alone enabled the Jewish prisoner in Auschwitz to remain alive' (**Begov**, 1983: 94). Lucie Adelsberger also employs religious imagery in describing the mass extermination: 'Day by day we saw them [going to the gas chambers]. The people were different, but the image was always the same of many pilgrims going to their death' (**Adelsberger**, 1956: 105). But the comparison seems inappropriate, like many others used in the concentration camp literature. Pilgrims usually set out on their journey voluntarily, and with an awareness of what they are letting themselves in for. In her description of the behaviour of people newly arriving at Auschwitz, Lucie Adelsberger turns to an image from Jewish ritual food requirements: 'the survivors, on being unloaded, threw themselves like unclean creatures with overpowering thirst on the murky puddle water beside the tracks' (**Adelsberger**, 1956: 103).

In one exceptional case, religious metaphor documents the survival of Christian anti-Semitism behind the barbed wire, precisely among the interned priests. Thus, the Austrian Father Lenz abuses a colleague who renounced his vocation in Dachau as 'a Judas' (**Lenz**, 1956: 207).

The religious metaphor is derived from very different sources, reflecting not so much the author's own affiliation – Adelsberger, though Jewish, employs the Christian theme of 'pilgrims' in the context of the Judaeocide – as a general socialization in Western civilization. The mode of use ranges from metaphors such as 'a Mount of Olives fear of death' (**Drexel**, 1980: 69) or 'vitamin miracles' (**ten Boom**, 1954: 97), through comparison of the camp to Sodom and Gomorrah (**Schupack**, 1984: 118) to more extensive passages. Mostly the religious imagery is to be found in comments on people's torments – which Joseph Schupack, for example, compares to 'the twelve plagues of the Pharaoh' (**Schupack**, 1984: 156)[21] – and in accounts of the day of liberation. 'Finally we heard the still distant rumble of the approaching front, announcing the reappearance of firm ground from the Flood' (**Fritz**, 1986: 121). These words of Mali Fritz's record the first signs of the war's end and hence the prospect of an end to her days in the camp.

The following quotation from Margarete Buber-Neumann's testimony occupies a special place among biblical imagery for liberation. By means of a metaphor from Genesis, she describes liberation not from the camp but from the darkness of the 'bunker' or camp prison:

> [T]he blinds were raised and there was Light. I no longer know whether I prayed or cried or sang. I climbed with great effort up to the open window. With one foot resting on the folding table, I wedged my face into the tiny opening of the window. I felt summer air, and beyond the camp wall I could see the sun shining on the new chimney of the crematorium, blue sky and, far away to the right of the chimney, the spire of a church tower. Until my eyes grew weary, I drank in the view of sun and daylight and was intoxicated by the joy of being allowed to live. (**Buber-Neumann**, 1968: 254)

This idyllic view over Ravensbrück is disturbed by the chimney, whose smoke, far from being part of a framing image of hut and hearth, is a symbol of annihilation. At the moment when Buber-Neumann experiences her vision, however, this symbol loses its power over her. She has been permitted to live a little longer. The light imagery in the quotation applies the dichotomy of light and darkness not to camp and outside world but to the camp experience itself. The difference between camp and freedom blurs at that moment into a gradation. The paradox of the prison within imprisonment causes a revaluation of the camp, which itself suddenly takes on the status of freedom. The horizon opens out for Buber-Neumann, transcending the camp perimeter and taking in the outside world (church steeple).

Given the poor and extremely inadequate nourishment in the camps, especially towards the end of the war, it is not surprising that prisoners were almost constantly preoccupied with *food*. By exchanging recipes or imagining especially tasty dishes, they often compensated in their minds for the deficiencies in reality.

In their subsequent reports, survivors try to grasp in metaphor – and hence to convey to others – what bread meant to them. Thus Mali Fritz recognizes that bread can 'weigh differently': 'where hunger is raging, it has the weight of snowflakes' (**Fritz**, 1986: 31); for Grete Salus, it was like 'a solid island in a sea of watery soup' (**Salus**, 1981: 60). Both images associate the meaning of this main contributor of energy with the small quantity of it that prisoners received. But the metaphors gradually become distinct from each other. Whereas Fritz establishes only a relation of quantity or weight, the adjective 'solid' in Salus's image refers, beyond the distinction between solid and watery, to the substantiveness of bread as food.

This helps us understand the quite different metaphors which refer to the poor quality of the food that caused prisoners so much suffering, especially at the beginning of their captivity. They concern the stew-like substance (Salus's 'sea of watery soup') that was the main meal each day. Matejka calls it 'the midday muck' (**Matejka**, 1983: 114), and Isa Vermehren says affectedly that it was only 'with great application that she could (bring) her examination of the contents of the metal dish to some kind of conclusion' (**Vermehren**, 1979: 119). But as far as the camp food is concerned, both of them speak from a position of relative strength that was not at all typical for the ordinary internee. Especially in Auschwitz and Bergen-Belsen hunger did not permit prisoners to be critical of the food. All that counted for them was quantity. The significance of food, despite its great deterioration towards the end of the war, should therefore not be underestimated. It may be seen not least in the transfer of eating metaphors to situations that had nothing directly to do with food, where physical satisfaction was the main *tertium comparationis*. Mali Fritz says that she 'sucked up' a report about the Greek partisan struggle, and significantly adds that 'it brought to life something inside me' (**Fritz**, 1986: 56). Prisoners received news about the war situation as greedily as they did food. Temporary periods outside the camp, when it became possible again to observe a long-missed Nature, aroused in them memories of freedom that were also experienced in terms of food metaphors, as the following quotation illustrates: 'In these minutes of freedom we romped thirstily around, scarcely thinking that we were in fact prisoners.' Or: 'For two and a half years my eyes had seen nothing of Nature, and now I sucked in the fast-changing landscape like someone parched with thirst' (**Elias**, 1988: 121, 167). Although food imagery is also quite common in normal speech situations, one has the feeling that the defective and unbalanced nourishment occupied the prisoners' minds so vividly that it moulded their perception of the surrounding world. One indication of this is Albert Drach's image of the transport wagons, 'packed tight' as they 'deliver human food for the German cannibals' (**Drach**, 1992: 134).

Metaphors appear in the concentration camp literature mainly when survivors think back with heightened emotion to their captivity. As one would expect, this occurs at especially sensitive points such as the approach of liberation or encounters with death. Another event that had a similar function to information about the state of the war was the sight of Allied aircraft flying over the camp. Bombing raids, in particular, gave them hope that rescue was at hand (see also Langbein, 1980a: 149), and the noise of tanks also did a lot to raise their spirits. 'The whole night long,' recalls Grete Salus, 'we lay awake listening to heavy artillery roll through the village. Our nerves were stretched to breaking point, and we were no more than embodiments of hope and wishing' (**Salus**, 1981: 77). Here, however, the traditional image is no more adequate to express the prisoners' feelings than is the comparison of an air-raid warning to the sound of music (**Salus**, 1981: 80). The way in which Albert Befford aestheticizes the visual impression of a bomber group, however, conveys more convincingly the anxious joy at the approach of the liberators:

Far to the west and the north, the first swarms of bombers glint in the sky. Some formations head unwavering and unhindered towards the camp, and are suddenly there, like well-ordered strips of little black crosses, in the blue of the sky vaulting above the camp. Suddenly there are also countless little white clouds of flak. Then a white line [of bombs] detaches itself from the first bomber group, followed by another and another! The lines fall deeper and hang like exclamation marks of warning above the camp. (**Befford**, 1947: IV/10f.)

In Befford's description, Nature and the liberators' aircraft form a compound; the image carries the autograph of the oppressed. The witness sees the inevitability of approaching freedom in the geometric disposition of what he observes. As in Belshazzar's writing on the wall, the observer's predisposition to see things in this way is obscured. In Heine's poem 'Belsatzar', it is the guilty conscience of the Babylonian king that directs the interpretation of the letters of fire, while in Befford's text it is the prisoners' wish for an end to their captivity. Religious prisoners also saw in this sign in the sky a message from God, and thought they could discern its immediate effect in the reaction of the guards (cf. e.g., **Stojka**, 1988: 37f.).

Coping with the omnipresence of death was another reason for inmates to resort to metaphor; they did not have the usual rituals or social system to help them come to terms with it. Moreover, they had to face not only the genocidal minimization of individual existence, but also a factory-style removal of the dead. Officially, they were not supposed to know of the gas chambers or to mourn their dead, even if they had died a 'natural' death in the camp (cf. **Stojka**, 1988: 27). The methods of killing and of dealing with the dead resisted any religious or other attempt to ascribe meaning to them. Secular models, such as the idea of living on in the achievements of political struggle or work, did not operate either. The Nazi policy of extermination even robbed Jews, Gypsies and Slavs of the biological basis for living on in later generations (cf. Lifton and Olson, 1974: 76). Fundamental uncertainty about the future reduced the difference between the dying and the witnesses to one of gradation.

All this meant that death was constantly in the minds of prisoners, and their chances of survival were greatly influenced by how they faced up to it. Substitutes had to be found for the prohibited task of mourning work – a purpose served by attempts to become conscious through language of the *meaning of life and death* in the camps. The imagery used by survivors reflects this process of intellectually working through their experience of death; it makes us aware of their effort to make up for the deficit of meaning. One recurrent metaphor is that of being wiped out. 'The roll-call!' groans Mali Fritz. 'All the prisoners had to stand for hours in the early, very early morning and again in the evening, so that they could be more easily wiped out, without an obvious external application of violence' (**Fritz**, 1986: 19). Fred Wander uses the same verb: 'All around, the old and the frail – who were not going under canvas, because they would die there – sat crouching down; they did not lie but crouched down, because they knew that you are wiped out if you surrender to sleep – you fly silently away, like cranes' (**Wander**, 1985: 48). Both these examples underline the unspectacular character of death in the camps. It did not make itself conspicuous: not only because it was not supposed to be conspicuous, but because its mass scale meant that it simply could not be conspicuous. One dying individual made witnesses upset, but the sheer numbers depressed them. More than any others, those who worked in the sick bay had to come to grips with death. Mali Fritz was not the only one to suffer as a result: 'The groans and whimpers of the sick and dying pierce me through. By keeping my indignation on the boil, they may perhaps stop me from giving in to exhaustion' (**Fritz**, 1986: 86). The dying did her one last service by preventing her from giving up and dying herself. But it does not seem to have been uncommon that they themselves experienced death as a release from their torments. Erich Schweinburg, who only just escaped death himself, describes it poetically as 'a betrothal with the dearly beloved lady of the camelias whom I saw in my feverish nights' (**Schweinburg**, 1988: 265). This image, by associating death in the camps with an officially prohibited sexuality, enlists the trope of love intertwined with death. Similarly, Fred Wander writes of 'a heart like a glass bell – one simple jump and it no longer rings'. He ascribes to death a 'coppery gleam', and exalts a dying person as follows: 'The man's face is thousands of years old. The few years of his own life have fallen away, everything frail and inconsistent. The faces of fathers and mothers are left behind – the expression of a great effort to be human' (**Wander**, 1985: 63, 67, 129). Even if the man in question were to be the last in the chain, Fred Wander manages, by evoking the links between generations, to remove some of the meaninglessness from his death. Wander's metaphors generally give death in the camps an aura that the actual conditions denied it. Wander's literary coming to terms with the experience of death thus largely takes the place of an emotional coming to terms with it. It would seem that this is his way of trying to face, and to keep within tolerable bounds, his feelings of guilt towards the victims of Nazi murder.

Albert Drach, by contrast, rejects any poetic transfiguration in the face of genocide. His disrespectful question about a fellow-victim, 'In what oven was he smelted?' (**Drach**, 1992: 200), may be in keeping with what happened, but it remains a rhetorical question, since in most cases it was not later possible to establish where the Jewish victims (all of them marked out for death) were actually murdered. We know that SS doctors also killed prisoners with phenol injections, which Erwin Gostner evokes in the not very original image of 'death by needle'. Gostner also compares the Mauthausen camp, notorious for the mass murder in its quarry, to a 'killing field' – another hardly extraordinary image which does, however, take on a macabre significance: '[L]ike any killing field, the concentration camp also has its hyenas, since there is booty to be had even from its wretched dead' (**Gostner**, 1986: 151–2).

The periodic elimination of those too frail to work has gone down in history as one especially gruesome aspect of death in such camps as Auschwitz or Ravensbrück. These selections underlined the meaninglessness of life in the camp, before which even metaphor seems to break down. Grete Salus therefore, referring to the initial elimination on the 'ramp' at Auschwitz, limits herself to an exact reproduction of what she saw: 'Thus, at the waving of a hand, people went automatically to the left or to the right – a little wheel from life into death' (**Salus**, 1981: 15). This selection of the old, the frail and those unable to work did not at all mean an end to their suffering; often death was long in coming, as the capacity of the gas chambers and crematoria was not sufficient. Until their turn came, 'those who had been separated out ... were kept in a locked building; their murder was assured but they had to be patient – it might take days' (**Fritz**, 1986: 61). The waiting, usually without food and in hygienic conditions worse than elsewhere in the camp, was a horrible torture for those directly concerned, but it also depressed those who witnessed it, since it made them realize the complete hopelessness of their own situation.

Testimony about experiences as totally devoid of meaning as the selection process is thus the touchstone of the viability of metaphor in the concentration camp texts. The small number of examples shows that survivors were intuitively wary of using imagery in this context – which would appear to confirm the belief, sometimes expressed in the research literature, that mass murder and death camps are peculiarly resistant to metaphor (Rosenfeld, 1978: 180). This view, put forward especially in American studies of the Holocaust, is more a moral prescription than an ontological statement, but the lack of metaphor in texts dealing with the selections should really be taken to indicate the limits of what can be expressed in language. It is an example of what is known in the literature as the 'aesthetics of unrepresent-ability', which makes the helplessness of metaphor especially apparent. But whereas authors such as Franz Kafka (to whom this formulation is applied) avoid the unsayable by switching to a different semiotic system such as that of music,[22] this option was not available to survivors from the camps. They had to be concrete, if they wanted to be understood. In the search for a distinctive 'poetics of knowledge' (Vogl, 1990: 69) in these texts, one is hardly likely to explore the realm of metaphor.

Turning now to the origin of particular metaphors, we find that the experience of *sun and light* gives rise to one of the most extensive groups of metaphors in the concentration camp testi-mony. As the problem of evaluation is especially evident here, we should conclude by considering it in some detail. The contra-diction between trite formulations and the quite out-of-the-ordinary experience to which they refer is at its most striking in these images. More than the other groups of metaphors, they document internment in a concentration camp by means of clichéd language.

The special fondness of survivors for metaphors of light had a lot to do with their relationship to Nature in the camp. Many report that the varying natural conditions made a great impression upon them: they enjoyed the dramatic sight of a sunrise or sunset, as welcome distraction from an everyday existence that offered no aesthetic pleasure; and the rising of the sun could give them new confidence to face the morning roll-call, as it seemed to make visible the limits of their oppressors' power. This ideological charge of the experience of light, this association of light and hope going back to the Enlightenment and beyond, has long had a place in everyday metaphor.[23] And it was within this tradition that Erwin Gostner, for instance, greeted the first postcard he received from his mother in the camp, as the 'first sight of light' in his 'darkness' (**Gostner**, 1986: 38).

Essentially two tendencies may be distinguished in the textual recording of the experience of sun and light in the camps: it enlists the help of poetry either to indicate the meaning of that experience, or to transfer its meaning metaphorically to other situations and experiences. The metaphor of light is thus here inseparable from the conversion of an actual experience of light into a literary trope.

Especially good examples of this may be found in Fred Wander. 'The sun faded behind a wall of cloud.' 'It was no longer so fiercely cold; a sickly copper-red sun shone out intermittently among grey ribbons of cloud' (**Wander**, 1985: 25, 114). In the following passage, he evokes a link between the sun and the prisoners' situation:

> In the camp, too, there are sunrise and sunset. Many days fade away tired and colourless, like a discarded bunch of daffodils. But there are also the blazing evenings. And there are mornings when the sun comes up bloody, as from a battle. I remember one sunny red morning: the sun lay hidden behind veils of mist that gleamed now milky-red, now purple, like the cheeks of our tubercular brothers. (**Wander**, 1985: 58)

These quotations make us aware how narrow is the dividing line between authentic statements of camp experience and clichéd use of language. The first two examples, in particular, could easily come from some run-of-the-mill novel. What is involved here is not an exaltation of lived experience (common enough in Wander's report), but simply a wrongly conceived tone. However, one's assessment of literature from the camps must consider not only its use of metaphor but also its cognitive value: that is, whether it does justice to what was new and distinctive about the camps. And the longer quotation from Wander, over and above its three similes,[24] does perfectly characterize the prisoners' situation by using impressions of the sun in a figurative context.

Wander's suggestion of an intrinsic coincidence between the two is based upon the internees' receptiveness to 'signs' (cf. Blumenthal, 1963), which helped them to surmount the uncertainty of life in the camp.

In Lina Haag, the ideologization of light reads a little awkwardly:

> I am back in the good old cell, in a cell full of light. My eyes become moist – and not just because the light dazzles them. A ray of sunlight, shining down through the little window, goes straight to my heart. I do not think I have ever been so grateful in my life as I was at that moment. (**Haag**, 1985: 62)

Even the banalizing mode of presentation, however, cannot diminish what the light must have meant to Haag at that moment. Indeed, it shows that the experience overtaxed her ability to express it in language.

The figurative use of light was not confined to the sun, as a quotation from Erich Schweinburg's testimony will illustrate. Together with his fellow-captives in Dachau, he interpreted a source of artificial light as a symbol for release. From the length of time that a lamp shone in the prisoners' storehouse (where belongings were collected on the eve of a prisoner's release), they tried to guess how many would be set free the following morning at roll-call: 'The effect of the light on our emotional state,' writes Schweinburg, 'had something of the comfort that lost travellers have felt from time immemorial at the sight of an illuminated cottage window' (**Schweinburg**, 1988: 227). In this example, light is associated with a specific experience in the camp, as a sign. Its figurative character is thus grounded on a concrete situation.

Very few survivors seem to have been conscious of this figure in their experience of light. One of the few is Antonia Bruha: 'Actually one ought to have been happy to see the sun again after a year's imprisonment! But this sun is so cold: it does not warm either the body or the soul. It is alien and hostile' (**Bruha**, 1984: 96). The so-called Prisoners' Chorus at the end of the first act of Beethoven's *Fidelio* is the unmistakable background to Bruha's picture and to others like it, although in her case the sun fails to have its effect in heralding new hope.

Metaphorization of the experience of light underpins a bipolar presentation in which the sun is either present or absent. In this sense, metaphorization in the concentration camp texts should be understood as ideologization. The sun is simply associated with lost freedom: 'Through the little flap before which I took painful farewell yesterday from the sun of a past life, the Germany of the so-called "Third Reich" stared at us with an alien and hostile countenance' (**Begov**, 1983: 78). Here Lucie Begov is being transported by train from southern Italy to the death camp at Auschwitz. The experience of losing the sun corresponds to a geographical reality, which the author ideologizes in her text.

If the sun is replaced by an artificial source of light, the positive character of the experience is no longer assured. Schweinburg writes of the 'floodlight of destiny', which casts 'its light upon Nikolaus Deutsch', a fellow-deportee on the train to Dachau (**Schweinburg**, 1988: 75). Deutsch was anything but favoured by destiny: the glaring light illuminated his maltreatment and eventual murder at the hands of those in charge of the transport. Whereas the floodlight or spotlight is a positive metaphor in everyday usage – for instance, in the context of public success – it did not admit of this meaning in the camps.

The figures of sun and light in the camp testimony have their roots in the realm of myth and religion. Because of its immateriality, light is there 'a symbol of the celestial and transcendent' (Langen, 1963: 450) – especially in Romanticism, where the daily rhythm of sunrise and sunset played an important role. One of the themes in which this Romantic symbolism of light finds expression – as the paintings of Caspar David Friedrich well illustrate – is the 'mountaintop view', with its 'uplifting movement toward heaven, the homeland of divine light' (Langen, 1963: 460, 462).

The textualized impressions of light in Romantic literature have parallels in the testimony from the camps. It would be wrong to conclude, however, that survivors took these metaphors and tropes directly from Romanticism. For the themes had become so widely available that they hardly expressed a personal experience any longer – a fact confirmed by their popularity in light fiction, which does indeed seem more likely to have been a source of imagery for the authors of concentration camp texts. Hermann Glaser has shown how the 'trivial Romanticism' characteristic of nineteenth-century and early twentieth-century Germany was mediated by the discipline of German studies (Glaser, 1979: 53–6: 'Spießers Romantik'). In the form of a 'perverted Romanticism', it influenced the blood-and-soil mysticism of Nazi attitudes to life.

Other romantic themes in the camp testimony are derived even more clearly from trivial forms of popular fiction. The moods of Nature supply the main clichés (cf. Weiss-Laqueur, 1971), especially in diaries and journals (which cannot be examined further here).

One symptom of cliché in the use of romantic themes is the lack of any critical reference to contemporary issues, of the kind that precisely the Romantics once expressed in their symbolism of light (Langen, 1963: 471). The camp texts resort to imagery in a purely affirmative manner. Indeed, the prisoners themselves clung to romantic moods, which were often their only form of aesthetic experience in the camp. In a way, this seems to have strengthened their trust in their own humanity. Anything that more nearly approached critique called for self-assuredness, and prisoners hoped to win this back precisely through an affirmative immersion in Nature. In their immediate situation, critique based on metaphor would have been a masochistic act.

In their use of metaphor, as in their choice of genre, the camp reports display little inclination to novelty. Formally, the imagery is very traditional, in many cases involving no more than a simile or a simple equation of two things. Only at the level of content do the survivors use their imagination more. Now and then, a thoroughly individual effort to come to terms with the experience finds expression in a striking image for starvation or death in the special conditions of the camp. In comparison with the aspect of genre, however, the prevailing lack of metaphorical originality weighs more heavily in the balance. Clearly the authors run the risk, by adopting an image without comment, of also taking certain ideological elements on board that contradict their own political standpoint. Not only in terms of content, but also in their fondness for metaphor, the survivors remain trapped in the mentality that they denounce. For by using images passed down from previous writers, they make a purely instrumental use of language that threatens their account with the loss of intellectual depth (cf. Horkheimer, 1985: 30; Habermas, 1991: 366–99) and even at times a descent into purely mechanical writing. Nevertheless, we should recognize with Peter Weiss that the conventional modes of expression are consciously employed, and that 'these hardly suitable means [are] better than silence and bewilderment' (P. Weiss, 1968: 76). In these conditions, the act of writing becomes more important than the form. For writing itself appeared to some survivors as the appropriate way of protecting their humanity against the threat of nihilism (cf. Rosenfeld, 1978: 13).

The way in which a prisoner uses metaphor can give us some idea of his or her linguistic socialization. *Heimat* literature and trite popular fiction left stronger traces than other genres did.

The authors in question make only very conditional use of the cognitive function of metaphor, and sometimes their imagery does more to blur than to clarify. Judging by this, they would seem to have an extremely limited and, above all, merely second-hand understanding of the world. Moreover, the examples given above mostly confirm that the use of readily available elements restricted the power of language to express what survivors had actually experienced in the camps. The reports apparently illustrate an insight of the Formalists: namely, that established patterns of expression have a tendency to spread and become automatic (cf. Arnold and Sinemus, 1983: 361). It seems obvious that authors without a literary background would have found it especially difficult to replace these automatic patterns with new ones. The formalized language of the camp texts, with its deep debt to tradition, should therefore be regarded as expressing helplessness in the face of a monstrous experience.

Humour and irony in the concentration camp literature

Irony, like metaphor, is a non-literal form of speech. In contrast to the purely content-centred definition that marks traditional theories of irony, recent research has turned to the linguistic study of texts to interpret its pragmatic or (in Noam Chomsky's terminology) its 'performative' function. Urs Engeler (1980: especially 96–184) defines irony accordingly as semantic opposition. Whereas, in actual usage, the meaning of a lexeme is determined by nearby meanings, an ironically textualized lexeme takes on the exactly opposite meaning. The crucial feature of irony is thus negation – a negation, however, which results from the wider context. Irony can be understood only if the recipient shares in what Engeler rather unfortunately calls the 'cultural grid'

(Engeler, 1980: 116). This 'grid' should, of course, be thought of as very widely spaced; it must also include social, situational and emotional components. But the 'grid' heuristics does allow one key function of irony not mentioned by Engeler to be explained: namely, its role in the constitution or reinforcement of group identity. Irony can be used as an effective weapon by the otherwise defenceless; its aggressive potential lies in its partner-oriented disposition, which, as Freud established, it has in common with jokes (cf. Stempel, 1976: 219). Although classical rhetoric already treated irony as 'one of the most important means of casting doubt upon the trustworthiness of a person or a thing' (Ueding, 1991: 80), a typically ironic constellation does not merely involve the 'negative solidarity' of two people unmasking a third, since the user of irony may also count on gaining prestige (Stempel, 1976: 219ff.). In any event, if irony is to be effective, it needs a receptive listener.

Whereas an affinity with aggression is essential to irony, humour presents itself as, so to speak, its 'civilized brother'. As a kind of real statement, it arises out of the discrepancy between expected norm and presented facts. In terms of the aesthetics of reception, humour has, alongside its effect of affirmative unburdening, the function of critical protest, and may also serve to develop ties of solidarity (cf. Jauss, 1976: 105).

Humour and irony are deployed at different moments of the process of coming to terms with the experience of the camps. Humour, without itself being part of the facts in question (cf. Preisendanz, 1976: 156), is principally an immediate reaction of prisoners to a particular experience; whereas irony, as a linguistic phenomenon, belongs at the level of reflexion and literary composition. One might say, therefore, that humour operated more directly than irony in the process of coming to terms with the experience of the camp. Both underline the antagonism between prisoners and SS, through group integration (cf. Zijderveld, 1976: 185f.) as well as exclusion. Both always raise the self-assuredness of those who use them at the expense of their object (regardless of whether that object is aware of it or not). Under such conditions, humour strengthened the prisoners' morale and even permitted them a kind of resistance, however externally ineffective. Not surprisingly, therefore, Hugo Walletner criticizes humour directed at other prisoners, because it jeopardized the solidarity among them (**Walletner**, 1945: 73). Walletner's point suggests that humour in the camp also served to bolster particular group structures within the camp population. This would have been altogether in the interest of the SS, which used a rigorous hierarchy based on reasons for detention (and later on nationality) as a way of encouraging the formation of rival groups and thereby nipping any resistance in the bud. In this sense, the actual targets of camp humour may be regarded as a measure of the effectiveness of SS strategy.

Humour in the concentration camp texts, let it be said at once, mainly takes the form of situation comedy. In fact, it was usually sad or dangerous situations that roused the former prisoners to laughter. Superficially, the attempt to come to terms with life in the camp by means of humour may therefore appear as a kind of evasion; laughter worked because it created a distance from the prisoners' actual experience, and because it made them forget for a moment the seriousness of their situation. Albert Drach criticizes the unthinking drive for amusement, especially on sexual themes, which he considered incompatible with the ending of life in store for them (**Drach**, 1992: 45). Most of the former prisoners, however, endorsed humour as one of the few means left to them of temporarily escaping the stress of camp life. Benedikt Kautsky distinguishes two kinds of humour in his report: 'Humour in the camps. What I mean is not the bitter joking with which prisoners accompanied events in the camp, but that liberating laughter which helped you get through many a situation' (**Kautsky**, 1946: 187).[25]

Bruno Heilig testifies that prisoners in Dachau tried to look on the 'humorous' side of a potentially fatal situation. Once the camp commandant, as a measure against frostbite on the prisoners' hands, ordered that 'blood circulation should be stimulated through the carrying of heavy loads'. Heilig comments: 'This was a spiteful order, yet we could not help laughing at it. Malignity of that sort can only be met with laughter' (**Heilig**, 1941: 241). Humour, he hints, had also to be seen as a symptom of helplessness, which was still felt when writing about it: 'If I may say so,' writes Rudolf Kalmár, 'it is actually not possible to remain serious when recalling that whole monstrous business, even though the humour has a bitter taste' (**Kalmár**, 1988: 175). Humour in the camps, then, is at least as much an expression of the prisoners' helplessness as it is of their contempt for the oppressor.

The SS provided many involuntary occasions for mirth, which were understandably taken up by prisoners. Feeling themselves to be mentally inferior, many low-ranking guards sometimes made up for this by treating intellectuals with special brutality. However, this tended to strengthen the prisoners' self-assurance, and their laughter at the frailties of the SS took away some of their fear. Feelings of superiority were not uncommon:

> The pleasure we took in laughing at stupidity did not make us different from other people. It was just that this need of ours became part of the perpetual conflict between SS and prisoners. Stupid SS types provided especially effective material for laughter. The things they said were diligently spread around. The whole camp laughed at them. (**Röder**, 1985: 316)

The meaning of humour for the prisoners can be seen in the fact that they did not leave it to chance, but stored humorous situations in speech and could thus call them up at any moment.

For many prisoners, laughter already relieved some of the stress at their induction into the camp. Women in particular, whose self-esteem was threatened by the 'fitting out' process, tried to be humorous about its inherent nastiness: 'Some of us,' Lucie Begov recalls, 'even summoned up a little bit of gallows humour as we scrutinized each other with astonished horror and ran our hands over our shiny pates' (**Begov**, 1983: 116).

The psychologist Viktor Frankl considers humour to have been the newcomer's 'first reaction' to the situation in the camp. 'It was a spiritual weapon in the struggle for self-preservation. Indeed, it is well known that humour is suited, as hardly anything else is in human life, to establish a distance and to raise a person above the situation, if only for a few seconds.' In his view, the 'will to humour' in the camps was a 'ploy, in the sense of a way of living' (**Frankl**, 1977: 74f.). By this he means a flight from the reality of the camp, similar to what Joel König describes: 'Unaccountable horror was constantly before our eyes, and yet we were still able to laugh. Amid all the perils, we experienced scenes of irresistible comedy' (**König**, 1983: 272). The will to humour should be interpreted as a drive on the part of concentration camp inmates and other victims of Nazism to uncover the comical side of a situation. This drive is what distinguishes the prisoners' 'gallows humour' from more normal kinds, as Lucie Begov recognizes: 'I felt that it was not my, not our usual laughter; that we ... were also trying to laugh off the vague and anxious forebodings that this camp aroused in us with its anomalous paraphernalia and its uncanny customs and mores' (**Begov**, 1983: 188).

Karl Röder, however, on somewhat arbitrary grounds, considers the term 'gallows humour' to be inappropriate here:

> Evidently the need to laugh is directly related to the situation in which one finds oneself. The more hopeless this is, the stronger is the need for laughter. For us this had nothing to do with gallows humour, which is restricted to individuals who can no longer avoid a certain event ... Our laughter was a reaction inspired by community. It was not able to suppress thoughts, but was rather proof that we were grappling intellectually with our surroundings. (**Röder**, 1985: 316)

Röder here marks out a further key characteristic of humour in the camps: it signalled that the mind was at work. This contradicts the frequently held view that mirth merely served as an escape from reality. For humour and irony have in common a piercing of reality in thought.

One side of humour in the camps was, however, always directed against the prisoners as a group. How many reports testify that the sadistic 'humour' of the SS had none of the relative innocuousness of the prisoners' humour, and that it quite often had fatal consequences for the person on the receiving end! An internee's life counted for nothing in the eyes of the SS. Many survivors suspect that their oppressors tormented them out of sheer boredom. A number of reports speak, for example, of how the guards threw a prisoner's cap close to the electrified wire fence and then told him to go and fetch it. If he obeyed, he was shot for 'attempting to escape' or for being close to the fence without permission.[26] But if he refused, he became guilty of an offence punishable by death. The SS man gloated over the prisoner's desperate indecision; while the other inmates, aware of their total helplessness, tried to avoid being the butt of this kind of deadly 'humour' by making themselves as inconspicuous as they could.

All the essential functions and effects of humour in the camps may be studied in an event that Wolfgang Langhoff experienced and partly shaped at the Börgermoor camp in 1933. In his report, he describes it under the title 'Zirkus Konzentrazani'. Together with some theatrically gifted fellow-prisoners, he put on a circus performance for his comrades and the SS that was probably the only one of its kind in the history of the camps.[27] Despite the misgivings of many other inmates, he carried out his idea on the grounds that it would demonstrate their (moral) strength to their oppressors, as well as fostering solidarity in their own ranks. To take the SS's need for entertainment into account was, for Langhoff, to equate humour with resistance. His calculation proved correct, and the camp commandant put nothing in the prisoners' way. The demonstration of strength and solidarity also involved the idea of making a subtle critique of the SS and its running of the camp, mainly through consciously ambivalent allusions such as that contained in the title. For 'Zirkus Konzentrazani' not only shared (albeit in reverse order) the familiar German initials of the concentration camp [*Konzentrationslager* – or *KZ*]; it also cast ridicule on the thinking behind the camp's structure. Even the promise contained in the announcement of the performance – that 'the biggest oxen'[28] would be on show there – is as ambiguous as one could possibly wish. This subversive humour, hardly ever expressed so openly elsewhere in the camps, indicates a desire to rise above the situation in an act of 'mental rebellion', as George Orwell might have put it (Albrecht, 1984: 676); it really did erect a 'counter-reality' (Moll, 1988: 154). Langhoff even gives the following explanation of this prisoners' initiative:

> We who no longer lived the lives of human beings had dared for a few hours to decide something for ourselves, without orders or instructions, just as if we were our own masters and there were no such institution as a concentration camp! This feeling could be plainly sensed among the mass of spectators. (**Langhoff**, 1986: 173)

This point of Langhoff's is important for an understanding of intellectual activity in the camps. Degradation at the hands of the oppressors and the removal of autonomous responsibility felt especially painful to internees. Any activity that suggested freedom to operate and take initiatives was therefore eagerly taken up.[29] The reaction of fellow-prisoners also made an impression on Langhoff at his 'circus performance'; he felt himself vindicated by the merriment around him.

Humour was therefore well suited to demonstrate resistance in the camps, because it involved resistance without aggression.[30] It was not only the extreme repression of all personal emotion that checked the prisoners' potential for aggression; the hard labour with insufficient food also played its part. Only when inmates temporarily won back a minimal sense of freedom – as at the 'circus performance' in Börgermoor – did aggressive joking begin to develop. Thus, whereas it has been possible to publish a collection of so-called 'whisper jokes' from the Nazi period (cf. Danimann, 1983), there is an absence of jokes in the recollections of concentration camp inmates.

In the camp reports, *irony* is essentially used either for criticism of the SS or for self-criticism, as former prisoners seek to rise above themselves. Irony, as Albert Drach once said in an interview, is the only means of coping with oneself and with others (cf. Riepl and Stürzl, 1991). Lying behind ironic remarks about the author's former tormentors is often the fear reawakened by the memory. A display of strength is needed to conceal the weakness.

Irony also enables survivors to generate a view common to both themselves and their readers. By presenting them with the role of ironic observers, they try to gain the readers' attention for their own torments. Thus it was only in his later report that the experience of Auschwitz turned Tadeusz Borowski into a wielder of irony. Statements by his fellow-prisoners confirm that this pose was the diametrical opposite of his behaviour in the camp (cf. Mitosz, 1985: 115f.).

In the texts from the camps, irony is expressed in compounds such as *Vernichtungsdisziplin* or 'annihilatory discipline' (**Begov**, 1983: 182) and in short epigrammatic remarks. But sometimes it is embedded in a lengthier context. Viktor Matejka's interpretation of the camp as 'concentrated unfreedom', or his description of Dachau as 'the camp of unrestricted impossibility' (**Matejka**, 1983: 89, 102), belongs in the first category. And Gerhart Seger also uses this means of expression when he speaks of Oranienburg as one of 'the Third Reich's sites of cultural interest', or characterizes work in the camps as 'intellectually scintillating varieties of the national labour of construction' (**Seger**, 1979: 13, 14).

The figurative mode has two overriding functions in the camp literature: criticism, and coming to terms with experience. Just as in the case of humour, the victims use irony to express their sense of intellectual superiority over the SS. Inge Deutschkron, for example, lashes the incompetence of a Nazi official in the following words:

> I guessed he was Eschhaus, the infamous director of the Labour Department for Jews. Years ago he trained (not very successfully) under a Jewish textile dealer, since when he has hated Jews and treated them accordingly. This was his only qualification as director of the Labour Department for Jews. (**Deutschkron**, 1978: 71)

Deutschkron's ironic comment 'exposes' anti-Semitism as sociologically and economically determined. But this overlooks the fact that racist anti-Semitism was precisely the ideological foundation of the Nazi Judaeocide. Deutschkron's irony thus obscures the facts more than it explains them.

Kurt Hiller ironically illustrates the contradiction between Nazi propaganda and the way in which prisoners were treated (**Hiller**, 1934–35: 1648). Antonia Bruha contrasts the peddling of a 'superman' consciousness with the cowardly behaviour widespread towards the end of the war, when she takes up one of the keywords used by her oppressors and turns it against them (**Bruha**, 1984: 126). As a 'boomerang technique' (Schlüter, 1974: 36f.), this kind of irony is common enough in everyday communication. Gerhart Seger similarly comments on the inadequate provisions in the camp: 'After a few weeks . . . , under the model administration of the Third Reich, arrests and deportations to the camp were taking place considerably faster than deliveries of straw-filled mattresses' (**Seger**, 1979: 15).

In these examples, the incompatibility between Nazi ideology and the SS's behaviour in the camps is the basis of the ironic account. One of the uses of irony already known in classical rhetoric is criticism of the enemy. In the texts from the camps, however, it is directed not only against the oppressors but also against zealous collaborators in the prisoners' ranks. Joel König, for instance, calls one informer 'an especially conscientious member of the Jewish community' (**König**, 1983: 98). Here the irony operates in two stages: condemnation of a show of conscientiousness put on for the oppressors refers to the exact opposite of what König literally says: namely, a 'lack of conscience'.

Irony deployed by authors against themselves forms a special complex in the concentration camp literature. The Romantics already knew the aspect of self-ironical elevation above one's own weaknesses, which arose from recognition of the unbridgeable gulf between ideal and reality. Thomas Mann was the first to turn this into a means of self-preservation (cf. Wilpert, 1969: 362). The former prisoners also use it to rise above taboos such as that surrounding death. Thus, Lévy-Hass casually associates the inadequate camp food with death: 'We shall eat these turnips all winter long – unless we die first' (**Lévy-Hass**, 1979: 40); and Erwin Gostner's talk of 'the Mauthausen slimming diet' is on a similar plane (**Gostner**, 1986: 145). Both examples, in the context of the death camps, are not without an element of the macabre. In order to be able to describe their strongest impressions from the camps, the authors consciously belittle them in retrospect and thereby place them at a more bearable distance. By speaking ironically in general terms, they are best able to protect themselves from the fresh shock that accompanies any recollection of traumatic experiences.

Even if self-irony appears to have a purely descriptive function in these texts, it may possibly be concealing the abyss. This may be seen in Lina Haag's account of her 'occupation' of a new cell:

> You explore and investigate . . . you discover with sudden joy that you can lift away the stool. But here too the table is screwed tightly down. Still, the corner with the toilet bucket is boarded off, so the stench from it is not too great . . . Blessing upon blessing! (**Haag**, 1985: 50)

Haag here waxes ironic about how shamefully undemanding she has become. Moreover, she tries to restore her self-esteem by generalizing the unpleasant memory with the help of the German impersonal pronoun *man* ['one' or 'you'].

The concentration camp victims speak with irony about their degradation as individuals and social beings. Ruth Elias, for instance, describes as follows her journey to Theresienstadt: 'This time my star of David was glowing on the left of my chest. I no longer had to fear being caught and locked up by the Gestapo for unauthorized travel. This time I was travelling with official approval, for that is how one travelled to the ghetto' (**Elias**, 1988: 78). The relief ironically expressed here by Elias does, however, correspond to a thoroughly genuine feeling that other authors report after unsuccessful attempts to escape a transport. Their eventual deportation freed them from the physical and nervous strain of having to remain concealed, and faced them with facts which they thought they could to some extent evaluate.

The social helplessness that inmates felt whenever they were forced to be present at the public flogging or even murder of a fellow-prisoner is also expressed with irony in their reports. Erwin Gostner describes one such scene at Mauthausen:

> The camp elder orders: 'Sing!' Then, to the strains of *I'm only a poor wandering soul, good night, sweet maiden, good night*, the whipping begins behind our backs. . . . We add *Dark brown is the hazelnut* and *No finer land to be seen today than the length and breadth of ours*. To conclude, those who have just been whipped join the ranks again and sing along with the rest. It is all very clever. (**Gostner**, 1986: 91)

The forced singing and the gaiety of the lyrics not only underline the sadism of the SS thugs, but also reinforce the prisoners' feeling of impotence at not being able to help their comrades. The ironic mode of expression is subsequently used in the text to compensate for that impotence.

Although humour and irony in the concentration camp reports demonstrate the prisoners' effort to make sense of their experience, they reveal more tellingly than other literary devices the failure of that effort. For it is not the global meaning of their internment and suffering which they seek to clarify for themselves with the help of humour or irony, even the sense of detail with which they hope to compensate for the general lack of meaning largely escapes their grasp. What nevertheless appealed so much to former prisoners was the illusion that irony gave them of coming to terms with their experience.

Notes

1. See, for example, Patzig (1966), Hillmann (1977), Gadamer (1986). On the connection between speaking and thinking, as the young Wittgenstein describes it in the *Tractatus*, see S.J. Schmidt (1968).
2. For example, Ilse Aichinger with her *Aufruf zum Mißtrauen* (1946) or Wolfgang Borchert with *Manifest* (1946) (cf. W. Weiss, 1972: 442).
3. See the work of the Vienna Group, of Heissenbüttel, Enzensberger and Gomringer. In connection with the camps, the name of Paul Celan should be mentioned in particular.
4. This has already been convincingly done in Michael Moll's *Lyrik in einer entmenschlichten Welt* (1988).
5. On Aichinger, see also my essay 'Die Erfahrung des Holocausts und ihre sprachliche Bewältigung. Zu Ilse Aichingers *Die grössere Hoffnung*', *German Life and Letters* 49/2

(April 1996), Special German-Jewish Number, pp. 236–42. (A greatly expanded version of this article appeared under the title 'Die Erfahrung des Holocausts und ihre sprachliche Bewältigung' in *literatur für leser* 21 (1998) 3, ed. Bernhard Spies, pp. 275–86).

6. See Gerhard Wahrig (ed.), *Wörterbuch der deutschen Sprache*, Munich: Deutscher Taschenbuch Verlag (1986). On the use of '*organisieren*' in the camps, see **Matejka** (1993: 75–80: 'Josef Pospisil oder das Organisieren').

7. The theory of cognitive dissonance has vividly formulated this alternative. It states that two or more contradictory interests set up a pressure which causes their respective attractiveness to be manipulated until one or the other has a clear advantage (Festinger, 1978). The theory of cognitive dissonance is thus essentially a theory of how we come to terms with lived experience. Since the structure of our experience does not admit of long-term incompatibility, we are constantly led into attempts at harmonization. The same was true *a fortiori* for concentration camp prisoners, who constantly had to react to experiences that clashed with their experience potential. According to the theory of cognitive dissonance, prisoners had two possible ways of resolving the dissonance: either they changed the notions and value concepts brought in from the outside, or they interpreted their impressions of the camp in such a way that these did not blatantly contradict their earlier experiences.

8. 'Interpretative models already formulated in language have ... a considerable power of initiation, organization and direction for and in the development of unfamiliar or vaguely familiar (anyway not clearly known) regions and conditions' (Hillmann, 1977: 151).

9. In contemporary reception theory, it enters into a definition of the image as 'an attempt to imagine what can never be seen as such' (Iser, 1976: 121).

10. This applies, for example, to the texts published by Ella Lingens-Reiner and Bruno Heilig in Britain and by Bruno Bettelheim in the United States.

11. As Helen Epstein shows in *Children of the Holocaust* (1979), many refugees who emigrated to the United States after their release tried to keep their children away from anything German, although she also mentions the opposite extreme of a couple who sent their children to a German school in South America.

    Recently, the German-French writer Georges-Arthur Goldschmidt remarked – in connection with his return to the German language after fifty years, in *Die Absonderung* – that for a long time German was for him 'the language of rejection and guilt' (*Der Spiegel*, 35/1991, 11–12).

12. I owe this term to Bernard Spolsky's lecture 'Language in the Old City of Jerusalem, a Socio-Linguistic Survey', delivered on 5 March 1987 at the University of Southampton.

13. Walter Weiss speaks in general of a 'Humboldt renaissance' in contemporary literary theory (W. Weiss, 1972: 669–93).

14. The philosophy of language characteristic of German Romanticism thought that the existence of a 'primal language' could be detected in this fact (cf. Zimmermann, 1978: 247). On the significance of this for the situation of concentration camp prisoners, see Pingel, (1978: 17f.), who refers to Diether Cartellieri, 'Erinnerungsveränderungen und Zeitabstand', in Erich Maschke (ed.), *Zur Geschichte der*

deutschen Kriegsgefangenen des Zweiten Weltkriegs, vol. 15, Munich, 1974, pp. 105–83.

15. [*Die Fackel*: the famous journal founded by Karl Kraus in 1899 and continued until 1936, mostly consisting of satirical material written by himself – *trans. note.*]

16. Apart from 'the Jewish question', another key term in the enemy images of the Nazi world-view was the 'masonic problem' (Broszat, 1983: 346).

17. It is well known that the labour camps were organized on a single-sex basis, Theresienstadt being an exception in this respect. In Auschwitz there was a male camp (the so-called *Stammlager* or original camp) and a female camp, Birkenau – a situation that offered the possibility of (secret) contacts. In the gypsy camp and the Theresienstadt family camp at Auschwitz, however, there was for a time not a strict separation between the sexes.

18. On the significance of people's experience of life before deportation to a concentration camp, see Pingel (1978: 151f.).

19. See Comité International d'Auschwitz, *Das kulturelle Leben im KL Auschwitz. Informationsbulletin* No. 2 (167), Warsaw, February, 1975.

20. In fact, Köhler's interlocutors were not former concentration camp prisoners, but people who had survived life underground and in the resistance. Nevertheless, the experiences are to some extent comparable.

21. Schupack actually misquotes from Exodus, which speaks of the *ten* plagues of Egypt.

22. This happens, for instance, in the short story 'Investigations of a Dog'. For a discussion of this problem, see also Vogl (1990: 224).

23. See, for example, the title of the annual Christmas promotion in Austria: 'Licht ins Dunkel' (Light into Darkness). Cf. also Blumenberg (1957).

24. For a critique of simile in poetry, see Benn (1959: 494–532).

25. How seriously **Kautsky** took humour in the camps can be seen from the fact that he devoted a whole section of his report to it (187–9). Other survivors also discuss the topic at some length (e.g., **Röder**, 1985: 316–32: 'Worüber wir lachten').

26. 'The boundary was an untouchable taboo, its violation an affront to absolute power' (Sofsky, 1997: 57).

27. Bruno Apitz reported that he performed several sketches written by himself in Buchenwald in 1943–4 (cf. Schneider, 1976: 126–8), but they do not seem to have made an impact on any but a small circle of prisoners.

28. [The German word for ox is also used with the meaning of 'numbskull' – *trans. note.*]

29. This is striking evidence against Bettelheim's thesis of 'infantile regression' among camp inmates.

30. Anton Zijderfeld has shown that, in the view of Sigmund Freud, humour differs from joking by its lack of aggressiveness (Zijderfeld, 1976: 175).

4

The narrative of lived reality

The function of narrative in and after the camps

In their testimony, the concentration camp survivors stress how much it meant to them to tell their story, both during and after their period of captivity. One major function, of course, was the bearing of witness, but even more important was the therapeutic effect they expected from it. In the camp itself, some temporary relief might be gained from the torments of reality, while afterwards a kind of catharsis might enable them to come to terms with what they had lived through.[1]

A precursor of this function may be found in the storytelling tradition of the Jews of Eastern Europe, which has already been considered in some detail in relation to Fred Wander.

Without having reflected on the matter, other survivors confirm the effects of storytelling. The wish to make their 'past' life come alive again and to share it with their fellow-captives appears to have been especially marked in the concentration camps. 'There is talking everywhere' – writes Tadeusz Borowksi – 'on the way home, during work, in the evening on the plank beds, at the roll-call. We tell stories; we tell about our lives' (**Borowski**, 1983: 164). Prisoners lived 'their lives again' by talking about them (**Wander**, 1985: 49). Nor was it just their own lives that they narrated, but everything connected with freedom was suitable material to bring the time before the camps back to mind. Many reports mention so-called 'strolls', in which prisoners wandered through their native streets telling one another what they saw and experienced there. The following from Jenny Spritzer's testimony may serve to illustrate this:

> We sat as friends in a circle and discussed all possible topics. Our
> favourite was 'going on a trip', as we called it, when we would meet in
> a town in the wonderful freedom outside, each in the company of his
> [*sic!*] dearest, if he still had one. We then described our life as we
> pictured it in our imagination. (**Spritzer**, 1980: 121f.)

The psychological effect of this storytelling was to place prisoners
in a condition of normality, so that for the duration of the
imaginary trip they had the illusion of being human among other
human beings.

Numerous reports testify that debates about scientific problems –
especially in the natural sciences – also fulfilled the function of
making prisoners forget, perhaps just because they did not evoke
any intimate personal memories. Faced with the chaotic world of
the concentration camp, many inmates found escape in the
orderly world of mathematics. Exposed every day to arbitrary
powers, they sought a fixed and stable point in the predictability
and verifiability of mathematical axioms and theorems.

Internees generally experienced the ability to speak as liberating; indeed, it may be seen as serving a kind of psychological
hygiene. Prisoners instinctively tried to come to terms with humiliation, mistreatment and loss by turning them into language. Ruth
Elias describes the mechanism and the effects of this: 'At first I
began to speak falteringly, but then the words flowed from my
mouth. I found comfort in speaking, and I was grateful to have at
last found a patient listener' (**Elias**, 1988: 188). Although Karl
Röder stresses that even without a listener he satisfied his urge to
speak (**Röder**, 1985: 147), most of the prisoners felt the need for
one. Receptiveness did not seem all that important, however, as
Albert Drach learned:

> Anyway it's more important to me to report things to someone than to
> receive reports myself. The fact that Mrs von Quanten may not hear
> me plays a minor role. It's enough if I hear myself, and have the
> illusion of being heard sometimes. (**Drach**, 1992: 184–5)

For Drach, hunted by the Germans in France, his listener's poor
hearing actually had the advantage that she could not use his
words to betray him.

It is clear from many reports that fellow-inmates who functioned as listeners assumed a certain duty towards those who
confided in them. Sometimes people told their story in the

desperate hope of finding strength from others. Antonia Bruha reports that she even drew strength from the trust that a cellmate placed in her: 'I should stop being sad and stop brooding; Ruth is there, and she has a claim on my good temper' (**Bruha**, 1984: 58). Here the social function of storytelling is associated with its psychological effect. And it is also at the centre of the Sunday congregation around Mendel Teichmann that is described by Fred Wander. Storytelling created a personal bond between narrator and listener that proved to be of exceptional importance, precisely amid the isolation that defined the atmosphere among prisoners in the camps.

Storytelling in the camps seems to have had a physiological as well as a psychological effect. This is apparent in the parallel between narrating and eating that often occurs at the level of metaphor in the survivors' reports.

Sometimes in the camps, storytelling had to replace a lack of food – a function which Adolf Muschg actually ascribes to art in general (Muschg, 1981: 177) – although this physiological effect could obviously last for only a limited time. On the other hand, as Viktor Frankl attests, former prisoners found that their tongue loosened more easily when they sat down to a copious meal shortly after their release (**Frankl**, 1977: 142).

When they did not prefer to remain silent, survivors told their story in the hope both of coming to terms with what they had lived through and of starting a new life. But they also saw the bearing of witness as the paying of a debt that they owed for their own survival, which would confirm the 'reciprocity' of surviving and testifying (Des Pres, 1976: 31). In the same way that survivors write so that the past should not be forgotten, they sometimes declare their willingness to speak in public about what they remember.[2] In any event, many must have given testimony about their life in the camps – all trace of which their oppressors had intended to disappear – with the conviction that they owed it to those who were murdered there. Having survived, they felt a duty to others who had not.

Already in the camps, prisoners were kept going by the thought of one day telling a wider public about what had happened (e.g. **Naor**, 1986: 56). In the act of narration, they subsequently tried to understand the experience – that is, to come to terms with it intellectually. This cognitive function, however, was impaired by the widespread lack of reflective distance (cf. Apel, 1980: 33), so that the act of narration often had the opposite of the hoped-for effect. In such cases, recollection of what they had been through proved so overwhelming that many preferred to remain silent.

There were also other reasons for this: not only the negative reaction of contemporaries who had not shared the same experience, but also the belief that everything capable of being expressed can also be entertained in thought and therefore made to happen again. 'That which finds a form loses the danger of chaos,' writes Peter Bichsel in his Frankfurt lectures on poetics. 'A story carries within itself an alleviation of the real world' (Bichsel, 1982: 11). It was precisely this effect that those who survived the concentration camps wanted to avoid. Mali Fritz, who wrote her report quite a long time afterwards, has shared with the public her thoughts about this delay:

> There were times when I wondered if we should speak at all about the mass killings, because then people would think that something like that was possible and could happen again. But I do not want it to become thinkable. People have also taken over Nazi language, which did not cover anything up. '*Bis zur Vergasung*' [literally: 'as far as gassing'], for example, is said in the most uninhibited way. I thought that many words must not be uttered; so that it will not have happened and cannot happen again – so as not to let all the horror into our lives. (**Berger**, 1987: 274)

Jorge **Semprún**, a Buchenwald survivor and later Spanish Minister of Culture, said something similar in an interview [1989; also 1994]. He reported on his experience in the camp only sixteen years after his release, and even then *The Long Voyage* filtered it, as it were, by concentrating on the train journey to Buchenwald.

Words were certainly capable of exercising a 'magical power' over prisoners. After they were liberated, however, their view often coincided with that of the early Wittgenstein of the *Tractatus*: that is possible which is thinkable – that is, which can be grasped in language.

The tension between the impulse to communicate and the psychological or intellectual barriers in its path acquired a new quality as soon as former prisoners made up their mind to write down what they remembered. Apart from a tiny minority, they had had no previous experience of writing. They therefore had to decide *how* they should present their memories, what means they should use.

Fictional literature: the example of Bruno Apitz's Nackt unter Wölfen

In the mid-1960s Wolfgang Hildesheimer, a survivor (though not directly of a concentration camp), defined his Jewishness with some reservations as 'membership of a common destiny' (Hildesheimer, 1986: 219). In a well-known statement, he also proclaimed the end of fiction, as evidenced both by the strict rules surrounding Socialist Realism in the German Democratic Republic (GDR) and by the 'organic demise of bourgeois literature' (Hildesheimer, 1984: 103–22). Hildesheimer stuck to this view, following his great novels *Tynset* and *Masante* with a semi-biography, *Mozart*, and even giving the biographical treatment to a fictional character in *Marbot*. In the end, he bade literature adieu and turned his attention to the fine arts.

For many survivors of the Nazi concentration camps, the choice between novel and authentic report was posed differently from the way it was for Hildesheimer. It is true that an overwhelming majority opted for the report – there seems to be no really significant novel in which a death camp is at the centre of events (cf. Cernyak-Spatz, 1985: 49)[3] – but some did choose the novel form and thereby founded a distinctive genre. One of the best-known examples is Elie Wiesel, whose whole work – and especially his Elisha trilogy – cannot be understood without his experience of the camps. There are other authors, however, who have dealt with the camps without having personal experience of them: André Schwarz-Bart, for example, in *The Last of the Just*, or Anna Seghers in *Das siebte Kreuz*.[4] These fall outside the frame of reference of this study.

What, then, distinguishes a work of fiction set in the camps from an authentic report? To answer this question, we shall take the case of a successful novel published in the late 1950s in the GDR: Bruno Apitz's *Nackt unter Wölfen*, which has been chosen not so much for its literary merit as because its central event has since been the object of a report by Zacharias Zweig: *'Mein Vater, was machst du hier ... ?' Zwischen Buchenwald und Auschwitz*. In this report a Polish-Jewish lawyer who had emigrated to Israel after the war set out, with the encouragement of the Yad Vashem Documentation Centre, to describe his struggle for survival in Buchenwald (**Zweig**, 1987: 5). What makes this document different from other survivors' reports is the same fact that provided the focus of Apitz's novel: namely, Zweig was able to save not only his own life but also that of his three-year-old son, Jerzy. When he was sent from a Polish labour camp to Buchenwald at the end of 1944, the secret Communist committee there decided to take responsibility for the child's safety.

Apitz makes up a story around this material, whose historical kernel he himself witnessed in Buchenwald. Marcel Reich-Ranicki, another survivor of the Nazi terror, has already drawn attention to the weaknesses of this book (Reich-Ranicki, 1991: 24–7; 456–60), which cannot here be either refuted or confirmed in detail. Rather, this fictionalization of material from the camps will be used to illustrate the difference between a novel and a report of lived experience.

Since autobiographical texts, like other epic forms, have so far been analysed mainly from the point of view of their historical content (cf. Petersen, 1993: 2), there were neither categories nor models available for the following analysis. I have therefore adopted the narrative system used by Jürgen H. Petersen to describe epic texts. In contrast to earlier 'theories' of narrative, Petersen develops a convincingly logical and consistent list of categories, which may be applied by analogy (although he himself does not mention these forms) both to autobiographical writing and to the recollections in question here.

The concentration camp reports, like any epic text, obey laws of narrative, but they differ from works of fiction in not having an intermediary voice at their disposal. Some of Petersen's criteria are therefore irrelevant, while others – such as narrative form, attitude or presentation – may be established even if they do not have the same function as in fictional texts.

As far as the majority of concentration camp texts are concerned, they conform to the genre in their use of first-person narrative. The authorial self is thus identical with the subject of the experiences. What distinguishes them from first-person fiction is that they mainly forego what Petersen calls '*the ego's identity in difference*' (Petersen, 1993: 56; emphasis in the original). The self here is not an intermediary but the real self, though usually somewhat older than the subject of the experience. Primo Levi, for example, gave thought to this distinction (cf. **Levi**, 1987a), but most of the testimonies convey the illusion that experience and presentation overlap with each other. In fact, even the knowledge of eventual survival is situated at the respective time of narration, although in this matter the limits set by the genre anyway leave no option.

Not all the reports discussed here necessarily conform to the genre. Two examples may be mentioned which, right from the outset, appear to clash with the distinctive structure of autobiography: namely, the third-person narratives of Ernst Wiechert and Cordelia Edvardson. No doubt, experience or disposition as a writer played a role in both these cases. Wiechert's report begins as follows:

> Johannes – let this be the assumed name of the one who acts and suffers in these sketches – had already passed the middle of his life when, at the peak of a seemingly secure and enviable existence not lacking in repute, the things of this world and notions of a hereafter became shaky and unstable and an ever-increasing darkness of the soul overshadowed his days and nights. But while his musings circled fruitlessly around the ideas of justice, human dignity and God's kingdom on earth, these were dimmed and weighed down by troubled, almost shapeless dreams of a kind familiar to him from previous crises in his life. In these hours removed from the growth and the materiality of life, not only did his soul seem to suffer from the day that had just been and gone, but the future, a disastrous future, seemed to stand silent and admonishing at the darkened threshold of his consciousness, formless, speechless and even faceless, right down to a pale hand, unlike all human hands and already part of an obscure twilight zone, which raised itself movingly, almost threateningly, from the shadows between dream and waking in order to point out something still hidden from the sleeper. (**Wiechert**, 1984: 74)

Already in the first sentence of his report, which calls to mind the opening of Goethe's *Elective Affinities*, Wiechert makes it clear that it will be told within an interior perspective. The personal conduct of the narrative, from which the reader learns of Johannes's fate, is subsequently reinforced when the first name gives way to the personal pronoun and the personal narrator draws closer to the reflector. The third sentence departs from the interior perspective: an authorial narrator is concealed behind 'not only did his soul seem ... '. But the very next sentence returns to the standpoint of Johannes's lived experience, the hallmark of which is the use of verbs of cognition and feeling.

With regard to content, the opening of Wiechert's report provides a thumbnail sketch of his own previous history, verifiable from the biographical data known to us. The text is thus a reality statement, in which the meaning of the past inheres in the use of the preterite tense. The narrative attitude of the authorial person proves to be misleading, since here it is evidently Wiechert himself and not an intermediary who is speaking.

Edvardson uses a good part of her book to impress upon the reader what her life had been like before the camp. Yet she too presents verifiable data and hence a real-life report. Although she apostrophizes her childhood self as 'the Girl', the two are obviously identical. By frequently repeating this term, however, instead of passing to the personal pronoun, she appears to maintain the distance between subject of experience and narrator. In her report too, the interior perspective is dominant, as the following kind of question to the implicit reader serves to emphasize:

> When the Star of David came along ... – that sounds like 'when school began' or 'when autumn fell', as if it were the normal run of life, completely lacking in drama. Can it not be said differently? Are there no other words? No, not for the Girl. (**Edvardson**, 1986: 55)

In both texts, everything in the content indicates that the third person inserted between the author and the events is actually identical with the author, or at least was at the time of the experience in question. Verifiable facts prevent a fictional intermediary from being slipped between author and text in the reader's imagination; the identity of the two means that the 'he' or 'she' form is only a pose on the author's part, designed to signal the temporal distance between experience and narrator. Here, then, it is content which gains the upper hand over narrative system and identifies an ostensibly fictional account of personal experience as a statement about reality. In the case of Wiechert, the generic denomination 'report' predisposes the reader to receive the text as an account of actual facts. Edvardson's book, first written in Swedish and translated into German, is designated on the dust-jacket as a 'novel', but this is contradicted by a photograph that is obviously of the author as a child. Interestingly, there is no such generic designation on the title page inside, and the promotional blurb explicitly refers to the 'terrible reality' that befell the daughter of the writer Elisabeth Langgässer. The multiple advice to take the text as an account of reality therefore excludes it as a piece of fiction.

The generic term 'tale' that Fred Wander gives to his book of recollections proves to be similarly deceptive. For not only is it a first-person narrative, but it also allows eighteen of his fellow-prisoners to have a say for long stretches of text. When he reports what his companions were thinking, he justifies this discursively in the following way: 'How do I know this? He often spoke of the Seders in his home, the rich farmer Meier Bernstein. All the Jews from Eastern Europe enjoyed telling stories about festivities' (**Wander**, 1985: 44). In another place, as we shall see below, he uses the German tense system to mark out what is mere supposition. 'Story' in Wander's work should thus be taken in the sense of the 'Hasidic tale', which is also based upon real events (cf. Eliach, 1985).

Things are quite different in the case of Bruno Apitz's *Nackt unter Wölfen*; it too bears the title 'novel', but here this unambiguously indicates a work of fiction. It is true that the action is situated in real topography – Ettersberg is mentioned in the very first sentence, and Buchenwald a little later – yet the epic preterite immediately introduces the recipient to an atmosphere outside real time. The work remains throughout a traditional third-person novel, in which the narrator's voice never acquires a personal profile. Narrative report alternates with passages of dialogue (usually without an introductory 'he said' or 'she said'), in which the intermediary completely withdraws.

The narrator's purview covers both the prisoners as a group and the SS. Although the author draws on his own experience, his narrator plays no part in the world of the imaginary figures. The 'narrative distance' (Stanzel, 1985: 305) – that is, the sovereign independence of the intermediary voice from the world it depicts – gives the novel a multiperspectival character. The reader discovers in the same way how the prisoners and the SS judge events. Yet the univocal evaluation of their conduct, expressed through black-and-white characterization, lets us see the subjective opinion of the presenter of the story. The selection and drawing of the characters, which provide the social spectrum in which the action unfolds, take their inspiration from the historical novel (cf. Foley, 1982: 345).

The narrator's partly limited knowledge, together with his switching between prisoners and SS, is used by the author to produce the tension or suspense in *Nackt unter Wölfen*. For suspense is the higher category which Apitz's narrative system is made to serve. It is generated with the help of the novel's 'dramatic' structure, in which the dialogue plays an important role, as mentioned before. After 1945, Apitz would use this exercise in the genre of drama for the writing of radio plays – indeed, he adapted *Nackt unter Wölfen* itself for the radio soon after publication, and turned it into a film for the fifteenth anniversary of the liberation of Buchenwald (cf. Reißland, 1976: 62–76).

In the view of Emil Staiger, dramatic tension may be stylistically expressed either as pathos or as a problem. In Apitz's novel it is mainly a question of problematic style, in which tension is 'generated through the lack of independence of the individual parts' (Staiger, 1983: 115). The fate of the characters and the various episodes in the novel are narrated with each other in mind: that is, they stand in an interrelated tension that is resolved only at the end of the narrative. Since suspense is meant to hold the reader's interest and only becomes actual in the process of reception, the concentration camp novel, as represented by *Nackt unter Wölfen*, may be described as reader-oriented.

The exposition of the novel already supplies what is needed for the suspense in the plot structure. Departing from his historical source, Apitz has the child arrive in Buchenwald only at the beginning of 1945, so that the narrative is limited to the final months before the camp was liberated by the Americans. Apitz evidently chose this period because the radical turnaround associated with the end of SS rule in Buchenwald was favourable for the generation of dramatic tension.

In Apitz's text the child is smuggled into the camp in a trunk; his arrival is not open and public as it was in historical reality. The novel thus begins at a strategic moment which, being also crucial for the building of tension, represents what Georg Lukács called a 'significant landmark' (Lukács, 1971: 81f.). At first the child remains hidden from the SS. The reader's anticipatory sense focuses on how those running the camp will eventually find out and then react to that knowledge. The saving of the child is thus the nucleus that has the potential to generate suspense in the novel.

There are three strands to the plot. Höfel and Pippig in the prisoners' storehouse discover the child and decide to conceal him – in Höfel's case through thinking about his own son. But Höfel belongs to the secret political organization in the camp, the International Camp Committee (ILK),[5] where he has an exposed position as military instructor. The third strand shows the camp elder Krämer, who is also linked to the ILK, receiving orders in the commandant's office together with the headman. Among the top SS people in the camp, a conflict is raging between the commandant Alois Schwahl, who is already making provisions for the end of SS rule, and the bloodthirsty headman Kluttig and his friend Reineboth.

Right from the beginning, these three strands suggest the difficulties to be overcome: Höfel, in Schillerian mould, must choose between two duties: his humanitarian feelings and his loyalty to the ILK. This personal conflict of his divides the prisoners. The temperaments of Kluttig and Reineboth lead one to expect a clash between the SS and the inmates.

Höfel wants to keep the child, even against the orders of the ILK leader, Bochow, who considers him to be a danger to the committee and ultimately to the 50,000 prisoners in Buchenwald. Bochow therefore intends to have the child sent away on the next transport, even though he is aware that it will take him to certain death in another camp. In the end, Kluttig and Reineboth plan an operation against the prisoners, to smash the secret political conspiracy of which they still have only an inkling.

The reader's interest is now directed towards the solving of personal and interpersonal problems triggered by the child's arrival, and to the outcome of the conflict between the prisoners and the SS. This, however, reduces the camp background to a factor not directly relevant to the development of events.

The medial structure of the novel ensures that its conclusion is relatively open: neither the child's survival nor that of the other protagonists is certain until the very end. The plot development therefore requires a few victims, even if these do not come from among the main actors. It is true that Krämer is shot in revenge by Kluttig in the closing minutes, but the prisoners' doctor is able to save his life.

If suspense in *Nackt unter Wölfen* were generated only through the novel's structure and the sensational character of the events described in it (to which the title also alludes), then it would presumably not have been the success it was. Epic elements, however, maintain the reader's curiosity, as they do in the traditional novel. Unlike in the witness report, their effect is to heighten or to lower the suspense, as the author strategically narrows or broadens the narrator's intermediary viewpoint on events. For example, Apitz employs retrospective to slow down the action, and not, as the reports do, simply to insert information about things experienced in an earlier period. He has Rose reflecting in the prison bunker about his arrival in Buchenwald, as he waits to be taken for interrogation and probable torture (**Apitz**, 1982: 249ff.). The agony of waiting is thus shared with the reader, even though narrative time and narrated time do not entirely coincide.

The limited knowledge of the narrator is also used to heighten the suspense. When the child, who has so far been relatively safe hidden in Block 61, is taken by an unknown prisoner at night to another place in the camp, both the identity of the 'kidnapper' and the exact destination remain unknown even to the ILK. Only at the end is it revealed to the reader and to the ILK that, on the orders of one member of the committee, the child was concealed by another prisoner in the SS pigsty and came to no real harm.

A third example of how the author tries to maintain the suspense throughout is the constant shortening of the scenes towards the end, which creates an illusion of simultaneity (**Apitz**, 1982: 420ff.). This technique is also meant to anticipate structurally the hectic scenes that will precede and accompany the long-awaited arrival of the liberators.[6] The spotlight, as it were, shifts from Höfel and Kropinski in the bunker to Bochow and his decision to restrain the ILK in the face of the threatened 'evacuation' of prisoners, then to the jumpiness of the SS still left in the camp, then back to the bunker. These repeated scene-changes over only a few pages underline the reader's impression of the dramatically staged structure of the novel.

Besides the use of suspense in *Nackt unter Wölfen*, another aspect is also significant for its fictional character. As we have already seen, the report written by the father of the child who served as Apitz's model was published in the late 1980s. Moreover, the saving of that child in Buchenwald is one of the few events in the camps that are identifiable from the testimony of a number of survivors; its exceptional character made it the stuff of legend already in the camp, by temporarily restoring its original dual function as entertainment and source of strength. Events such as the child's arrival in Buchenwald helped to raise the prisoners' morale, and active participation in his safety gave a certain meaning to their life in the camp.

A similar effect was produced in Auschwitz by the bold presence of mind of a young Jewish woman, who killed the SS man Schillinger with his own service pistol in the changing room attached to the gas chamber. This incident, too, was immediately stylized into a legend.[7] In his analysis of it, James Young demonstrates how various witness reports modify and embroider the narrative core and subject it to distinct interpretations – which is the sign of fictionalization – yet still preserve its essential identity as a prisoner's act of resistance to her killers (cf. Young, 1987b: 46–50). Bruno Apitz, too, changes the real-life core to his novel, so that it accords with the message that the integration of the ILK was furthered by the saving of the child. *Nackt unter Wölfen* is thus a good example of how events with the potential to become a legend, because of their usually sensational character, are especially susceptible to novelistic treatment.

The fictionalization of concentration camp material, as in Apitz's novel, affects the whole of the text. It underlies the structural conception and seeks to convey a definite message. *Nackt unter Wölfen* demonstrates the triumph of individual humanitarian action over party exigency, which is Reich-Ranicki's explanation for its success in the GDR (Reich-Ranicki, 1991: 459f.). The meaning-potential inherent in the novelistic form (cf. Lukács, 1971: 40f.) not only permits the camp survivor, like Bruno Apitz, to transfer historical meaning onto something new, but facilitates the invention of meaning in general in a potentially meaningless world such as that of the concentration camp. In this way, that which is reported acquires the 'appearance of ideality' (White, 1987). *Nackt unter Wölfen* bears out what Hayden White holds to be the essence of historiography: namely, that the representation of an event takes place from a particular moral point of view; that moral significance is expressed in the plot, which is 'superimposed' on the events and gives the whole a greater unity (White, 1987: 20).

Suspense may therefore develop within the unity of the novel, because its structure is directed to a definite goal (cf. Schulte-Sasse and Werner, 1990: 141). This teleological character of the novelistic treatment underpins the diverse ways of linking together the narrative sequences (cf. Schulte-Sasse and Werner, 1990: 145) and itself produces 'problematic style' (Staiger, 1983: 116). But it is also this orientation to a particular goal which helps the author to ascribe meaning to what is reported. From the beginning, such authors as Bruno Apitz must keep in mind the meaning of the whole. Problems that arise along the way will then perhaps delay, but not prevent, achievement of the goal.

From the point of view of structure, then, the novel differs fundamentally from the report, which is in this respect more akin to a chronicle; it lacks 'that summing up of the "meaning" of the chain of events with which it deals that we normally expect from the well-made story' (White, 1987: 16). Precisely this meaning was closed to survivors who limited their writing to reported experience. Details accumulate in their texts, but they are not subordinate to a recognizable goal. Staiger speaks of the 'epic style' in such texts (Staiger, 1983: 116). Often the former prisoners write of their experience in order to clarify what meaning their survival may have had. The only meaning they perceive at first lies in the writing process itself, as a means of bearing witness for themselves and for others who have not survived,[8] and as a means of freeing themselves of what they lived through.[9]

Fictionalization of the concentration camp subject, in a novel such as *Nackt unter Wölfen*, therefore concerns not the material as such but its presentation, that is, the way in which the author makes his or her experience serve the goal of clarifying a message and confers a particular modality on that experience. It is true that such fictionalization makes concessions to the reader's experience of life and may therefore obscure the dehumanized reality of the camps (cf. Foley, 1982: 348); in so far as it is practised by survivors, however, it has nothing to do with a falsification of the facts, such as one associates, for example, with the camp at Theresienstadt. In the 'ghetto' there, and not only through 'prisoners' self-administration' or 'leisure organization', the SS cultivated the reputation of a 'showcase camp' and the illusion of a 'family' or 'old people's' camp. In order to deceive delegations from Denmark and the Red Cross in late 1943 and early 1944, prisoners were even made to put on a sham city life that had nothing in common with their true situation.[10] With the reality of the camp hidden beneath dummies and euphemisms, a film was made of the whole sham in the late summer of 1944 and exploited in the autumn for Nazi propaganda about the Jews (Adler, 1960: 184).[11] Immediately after the shooting of the film was completed, one of the largest-ever deportations began to Auschwitz – and it included some of those who had 'acted' in the film (cf. Wolfberg, 1991: 44). A clear distinction must be drawn, therefore, between SS fiction designed to fool its international critics, and an account of experiences in the camp that is fictional in the sense of not being subject to the categories of truth and falsity.

Literary crafting in the concentration camp reports

It should therefore be stressed that the concentration camp reports present empirical-historical reality from the point of view of personal experience. This orientation of the content determines the narrative form. If narrative texts represent a 'medium-specific realization of a structure of narrative logic',[12] then the task posed for survivors was to find an adequate narrative means to represent the structure of memory. This is how Hayden White should be understood when he says of form that it 'is found rather than constructed' (White, 1987: 27).

The witnesses are aware that they cannot exclude their feelings when they write down their testimony. Nevertheless, they make every effort to give as objective a report as they can of their experience, and in so doing they unconsciously join a tradition that already guided the compilers of the Bible (cf. Auerbach, 1968: 8–23). The striving for objective truth goes so far that Grete Salus, for example, extracts from the rest of the text what she has to say about the personal meaning of her experience and presents it in the form of poetry. It is, however, their subjective character which gives these lyrics an informative content that should not be underestimated. In her poems, most of which she probably composed in the camp, something is preserved of the immediacy of her instinctive reaction to what she was living through. A wealth of poetic codes, as represented in lyrical verse, convey in a short space more information than prose does; for it is not only the content but also the form of poetical discourse that is a bearer of information. In other words, if we follow Roman Jakobson in interpreting the production of a text as selection and combination, then the poetic function may be recognized precisely in the ordering of the chosen material (cf. Jakobson, 1979: 94). In the ideal case, then, poetic language will also be better than prose at capturing the atmosphere of the camps, but only if the author manages, as Paul Celan did, for instance, to break free from ossified forms. In most cases, however, the traditional forms of poetry employed by survivors seem to have put a clamp on the immediacy of their message (cf. Moll, 1988: 246).

A minority would have liked to write about their feelings, but like Ella Lingens-Reiner did not think themselves capable of doing it in verse; she therefore contented herself with a 'sketchy picture' of the story of her survival (**Lingens-Reiner**, 1948: x). And yet, linguistic dexterity would not have removed her fear of the fresh torments associated with recollection.

However different the concentration camp texts may be in terms of the camp they describe, the length of internment and the date on which it started, they all share with the autobiographical genre, and also with novels that draw on material from the camps, the problem of how to present the facts in the form of a narrative. Furthermore, they all require to be structured with a beginning, a middle and an end, as we shall now see.

Typically, the concentration camp texts follow a chronological order.[13] They begin with the initial internment, or (more rarely) with the events that led up to it, and end with the liberation. These two moments in time that frame the experience of the camps are described in considerable detail, and this distinguishes them from the middle part where particular aspects of camp life such as hygiene, food or work are gathered together and spoken about in general terms (sometimes in explicitly thematic sections). This structure of the report follows the structure of life itself; the choice of a beginning and end conforms to their significance for the period of life in question. By contrast, the corresponding parts in the traditional novel are subject to the requirements of narration – that is, to the generation of suspense. In a few cases, reports employ a figurative mode of presentation as in a fictional text. One of the two examples that may serve to illustrate this is the passage already quoted from *Der Totenwald*, by the writer Ernst Wiechert. But first let us look at the moment in Antonia Bruha's report where she refers to a dream that encoded and summarily reproduced or partly anticipated her destiny:

> Nowhere do the chestnut trees blossom as beautifully as in Vienna: the Prater is filled with their fragrance, and their candles are large, white and pink. Everything is blooming and greening; everything is fresh, white and lilac-coloured, and a breath of wind carries the overwhelming scent along. One would like it to remain forever spring.
>
> Suddenly there is a wind, a raging and roaring in the air. The storm tears at the leaves, pulls at the blossom. One leaf after another falls down, and the chestnut candles grow weary and droop their heads.
>
> Please, leave just one blossom standing, the blossom of hope and faith! But the storm is not open to persuasion: it roars and rages and whirls. Suddenly, amid all the din, a baby's crying sounds softly, then more loudly and insistently, and all at once rings out like a scream for help.
>
> Ah yes, the baby is crying. One need only stretch out one's left hand and gently move the pram that stands beside the bed. I stretch out my hand – but no pram is there. My hand clutches at thin air. It falls heavily, and now I am sitting wide awake on the straw mattress.
>
> (**Bruha**, 1984: 9)

The telling of the dream is a perfect example of a personal narrative stance. The perspective is one of interiority, and we hear the beginnings of an internal monologue: 'Please, leave just one blossom standing!' and 'Ah yes, the baby is crying'. After the non-temporal judgement of the opening sentence, Bruha passes to the reporting of narrated time. The double use of 'suddenly' marks the coincidence of narrated time and narrative time, and from then on Bruha makes the temporality more and more precise. Similarly, with regard to the experiential subject, she progresses from a generalizing 'one' to a specifying 'I'.

This grammatical analysis is supported by the content. Strictly speaking, the passage concerns a dream within a dream: a dream of freedom, ended by the baby's crying, contains within it a prison dream from which the narrator is woken by the missing baby. The two dreams differ only in how they end. The symbolic charge of the sudden change of weather in springtime Vienna, and the allegorization, belong to both dreams. It is an open question whether Bruha actually experienced the dream within a dream as she records it. But it enables her to pass from her previous reflections – which sought to clarify a political situation super-elevated to the level of natural myth – to her own family situation at the time of her internment and then directly to her prison surroundings. The dreams further give us an idea of her state of mind, and more generally attest to the tendency of prisoners to escape from a loathsome present into reverie and bygone days. Whereas the exposition of a fictional work often anticipates, as in a nutshell, all its main themes,[14] the first couple of paragraphs in Bruha's report are of little structural significance for what is to follow.

Things stand otherwise in Ernst Wiechert's *Der Totenwald*. His recollective testimony begins by establishing a distance from the recollected self, so that he almost draws an intermediary into the narrative situation. The distance is increased by the use of a fictitious name for his protagonist. Only somewhat later does it become clear that there is a programmatic objective in this, when he thinks he can see John the Baptist's face in his first dreams during captivity.

> Then Johannes recognized that he had been destined to suffer together with that head. Not that he would save it, or even help it. But from that still, lonely gaze, he would draw the strength and the duty to step from security to insecurity, from silence to speech, from bondage to freedom – even if it was only freedom of conscience.
> (**Wiechert**, 1984: 13)

The religious imagery modelling this dream (itself an allusion to Pastor Martin Niemöller, in whose defence Wiechert had publicly spoken out) gave him the strength to live through the camp. In his report, he employs it as a theme that imparts meaning: his torments acquire a certain sense from the martyrdom of a saint.[15] (The comparison does appear rather forced, though, because Wiechert's religiously motivated criticism of the Nazis brought about his imprisonment in a camp (cf. **Wiechert**, 1966) but did not put his life in serious danger.)

Looking back, Wiechert fits his own experiences into the interpretive schema of a Passion (cf. Peitsch, 1990: 177–91). Moreover, a comparison with his prison diary and letters (which were not at hand when he composed *Der Totenwald*) allows us to see the extent to which he reworked his experiences in the medium of writing.

The general structure of Wiechert's text places it somewhere between the report based on personal experience and the novel. As the testimony of a writer, it is an exception within the group of concentration camp reports. In the great majority of these, the structural functionalization of narrative devices is very limited, and any judgement of occasional literary effect has to make allowances for the author's aim of coming to terms with experience (cf. Anderegg, 1983: 155). In the narrative fashioning of lived reality, they scoop out part of the 'pre-given meaning' that reality as such includes (cf. Glinz, 1979: 120).[16] With direct speech, generalization, cumulative repetition, forward view and retrospective, and with tenses dictated by content, they use the same 'narrative building blocks' (Lämmert, 1983) that are found in the novel. What is different is the functional deployment of these devices, which, because the author and narrator are identical, cannot be the same as in a fictional text presented through an intermediary. Let us consider this point more closely.

The choice of *tense* plays an important role in the reception of any narrative text. Käte Hamburger, in various essays and in her book *Die Logik der Dichtung* (1957), was one of the first to draw attention to this substantive function of tenses in relation to the text. One of her core theses is that in the third-person novel – that is, in the textual working of material as fiction – the epic preterite loses its past significance. More recently, Jürgen H. Petersen has made a further contribution to the study of tense in the epic text, and what follows will to some extent be based upon his observations on this matter (1993: 21–30). Petersen also starts from the non-temporal significance of the epic preterite. But he further argues that, if the narrator makes any intervention in the present tense, the preterite provisionally acquires an '*immanent* temporal function *within the text*' (Petersen, 1993: 23 – emphasis in the original).

From their retrospective narrative stance, one would expect the concentration camp texts to employ the preterite, which, because it is a question of a statement about reality, also has a past significance. What one finds, however, is an above-average number of texts written almost entirely in the present tense. This indicates, of course, not so much a modernist narrative strategy as an emotional use of tense; the witnesses are literally reliving the torments of their captivity. Even the reports composed in the preterite repeatedly fall into the present for whole passages. Antonia Bruha, for instance, in the account of her internment, switches from the preterite of recollection to the present tense:

> And so I was put in that cell. Now I am lying there, for I know not how long. No one brought me anything, no one called me, no one any longer asked me about anything. I heard nothing from the outside world – only the heavy steps in front of the door. Three times a day the flap opens in the cell door, and food is reached through to me. In the morning coffee and a piece of bread, at midday and in the evening an indefinable soup. (**Bruha**, 1984: 18)

The verbs in the present tense here signal a historic present, which underlines Bruha's situation at the time in question. Then the anaphorically structured factual report breaks through again, followed by a further passage in the historic present. Within one paragraph, then, the narrative shifts several times from the tense of the narrated world – to use Harald Weinrich's term (Weinrich, 1964) – to the tense of the talked-about world, and hence from a relaxed narrative posture to one that is much more taut. The author appears to make the changes of tense intuitively, although a certain purpose may be seen in the fact that sentences in which she alludes to her mental and physical condition are placed in the present. The last two sentences show, however, that she also employs the present for the narrative report.

In any event, the present tense lends authenticity to the event or situation described and carries a suggestion of immediacy. It becomes especially interesting where the time of imprisonment and the time of writing are brought into relation with each other: that is, where the remembered event is reflected upon from the compositional present. Thus, at another point the author describes in the preterite a dream about her internment, and goes on to write in the present about the effect that the event continues to have on her (**Bruha**, 1984: 104), so that the use of the present tense involves a statement about her situation as it is today. This passage acquires structural significance if one considers its context: it is preceded by an account in the preterite of the deficient medical care given to prisoners in Ravensbrück; and it is followed by Bruha's report of an incident in the prisoners' sick bay, also in the preterite. The dream on which she comments in the present tense thus serves as a way of passing from the general to the concrete. Elsewhere in the same report, the significance of the past for prisoners in the camp – a significance reflected upon in the present tense – serves as a transition to a passage where the author looks back at some length on the time before her internment (**Bruha**, 1984: 11).

Another example will illustrate this strategic use of the present in the concentration camp texts. 'Hermi has the patience of an angel,' Mali Fritz praises a new-found friend. 'She is a really good comrade; it's probably time I asked and listened to her again about her "former life". I didn't know her in the camp. I learnt a lot about her en route, but I'd like to know more. Hermi speaks of "then" – it lies infinitely far away' (**Fritz and Jursa**, 1983: 71). At the time of writing, the need to enquire no longer exists for the author, but only for the reader. As in Bruha's case, however, Mali Fritz's statement also serves to justify – and shows that she feels a need to justify – her interruption of the chronology of the report with information about events prior to her internment.

Fred Wander's use of tense changes falls into a category of its own. Often he appears to leap arbitrarily back and forth between present and preterite, but usually it is possible to see some motivation behind it. It is not, as Birgit Kröhle believes, just a question of making the experience more authentic or historicizing it within the report (Kröhle, 1989: 100f.). Wander changes tense quite consistently, for example, when he lets one of his eighteen fellow-prisoners speak. When he himself reports in the present, he has the other voice begin in the preterite – and vice versa; the tense change serves to show that someone different is speaking (e.g. **Wander**, 1985: 12f.). When the reporter recalls an earlier stage of detention or his own escape, 'the images come over him' (**Wander**, 1985: 82); he therefore brings them to mind in the present tense.

The central chapter discussed earlier, '*Woran erinnert dich Wald?*', which deals with the death of a young fellow-prisoner, uses a strikingly frequent change of tense to express the high emotion that grips the writer as he is composing the report. Here the shifts are completely in the service of structure: the restaurant scene acted by Tadeusz Moll, for example, is reproduced in the present tense; and Wander's intention is even plainer in the account of his death. He tries to imagine Moll's thoughts in 'fictional' form (**Wander**, 1985: 118–21), and for this he employs the present tense. Then follows an attempt in the preterite to describe the 'probable reality': 'To hell with all this pompous stuff. He no longer loved anybody, anything' (**Wander**, 1985: 122). Wander's use of tenses is altogether in the tradition of the modern novel, as exemplified by Christa Wolf's *A Model Childhood*, but especially here it also recalls the so-called 'fictional present' (Petersen, 1993) which, in Max Frisch's *Mein Name sei Gantenbein*, marks the narrator's recurrent 'imaginings' and sets them apart from the reality narrated in the epic preterite which has no reference to actual time. To similar effect, the fictional present breaks into Wander's report in the depiction of the real past, where he seems to make fertile use of a modern narrative procedure to represent reality.

It is quite clear that the time which elapses between an experience and a report about it has an influence at the level not only of content but also of narrative structure. The manner of presentation generally acquires greater weight with the passing of time, with reflection (which also takes up more space) and increasing knowledge. In the concentration camp texts, this may be expressed in a viewing of the experience not in isolation but as part of the total life of the person concerned. By incorporating the experience as an 'episode' in an autobiography or memoirs, it may in a sense be possible to relativize and thereby come to terms with it. It is not surprising that hardly any Jews are among the public figures, such as politicians or writers, who have handled their past in the camps in this way (**Maleta** (1981), **Matejka** (1983); an exception: **Edel** (1979)). Even at a greater distance, the Jewish authors tend to view the period of their internment as the really decisive part of their life; they try to come to terms with it by keeping to existing models of interpretation, such as those provided by religion (Wander) or literature (Drach). Both kinds of 'treatment' – relativization as well as singularization of a personal past – are instrumentally connected to the search for meaning in what has been experienced.

Analysis of Bruno Apitz's *Nackt unter Wölfen* has shown that it has a relatively tight teleological structure; it was conceived with a certain message in mind. Reports based on personal experience are also written with knowledge of the ending: the day of flight (Seger) or release (e.g. Gostner) or liberation (Wander) influences to a degree how the experience is interpreted. In a few cases,

it is true, particular experiences are presented as absolutely necessary to the achievement of the goal, but they are seen within a
temporal framework that gives a certain unity to the experience of
the camp (cf. Jauss, 1982: 422). Not by chance are beginning and
end the key moments in most of the reports, which lend retrospective significance to the events in between.

Microstructurally, subsequent interpretation (that is, knowledge) is expressed in the choice of narrative devices, one of which
is precisely the tense of verbs. *Temporal structure* in the concentration camp texts, as in other epic texts, is achieved through the
devices of compression, anticipation and retrospection, although
all of these have a special function in the report based upon
personal experience.

Mali Fritz opens her account of a specific memory ('this time it
is hard again') with frequentative and durative indicators of time
compression, such as 'once again' or 'constantly' (**Fritz**, 1986: 24).
Since she has not kept each event alive in her memory with the
same vigour – and quite apart from the fact that she could not
report each one in the same detail – the device of compression to
some extent reproduces the structure of her recollection. Her
memory can be claimed as genuine to the extent that this
structure permits conclusions to be drawn about the effect of
certain experiences upon those who survived them. It is a truism
that more striking impressions are remembered more readily and
with greater accuracy. As psychologists dealing with long-term
damage suffered by former inmates of a concentration camp have
repeatedly confirmed, memory in these cases fluctuates between
amnesia and hypermnesia, forgotten details and overly clear
images. There is indeed plenty of evidence of this in the reports
themselves. We have already pointed to their rough uniformity of
structure, with arrival at the camp and eventual liberation often
recorded in sharper detail, and the intervening time more or less
compressed so that only some particular experiences stand out in
the narrative.

Compression is also apparent where a number of experiences
at discrete points in time are treated as a single continuum.
The following example from Erwin Gostner's report depicts a
situation which he probably experienced several times in that
or a similar way, and about which other prisoners have also
spoken and speculated. Gostner describes his 'observation' of how

a prisoner was shot by the camp guards: 'The desperate man collapses; he is dragged badly wounded into the guardhouse. The machine-gunner is immediately relieved and has to report to the camp commandant. He receives a commendation' (**Gostner**, 1986: 69). If Gostner had been close to the scene, he might just have observed the wounded man being dragged into the guard-house, but otherwise he would have been drawing on knowledge he had acquired during his period of captivity – whether before or after the event is, in retrospect, immaterial. Gostner may also have seen that the SS man who committed the murder was 'relieved'. But the rest of his 'description' is certainly based on sources other than direct observation.

Along with compression, the device of generalization temporally concentrates experiences in the report. Salus, for instance, describes through generalization the danger of disease in the camps: 'The dirt and the living on top of one another were among the worst scourges of the concentration camp, for they helped to produce epidemics and cost many people's lives' (**Salus**, 1981: 61). From the individual experiences of illness and death that she witnessed in the camp, she abstracts a general statement. Such use of generalization, as a pendant to an illustrative description of a particular incident, helps the reporter to conceal gaps in his or her memory. Furthermore, generalization underlines the mediated character of what is reported, the filtering function of the witness, which should not be confused with that of the intermediary in the system of fictional narrative.

Anticipations, which by no means contradict and may even accentuate the chronological presentation, may be found in a few of the texts. Usually, as in the following instance, they involve advance warning of a tragic event. 'I knew there were worse things than death,' writes Joseph Drexel, 'and I would learn it still more clearly, up to the most bitter realization that it is reserved to man to besmirch even death' (**Drexel**, 1980: 72). Immediately, however, he takes this back with what seems like a half-apology: 'But I had not yet reached that point, or anyway had not gone beyond an unwelcome suspicion which, in order to become actual knowledge, still had to pass through much suffering along the way.' By thus qualifying his anticipation, Drexel seems to be trying to preserve the chronology of his report, but this serves to heighten the element of suspense.

The concentration camp reports, then, are also indebted to the categories of the narrative system, even if the lack of an intermediary gives them a different function from the one they have in a work of fiction.

The presentation of material such as the experience of the camps does, however, require the use of stylistic devices. A pathos-filled account of an event may immediately suggest itself. Whereas, according to Emil Staiger, pathos generates suspense in dramatic verse, it presupposes an 'oppositeness' in the case of a prose text, which the pathetic style 'strives to overcome, whether the speaker wins over the listener, or the listener is crushed by the force of the speech' (Staiger, 1983 107). In the prose text, pathos takes shape through the hammering repetition of words and the rhythm of sentences. Pathos mainly generated by rhetorical means is characteristic of 'poetry written in the consciousness of crisis' (Hegele, 1963: 92), such as that which expressionism produced in the early twentieth century. Genuine pathos, supported by an experience, lacks all calculation and is therefore indifferent to aesthetic evaluation. It is found not only in 'lofty' verse, but also, for example, in the lyrical poetry based on personal experience that was written by the victims of National Socialism.

Concentration camp survivors also employ the device of emphatic expression. The use of elevated language, for example, gives certain passages an expressive urgency, and many authors strike a pathetic tone when it is a question of the suffering in the camps: 'We go past the Jewish blocks. Their ranks have thinned. Many little snow-covered heaps, from which human arms stretch in rigid accusation, testify to a tragedy of which we are the witnesses' (**Gostner**, 1986: 68). With these words Erwin Gostner depicts the aftermath of a night-long line-up in Dachau – 'a temporal sanction, a mode of punishment that used time itself as means' (Sofsky, 1997: 79), imposed collectively by the SS when a prisoner escaped from the camp. The reported gesture of the dead is not open to empirical verification – indeed, it is unlikely that Gostner actually saw it in this way. But that is of no consequence. What matters is that he *experienced* it thus in his memory; factuality takes second place to a '*higher reality*' (Kronsbein, 1984: 91 – emphasis in the original), and authenticity takes on a different quality. For Gostner's account implies that he recognized the scale and permanence of the suffering inflicted on the Jews in the camp; and that only death made them, the lowest in the prisoners' hierarchy, into accusers. Apart from the fact that their lives mattered less than those of Poles to the SS thugs, they also suffered from the anti-Semitic attitudes widespread among their fellow-prisoners. Gostner's choice of words, therefore, tells us not only what he experienced but also the impression it made upon him. The emphatic use of language has an eminently cognitive function.

Gerhart Seger describes in similar style the line-up that took place on his arrival at the camp. Here he is trying to make the effect of this harassment intelligible to his readers:

> You are transferred to Oranienburg. Now one stands there: one hour passes, a second hour seeps away, then a third, a fourth, ... The bleakness of it grows, the repugnance becomes ever stronger: that something like this concentration camp is possible, that human beings can do something like this to other human beings! The fifth, the sixth, the seventh, the eighth hour – without end. Abandon all hope, ye who wait here! The ninth hour, the tenth hour – our knees are shaking; the whole physical pain, the feeling of disgust rises up to the throat. Reception in Oranienburg! (**Seger**, 1979: 56)

Seger's urgent language draws its imagery from a number of different sources. The dominant model of the counting of hours recalls Christ's Passion; the Social Democrat Seger uses it to record the slow passing of time up to the moment of the sacrifice. Also of religious origin, though mediated by literature, is the 'Abandon all hope!', an allusion to the sign hanging over the Gate of Hell in Dante's *Inferno*. (Seger is certainly not alone among the concentration camp authors in drawing upon a literary stock of meaning.) Similarly, the German verb *überführen* [originally 'carry or ferry across', here rendered by 'transfer' – *trans. note*], which is used by Seger to indicate that he is now counted among the dead, belongs to the semantic zone of dying that dominates the passage. The subsequent change from the personal pronoun 'you' to the impersonal 'one' is a sign of depersonalization. Seger experiences his deportation as an entombment.[17]

Pathos of style, which is deployed in the camp texts to win the recipient over, makes use of the argumentative strategies of classical rhetoric. Thus we find leitmotifs and devices such as antithesis, chiasmus and anaphora, as well as other kinds of emphatic repetition of words. The bold and simple use of antithesis (cf. Skreb, 1968: 49–59) lends a vivid quality to Lina Haag's account of her fate and enhances its moral status. She thereby also evinces a certain political insight:

> Seated not far from me, a beautiful woman is leafing through a journal with an air of boredom. In one day she certainly spends more on beauty care . . . than I earn in one week. Pearls shine on her chest. On my chest no pearls shine; instead I carry half a razor blade sewn into my bra. The fair and splendid lady has no need of that; she has never distributed any forbidden leaflets or done time in a concentration camp; presumably all she has done is make love. The good-looking, supple old gentleman with silvery hair and precisely trimmed white moustache who is now greeting her with a tender kiss is probably the husband for whom she has been waiting. I too am waiting for my man, but I wait in vain, because he won't be coming in such a hurry after today's decision in Prinz-Albrecht-Strasse. If he ever comes back from there, he'll have work to do in the Mauthausen quarry. That is the difference. (**Haag**, 1985: 156f.)

Haag's counterposition of two worlds enables her to characterize conflicting political attitudes in a way that makes her appear a proud outsider. The ironic undertones reveal the narrator's self-assured feeling of superiority, which she shortly after dresses up in the rhetorical question: 'Are they better than us, the people standing around here and lying in easy chairs?' 'No,' she answers herself, 'they've never thought of anything but themselves' (**Haag**, 1985: 157) – and with that she overlays her political judgement with a value judgement.

In addition to its structural function, antithesis also has a cognitive function in the concentration camp reports. This is especially clear in the terse form of Primo Levi's judgement on the so-called 'musulmans' in Auschwitz: 'Their life is short, but their number is endless' (**Levi**, 1987a: 96). Levi uses the epigrammatic figure not as an empty stylistic device, but to express an insight gained from observation of life in the camp: no prisoner counted as an individual. Only the mass played a role, and it seemed inexhaustible. As in classical rhetoric, antithesis here replaces a lengthier presentation of the argument.

The formal quality of antithesis is enhanced by chiasmus, as in Primo Levi's statement: 'There were twelve goods wagons, and six hundred and fifty were we' (**Levi**, 1987a: 22);[18] the symmetrical arrangement generates a certain urgency. Cordelia Edvardson, the daughter of Elisabeth Langgässer, unites chiasmus with alliteration to serve a quasi-mythological characterization of her oppressors in Auschwitz: 'Mengele and Mandel, Mandel and Mengele, the fair-haired headwoman Maria Mandel in Auschwitz-Birkenau and the dark-haired Dr Mengele, who carried out the selections. The king and queen in the kingdom of the dead' (**Edvardson**, 1986: 84). Parallelism at the level of language here matches the myth, evoked as thoroughly conforming to the reality (absolute power enabled the SS thugs to achieve that). Edvardson writes from the viewpoint of herself as a girl, who was aged 14 when she was deported in 1943 to Theresienstadt and then on to Auschwitz. She brought with her into the camps the airiness of fairy tale and myth that had marked her childhood (**Edvardson**, 1986: 63). Familiarity with this literary world was also a major influence on how she grappled with the experience of the camps.

In his case, Primo Levi stresses the parallelism by combining a pair of opposites into anaphora: 'One hesitates to call them living: one hesitates to call their death death, in the face of which they have no fear' (**Levi**, 1987a: 96). The rhetorical figure underlines Levi's judgement on the state of the 'musulmans' in Auschwitz. Neither life nor death had any meaning for them. While still alive, they counted among the dead.

In other texts, the figure of anaphora is used to reconstruct the author's despair at the hopelessness and finality of his existence in the camp. Erich Altmann's words: 'That was our life. One starves, one hopes, one dies – and all with musical accompaniment' (**Altmann**, 1947: 81f.), with their sudden shift from first person plural to impersonal 'one', underline the individual's feeling of desolation amid the mass. Especially emphatic is the anaphoric repetition of a number. Wolfgang Langhoff, for example, observed the dismay of prisoners exercising in Lichtenburg: 'Soon there were two hundred men in the yard, being drilled in their old blue uniforms. Two hundred shaven heads, two hundred pale faces, two hundred machines with legs and arms' (**Langhoff**, 1986: 286).

Erwin Gostner makes similar use of this device: 'Four months of the bunker, four months of darkness, four months of hot food only every fourth day!' (**Gostner**, 1986: 35). Levi, by emphatic repetition of an adverb, tries to convey the impression that his arrival in Auschwitz made on him: 'They [the prisoners who received the new arrivals] walked in a large circle around us, never drawing near, silently began to busy themselves with our luggage, silently climbed into the empty waggons, and silently came out again' (**Levi**, 1987a: 26).[19] Levi's account vividly records the sense of fright at how little he mattered as a person to those who would soon be his fellow-inmates. It is evidence of the 'affect rigidity' (Pingel, 1978: 155) to which new arrivals were exposed, and which denied them the solidarity they needed so much in the first few days. The shattering impression of a complete loss of communication, after terrible days spent on the train, is imparted to the reader through the mythologizing quality of Levi's emphatic repetition. The anaphoric structure suggests a manageable world – somewhat of an anachronism when applied to the concentration camp, as the stylistic device simulates an openness to interpretation that was not available to the inmates at the time. Structurally, anaphoric sequences generate pathos by spurring the narrative forward; Emil Staiger therefore considers them closer to the genre of drama than to epic (cf. Staiger, 1983: 106).

The structural function of word *repetition* is even more powerful where more than one word is involved. In Wolfgang Langhoff's report *Die Moorsoldaten*, for example, the author compares a directive issued by Hitler's deputy Rudolf Hess with the actual conditions of life in the concentration camps. The key sentence in Hess's statement: 'It is unworthy of a German man to mistreat defenceless prisoners' is antithetically confronted with four events in the camp (**Langhoff**, 1986: 89), so that the resulting contradiction serves to demonstrate the moral hypocrisy of Nazi rule.[20] Whereas Langhoff's anaphoric constructions express the awareness of someone at the mercy of an arbitrary and criminal regime, Joel König uses them to underline the narrator's despair and to appeal to the reader's emotions (cf. Ueding, 1991: 70). Thus, there is no euphoria in the 'we go on living' in the context of *David. Aufzeichnungen eines Überlebenden*: 'We go on living. We hoe and dig, we dig and hoe; we lock ourselves in the lavatory' (**König**, 1983: 190). Life had become meaningless for the group of young Jews who, as late as 1942, were still training in a country house in Germany for pioneering work in Palestine. The deportations then under way in circles close to them had taken all the zest from their existence. Yet in his later account of that time, König also accuses himself of a certain blind indifference to the processes of the persecution of the Jews. He and his group went on with their naive, blank existence, while people around them were already being deported to the death camps.

A *refrain-like repetition* of short sentences is also frequently used when authors are describing an experience that especially affected them. Not surprisingly, it is mainly survivors with some experience as writers who make use of this device. When the Pole Tadeusz Borowski, for instance, uses the expression 'and they all went – the one way' (**Borowski**, 1983: 198f.) to depict a mass killing of Jews, he singles out one element of the historical reality. And by repeating this phrase in isolation, he conveys something of the mechanical compulsion of events happening with the inexorability of a law of nature, which would have been lost in a more straightforward description. This may even be interpreted, as in Andrzej Wirth's afterword to the German edition of Borowski's short stories, as diminishing the enormity of the crime. The detached standpoint of the narrator, however, who is neither one of the perpetrators nor one of their victims, makes the reader grasp the event in all its horror, precisely because it appears 'almost as a natural matter of course' (**Borowski**, 1983: 276). Borowski gives some idea of the time duration by slightly modifying the repeated sentence: 'Day and night people went – the one way and the other', and 'more and more people went – on and on'. The increasing lack of concreteness in the second half of the sentence leaves what actually happened unclear – which eloquently expresses that which cannot be described. Borowski's repetition thus displays an awareness of style which goes beyond purely emphatic repetition of individual words.

Albert Drach, through the strategic repetition of sentences, lends them the status of *leitmotifs*. Three different themes may be recognized as having this function. First, people who will soon die an anonymous death gain an identity in his story; even the description of a particular companion is sometimes repeated as a leitmotif. In epithets such as 'candidate for a posthumous child' and 'would-be paterfamilias', which he uses for a young Jew deported a few days before his marriage to a woman expecting his child, or 'SS Kohn' for an old Jewish man whose daughter is married to someone from the SS yet can do nothing for him, and must later even renounce him, Drach compresses the lives of individual people encountered on his 'unsentimental journey' – not only their identity, but also the tragic fate awaiting them in the death camps.

The second motif is associated with, and indeed clarifies, the title of Drach's report (see Chapter 2). The journey he undertakes is indeed not sentimental but unsentimental, with death as its destination. Hence the similes such as 'narrow as a coffin' for a room, or the statement that 'dead people do not weep'. The third motif refers to the experience of sexuality in the face of death: 'stories about things related to reproduction could sound like mockery on the way to annihilation' (**Drach**, 1992: 45). Drach's leitmotifs are connected by the mortal danger in which the narrator constantly finds himself.

In Gerti Spies's Theresienstadt journal, the aesthetic effects are more questionable: they do not serve to evoke an unusual experience, but, on the contrary, strive to generate an illusion of normality:

> In the evening, a stroll arm in arm with Martha beneath the stars. We have to be careful not to stumble over lovers fondly whispering in the barrack shadows. Everyone must be home by nine. But many occupations require people to stay out longer. These are given a pass from their place of work, and they can spend more of the evening with their sweetheart. It is a wonderful starry night. Here and there a farewell kiss can be heard fluttering through the stillness. (**Spies**, 1984: 105)

In this passage, it is not only the romantic tone but the scene itself which idealizes, indeed trivializes, what it was like to live in the camps. Since, by this point, the deportations from Theresienstadt to the death camps were running at full steam – the journal entry is dated 19 September 1944 – an almost deliberate blindness seems to be involved. Such examples of bad prose, which admittedly do not occur in most reports, are nevertheless proof of the degree of self-deception of which human beings seem capable in a situation of existential stress. They correspond to the unwillingness of many prisoners to face the reality of the camps.

Part of this reality was the complete removal of the internees' powers of decision. Zacheusz Pawlak projects this loss of sovereignty onto the forces of Nature: 'The hut's structure creaked. The dried boards had started to leak and displayed wide cracks. The storm spied them out well. Now it was pouring white snow

through them, whose starry down twinkled a hundred times over.'
As an actor, the storm also has to cover the harsh reality. The cold
of the snow is ironically aestheticized as warmth-giving down, and
this evokes a trope well known from fairy tales. Pawlak again
compensates for the intolerable housing conditions in the camp
when he recalls 'mountain scenery' and skiing and 'the women
from (his) native Zwolén', who 'travel by sledge to the Thursday
market' (**Pawlak**, 1979: 46). Only his cold limbs bring him from
this childhood idyll back to the reality of the camp. But the prose
reports share such flights with poetry originating in the camps.
According to Michael Moll's analysis of 548 poems from the
concentration camps, a total of 225 – approaching a half – come
under the heading 'love poetry, idyllic verse, poems on purely
spiritual themes, general reflections' (Moll, 1988: 59, 270). This
confirms once more the willingness of prisoners, when possible, to
escape the reality of the camp.

By and large, survivors seem to have been aware of the danger
lurking in a pathos-filled aestheticization of their camp experience. To avoid falsifying the reality, some authors prefer to avoid
all pathos. The unemotional mode of presentation from a position
of apparently total detachment forms a kind of pendant to the
accounts that have recourse to pathos. One instrument of *laconic
style* is the successive enumeration used by Zacheusz Pawlak and
others to convey the lack of meaning and hope in the captives'
existence. The ritual of 'reporting', which internees had to
undergo on leaving or entering a section of the camp, was for him
the perfect example of meaningless action:

> The same ceremony for the return with the empty manure cart. The
> vehicle is wheeled through the gate, caps are taken off, a line-up in
> five rows, counting by the SS man, caps put back on, pushing of the
> manure cart to the latrines, filling it up again. (**Pawlak**, 1979: 23)

Both the passive form of the verbs at the beginning and the later
verbal nouns convey the feeling of extreme depersonalization and
lost consciousness of time, which the activity of pushing the
manure cart left behind in the author. Because of the conditions
under which the prisoners were forced into it, even an intrinsically
meaningful (if also degrading) task such as the removal of liquid
manure caused their estrangement from the activity and a disturbance in the way they related to reality. The concentration camp

inmate had to function like a machine – predictably and with no idle moments – and was eliminated when he or she was no longer any good. 'Repairs' were carried out only in a few cases. Things that were designed to strangle at birth any will to resistance were experienced by prisoners as sealing their fate. Later damage resulting from the period of internment is thus often attributed to the working conditions in the camps (cf. Matussek *et al.*, 1971: 247). In their reports, survivors sometimes try to describe the mechanics of slave labour by focusing on particular details, and hence to grasp for themselves the historical reality.[21]

Take, for example, Gerhart Seger's description of a typical day in a camp (**Seger**, 1979: 21–6). His detailed visualization is supposed to compensate for the general uncertainty of the time he spent there, and thus to overcome the absence of meaning. Especially when they depict the physical abuse of prisoners, the authors of such reports continually have recourse to detail. Mention of their tormentors' names serves this same purpose.

Another strategy for objectifying the loss of reality is the thematic discussion of 'aspects' of camp life, such as 'hygiene', 'food' or 'selections'.[22] Indeed, this is how most chapter divisions in the reports come about. What at first looks like a structural feature turns out on closer inspection to be a strategy for handling certain experiences. By objectifying them in this way, the former inmates gain the distance they need to come to terms with them.

The method of laconic presentation does not, however, serve only to objectify experience. Some witnesses find that it too, like emphasis, is a good way of transcending the limits of communicability. Zacheusz Pawlak, for instance, describes a situation in which a fellow-prisoner, being unable to hand in his ring because of a swollen finger, refuses to obey an order: 'The Kapo Wydenko and the block elder, together with other inmates employed in the camp office, then cut off the prisoner's finger with a kitchen knife. Biatowas died a few days later, probably as the result of infection' (**Pawlak**, 1979: 43). Pawlak only describes what happened to the prisoner, not how he reacted to the ill-treatment. On the other hand, he is quite precise about the instrument of torture: his mentioning of the kitchen knife underlines the sadistic brutality of the incident, without putting any feelings into words. The purely factual style of presentation conveys an impression of detached observation, but it may also be due to a sense of helpless outrage.[23] In any event, this bare, laconic language has a more lasting effect on the reader than effusive pathos; cool description, in which the reporter stays right in the background, allows things to stand out by themselves.

As the above examples show, survivors employ strategies of poetic formulation in describing their experience of the concentration camps.[24] The criticism that these strategies are inappropriate to the subject is misguided, because the function they fulfil is that of communication. Certainly they tell us a lot about how the survivors themselves were affected by the experience, and also, in the most interesting cases, about the impact of the everyday routine on other prisoners. On the other hand, the conventional kind of stylistic device preferred by most survivors quite definitely weakens the individual character of their statement. Where a boldness for linguistic innovation is lacking, the individual's attempt to come to terms with the experience may be seen in the choice of stylistic devices. To use the regular literary criteria in evaluating this choice would therefore be to misjudge its significance. Indeed, the very fact that an author who actually lived those experiences stands behind the text has a major effect on how the text is received; aesthetic judgement takes second place (cf. Moll, 1988: 90). Our critical appraisal here has thus been concerned only with the models and the performance of narrative strategies in the concentration camp texts.

Although the authors of survivors' reports often stress in a preface that they have tried to give an objective account of their impressions, they hardly ever reflect upon its narrative character. They take for granted the use of certain narrative and stylistic devices, and assume that these do not conflict with their striving for objectivity. We have seen, however, that there is a purpose in the various literary strategies: whether it is a question of verb tense, generalization and anticipation, pathos or laconic style, the authors never resort to them as ends in themselves. Of course, the mode of presentation may endanger the empirical reference to the facts – yet there is no other way in which these can be grasped (cf. Adorno, 1990: 336).

Witnesses are only exceptionally, if ever, conscious of this dilemma, whereas the historian, not having an intersubjective scientific language for the discipline of history, has to keep solving the problem of narrative 'authenticity' over and over again (White, 1973: 3, n. 13).

Survivors also differ fundamentally from writers of novels, as we have been able to show. For whereas the latter in the main know the meaning of their story before they sit down to write, and choose their mode of presentation accordingly, the former struggle as they write to find the meaning of what they have lived through.

This lack of a higher meaning gives the concentration camp reports a depressing character.[25] Even the worst circumstances are relatively bearable in the traditional novel, because they are made to serve a particular end. When Ernie, 'the last of the Just' in Schwarz-Bart's eponymous novel, and his fiancée Golda accompany the children placed in their care into the gas chamber, they do so with confidence that something better lies beyond. This idealistic, cathartic turning-point may be criticized (e.g. Foley, 1982: 348), and such a positive vision was anyway denied to most of the survivors. Even if, in the camps, they still had some expectations about what life would bring after liberation, these mostly turned out to be illusory.

The function of historical and literary associations

Cashier (pushes the cylinder back, takes cigarettes from a golden case, lights up). Off to the fight, torero. Everything that comes to one's lips. One is loaded up with it. Everything, simply everything. Torero – Carmen. Caruso. The swindle read somewhere – stayed in the brain. Piled up.

(Georg Kaiser, *Von morgens bis mitternachts*)

In a series of lectures on poetics that he gave in Frankfurt in 1984, Peter Härtling argued that storytelling and writing should not be treated as if they were separated off from any associations. Referring to the origins of Theodor Fontane's novel *Effi Briest*, he showed how elements from the author's memory went into the making of both plot and characters. Memory had been like a 'place of confinement' for 'forgotten, repressed life' (Härtling, 1984: 13).

In a special sense, memory is also at work where the cultural tradition – that is, the cultural heritage of educated members of

169

society – finds its way into a text. But associated memory not only serves the author in the production of a text, but also plays a role in the process of its reception, where various patterns condition 'the reader's point of view' by providing an 'empty form into which the reader's sedimented knowledge, varying both in scale and nuance, flows' (Iser, 1976: 232, 233), yet leave sufficient leeway for the subjective outcome to be thoroughly individual. This is true also of non-fictional texts and concentration camp reports. The subjectivity of the reader's interpretation may appear to be a disadvantage, but he or she can grasp what is conveyed in the report only to the extent that the patterns offered there evoke imagery available through (subjective) recollection. Here lies both the strength and the weakness of the literary and historical associations in the concentration camp texts.

Characteristically, the authors of these reports draw upon a stock of historical and literary situations already familiar to them, when they struggle to find the right expression to depict life and work in the camps, to convey indescribable things such as the effects of torture, or to reflect on the meaning of the time spent there. Quite consciously, though of course without motivating it theoretically, survivors deploy these 'empty forms' where they are unwilling or unable to offer a direct description. It is astonishing how unoriginal the choice of these usually is. Both the historical and the literary associations cluster around a few generally known authors or events.

If we take associations, as reception theory does, as the limited and isolated appropriation of literary or historical models inserted by the author from the angle of a certain meaning, where they refer not to the work or source-event itself but to a certain interpretation of it, then associations in the camp texts should be judged by the extent to which the author follows or deviates from a current interpretation. What makes Iser's patterns aesthetically relevant is their modalization in the text. In so far as the memory images that a text evokes in the reader appear 'negated, transcended, segmented or no longer valid', the 'knowledge whose validity is cancelled' functions 'as an analogue through which the intended content should be imagined' (Iser, 1976: 233). As we shall see, this is of the greatest significance for discourse about the camps. Modal patterns help survivors to speak about impressions and experiences which contradict everything previously known or experienced. They thus have a linguistically creative function at the outer limits of communicability, even though, precisely as traditional associations, they tend to cancel the particularity of the event.

Among the historical models, archetypes of oppression – archetypes in the sense of Northrop Frye's 'associative clusters' (Frye, 1957: 124) – are predominant. The fate of galley convicts is repeatedly appropriated by the survivors. The Middle Ages, with their inhuman use of torture, and the Catholic Inquisition are also models of persecution and torment, which authors use to conjure up what they lived through. Similar reference is made to works of literature, especially Dante's *Divine Comedy* and its archetypal description of Hell as the site of pain and torture. Terence Des Pres rightly points to the danger that this image will not do justice to the survivors among the victims, because it denotes not only spiritual mutilation but also physical death (Des Pres, 1976: 172).

Of greater interest are a number of other themes that are not already part of the standard repertoire of historical and literary comparisons. Only their use to interpret experiences of concentration camp survivors lends them the status of (individualized) archetypes (cf. Young, 1988: 99–116).

The choice of historical or literary model appears to depend not only on the cultural background of the former camp inmates, but also on their interests and beliefs. To take one revealing example, the poverty of life in Dachau reminded priests interned there of the story of Jesus's childhood (**Steinwender**, 1946: 28; **Lenz**, 1956: 183), whereas the Communist Glas-Larsson thought of Auschwitz as more reminiscent of Sing-Sing, the US penitentiary for serious criminals (**Glas-Larsson**, 1981: 132). Now and then, even the name of a fellow-prisoner might trigger associations. Thus for Lina Haag, 'Johanna is not a heroic maiden like the saints of old, but a clever lass' (**Haag**, 1985: 50). In this comparison, the metonymy exemplifies one characteristic of associations in the camp reports: namely, that their effect is very rarely based on full congruence with the experience in question. Sometimes the similarity is only partial, sometimes it is lacking altogether. The explanatory potential of 'negative' comparisons lies in a qualitative difference between situation and association; medieval torture, for instance, is often mentioned with the caveat that the Nazis' use of it was far worse.

Comparison with model *historical* situations occurs in the reports when the camp itself is being described – which is relatively uncommon. What these authors seem to have found a problem was not the description of general conditions in the camps, but specific situations such as torture or 'extermination through work' that threatened their further survival. This, more than any other aspect of the camps, brought out the lack of suitable expressions – a lack compounded by the recourse to associations derived from the atrocities of previous centuries.

The image that most frequently came to the mind of former prisoners was that of *slaves*. Nowadays scholars distinguish the terroristic labour in the camps from slavery proper, yet 'comparison with the social form of slavery has heuristic value' (Sofsky, 1997: 171). Like slaves, the internees neither had any say over their conditions of work, nor drew any kind of benefit from their labour product. On the other hand, the personal dependence from which the slave-owner drew his economic profit was not present in the camps. Bondsmen and bondwomen had a certain value, and it was in their owners' interest to preserve it. The concentration camp, in contrast, knew no 'economy of value maintenance and enhancement' (Sofsky, 1997: 172).

Such trains of thought did not sway the former internees, however, when they used the comparison for certain labour processes. In particular, the systematic 'undermechanization' (Sofsky, 1997: 188) of labour based on terror forced the image of slavery into the minds of survivors. Rudolf Kalmár associates all the rigours of the pre-industrial age with the pulling of concrete drums in Dachau to keep the Appellplatz smooth and level: 'It was a sight as in pictures of the building of the Egyptian pyramids. This was how galley slaves were fixed to their oars, or how Volga boatmen hauled their barges upstream' (**Kalmár**, 1988: 54). But unlike those creatures, the camp inmates of the mid-twentieth century could have had their work made easier by machinery. There was no longer any necessity for such grinding toil: it served only to break the prisoners' morale and to bring them to death's door. In an ironic remark at the end, Kalmár alludes to a book by Nazi ideologue Alfred Rosenberg: 'The myth connected with this barbarity was the myth of the twentieth century.'

Other survivors who employ the image of slavery mainly do so without referring to the changed economic conditions. When

Bruno Heilig, pointlessly shovelling soil in Dachau, is reminded of the rowing galley slaves (**Heilig**, 1941: 52), it escapes him that that application of physical strength at least propelled the ship forward, whereas the shovelling by Dachau's slaves does not even serve to move soil to a different place. It is well known that work had different meanings in different phases of the concentration camp system. If at first, especially in Dachau, its main function was to demoralize the mostly intellectual inmates, after the beginning of the war it increasingly became a factor in economic exploitation (cf. Broszat, 1984: 46ff., 108ff.). Slave imagery, however, obscures this shift in meaning. Lisa Scheuer compares the allocation to work detachments in the factories around Auschwitz to the operation of slave markets, 'organized by the miracle-working nation, the flower of European culture, the master race, as they self-righteously described themselves. The men walk slowly along our ranks and carefully pick out girls and women to work in their factories' (**Scheuer**, 1983: 46). The irony in this quotation, however, makes any comment unnecessary on the suitability of the comparison.

Often enough, the former prisoners are actually aware that an analogy is inappropriate, yet they use it repeatedly for lack of anything better. The association between the status of concentration camp prisoner and the slave world of antiquity and the Middle Ages falls short in a number of ways: it conflicts not only with the fundamental economic change, but also with social conditions in twentieth-century Europe. Hence the survivors' use of slave imagery detracts from serious analysis, and indeed blurs the real situation in which they lived.

Apart from the collective harassment that affected everyone working in the camps, survivors often write of the torture that was administered on an individual basis. This was by no means only a question of physical suffering; it also meant the most painful mental ordeal. Thus the reports not only make comparisons with medieval torture, but also understand the subtle psychological terror as constituting a model in its own right. Gerhart Seger, for example, in order to conjure up the effects of uncertainty and the fact that inmates never had any time of their own, refers to Chinese methods of torture:

> in which the victim is tied down and constantly subjected to the dripping of water on a certain part of the head; the person never has

a moment's peace, because the nature of the human mind is such that, after one drop has fallen, it focuses on anticipatory fear of the next, and so on. (**Seger**, 1979: 25f.)

This comparison puts in its true light the effect that forced disquiet had upon the minds of concentration camp inmates. Superficially, this may not seem worthy of such great mention, but in the conditions of the camps it assumed the quality of torture. The force of the image lies not so much in the interpretation of a subjective experience as in its authentication.

Bruno Heilig, as the title of his book indicates, takes the image of crucifixion to represent the torture of fellow-captives that he was forced to witness:

> Never had I heard such screams as those. They were no longer human voices ... Pictures of crucifixion came into my mind: after all, what these people were doing was the same as crucifixion. Except that the Romans let people hang until they were dead, while here they took them down perhaps some time before. (**Heilig**, 1941: 25)

It may seem surprising that a Jew should make use of the very image from the Christian story that has been at the root of traditional Christian anti-Semitism. But David Roskies confirms that, in the Jewish literature of Eastern Europe, the image of crucifixion was deployed as a new archetype to interpret the Judaeocide (Roskies, 1984: 258–312). Since this most recent catastrophe to befall the Jews was so radically different from all previous ones, the traditional archetypes were no longer sufficient to record it. And the figure of Jesus, when separated from the context of the early twentieth-century Christian Church, became an acceptable archetype also for Jews. Whereas Jewish writers and artists had taken it as a mythical archetype, however, the Nazi persecution of the Jews turned it into an apocalyptic omen (cf. Kermode, 1967: 29). In this way, the image of the end of time overcame the 'symbol degradation' that had affected social-revolutionary and lifeworld apocalypses (cf. Pfeiffer, 1982: 181–96) and reverted to its original religious content.

The historical associations present in these examples have the common feature of mainly stemming from distant centuries. This ensures the relative openness of their interpretation, and there-fore a wide scope for application. Furthermore, the methods of torture practised in antiquity and the Middle Ages were more 'vivid' than the subtler (often psychological) ones of the modern world, so that a comparison with the Middle Ages suggested itself when the Nazi persecution of the Jews – for example, through public labelling and ghettoization – reactivated such methods.

Wolfgang Langhoff chooses a more recent historical event as the image for his experience of the camps. The winter conditions of work at Börgermoor make him think of Napoleon's Russian campaign: 'The guards have had big fires lit for themselves. In the frost-covered countryside, the fires glow all around as Napoleon's bivouac fires did on the Berezina' (**Langhoff**, 1986: 191). Everything suggests that Langhoff had a visual impression of this scene in his memory. Just as the remembered image, probably in Romantic style, passes over the soldiers' shivering and other harsh facts of a winter war, so does Langhoff's own reference to it stand out, as it were, from his account of poorly clad prisoners and harsh working conditions that precedes and follows it. Langhoff's recollection speaks only of aesthetic fascination with the view in the picture, which seems to have helped him get over the lack of meaning in his experience. His choice of mode thus contradicts Michael Moll's view that, 'where scope for transcendence and the attribution of meaning existed only in tiny niches', literary presentation became 'a direct indictment of the situation' (Moll, 1988: 130). This judgement may hold in particular cases, but it cannot be generalized – at least not in relation to the concentration camp reports.

'In the Girl's later life,' Cordelia Edvardson says a little exaggeratedly of her own experience in the camps, 'it was confirmed that one can literally live and feed off the words of a poem' (**Edvardson**, 1986: 15). Some of her companions in suffering clearly felt the same way. For if we judge by the use of *literary associations*, which are much more frequent than historical ones in the texts, former inmates did indeed feed quite intensely off their experience of reading. Literary associations offered themselves mainly for the description of life in the camps, and hence for the process of coming to terms with it. This superiority of literary over historical associations should be explained by the fact that a certain meaning is already inherited within them. A cross between the two are *religious and mythological associations*, which transcend situations by giving them an additional form largely derived from literature, as in the model: 'Baal, the fire god of the Assyrians, would have run rings round Hitler, the god of the Nazis!' (**Adelsberger**, 1956: 106). The appeal of mythological and religious imagery to those who wrote the concentration camp reports was that it was not fixed in time and had a more open content. Primo Levi, for example, uses a comparison from Jewish history for his description of a building in the Buna factory that was part of Auschwitz. Prisoners called the carbide tower they built there 'the Tower of Babel'. 'Its bricks,' Levi comments, 'were cemented by hate; hate and discord, like the Tower of Babel.' Nor is the resemblance limited to external features; it also concerns one special feature of the camp:

> And today, just as in the old fable, we all feel, and the Germans themselves feel, that a curse – not transcendent and divine, but immanent and historical – hangs over the insolent building based on the confusion of languages and erected in defiance of heaven like a stone blasphemy. (**Levi**, 1987a: 78–9, translation slightly modified)

Levi's association of the building with his historical image gives it the force of a symbol for the whole concentration camp. Yet this is of only limited validity, since the linguistic diversity in Auschwitz actually came about after the war had brought people in from occupied countries (cf. Broszat, 1984: 82); it was therefore not at all restricted to Auschwitz, as Levi's interpretation would suggest.

Confinement in Nazi concentration camps also reminded Jews of other episodes in the history of their persecution. Bruno Heilig, for example, thinks of the hard life of his ancestors in Egyptian exile, even if he rejects the comparison as inadequate (**Heilig**, 1941: 39).

Whereas Levi and Heilig use comparative imagery from the Old Testament, the Catholic priest Father Lenz chooses an image from the New Testament but succeeds in going drastically astray. Though directly confronted with the suffering of the Jews, Lenz is evidently unable to free himself from traditional Christian anti-Semitism. Thus, in his report on Easter Sunday in Dachau in 1945, he compares the attitude of SS men still hoping for 'final victory' to 'the blindness of the Jews at the fall of Jerusalem' (**Lenz**, 1956: 338). It is an open question whether this uncritical adoption of Catholic-anti-Semitic biblical exegesis stemmed from thoughtlessness, or whether Lenz was aware of its significance. In any event, it accords with the Church's historically verified failure to stand up against the Nazi persecution of the Jews.

Apart from allusions to biblical events with a mainly historical character, the camp reports also contain biblical associations at the level of reflection that have a more literary quality, either as direct quotations or in the form of metaphors. Again there is material from both the Old and the New Testament. The easily remembered saying from the Gospel according to St John (21:18): 'Someone else will fasten a belt around you and take you where you do not wish to go', is taken by Corrie ten Boom in the camp as a guiding thread, as well as being quoted by Cordelia Edvardson and used by Helmut Gollwitzer in the title of his report on Soviet military imprisonment (**ten Boom**, 1954: 53; **Edvardson**, 1986: 11; **Gollwitzer**, 1983). Both ten Boom and Gollwitzer had been in the religious profession before they were interned, in ten Boom's case as a result of her charitable work on behalf of persecuted Jews in Holland. Gollwitzer, who during the Nazi period was a lecturer at the illegal College of the Confessional Church, ended up in 1945 as a military prisoner-of-war. In all three authors, the sentence from John's Gospel expressed a faith that enabled them to grasp their internment as part of an inscrutable divine will. Sayings from the Bible could thus help religious believers to survive in the camps, as Viktor Frankl also felt when he saw his love for his wife revealed in *The Song of Songs* (**Frankl**, 1977: 67). He stressed that the life-preserving effect of this love had not been influenced by the fact that his wife had by then already been murdered.

After the liberation, many former prisoners still extracted from the Bible guidelines on how they should behave. Lisa Scheuer explains her unwillingness to hate her tormentors with the words 'Revenge is mine, says the Lord' (**Scheuer**, 1983: 112). As her comment shows, she does not at all mean by this that the SS thugs should answer only to divine justice, but that she would rather entrust the task to qualified judges. The quotation on which she somewhat misleadingly bases herself should be seen in the context of her renunciation of the Old Testament principle of 'an eye for an eye, a tooth for a tooth'.

The appropriation of biblical precepts as aids to survival depends on their providing a (tried and tested) means to compensate for a meaning deficit. 'In the last few years,' writes

Gollwitzer, 'two biblical sayings had become clear to us as guiding threads of a true philosophy of life: "For you reap whatever you sow. If you sow to your own flesh, you will reap corruption from the flesh" (Gal. 6:7); and "For the measure you give will be the measure you get back" (Luke 6:38).' He then comments: 'Now "the" Germans got back the measure they had given to "the" Jews. Would they recognize the connection? When had there ever been such a clear example of the oft-mentioned divine providence?' (**Gollwitzer**, 1983: 14). Alexander and Margarete Mitscherlich's verdict on post-war German society constituted a well-known negative answer to Gollwitzer's question (Mitscherlich and Mitscherlich, 1983). But this does not detract from Gollwitzer's basic insight.

Religious ways of explaining the Unknowable have a solid place in cultures driven by tradition. In connection with the Nazi extermination policy, they would have to be called cynical if they did not come from the pens of the victims themselves. Religious belief permitted internees to free themselves at least spiritually, and temporarily, from the spell of the camp, since 'religions provide interpretive models that allow one to incorporate present events into a framework of expectation and to interpret them in the light of a fictive future' (Sofsky, 1997: 92).

Religious practice was largely repressed by the SS in the concentration camps.[26] Nevertheless, reports testify that even under the most adverse conditions Jews, for example, strictly observed the ritual fasts (cf. e.g. **Améry**, 1980: 34). Whereas Salus admired the 'inner strength' of a devout Jewish woman in Oederan (**Salus**, 1981: 73), other survivors criticized the bigotry with which Jewish fellow-prisoners said their prayers.

Christian internees such as ten Boom and Floris Bakels also report that religious gatherings took place in the camps. In 1940 priests at Dachau (cf. Weiler, 1971) managed to fix up a chapel (cf. **Lenz**, 1956: 183), and in 1941 introduced a Sunday mass duty [*sic!*] for those who did not have to work (cf. **Lenz**, 1956: 213). Lenz even declares that an ordination was performed on 17 December 1944 in Dachau (**Lenz**, 1956: 216).

The significance of religious practice was that prisoners involved in it were for a while able to leave behind the world of the camps, and to regard it as something merely temporary. Moreover, their faith helped them to interpret their tormentors' rule in more qualified terms. In both respects, there was a refusal to adapt to the reality of the camp or to subject it to close scrutiny. Although religious (or any other) convictions – whether expressed as an 'ideological' or a 'devout' attitude – made it easier for prisoners in the camps to live or to die (cf. **Améry**, 1980: 34), their subsequent use of religious associations to interpret the experience shows that they were still rather a long way from coping with their memories.[27] For such imagery, more than other adopted uses of language, took them away from a personal confrontation with what they had lived through. One exception is Primo Levi, whose attitude to the Bible is quite nuanced: 'Today I think that if for no other reason than that an Auschwitz existed, no one in our age should speak of Providence. But without doubt in that hour the memory of biblical salvations in times of extreme adversity passed like a wind through all our minds' (**Levi**, 1987a: 163–4). Levi thus distinguishes very precisely between the attitudes he had before and after liberation. The special circumstances of the camp sanctioned an interpretation that he could afterwards no longer accept.

Undoubtedly, most of the literary associations have to do with *the classics*, and a special role is played here by identification with their authors. Survivors from Buchenwald, for obvious reasons, return time and again to Goethe, who is said to have frequently visited the Ettersberg near Weimar, where the camp was situated. Former internees were prompted to reflect upon the change that the site had undergone since the days of Goethe. Only Ernst Wiechert asserts that he drew strength from the realization that he was, so to speak, walking in the footsteps of the great poet (**Wiechert**, 1984: 71), to whose immortal work he felt inspired to cling:

> He looked out for a while, as alone as if he were the last man on earth, and tried to recall all the verses he knew by the poet who might have stood right there a hundred and fifty years before. Nothing had been lost of that great life, and even if he were to be chained in a galley for fifty years, still nothing would be lost of it. 'Noble, generous and good . . . '[28] No, not even that would perish, so long as a single human being kept speaking it and tried to preserve it until their dying day. (**Wiechert**, 1984: 94)

Posing as a direct heir and sole keeper of Goethe's humanity, Wiechert even derives from it a certain meaning of his internment in Buchenwald. He thus withdraws into a spiritual freedom based on art, as a way of distancing himself from his present situation. This amounts to a splitting of the ego, which Bruno Bettelheim described as a typical reaction to the camps (Bettelheim, 1979: 65ff.).

The Dutch journalist Nico Rost employs the name of the Weimar classic in the title of his testimony, *Goethe in Dachau* metonymically evoking his own 'survival through literature'. In the Flossenbürg camp, an educated middle-class prisoner is in turn fortified by the rather different tradition according to which it was the scene for Schiller's *The Robbers*.

Most of the camps, however, could not serve up this kind of association with literary history; the works themselves then had to form the basis of imaginative comparison. In her report, Margareta Glas-Larsson nevertheless testifies to one functional updating of Goethe's work that worked against the prisoners' will to survive. For the oppressors knew 'their' Goethe: Josef Mengele, for example, the much-feared SS doctor at Auschwitz, is said to have cynically quoted *Faust, Part Two* at a large-scale 'selection' of Jewish prisoners:

> *Faust*: Ein Sumpf zieht am Gebirge hin,
>   Verpestet alles schon Errungene;
>   Den faulen Pfuhl auch abzuziehn,
>   Das letzte wär' das Höchsterrungene.
>   Eröffn' ich Räume vielen Millionen,
>   Nicht sicher zwar, doch tätig-frei zu wohnen.
>   (**Glas-Larsson**, 1981: 152f.; *Faust* 11559–64)[29]

Although it is questionable, of course, whether Mengele quoted these lines in full at that time, they could well have been misused as a 'classical' source justifying the Judaeocide. The fact that Mengele should have spoken these very words, moreover, says something about the man, as the abhorrence of mud, swamp and slime, of anything weak and moist, was characteristic of fascist thinking (cf. Theweleit, 1980: 403–10). If Wiechert recalled some lines from Goethe to strengthen his resistance, the effect for Margareta Glas-Larsson was rather one of cruel sarcasm: they drove home her exclusion from the society into whose culture she had been socialized. The German-speaking Jews still felt part of the German culture, at a time when its avowed proponents were mercilessly persecuting them, and so the Nazi use of classical literature to malign the Jews was bound to intensify their identity crisis triggered by conditions in the camps.

Albert Drach's approach to the Weimar classics is different again: he does not separate out his quotations but merges them into the rest of the text. Towards the end of *Unsentimental Journey* he puts the following words into the mouth of Darling Withorse: 'It seems to me as if a devil had come from hell and were dragging Pierre [i.e. Kucku] and me into it. I have a feeling that I'll be able to free myself but Pierre won't any more. I don't have the strength to pull him up' (**Drach**, 1992: 340). The allusion is unmistakably to Goethe's 'eternal feminine that raises us up', thanks to whom Mephistopheles finally has to release Faust from their pact. Such idealism no longer works for Drach; Hitler's reign of terror against the Jews has destroyed it. Drach's text may therefore be read as a corrective to authors in the mould of Wiechert. It is more in tune with 'modern' times, in which the changed conditions forbid an affirmative evocation of the great classics.

These examples illustrate the variety of ways in which literature is received in the camp reports. Sometimes former prisoners associate with an author's person, sometimes with his or her work as an indestructible value. Or else they may offer it as a contrast to their own situation, with the argument that not even a great writer's imagination could picture the misery they are being made to suffer.

Of the other classic writers, Friedrich Schiller seems to have been the most frequent source of associations. Erwin Gostner brings to bear an often misquoted line from Schiller's *Die Verschwörung des Fiesko zu Genua*, when he comments on the public execution of a prisoner who had attempted to escape from Mauthausen: 'The play has served its purpose: better to die in the quarry than on the noose!' (**Gostner**, 1986: 114). Gostner here changes not only the wording but also the meaning. For whereas these words tell the Moor in Schiller's work that he has been used as a tool and is no longer needed, Gostner wants to express the fact that the execution he was forced to attend had the effect upon him intended by the SS. This is a good example of adaptation of a classical source, which often occurs in colloquial language, too.

In another report from the camps, in which Schiller's *Die Bürgschaft* serves as the comparison, Bruno Marcuse describes a father who offers to sacrifice himself in place of his condemned son. But whereas Schiller's tyrant eventually permits himself to be swayed by the ideal of loyal friendship, the laws of the concentration camp system allow of no human feeling (**Marcuse,** 1946: 15).

This kind of 'negative' reception of the classics usually refers to the sentiment of humanity (*Humanität*) that was the main characteristic of that epoch in German literature. The classical model of the hero actually stands in direct contradiction to the state of things in the camps. Prisoners there were no longer actors in the classical sense, nor were they free to choose between good and evil. In the Nazi camp system, greatness of character counted for nothing. The representation of suffering therefore required a new conception of tragedy (cf. Kröhle, 1989: 244) that had room for cynicism, irony and even moral indifference, with the result that associated images from the literature of classical antiquity appeared especially jarring and anachronistic. The term *Tantalusqualen*, (**Salus,** 1981: 81) then already in common usage to signify agonizing frustration, did as little justice to people's sufferings in the camps as did Odysseus's journey into the underworld (**Wander,** 1985: 97). In the closed world of the Greeks, suffering had still had a meaning (cf. Lukács, 1971); now the world of the Nazi camps poured scorn on it. Thus, whenever survivors tried through quotation to share in that meaning, it had the opposite effect. Their reserve about comparisons with antiquity was based not so much on lack of education as on an awareness that they would be inappropriate.

Dante's *Divine Comedy*, as we have seen, occupied a special place among classical works and was quoted on many occasions. It offered itself as a comparative model because it did not depict the individual as sovereign (which is what Odysseus remains even in the descent to Hades), but showed him as the plaything of fate. The titles of several reports from the camps already refer to this explanatory model (e.g. **Lundholm,** 1988). And especially in the description of Inferno, many authors see parallels to what they went through. The comparison, however, is typical of how metaphorical language could be and was used for very different situations. Lisa Scheuer even thought of the bombing of Dresden in terms of Dante's *Inferno* (**Scheuer,** 1983: 76f.). And in the material about the camps, its application ranges from the relatively 'mild' early camp at Oranienburg, through others where extermination through work was practised, to the factory-style killing of Jews in Auschwitz. Joseph Drexel explains as follows to his readers what a period in Mauthausen meant:

> Before entering a concentration camp, one does well to draw a line under the previous chapters of one's life ... and to begin a new page, preferably with the words: *Lasziate* [sic] *ogni speranza* – Abandon all hope. Dante's Hell really is the right place with which comparison stands. (**Drexel**, 1980: 59)

When Simha Naor, on the other hand, looks at a new transport arriving in Auschwitz, she thinks that even Dante's imaginings of Hell are no longer suited to the reality (**Naor**, 1986: 39). Filip Müller agrees with this. His chapter on the annihilation of the Hungarian Jews in Auschwitz is entitled 'The Inferno':

> There were now nine of those large pits in addition to the cremato- rium ovens, making it possible to burn an almost unlimited number of corpses. All these installations originated in the brain of mass mur- derer Moll, who had succeeded in turning a small corner of the earth's surface into something of such unspeakable vileness that it made Dante's Inferno appear a pleasure garden. (**F. Müller**, 1979: 133)

The Divine Comedy plays quite an important role in Primo Levi's report. At one point, he describes how he desperately tried to impress the verse on a young companion in suffering; it was more important to him than his insufficient daily food that the young person should get to know the work before it was too late. Levi attaches great importance to the text for the existence of the camp prisoners:

> The canto of Ulysses. Who knows how or why it comes into my mind. ... Here, listen Pikolo, open your ears and your mind, you have to understand, for my sake:
>
>> Think of your breed; for brutish ignorance
>> Your mettle was not made; you were made men,
>> To follow after knowledge and excellence. (**Levi**, 1987a: 119)

Even when it is only a question of sheer survival, human beings must remain true to their spiritual existence. In opting for this interpretation, Levi makes direct use of Dante's work as an aid to survival.

An association with *The Divine Comedy* helped Peter Weiss to assure at least some of the concentration camp texts a place in literary history. In parallel with his writing of the documentary play *The Investigation*, he made a close study of Dante's work, and especially the *Inferno*,[30] trying to get a feel for the details, the specific 'aberrations, doubts, longings, fears and hopes' that alone make Dante understandable. He also has some harsh words to say about Dante's failure to take a moral position on what he portrayed, but in the end becomes convinced that authorial distance is essential for the presentation of material such as Dante's. Weiss considers that, for writers like himself, Dante's portrayal of the horrors of Hell sets a paradigm: that the problem is still Dante's one of having to convey events and experiences for which there is no language, and only by making of them a work of art is it possible to overcome this lack. Weiss – who, being defined as a 'half-Jew' under the Nuremberg Laws, spent the years of the Third Reich in exile, first in England, then in Sweden – firmly insisted that it was only the updating of Dante's work which made it accessible to him. He received *The Divine Comedy* by replacing what is described there with his own knowledge of the Nazi Judaeocide and the Second World War. In this way, it acquired programmatic meaning for his own creations, especially *The Investigation*.

Although concentration camp survivors who invoked Dante did not do so from the same theoretical point of view, they pursued similar strategies of 'updating' and criticizing. The essential difference lies in their attitude to the artistic use of Dante's work as a model. For whereas Peter Weiss felt especially close to Dante the writer, who had succeeded in presenting the unimaginable through emotional distance and strategic use of the means of expression at his command, the survivors were unable either to distance themselves completely from their memories or to make use of the necessary means of expression. In a much more direct sense, then, they were in the hands of their model.

Compared with the literature of classical antiquity or Weimar classicism, more recent writers such as Heinrich Heine have drawn pictures or described situations that are better suited to throw light on the experience of the camps. A number of survivors refer to the tale of the writing on the wall that announced to the Babylonian ruler Belshazzar his imminent demise. Fred Wander invokes it to greet the approaching liberators: 'We would have liked to embrace those who were dropping bombs. Their signature in the blue sky meant victory' (**Wander**, 1985: 105). Peter Edel even claims for himself the role of prophet of doom:

> If words can strike like lightning, those sentences did it. They grew bigger and bigger before me, as if they were not printed like all the others in small gothic letters, but serrated and raised in a huge shape – *and wrote and wrote letters of fire on the white wall and wrote and disappeared* [emphasis in the original] . . . An image suddenly flares up: Menetekel in Belshazzar's royal hall. And why not Menetekel on another wall? On a house wall in the middle of Hitler's Babylon! (**Edel**, 1979: I/290f.)

Impressed by his reading of Heine, the young Edel became active in the resistance to Hitler. In the romantic, half-adventurous role of the 'writer on the wall', he covered house walls in his native Berlin with anti-Hitler leaflets. The identification with his literary model came to an end, however, when he was arrested by the Gestapo and eventually interned in a concentration camp.

Wolfgang Langhoff, forced by the Nazis to emigrate to Switzerland, identifies with Heine's oft-quoted lines in exile: '*Denk ich an Deutschland in der Nacht,/Dann bin ich um den Schlaf gebracht*'.[31] Charlotte Müller also shows that the poems of Heine, especially those referring critically to Germany, could fire a mentality of resistance among the concentration camp prisoners. She herself is reminded of 'The Silesian Weavers' as she gets down to forced labour in Ravensbrück (**Ch. Müller**, 1981: 19).

The verse which such prisoners think about either expresses their feelings or clothes their will to resist in words. What Nico **Rost** (1983: 22, 28), Karl **Röder** (1983: 293f.) and Ernst **Wiechert** (1984: 49f.) say about their choice of reading in the camps – and this is echoed by Joel **König** in his hiding place in Berlin (1983: 224ff.) – also applies to their memory of things read earlier: it had to fit the situation in which they found themselves, to give them strength and hope and to provide formulations in which they could express contempt for their oppressors.

Allusions to *fairy tales*[32] and *scenes from light fiction* have the same function as religious associations in the camp reports. They too were a means for former prisoners to describe and explain their experience, and in the camp itself served as a moment of escape. Contact with fairy tales called forth both pleasant and unpleasant ideas. Isa Vermehren felt after her release, like Iron Heinrich in

'The Frog King', that the rings placed around her heart to handle her sorrow were gradually breaking (**Vermehren**, 1979: 158). Lina Haag, on the other hand, was reminded of the frightening side of children's stories by the prison in which she was confined (**Haag**, 1985: 50). This paradoxical ambivalence of the fairy tale stems from its very structure, in which the good are played off against the bad. Krysztyna Zywulska draws a parallel with the 'antisocial' Kapos:

> We had all heard fairy tales in our childhood. In nearly every one there is some evil spirit, some witch, who whirs through the air on a broomstick. If such a fairy tale witch were brought to life, she would probably look like the German woman with the black triangle. (**Zywulska**, 1980: 14)

This seemingly naive belief in childhood tales is in striking contrast to the prisoners' experience, simply because the underlying pattern of bad people punished and good people rewarded had evidently been reversed in the camps. The reception of fairy tales there seems to confirm what Bruno Bettelheim says about infantile regression among internees (cf. Bettelheim, 1979: 75ff.).

Bettelheim, who has made a well-known study of the importance of fairy tales in a child's development, argues with reference to Tolkien[33] that a good fairy tale brings above all else fresh heart, escape and consolation; the child finds in it the meaning sought in his or her own life. The fairy tale shows the child by example how to behave in certain situations (mostly ones of mortal danger) in order to come out of them unscathed.

Yet, when internees try to apply the problem-solving mode of the fairy tale to their experience of the camps, this is seen by Bettelheim as deliberate blindness on their part. The feeling of abandonment was not there the product of childishly exaggerated anxiety fantasies; it was harsh reality. To trust in the strategy of model-case problem-solving, which had once brought them consolation as children, was therefore evidence of infantile regression. And the significance they attached to fairy tales, he claims, indicated childish behaviour in the face of the punitive SS.

The reception of fairy tales in the camps was fostered, however, precisely by the fact that they offered a temporary escape from reality. This may be seen in the associations with Vienna that colour Spritzer's return to the ideal world of childhood (**Spritzer**, 1980: 87f.), where the 'Wurschtl'-Prater[34] forms a make-believe world in which problems turn out to be illusory or capable of a miraculous or jocose resolution. Similarly, the horrors of the journey to Auschwitz impress themselves on Lucie Begov as a trip to the 'haunted castle'.

> It went through my mind that I had seen such images before, and I immediately knew where. It had been in Vienna's 'Wurschtl' Prater, in the 'Haunted House', where you could get a creepy feeling for a couple of pennies. The sight that we in the trucks were offered in the flickering candlelight was so improbable and so uncanny that this comparison forced itself upon me. (**Begov**, 1983: 76)

Although, on the journey to Auschwitz, her experience of fear was no longer of her own choosing, and although it was not in her power to put an end to this learning process, Lucie Begov still clung to the association. The thought that she had once before come through a similar situation unscathed would certainly have been a dubious way of comforting herself, if it could not be taken as a case of gallows humour.

Light fiction also suggests the idea of problem-solving in a safe place with a fair guarantee of success.[35] Allowance must be made for the fact that survivors identified only ironically with characters from this literary genre, but their wish is evident to usurp for themselves its way of solving problems. This is especially clear in the following two examples from concentration camp reports. In the first, Kurt Hiller at one point describes himself in rather awkward German as 'unshaven, unshorn, without a collar, with trousers that slip further the thinner you get, with unpolished laceless shoes – to be imagined as a highway robber from a children's fable, or a common criminal in a humorous magazine' (**Hiller**, 1934/35: 144). The external change signals his exclusion from the respectable bourgeois world. But his perception of this change as open to revision can be seen in his association with a model from literature rather than from reality.

In the second example, Lisa Scheuer expresses a sense of superiority without saying as much:

> There's nothing quite like hierarchy! Yes, after I had boiled the things [beetroots] till they were done, I peeled them so thick that half was left for me; the chief was content, and I the cook was too ... The old

farce of the swindler swindled is being acted out. (**Scheuer**, 1983: 57f.)

Whereas all the authors so far mentioned empathize with a literary model, Grete Salus does not trust reality precisely because of its resemblance to an example from literature. 'I could not believe,' she says of her liberation, 'that Theresienstadt really was to be the end of our road, at the very place where it had begun. It seemed like the happy ending in some trashy novel' (**Salus**, 1981: 85).

Fairy tales and light fiction offered themselves, more readily than other literary forms, as a model for survivors to come to terms with the experience of the camps either because situations in life were archetypally represented in them, or because they left a lasting impression on the reader. Their widespread use for interpretive purposes throws as much light on the authors of these reports as it does on the genre itself.

Literary associations, like literary genres, may be analysed as having two functions in the concentration camp texts: to describe the camp itself, and to master and clarify the question of meaning. In practice, however, these two cannot be separated.

In their use of literary associations to help them describe the camps, the former inmates are concerned to be as truthful and convincing as possible. The less familiar the author or work that they associate, the more convincing is their personal effort to come to terms with their experience through language. In the following examples, however, which share this quality that sets them apart from clichéd associations, the most striking feature is not so much the individual attempt at interpretation as the breadth of the author's reading. All the associated literature depicts torment and suffering, in many cases – as in that of Dostoevsky – in a situation similar to the internee's.

Both Ernst Wiechert and Viktor Frankl are reminded in the camps of Dostoevsky's works: his autobiographical *The House of the Dead*, in which he describes his four years in a Siberian prison camp, lends itself especially to such use as a comparative model. In the tone of sorrowful resignation characteristic of his report, however, Wiechert shows that for all the similarity there was a fundamental difference between the Russian system described by Dostoevsky and Buchenwald. This first occurred to him at the time of his release: 'Everywhere people signalled to him, surreptitiously, using almost nothing but their eyes. "With God! With God!" called the prisoners in Dostoevsky's *House of the Dead*, but here they could not call out "With God!" God had deserted them and died' (**Wiechert**, 1984: 151). By contrast, Frankl identifies with Dostoevsky in his concern to preserve his integrity:

> Dostoevsky once said: 'I am afraid of one thing: that I won't be worthy of my torment.' These words inevitably went through your head quite often, when you got to know those martyr-like people whose conduct in the camp, whose suffering and death, bore witness to the ultimate and inescapable inner freedom of man that was being placed in question. (**Frankl**, 1977: 109)

These local similarities between the situation of the concentration camp prisoners and Dostoevsky's experiences conceal the fundamental difference. Not only was there no comparison between the nineteenth-century penal system and twentieth-century terror, but in his *House of the Dead* the Russian author could still find a meaning that was radically missing in the concentration camps. There imprisonment could appear as a true liberation.[36] Wiechert's and Frankl's associations thus display an essentially narrow interpretation of their reading.

Dostoevsky was not the only fruitful model for accounts of the horrors of the camps; situations depicted by Heinrich von Kleist also came to mind in certain circumstances. Ernst Wiechert, for instance, associates Kleist's novella *Michael Kohlhaas* with the fate of a fellow-captive – who owed his internment to an unwavering sense of justice (**Wiechert**, 1984: 120) – and thereby makes it clear that the purpose of literary association in the camps was not always necessarily to relieve suffering. Sometimes it helped inmates to accept their unchangeable fate while still preserving their self-respect. The story of Michael Kohlhaas may thus have served as a symbol of innocent suffering and kept alive the hope that justice would one day be done. Such hopes for rehabilitation were, so to speak, the *tertium comparationis* between the camp prisoner and the figure of Michael Kohlhaas.

E.T.A. Hoffmann enjoys a reputation among concentration camp survivors as a writer who knew how to depict ugliness. Isa Vermehren describes the men from the Ravensbrück 'security service' with the help of an allusion to Hoffmann (**Vermehren**, 1979: 115). And Walter Adam characterizes the general factotum at the Dachau detention centre by alluding to the same poet of the romantic and the scurrilous (**Adam**, 1947: 49), although here the association is more with the mystery in Hoffmann's work than with ugliness.

Former prisoners also draw on the works of *philosophers* to explain what they lived through in the camps. Viktor Frankl, for example, defines happiness there *ex negativo* as a Schopenhaurian 'freedom from suffering' (**Frankl**, 1977: 79).

Survivors derive meaning mainly from an affirmative relationship to literary models: Nico Rost, for instance, from emphatic agreement with Grillparzer's dictum that 'poetry is the overcoming of the limitations of existence' (**Rost**, 1983: 61). Sometimes, however, an interpretation may involve the repudiation of a statement previously held to be correct. Thus, Karl Röder describes how he tried to cope with the news that his girlfriend had left him:

> It serves me right. Just keep giving it to me! That's not enough at all. There's a lot more to cope with. 'Tear me apart with all the tears and all the suffering of humanity, and I will still remain on top, like a drop of oil on water.' How dreadful it is, this Nietzschean pathos that dramatically lights up despair. As if the opposite were not true – I see it every day. (**Röder**, 1985: 22)

Basing himself on personal observation, Röder feels compelled to expose the philosopher's saying as 'pathos'. Despair in the camps, he knows, is not an element with low specific gravity, as Nietzsche's metaphor expresses it.

In comparison with the 'serious' literary allusions discussed up until now, humorous ones had the advantage that they appeared to help more in coming to terms with experience. *Associations with humorous or tragicomic situations* in literature, like all other associations, invite readers to complete the report with their own knowledge of literature. They also have the effect, like all humour in the camps, of providing prisoners with some temporary relief. One example of this is Wladyslaw Bartoszewski's comparison of his flight from the Nazis to the story of Captain von Köpenick (**Bartoszewski**, 1984: 82). But the association may not go beyond ironic commentary, as in Lina Haag's account of a change in her place of confinement: 'From Gotteszell to the Lichtenburg, I think – the very Story of the Grail' (**Haag**, 1985: 124).

Karl Röder describes the following scene: 'Two shapes appear amid the tumult. They attract my attention, because they look like Don Quixote and Sancho Panza, the one tall and skinny, the other plump and rotund' (**Röder**, 1985: 27). As the quotation from Haag's report already shows, observation and association keep the author's thoughts in thrall. Haag is obviously amused at the moment of making the association, and this takes her mind off the fact of her internment. For a few moments, the thought of Cervantes's two characters distracts Röder too from his own wretched existence. In contrast to Haag's literary 'digression', however, Röder's does not work only once but has the potential to become repetitive: for subsequently, whenever he sees his two comrades in the camp, the same distraction comes into play. It is significant for Röder's awareness of himself as a concentration camp prisoner that he does not focus only on the comic association of Cervantes's figures. He admires the mathematics lessons that 'Skinny' gives 'Shorty' in their free time, so that the pair become 'an astonishing symbol of man's spiritual endeavour' (**Röder**, 1985: 28). This confidence in the prisoner's intellectual existence keeps Röder himself going in the camp. He sees in it the meaning of his internment.[37] Beyond the humour, he repeatedly grasps this as the basis of his existence.[38]

Kurt Hiller, referring to Ferdinand Raimund, expresses a sense of intellectual superiority over the oppressors: 'In the Berlin political police, it seems, people quarrel about me. My freedom has ended up a pawn in the game between a German national clique and a National Socialist one; how delightful!' Here the author's satisfaction at his oppressors' disunity over whether to release him allows the urgency of it all to be overlooked. When one thinks how many intellectuals from the Weimar Republic did not come out of the camps alive, one cannot but be surprised at the carefree way in which Hiller plays the matter down with the help of the well-known first line from the 'Hobellied'.[39] The same reproach may be directed at Lucie Adelsberger, who uses the following image to describe the forced departure of the sick on the death march out of Auschwitz:

Eulenspiegel bets a lot with the hospital chief that he will cure all the patients within twenty-four hours, however sick they are and however long they have been bedridden. Then he goes up to the patients one by one and whispers in each ear: 'It's thumbs down for the last still

> inside when the order comes to leave the hospital at once.' The next morning he calls on everyone to leave the building, and all the sick people rush out of bed. (**Adelsberger**, 1956: 160)

The macabre humour that a fool (here associated with the literary figure Eulenspiegel) allows himself at the expense of the helpless spells catastrophe in the serious context of the concentration camps. It later turned out that the sick people in Auschwitz who managed to evade the evacuation order had the greatest chance of survival. Unintentionally, Adelsberger's association goes beyond description of what she herself experienced; a tormentor's whim, and with it the whole system of terror based on absolute power, is made responsible for the prisoners' fate.

The above examples of literary association allow us to glimpse the typical canon of the educated middle classes in the first half of the twentieth century. For the former concentration camp prisoners, the works of German Classicism and Romanticism loomed as large as the Bible, whereas twentieth-century writers hardly figured at all. It is particularly surprising that there are only two mentions of Kafka's work, especially the short story *In the Penal Colony*, which has often been interpreted since the war as anticipating the use of torture in the concentration camps. In my view, this is only partly explained by the modest reception of Kafka's work in Europe before 1945.[40] It would appear to tell us more about the persistence of reading behaviour conditioned in youth.

The frequency of literary associations in the camp reports supports the hypothesis of a 'literary' coming to terms with experiences. With the help of experiences already given a shape by literature, former prisoners managed to speak about what they had been through or to place it in a certain perspective. Moreover, through the detour of literary association, events that potentially escaped any representation in language nevertheless gained entry to it. It may be a problem that survivors have tended to avoid making individual-personal interpretations of experience by leaning upon literary themes, more than upon metaphorical kinds of expression. But this is a problem mainly for literary historians. In so far as internees drew the strength to go on living from thoughts about literary models, the means fulfilled its purpose.

In the camps, as Nico Rost's journal confirms, literary associations were well suited to preserve or restore people's self-respect.

'Anyone who wants to cope with his suffering physically and mentally,' writes Manès Sperber, 'must be active, inventive and energetic. To withstand a system of oppression aimed at dehumanizing degradation, without become degraded inside yourself, you must every day re-establish the right to respect for yourself and what is yours' (Sperber, 1983: 16). Associations not only created a link to the past outside the camp, but also enabled inmates, at least temporarily, to rise above camp and oppressors and their hostility to culture. By turning their thoughts to examples from literature, they recognized themselves as the better people.

In alluding to the words of a poet or a historical situation, the authors of the concentration camp reports tried to objectify their personal experiences. But associations were not used as productively in the reports as they are, for example, in modern montage technique. Whereas virtuosi of montage, such as Hans Magnus Enzensberger, not only master language intellectually but are in danger of becoming completely captivated by its magic (cf. Grimm, 1961: 64), the relationship of camp survivors to language is marked by scepticism. Persecution has taught them the terrors of the word; they mistrust its secret potency. For Jean Améry, poetic usage completely drained words and made them impossible to employ for the communication of one's own experience.

> Those suffering from linguistic impotence (therefore) tend to forego statement and to push away with disgust the verbal apparition of potency ... Words, however their relationship to the world is posed, are to be repressed for the sake of reality's deadly honour. (Améry, 1982a: 122f.)

Consequently, many survivors preferred to remain silent. When they did speak, they remained in the grip of traditional forms and language – both because they had no experience of writing, and because many of their texts were composed soon after the liberation of the camps. In most cases, they literally wrote things down as they poured out of them. Only a few reports, composed by writers long after the events, display a careful literary crafting, and even then innovation is kept within limits, especially if they are part of a more general autobiography. Survivors take their bearings from the realistic style of the nineteenth century, in the belief that this is best suited to what they have to communicate.

The texts usually stay at a low level of reflection; even after a lot of time has elapsed, the authors still seem in the grip of what they lived through. Stylistic innovation is always a sign that the experience has been previously worked through, but it is precisely such a coming to terms with the past that the former victims hope to derive from the act of writing. More important still is their aim of presenting events in as objective a manner as possible, and this is why a majority opt for the form of the report. Distrustful of literary innovation, which they identify with imagination (that is, with untruth), they are not prepared to make use of its potential for conveying information to the reader.

Notes

1. Michel Foucault allocates a similar function to storytelling (Foucault, 1991: 141–60).
2. Austrian survivors – for example, Mali Fritz, Rosa Jochmann and Hermann Langbein – report that they have often been invited in recent years to speak at schools.
3. Lawrence Langer is quite categorical: 'An epic of genocide would seem to be a contradiction in terms'; and it would be equally impossible to speak of 'heroes' in that context (Langer, 1982: 85). A special case is that of Binjamin Wilkomirski's *Fragments* – see Epilogue.
4. For a survey of German-language novels set in the camps, see Cernyak-Spatz (1985).
5. On this political organization in Buchenwald, see Pingel (1978: 199).
6. On the actions that the political organization in Buchenwald has been shown to have carried out shortly before the liberation, see Pingel (1978: 221–7).
7. One example of the novelistic reworking of this material is Arnost Lustig's *A Prayer for Katerina Horovitzova* (Overlook Press 1987), to which reference is made in Foley (1982: 345).
8. Cf. Simon Wiesenthal: 'Survival is a privilege, which sets up obligations. I have repeatedly asked myself what I can do for those who did not survive' (Wiesenthal, 1988: 429).
9. Bettelheim says this on the matter: 'Writing about such things was unconsciously also an attempt to set aside my experiences by gaining a detached intellectual mastery over them . . . When one tries to grasp why something serious has happened to one, it often means an important development in the struggle to integrate the experience and its effects' (Bettelheim, 1980: 248).
10. Here and for what follows, see the detailed critical account in Adler (1960: 162–84).
11. The 75-minute film, of which only certain passages have survived, was not originally intended for screening in German cinemas (cf. Wolfberg, 1991: 43).
12. Manfred Smuda, 'Narrativität als ästhetisches Problem. Futurismus und Roman', unpublished lecture, quoted in Kronsbein (1984: 62).

13. On the various narrative schemas in concentration camp literature, see Peitsch (1990: 134–51).

14. Walter Weiss has shown, for example, that the opening passage of Thomas Mann's *Mario and the Magician* resembles a musical overture in already containing *in nuce* all the themes in the story (W. Weiss, 1964: 81–2).

15. In similar fashion, a number of priests aestheticized their maltreatment at the hands of SS thugs into a 'condition and new starting point for intense religious feeling' (Moll, 1988: 221).

16. Without saying so specifically, Glinz here goes beyond Käte Hamburger's view (Hamburger, 1973) that interpretation only applies to fiction.

17. Dostoevsky already interpreted his imprisonment as a burial (Dostoevsky, 1939: 7), and Seger employs the same trope without mentioning the precedent.

18. Translation slightly modified to accord with the German text.

19. Translation slightly modified to accord with the German text.

20. In his memoirs, Simon Wiesenthal quotes for special effect an SS police court verdict against an SS man who 'got carried away in acts of cruelty unworthy of a German man and SS leader'. Wiesenthal ironically comments: 'The German male kills cleanly' (Wiesenthal, 1988: 322).

21. Not only do survivors later use such details to focus on a strange world that was theirs for a shorter or longer time. In the camps themselves, an intense relationship to objects served the same purpose (cf. DeKoven, 1980: 74).

22. This is true especially of 'historical' accounts, such as Eugen Kogon's *SS-Staat*, Hermann Langbein's *Menschen in Auschwitz* or Benedikt Kautsky's *Teufel und Verdammte*.

23. This appears to contradict Michael Moll's view that the authors of these reports lacked sufficient distance to adopt a purely documentary mode, as a media reporter, for example, is expected to do.

24. Poeticity is here understood with Schulte-Sasse and Werner as a property of the text, not as a purely linguistic phenomenon (Schulte-Sasse and Werner, 1990: 124).

25. To explain this meaning deficit only by the lack of historical perspective, as Barbara Foley (1982: 343) does, is to fall much too short of the mark. In my view, it is due to a whole complex of reasons, not least psychological ones.

26. On religion in Auschwitz, see Klieber (1982).

27. On the use of metaphor in interpretations of the world, see Stoffer-Heibel (1981: 100).

28. [An allusion to the opening two lines of Goethe's famous poem 'Das Göttliche': '*Edel sei der Mensch,/Hilfreich und gut!*' – *trans. note.*]

29.   *Faust*: A marshland flanks the mountainside,
            Infecting all that we have gained;
            Our gain would reach its greatest pride
            If all this noisome bog were drained.
            I work that millions may possess this space,
            If not secure, a free and active race.
          (*Faust, Part Two* translated by Philip Wayne, Harmondsworth: Penguin, 1959, p. 269)

30. See 'Vorübungen zum dreiteiligen Drama divina commedia' (P. Weiss, 1968: 125–41). Weiss originally planned *The Investigation* as the third part of a 'World Theatre' project (cf. Baumgart, 1982: 51; Subiotto, 1991).
31. '[When at night I think of Germany, I cannot get any sleep' – the opening two lines of Heine's poem 'Nachtgedanken'.]
32. According to Helmut Gollwitzer, people in Soviet prisoner-of-war camps were even more likely to tell fairy tales (**Gollwitzer**, 1983: 52f.).
33. See J.R.R. Tolkien, *Tree and Leaf*, Boston: Houghton Mifflin, 1965.
34. [The part of the Prater district in Vienna called after the Punch-like figure of Hanswurst, whose puppet shows were once a common sight there – *trans. note.*]
35. In the afterword to his *Märchen-Verwirrbuch*, Iring Fetscher refers to the fact that light fiction nowadays performs the function that popular tales once had. The schoolchildren who, in his example, critically rewrote or continued tales by the Grimm Brothers were often, surprisingly often, using models from crime films that they may have seen on television (Fetscher, 1973).
36. See Rudolf Neuhäuser's 'Afterword' to the German translation of *The House of the Dead* (Dostojewskij, 1988: 428f.).
37. See also Sperber's dictum: 'Despite, indeed because of, this condition that had worsened into hopelessness, the intellectual vitality of the persecuted grew stronger' (Sperber, 1983: 113). What Sperber here noticed in his Jewish fellow-citizens also applied to many non-Jews in the concentration camps.
38. Although Jean Améry convincingly describes the special difficulties that intellectuals had in surviving the camps (**Améry**, 1999: 1–20), and although these were indeed intended by the SS at least in the early period of the camps, former prisoners report the lively life of the mind that developed there when the slightest possibility arose. This may be seen in the metaphorical usage that associated eating with activation of the intellect. Michael Moll even points to a reversal of 'existential relations' in the camps, so that 'hunger and life's immediacies ... temporarily became no more than indirect means of life, [and] an almost playful concern with things of the mind became an immediate elixir of life for many inmates' (Moll, 1988: 154).
39. The reference in the German original of Hiller's text is to a famous couplet in *Der Verschwender* (Act II, Scene 6) by the nineteenth-century Austrian playwright Ferdinand Raimund:
    Da streiten sich die Leut' herum
    oft um den Wert des Glücks . . .
    ['Since people often quarrel about the value of happiness . . . ']
40. On the reception of Kafka, see Hartmut Binder (ed.): *Kafka Handbuch*, vol. 2, *Das Werk und seine Wirkung*, Stuttgart: Kröner, 1979, pp. 624–35.

5
Text and meaning: from experience to report

The texts that have been considered in this study were written over a period of more than fifty years – between 1934 and the late 1980s. They record the survival of various categories of concentration camp prisoners, in different kinds of camp, and in different conditions. The earliest come from Communists or Jews who were released before the beginning of the war, or who – in a few cases such as Gerhart Seger's – managed to escape. Jews, especially those interned in the wake of the pogrom of November 1938, sometimes secured their release by undertaking to emigrate forthwith (e.g. **Heilig**, 1941; **Schweinburg**, 1988; cf. Kogon, 1985: 301). Only a minority of German 'Aryans' were released before 1945 (cf. Broszat, 1984: 121); in the later war years they could sometimes report for service at the front, but political prisoners generally tried to avoid this (cf. Kogon, 1985: 305f.).

The conditions that Austrian intellectuals found in Dachau in Spring 1938 can hardly be compared with those which prevailed a few years later, when, among others, priests critical of the regime were 're-educated' there (cf. Broszat, 1984: 46–55, 107). Dachau was different from Auschwitz, Buchenwald, Bergen-Belsen, Mauthausen or Theresienstadt, to name only the best known of the camps (cf. Broszat, 1984: 107).

The former prisoners had had many opportunities to discover the differences between, and indeed within, camps. Allocation to a penal work detachment or incarceration in the bunker made the rest of the camp appear in an almost rosy light (e.g. **Buber-Neumann**, 1968: 254) – a relativity expressed in the use of words such as 'sanatorium' or 'home' to describe this 'better' part. Even in Ravensbrück's detention block, one section seems to have been preferred by prisoners to the other on the dark and forlorn northern side (cf. **Vermehren**, 1979: 37). Certain work groups might also appear as blessed isles amid the hell of the camps. Thus, when Fania Fénelon first visited the 'rehearsal room' of the Auschwitz girls' orchestra, she felt she was in a 'paradise of music' (**Fénelon**, 1977: 26).

More commonly, survivors reflect on the differences between two camps, especially between Auschwitz and Bergen-Belsen or Dachau and Flossenbürg. Incredible though it may later seem to authors writing about it, prisoners did look back regretfully from Belsen to Auschwitz or envy those who had come from there; others welcomed the idea of going back to Dachau. This should be explained, however, by the shifting historical situation. When Auschwitz, in August 1944, began to be gradually evacuated in the face of the advancing Red Army, part of the camp population found itself being sent from a camp where it had been relatively well organized (not least through the action of the political prisoners there) to Bergen-Belsen. Once a relatively privileged internment camp mainly for Jews who might be exchanged for German prisoners-of-war, Bergen-Belsen was by then in a state of chaos caused by the level of new intakes. The accommodation was completely insufficient (Anne Frank, as is well known, died there in one of the overcrowded emergency tents), and food was always in short supply or so badly spoiled as to be unfit for consumption. There had been similar differences at an earlier period between Dachau and Flossenbürg – the former conceived as a showcase, with health and social facilities (including a library, for example), the latter newly created in 1939 with much harsher conditions.

In a sense, the reflections of former prisoners on the relative conditions in the camps show that they did, after all, retain a certain degree of realism. Those who could look back at better conditions did not sink into total apathy and were more likely to retain some will to survive.

A further problem in the way of comparing these texts is that some authors immediately wrote down their experiences, whereas others waited a long time before putting pen to paper. Those who were released before the end of the war offer contradictory testimony about the order forbidding them to speak about the camps (cf. Kogon, 1985: 304). Many say that it was a blanket ban, imposed on pain of fresh internment. This, for example, is what Erich Schweinburg was told when he was released from Dachau: 'Anyone who gets carried away and breathes a word about what he's seen here ... will be picked up and brought straight back. Of course, that's only as long as he's in Germany. We couldn't give a damn what you tell your friend Rosenfeld in America, or anyone else once you're out there' (**Schweinburg**, 1988: 331). In any event, most of the texts written before the end of the Third Reich were published abroad, the exception being those secretly written inside the country which became known only after 1945 (e.g. **Gostner**, 1986; **Haag**, 1985).

After the general liberation by Allied troops, a small group of survivors wrote down a report quite soon (cf. Peitsch, 1990: 101–231). Of the 130 or more texts consulted in this study, 13 were produced before the end of the war and another 42 came out before the end of the 1940s; the remainder – 60 per cent or so – were published between 1950 and the end of the 1980s. But these figures only tell us about the date of publication, which may have been separated by many years from the date of composition. Gerty Spies's *Drei Jahre Theresienstadt*, for example, appeared in 1984, without mention of the fact that it was an expanded version of a report written at the latest in the 1950s, kept then, as now, as a typescript in the archives of the Leo Baeck Institute in New York. Parts of it were published in the journal *Hochland*, in 1958.

From the late 1970s to the early 1980s, following the showing of the TV series *Holocaust* in 1979 (cf. Märthesheimer and Frenzel, 1979: 219–98), there was renewed interest in reports from the concentration camps. More than 20 per cent of our texts (30 in number) were first published after 1979, and the same number again were published for the second time; whereas only 10 per cent had come out in the preceding decade. The political situation in Germany in the 1960s and early 1970s (student unrest, extra-parliamentary opposition) does not therefore seem to have triggered the production of memoirs about the camps, or only did so with delayed effect.[1]

Although factual accuracy is a background issue in comparison with literary aspects, any analysis must take account of the time that elapsed between the experiencing and the recording of events in the camps. The greater the distance between the two, the more did survivors base themselves on explanatory models not directly connected with the experience, and the more they overlay that experience with models derived from literature or history. In the case of established writers such as Ernst Wiechert, in *Der Toten-wald*, this happened to some extent soon after the end of their time in the camps.

If one were to attempt a periodization, three phases of report publication would emerge: 1933–45, 1945–49 and 1950 onwards.[2] They all differ not only in the manner of production, distribution and reception of the texts, but also in their intended function.

The earliest texts were meant to inform the world about what was then happening in the concentration camps. They mostly appeared abroad, in Britain (Heilig) or the United States, although even there obstacles stood in the way of publication. Bruno Bettelheim's scientific psychological report, for example, was rejected by US publishers on the grounds that it was unbeliev-able (Bettelheim, 1979).

For those liberated by the Allied armies, the main concern was often not to secure publication but to come to terms with the experience through the act of writing. Nevertheless – and despite the widespread paper shortage – a number of books did come out in the years after the war.[3] In most cases, this was the author's first and only publication, but there were also some by established writers such as Ernst Wiechert or Albert Drach. For another minority – people like Fred Wander or Primo Levi – their autobio-graphical writing was the start of a literary career.

What is surprising, however, is not that there were only a handful of writers among the internees, but that so many non-writers who survived went on to put pen to paper. There were two reasons for this spate of writing: a wish to come to terms with what had happened, and/or a wish to bear witness on behalf of those who had been murdered. (It should not be forgotten that a number of dead relatives and comrades stand behind each verbal or written report (cf. Langer, 1991: 157).) Even if such victims as Primo Levi could find no meaning in survival, there was a feeling that the point was now to bear witness on behalf of life itself – so that Hitler should not prevail posthumously. The Jewish philoso-pher Emil Fackenheim called this the 614th command, referring to the Jewish tradition that God revealed 613 commands to Moses on Mount Sinai (Fackenheim, 1978: 22).[4]

In literary theory, when it is a question of coming to terms with an experience, one thinks of Aristotelian catharsis and its supposedly therapeutic effects. Literary activity as substitute behaviour[5] creates, for both writer and reader, a space in which life's problems can be solved. In his Frankfurt lecture 'Literature as Therapy?', Adolf Muschg expressed his doubts about this theory; literature had, to be sure, appeared to him as the only escape route from his biography, but he had not thereby solved his conflicts, only created a 'replacement body' for himself (Muschg, 1981: 105). Concerning his first work to be published, he asserts: 'I had been born! It was the start of my second existence, which was supposed to put my first to rights; my making good . . . began . . . the *other* life in the form of a book' (Muschg, 1981: 103; emphasis in the original). Speaking of the inner compulsion to write, he says that literature was the sign of a biographical 'defect'. But then he is quite categorical: 'This art – art *in general* – is *de profundis* anti-therapy' (Muschg, 1981: 84 – emphasis in the original). The object here of Muschg's criticism is a widespread tendency in the late-1970s' literary scene, stemming from various fringe groups, which backed the self-liberating potential of autobiographical writing and even led to the development of full-blown 'writing therapies' (cf. Mattenklott, 1992: 153–81). Whereas the model of 'text as communication' had as its motto: 'You tell others about yourself, so that their own story will become capable of being told',[6] former concentration camp internees earlier used the impulse to write autobiography as a way of coming to terms with their own memory.

Peter Bichsel, like Adolf Muschg, does not believe 'that the writer frees himself through writing, or that he, for example, overcomes his troubles [*sich die Sorgen vom Leib schreibe*]. The opposite is the case: he sinks more deeply into his troubles through writing [*er schreibt sich die Sorgen auf den Leib*]. Things, troubles, opinions: they get their weight from being described' (Bichsel, 1982: 61f.). But Bichsel, again like Muschg, downplays the importance of this for himself. Telling a story does have something to do with life, indeed it is the precondition for existence – '*only* by telling a story' can we continue to exist (Bichsel, 1982: 83; emphasis in the original). In his remarks, Bichsel is thinking of stories in and about the camps, and quite often explicitly refers to them. When he writes: 'Literature is the categorical explanation of things as meaningful. I am because I can tell a story, and it is because I can tell a story that I pull through in the end', he consciously places storytelling in the realm of coming to terms with life (Bichsel, 1982: 84). The empirical facts show that he is right. In the concentration camps, inmates were again and again concerned to share their experiences with their comrades. Fred Wander, for example, vividly describes how a prisoner transferred from Auschwitz to Buchenwald felt compelled to report what he had seen: 'He cannot wait, he must get it off his mind, to the first person who comes along, to the father or whoever takes his place. He trembles as he speaks, he has spasms as if he is going to vomit. I am terribly weary, my eyes close, my mind is smoky like the flame on a last drop of oil. I see a child to whom I must listen' (**Wander**, 1985: 98).

The compulsion to bear witness for murdered comrades and for life itself, even the wish to communicate one's experiences to others, are not enough to explain the mechanism that led to the writing of a report. How did former prisoners cross the threshold and start writing things down?

Sigmund Freud, among others, gave some thought to this phenomenon, as we can see in the short essay 'Creative Writers and Day-Dreaming' that he wrote sometime between 1903 and 1906 (Freud, 1985: 131–41). Heinz Hillmann, to whom the following remarks are mainly indebted, has tried to develop a system of aesthetic production on the basis of Freud's work (cf. Hillmann, 1977). He characterizes literary phantasy as a kind of day-dreaming, in which the dreamer places himself or herself at the middle of an egocentric structure (cf. Freud, 1985: 138; Hillmann, 1977: 19). Hillmann stresses that there is no qualitative difference between the writers' experience and that of ordinary mortals, except that at some point the former recognizes it as representative and decides to write it down. Both, then, conform to the underlying principle of experience: the ego within a certain situation. What is not necessarily known to this ego, but can nevertheless be communicated, is its reaction to the situation. This may be expressed conceptually, linguistically or pragmatically. The first of these expressions, which is usually the decisive one for the literary imagination, involves identifying a situation in accordance with the formula 'if x outside, then y inside', where the if-clause defines the situation in which the ego finds itself, and the then-clause defines 'the inner state of the ego located within the external situation or action' (Hillmann, 1977: 64). Together with Alfred Schütz,[7] Hillmann divides the external world into a 'surrounding world' [*Umwelt*] that directly affects the experiencing ego, and an 'accompanying world' [*Mitwelt*] with which the ego comes into contact only on certain occasions. The same law of the representativeness of experience that applies to writers in general also holds for concentration camp survivors who take up the pen. 'It should not become a sensational report', is how Abraham Hochhäuser begins his reflections (unusual in the camp material) on what impels a lay person to write (cf. Peitsch, 1990: 174). 'Rather, it should be the direct account of a man who has been deep down among a mass of people doomed to die; the personal experience of a man of the people to whom, under normal conditions, it may never have occurred throughout his life to pick up a pen and communicate to others his experiences and his thoughts' (**Hochhäuser**, 1948: 3).

Internees reacted emotionally to the situation in the camps, and already during their internment they sometimes tried to verbalize them through conversation with other prisoners or notebook sketches. By the act of narration, they made individual experience public and accessible to those who had not participated in it (cf. Hillmann, 1977: 71). It should be assumed that the reports genuinely reproduce these reactions to only a limited extent, and in any event they have been overlaid there with literary form.[8] Still, the author's description should enable one to conclude which circumstances in the camps triggered the reactions in question.

The dimension of understanding, which is what mainly interests us here, is also located in these reactions to experience. In particular, the writer's reaction in the camp reports signifies not least an attempt to come to terms with the experience intellectually. For this reason it is legitimate to read these texts as evidence of a working through of individual experience. Texts such as those considered here may give us some idea, if anything can, of the meaning that internees attached to their experiences. This meaning is already apparent in the subjective selection of material for the report, so that recollection may be seen as indicating the degree to which the subject was affected by events. Two groups of perceptions may be distinguished according to their accessibility for prisoners: one concerned the experience of their immediate surroundings (or *Umwelt*, in Hillmann's terminology), the other the world beyond the wire (or *Mitwelt*). Despite the differences between the camps, the moment of arrival and the first few days generally made a deep impact on those who endured them. This was the great depersonalization shock, which led to the sharpest reactions. Similar effects resulted from the completely inadequate food situation, and from the forced living together which meant that even privileged prisoners had scarcely any chance of withdrawal. Ella Lingens-Reiner, who enjoyed special privileges as an 'Aryan' doctor in Auschwitz, gives an impression of what it meant for her – towards the end of her internment – to be able to withdraw into a room of her own in one of Dachau's outcamps (**Lingens-Reiner**, 1948: 163). Nevertheless, prisoners also experienced contact with fellow-victims as functionally advantageous to survival; there is hardly one report that does not gratefully recall a camp friendship or 'family'.

Beyond their immediate surroundings, some areas of the world outside the camp remained in the prisoners' consciousness. Of course, only a minority – especially those who worked in war enterprises – could have any kind of limited contact with the local population. (cf. Langbein, 1980a: 502–22). More rarely, internees met craftsmen employed by the SS, who might even come into the camp; secret trading developed with them in Auschwitz, for example (open contact being a punishable offence), and this gave privileged prisoners access to food and little luxury items (Sofsky, 1997: 162). The resistance group in Auschwitz used some of these civilians as links to the Polish underground (cf. Langbein, 1980b).

Any information about the state of the war, especially after the Allied advance began, was strictly withheld from prisoners. It is hardly surprising, then, that the thirst for news helped the spread of rumours. The value of a piece of news was measured not by its truth content, but by whether it might strengthen the will to survive[9] – even if it also increased the tendency to escape from reality (cf. Sofsky, 1997: 91).

To establish the way in which prisoners experienced the camps. as we shall try to do now, we must again first draw a distinction. In the case of death camps such as Chelmno, Sobibor or Treblinka, only a small minority of people survived and there are hardly any reports in existence.[10] Auschwitz is, of course, an exception because of its status as both an extermination and a labour camp. But this does not at all mean that more humane conditions prevailed in the rest of the camps; indeed, the principle of 'extermination through work' often merely delayed the end for a while.[11] For a few, however, there was a chance of survival, and it is only their reports and experiences that can be considered here.

In normal life, perception of the surrounding world crucially requires memory of similar experiences in the past,[12] and the world of the camps, however radically different, did not change this dependence. Estrangement was certainly severe, but even there prisoners were subject to certain mechanisms of everyday life. Thus, paradoxical as it may seem – and the mass killings apart – most of the experiences in the camps differed from those of 'normal' life 'only' in their intensity. This is one further reason for the striking similarity of the reports, however different the camps and the characters.

The experience of discarding clothes before a bath or a medical examination is a routine event for everyone in Western civilization. What was new in the camps was its association with humiliation or even mortal danger. There could be nothing discreet about undressing *en masse* before the eyes of the SS. At the 'selections', the SS doctor examined naked bodies not to cure symptoms of illness, but to cut them away from the group (cf. Mitscherlich and Mielke, 1978). This experience forced prisoners to develop new forms of behaviour in order to survive. They had to suppress feelings of shame and make themselves appear as healthy as possible to the doctor.

Hunger taught prisoners to regard the palatability of food as a secondary matter; the general shortage largely ruled out distinctions between good and bad. Thus 'the amount of margarine used for soups ... was 60 to 90 per cent less than that provided for in the official menu for the week. Bread tasted sharp and was hard to digest; sausage for prisoners contained just a half of the fat of sausage meant for the SS'; corrupt duty-prisoners in Auschwitz made sure that their comrades received only 1300 to 1700 calories a day, instead of the scheduled 1700 to 2150 (cf. Auschwitz, 1982: 79). Survivors mention devouring even mouldy bread and rotten soup vegetables; many extol roast potato skins as a rare delicacy.

Most of the authors of reports describe how the process of cooking had to turn revolting scraps into something they could just about put inside them, but they also speak of fellow-prisoners who picked edible matter from the garbage; there were even said to be cases of cannibalism. At first, many internees resisted eating the camp fare, but hunger and the will to live soon made them change their mind. Tadeusz Borowski's point that the camp notables could be recognized from their having 'something to eat' (**Borowski**, 1983: 108) also indicates the function of food as a status symbol (cf. Kröhle, 1989: 179).

These are just two examples of how the camp forced prisoners to judge their perceptions differently from the way that 'normal' life had taught them. Much the same may be said for the value put on the world outside. The prohibition of any contact with the local population heightened the prisoners' sense of what it meant to be included or excluded. They welcomed anything that might put an end to this situation. Whereas the ordinary population experienced bombing raids as dangerous and potentially lethal, internees had two reasons to feel happy about them. First, air-raid warnings brought them temporary freedom by sending their guards off into protective shelters. Second, the bombs could be seen as heralds of the approaching liberators and lead to anticipatory feelings of victory over their oppressors; in Auschwitz even non-Communist internees waited impatiently for further advances of the Red Army. In this conflicting relationship to the external world, it was hoped that everything harmful to their tormentors – in an inclusive sense, the whole German people – would lead to their liberation. This explains the satisfaction that prisoners felt at the sight of bombed German cities, when they were sent to carry out clearing work there.

This kind of revaluation of experience took place amid the daily struggle for survival. Although the lives of prisoners had in some ways a radically different quality from what they had known before internment, certain structural features could be clearly discerned. The vague resemblance to the routine of 'normal' life had the result, in very many cases, that prisoners became aware of its power to create meaning only in a process of reflection.

Another group of events was more liable to create meaning spontaneously. In rare cases, internees were suddenly and unexpectedly, though quite consciously, confronted with an aspect of their life before the camps. Certain prisoners – as their choice of metaphor shows – seem to have been particularly open to moods associated with Nature; their romantic potential, in the utterly unromantic surroundings of the camps, apparently led to a mechanism rather like that involved in the reception of light fiction. In the desire to transcend an adverse reality, readers of such literature use certain tropes to sketch an ideal world that they increasingly substitute for their own (cf. H. Marcuse, 1956: 121). Similarly, the camp testimony suggests that inmates actually sought out, and tried to control the effects of, sensory impressions from their previous life outside. The meaning of such experiences should be attributed to the fact they were fundamentally different from the everyday routine of the camp, and lay outside the power of the oppressors. However minor and unimportant they may seem, their rarity in the prisoners' experience considerably enhanced their value.

Work outside the perimeter, or transfer to another camp, also brought prisoners face to face with their past. At the same time, they could often see people leading ordinary lives and going about their business. How such people behaved meant a lot to them, and many reports speculate about what was going through their minds. Some prisoners wondered how they themselves would have acted if the situation had been reversed;[13] others complained of the hostile attitude of the local population. In any event, such encounters set off a process of reflection and often led to idiosyncratic judgements about what they had seen. In *Holocaust Testimonies*, Lawrence Langer illustrates the change or inversion of values in the camps by a scene in which Edith P., an Auschwitz survivor, saw from her cattle truck a woman and child in a railway station and thought it was 'paradise' (Langer, 1991: 54–6). After long years of captivity, an everyday scene could present itself in a religious exaggeration that signalled at once longing and an acceptance of unattainability.

Since people's self-esteem is in large part defined through their occupation and work, what prisoners were assigned to do in the camps was potentially very significant. For new arrivals, the cynical motto '*Arbeit macht frei*' aroused false hopes that were soon corrected by the reality of extermination through work. Here absolute power 'broke free from the rationale of utility and

effectiveness, and subordinate(d) work to the law of terror'
(Sofsky, 1997: 168). To some extent this still applied after 1942,
when the concentration camps were more tightly integrated into
war production. Although, in principle, work did not guarantee
survival but undermined it, it served in individual cases 'to
determine whether a person would live or die' (**Améry**), particularly for intellectuals, who were special targets of the mostly
uneducated SS. When victims entered the camps, they were
robbed of their clothing and personal effects and, even before that,
saw their social identity erased. Nor should it be forgotten that a
craftsman was much more likely than a brain worker to find a job
appropriate to his training that would to some extent restore his
self-esteem. Only a few prisoners with an academic background,
such as Primo Levi, had the relative good fortune to be assigned
work in keeping with their training and not altogether unlike what
they had done previously.

Not for nothing do many survivors, especially those who spent
a long time in the camps, place their work activity at the centre of
their report, or even in its title (e.g. **Naor**, 1986), and give it as the
decisive reason for their survival. As the case of Glas-Larsson
shows, whether or not internees could practise their trade in the
camps depended not only upon mastery of definite skills but
crucially also upon their own individual initiative (**Glas-Larsson**,
1981). We have no wish here to adopt a psychologically reduc-
tionist approach. But with reservations, it should be noted that
under equal conditions certain character traits, as well as physical
ones (cf. e.g. Niederland, 1980), seem to have favoured one
inmate over another in the struggle for survival.

The illusion of a normal work activity enabled many prisoners
temporarily to put the everyday routine of the camp out of their
minds and even, astonishing though it may seem, to establish a
reflective distance from camp life and from their own suffering.
Psychologists such as Bruno Bettelheim and Viktor Frankl managed to bring their professional interest to bear, and thus for a
while at least to rise above the situation as it immediately presented itself. The following passage from Frankl's report explains
this effect:

> Almost crying from the pain in my sore feet, which had to tramp in
> open shoes through severe frost and into icy wind ... I limped the few
> kilometres in the long column from the camp to the place of work. My

mind ceaselessly occupied itself with the thousand little problems of
our wretched life in the camp ...

I already felt disgusted with this terrible compulsion, which meant
that my thoughts were plagued by such questions day in day out. Then
I used a trick. Suddenly I see myself standing at the rostrum in a
brightly lit, fine and warm lecture-hall, with an audience listening
with interest in nicely upholstered seats – and I am speaking. I speak
and give a lecture on the psychology of the concentration camp! And
everything that has been so tormenting and depressing me is rendered
objective, as I see and describe it from a lofty scientific standpoint.
(**Frankl**, 1977: 119f.)

There can be no doubt that such an objectification of suffering
required enormous intellectual discipline, which probably only a
few prisoners were capable of achieving.

Other internees who did not have the knowledge of a psychologist
tried every way of looking positively at their work assignment – to
take their mind off the camp, but also to make themselves
physically tired so that they could at least sleep at night. Work
that helped fellow-prisoners – in the care of the sick, for example –
was a source of special satisfaction. On the other hand, as one
would expect, sabotage of forced labour is first mentioned in
connection with work on arms production; not so much because
prisoners did not have other opportunities before working in that
sector, but because they had mainly been taken up with satisfying
the needs of the body. Moreover, sabotage of the kind of pointless
work inflicted on them in Dachau before the war would have
seemed politically meaningless and liable to backfire. Alfred
Schwerin reports, however, that during his time in Dachau the
Jewish prisoners were not allowed to work but had to exercise –
which suggests that not all prisoners then saw work as an extreme
form of harassment (**Schwerin**, 1944: 55). Only when conditions
improved a little did the political aspect of work output become
important for some prisoners, although even then ideas of sabotage competed with the wish for satisfaction through work (**Fritz**,
1986: 29, 80).

The evaluation of work-related experiences also relied upon
equivalents in life before the camp, but a feeling of greater
intensity stands out in the reports. This is particularly noticeable
when they talk about outdoor work. In the little strip of Nature
accessible to inmates, each object they perceived had significance.

Many viewed Nature as a witness that contradicted their oppressors' show of omnipotence, since even the suitably clothed guards suffered in Poland's cruel winter and scorching summer.

The Dutchwoman Renata Laqueur even associated her observation of Nature with her hopes for liberation: 'They cannot take from me this wonderful feeling when the sun's rays warm me through and the wind blows through my hair. One can hope in the future, dream of holidays to come. Switzerland!' A past sense of freedom is here directly associated with expectations for the future, as she makes even clearer later on. 'I think … it was precisely my eye for the beauty of Nature – which I tried to preserve without fail – that kept my strength up in this indescribable misery and stopped me from sinking into the dull indifference that would certainly have meant an early end' (**Laqueur**, 1983: 125f.). The sharpened focus on individual experience survives as an exceptionally clear memory. But, of course, former prisoners did not preserve every event with such clarity; more often they were faced with enormous blanks in their memory.

Although experience directly depends upon memory, the survivors' testimony shows that in the camps perception took on a dynamic of its own with regard to the attribution of meaning and the evaluation of reality. As we have seen, pieces of the surrounding world could in extreme cases become symbolically charged, so that prisoners used them with a certain meaning as signs for their own destiny.

When survivors, in their reports, later reflected upon this changed perceptual judgement due to their captivity, they took a first step towards understanding what had happened to them. Joel König tells us how, in the course of his struggle for survival, the very concept of that struggle changed its meaning (**König**, 1983: 166). The situation of persecution seems to have completely removed from the relationship between expression and content that reliability which alone makes communication possible. Ironically, at another place in his report, König acknowledges how his fellow-victims immediately adjusted to the changed meaning of a concept:

> The gathering did not go off as we had expected. Schilling did make
> a speech, but this time he struck the right chord. He explained that
> we were now prisoners for an indefinite time, and that none of us

knew what lay ahead. All the more should we direct all our efforts and plans to a future life in Palestine. What if, already in Germany, we were to get so far by our own efforts as to speak fluent Hebrew? Never before had a proposal of Schilling's met with such approval. What a happy idea to set ourselves such a goal right now! (**König**, 1983: 166)

It is understandable that König should have frowned upon the inappropriate reaction to mounting dangers. But in the situation in which he and his companions found themselves, a flight from reality was a legitimate option.

When they looked back, other former inmates realized that their thoroughly individual experience started a learning process which, in the ideal case, produced a balance between adaptation to the camp or persecution and the preservation of personal integrity (cf. Bettelheim, 1979: 48–83).

The written recording of experience is guided by an urge to interpret. By putting their painful memories on paper, survivors attempted to give them tangible shape: that is, to bring them within a formal structure that could stand independently of the suffering self. Hayden White, alluding to Northrop Frye's *Anatomy of Criticism*, speaks of explanation through 'emplotment', as a kind of codification which converts the facts of a chronicle into elements in a structured story (White, 1978: 83). In other words, the reported facts have a position allocated to them on the plane between beginning, middle and end of a text. Through 'emplotment', survivors were, in the ideal case, helped to establish a distance between themselves and their experiences, a distance which some accentuated by using the third person form for their report.

The camp experience hardly taught anyone to write (cf. Raddatz, 1989); for Primo Levi and Fred Wander, it is uncertain whether they would have written anyway if they had not gone through it.

In the camps themselves, the reception of literature played a fundamental role; almost every report mentions reading, or at least a longing to read.[14] Already in the title of his camp journal, *Goethe in Dachau*, the Dutch journalist Nico Rost points to the significance that reading had for him. Of course, he has in mind not only Goethe himself, from whose works he repeatedly drew strength and succour (cf. e.g. **Rost**, 1983: 22), but also the

Schlegel brothers (38), Gustav Frennsen (50), Franz Grillparzer (61ff.) and Jean Paul (80), among others. Rost kept notes on his reading and discussed books with fellow-internees. In September 1944 he even wrote an essay on Hölderlin's *Hyperion* (cf. 82ff.).

The importance of the printed word in the camps may be gauged by the multiple uses to which it was put. Books were regularly 'devoured' as food (**Graumann**, 1947: 97); books helped prisoners to feel human again (**Wiechert**, 1984: 140ff.) or to overcome forced idleness (**Hiller**, 1934/35: 1615). Lucie Begov even says that she and her companions used a collection of aphorisms to try to divine what was in store for them (**Begov**, 1983: 59). Altogether, reading must have strengthened the prisoners' will to resist (as it also did in Nazi prisons) (cf. Emmerich, 1976: 443). Not all camps had a library, and where there was one – in Buchenwald, Dachau or Theresienstadt (cf. Seela, 1988a; Richter, 1988) – not all prisoners had access to it. In the case of Buchenwald, Torsten Seela explains this by the different living and working conditions for different categories of prisoner (Seela, 1988b: 107). Viktor Matejka reports that in Dachau prisoners in the isolation block were denied use of the library (cited in Exenberger, 1992: 10). Books were not only administered but to a large extent financed by the prisoners, so that especially in Buchenwald Jews were asked to pay. The SS mainly ordered standard Nazi works such as Alfred Rosenberg's *Myth of the Twentieth Century* and Hitler's *Mein Kampf* (cf. Seela, 1988b: 103). If, nevertheless, the camp libraries did not become mere centres of fascist-style education,[15] this was due to the action of prisoners who, as Matejka reports in the case of Dachau, even managed to save and make available books that had long been subject to burning outside (**Matejka**, 1983: 89–93).

Although reading does not seem to have been explicitly banned in any camp (Seela, 1988b: 338), the reports indicate that the SS did not tolerate productive literary activity. (Theresienstadt, which enjoyed a kind of special status, was also an exception in this respect.) Although numerous survivors report that they felt a desire to write in the camps, the number of journals in existence today can almost be counted on the fingers of two hands.[16] For obvious reasons, when prisoners defied all prohibitions and wrote about the camp itself, they did so in the form of verse. The short story 'Esther', which Bruno Apitz wrote in Buchenwald (cf.

Emmerich, 1976: 444) stands out as a major work of fiction; while Viktor Matejka's *Pickbücher* occupy an interesting middle position between reception and production (**Matejka**, 1983: 108ff.).

Matejka, as he emphasizes not without a certain pride, was on the first transport of Austrian intellectuals sent to Dachau concentration camp on 1 April 1938. As an adult-education lecturer and educational adviser, but also as an open supporter of Austria's independence (cf. **Matejka**, 1991), he must have been considered especially dangerous by the new rulers. Then in mid-1944, nearly a year before the camp was liberated by the Allies, he was quite unexpectedly set free.

During his time in Dachau, Matejka managed to keep his head above water, mainly by working as a library assistant and as a 'clerk' attached to the SS training leader (**Matejka**, 1991: 102ff.). He tried to preserve his moral integrity by organizing educational activity with the help of some friends behind the backs of the SS. For this purpose they produced the so-called *Pickbücher*, collages from newspapers available in the camp or to which inmates could subscribe (cf. Klamper, 1981: 319f.). (Matejka recalls, for example, that in 1943 there were nineteen subscribers in Dachau just to the magazine *Kunst dem Volk*, edited by Karl Strobl (**Matejka**, 1983: 116).)[17] For the *Pickbücher*, Matejka also drew on his experience as an adviser for the Vienna Labour Office, when he had already been interested in the educational value of contradiction, and he assembled a collection of quotations and articles that were supposed to show the inordinate pessimism of the press about the capacity of the Soviet Union to survive. Among other things, he put together some three hundred pages of a book, 'whose various little parts had in fact already been written by others' (**Matejka**, 1983: 7). This philosophy of 'political education through contradiction' was all the more timely in that it could be fairly easily concealed from the SS.

Only in the course of Matejka's activity as a collector in Dachau, which he began in 1939 and continued despite the initial criticism of other prisoners, did it become clear that material from pro-Nazi publications was being pasted together in such a way that 'it fuelled opposition among non-Nazis and especially anti-Nazis, and encouraged them to think about what was happening' (**Matejka**, 1983: 112). As to form, Matejka referred to the model of John Heartfield (originally Helmut Herzfeld), the co-founder and illustrator of the Berlin Dada group and of the Berlin-based *Arbeiter Illustrierte Zeitung* (AIZ) who had placed photomontage in the service of political caricature. Matejka frankly admits that this activity in Dachau gave him pleasure, but he would certainly have wanted anyway to engage in instruction and persuasion against the new regime. From 1940 the collected texts, grouped by theme and pasted onto octavo-size paper, were bound into books and lent to politically reliable prisoners, some even being put on display in the camp library. The need for caution – all this was against regulations, and could qualify as sabotage since the sheets were bound at the SS bindery – naturally meant that Matejka's educational purpose did not go beyond the group of anti-Nazi or non-Nazi prisoners. But for those who received them, the collages served as a spur to discussion and promoted 'intellectual self-assertion' (**Röder**, 1985: 278). Matejka's friend Karl Röder has written about the importance of the 'power of thought' (for himself at least) in coming to terms with the experience of the camps (**Röder**, 1985: 285).

Apart from the *Pickbücher*, both Matejka and Röder filled volumes with texts of their own, which also served as a basis for discussion in a broader circle. Röder published a selection of these texts in his report: most of them are short, mainly consisting of a couple of lines, and only a few fill one page of a book. The propositions and arguments were probably worked out in the authors' heads before being put on paper in the time available (cf. **Röder**, 1985: 296). Röder writes at length about this 'literary' activity of self-preservation, because it was an important stage in the development of his own personality. The examples in his report include philosophical thoughts on the origins of religion, the requirements for an artist, and so on. There are also memories of life before the camp which, mainly written in the present tense, try to bridge the gulf between the camp and normal life outside. Not surprisingly, they are marked by a certain romantic nostalgia.

Röder and Matejka also wrote down impressions of books they read. Both stress the importance of discovering writers who had not been influenced by National Socialism, people who later entered into the history of literature as the 'internal emigration'. In this category they include the serialized novels of Ernst Schnabel and Stefan Andres, the essays of Sigismund von Radecki, and the art criticism of Jorg Lampe.[18] Nor was this all: Matejka filled whole letters to his wife with advice on what she and her wider family should read (cf. Klamper, 1981: 310–26). Internees greatly appreciated the anti-Nazi spirit of these authors, expressed 'in their fight against empty phrases, their free creative thought, their living relationship to the language, their realistic portrayal of life' (**Röder**, 1985: 91). As Röder's own reading notes show, however, it was also crucially important that the books widely respected by prisoners conveyed 'impressions (rooted) in the contemporary life-and-death struggle' (**Röder**, 1985: 313). Like other survivors, Röder thus recognizes that literature only really appealed to concentration camp inmates if they could relate to it in some way from their own special situation – although he refused to write about them during his internment, on the grounds that this 'would have meant doubling the suffering' (**Röder**, 1985: 295).

Viktor Matejka considers resistance as part of his life: not for nothing does he call his book *Widerstand ist alles* [Resistance Is Everything]. The 'unorthodox' (an adjective he uses about himself in the sub-title) and highly imaginative form of his resistance was expressed in, among other things, his literary work in Dachau. Although he did not dare to judge its effect, even in hindsight, his original idea succeeded in turning the minds of a small circle of friends to something other than the camp routine – which, as we have seen, is mentioned in many reports as a significant factor in individual survival. In an interview, Karl Röder once put his finger on it: 'We could do nothing against the physical annihilation, but we could do something against the psychological annihilation. That was the aim and meaning of what we undertook' (cited in Exenberger, 1992: 6). There is no question that in Dachau Matejka found an 'infrastructure' that was congenial to his operations; and that they would have been incomparably more difficult, if possible at all, in Buchenwald or Auschwitz.

Why, then, is this form of literary activity so interesting in relation to the concentration camps? Not only are the *Pickbücher* unique among written documents from the camps; Matejka found a way, in a climate extremely hostile to things of the mind, to use the alienation and surprise effects of collage to spur himself and other prisoners into creative intellectual activity. He cannot be said to have fully exhausted the potential of his material, since he simply placed set pieces one after another in sequence, without productively altering them as in montage proper. But that would have been beyond the possibilities open to him in the camp.

In any event, the *Pickbücher* testify to Matejka's great strength of character, which he was evidently able to preserve in the most adverse circumstances. With their help he resisted his oppressors, in that broad sense which included 'self-education of the individual resister, strengthening of his or her identity, encouragement of fellow-prisoners, tangible experiences of solidarity' (Emmerich, 1976: 442). On the other hand, the *Pickbücher* are evidence that – at least from 1940 – circumstances in the camp were such that Matejka's own life was not immediately threatened. Karl Röder himself makes the point that intellectual activity, especially organized in this way, could develop only in times of lesser physical danger. Like the camp humour directed at the SS, Matejka's activity helped to create and to strengthen solidarity among the prisoners. His *Pickbücher* thus differ from notebooks written in the camps by virtue of the fact that they aimed not only to preserve his own moral integrity, but also to undermine and destroy the enemy – even though he himself more modestly distinguished his *Pickbücher* from Nico Rost's *Goethe in Dachau* by the way in which the two were produced (cf. Matejka's Letter to Herbert Steiner, 2 May 1977, DÖW No. 12,839). It is no reflection upon Matejka that he himself derived a certain sense of purpose from this unusual occupation.

According to many reports, a sense of purpose seems to have been a major survival factor in the camps; so long as prisoners knew *why* they wanted to survive, the danger of giving themselves up for lost was considerably reduced. The reports also speak of the 'musulmans', who, in ceasing to look after themselves physically or even to get enough food, had already abandoned the struggle for survival. At the same time, internees were afraid of having to watch comrades in such a state (cf. **Frankl**, 1977: 121). Fear of seeing their own future writ large meant that they felt compelled to exclude the musulmans (cf. Sofsky, 1997: 199ff.). The danger of a 'crisis', as Viktor Frankl calls an accelerating loss of the will to live and hence a risk of suicide (**Frankl**, 1951: 178), was at its greatest in the first few weeks after arrival in the camp: not only because the encounter with a murderous environment sapped the prisoners' powers of resistance, but also because during that time they were either kept in quarantine (without doing any work) –

Erwin Leiser quotes one survivor whose six weeks quarantined in Auschwitz left worse memories than the rest of his time there (Leiser, 1982: 56) – or else immediately despatched to an especially unfavourable work assignment.

Work in a 'good' detachment might mean better living conditions for inmates (more opportunity for bodily hygiene, often extra food and special barracks), and it also gave their lives a kind of purpose. Not surprisingly, it was in many cases the non-material side of this activity which motivated prisoners to keep up the struggle for existence, especially when it involved caring for others and therefore took them outside themselves. 'Self-transcendence' is how Viktor Frankl calls this capacity in his theory of logotherapy, a 'motivation theory' that starts from the idea that a life which cannot find or set itself any purpose becomes impossible to live. In fact, the theory goes back to the period before Frankl's internment, but he developed it through his experience of the camps – where it underlies his observation of fellow-prisoners and his survival hypothesis – before finally publishing it at the end of the war. His conclusion that a purpose in life and a will to live were causally related in the camps, and that the latter had a significant influence on survival chances, may strike one as idealistic or even elitist, but it can hardly be gainsaid in the light of the survivors' testimony. Even Günther Anders's critique of the randomness of the ideals by which everyone lives loses its force with regard to the concentration camps (cf. Raddatz, 1985). Where physical existence is at stake, a noble concept of truth forfeits its relevance.

The axiomatic core of logotherapy – the achievement of distance from self [*Selbstdistanzierung*] or self-transcendence – relies upon the endowment of life with meaning. Frankl associates distance from self with the capacity for humour (Frankl and Kreuzer, 1986: 86), whose importance for psychical hygiene in the camps has already been discussed in the previous chapter (in the section on 'humour and irony'). In logotherapy, distance from self is converted into the so-called 'paradoxical intention': that is, 'the patient is directed to wish for . . . or to prefer the very thing that he or she has always feared so much' (Frankl and Kreuzer, 1986: 90; cf. Frankl, 1973: 205ff.). For prisoners in the camps, however, distance from self also meant an objectification of their suffering, as Frankl reports from his own experience. Conscious self-observation was supposed to divert the individual from a particularly unbearable condition and thus avert an immediate collapse into despair. If intellectual discussions and the telling of stories remained so persistently in the memory of former prisoners, it was because these at least temporarily carried them far away from the reality of the camp.

In keeping with the aim of logotherapy to make people conscious of living *for* something or someone – that is, of being responsible for something or someone (cf. Frankl and Kreuzer, 1986: 16) – the camp inmate had to turn his or her attention away from the immediate present: 'In the camps, those are lost who can no longer believe in a future, in their future .... Along with the future they lose a hold for the psyche and let themselves slip down, going into a decline at once physical and mental' (**Frankl**, 1977: 120f.). The danger in Frankl's approach was obviously that the hopes for the future would not materialize. He himself mentions a fellow-prisoner who dreamt that the war would end for him on a certain day, and as that day approached without any sign of liberation, he fell ill and died. 'My comrade F. died in the end,' comments Frankl, 'because his severe disappointment over the precisely awaited liberation suddenly lowered the resistance of his organism to a dormant typhus infection. His faith in the future and his will for the future faded away' (**Frankl**, 1977: 123). But even hopes invested in the period after liberation were often not fulfilled. Jewish survivors found themselves faced with the loss of their whole family, and former political prisoners, such as Jean Améry, were disappointed in their expectations of social change (cf. Schultz-Gerstein, 1978).

The real process of coming to terms with the camp, a process that put great demands on the individual, often began only at a time when physical survival as such was already assured. Numerous cases of suicide (only the most prominent of which became publicly known), and the widespread medical condition known as survivors' syndrome, allow no doubt that this is a major problem (cf. Niederland, 1980: 172f., 207) to which Frankl's theory is incapable of doing justice.[19]

Freedom is not an immutable space to be captured once and for all. It is a permanent process of more and more new liberations. (Jean Améry, *Hand an sich legen*)

For the former concentration camp prisoners, freedom was (and, as long as they are alive, still is) measured by success at reintegrating into 'normal' life. If we are to believe the expert psychiatric opinion (and there is no good reason not to), then reintegration has only very rarely, if ever, been a success. A study of a large group of survivors in the late 1950s concluded that 'not a single one ... has got over their time in the camps without suffering a permanent disorder' (cited in Niederland, 1980: 106). William Niederland, who escaped the persecution himself, devoted a large part of his professional career to the preparation of expert psychiatric evidence for reparation trials, in which he had to fight his colleagues' lack of understanding and empathy for the rights of survivors. His reports convey a picture of suffering that by no means ended with release from the camps; it was he, moreover, who coined the term 'survivors' syndrome'. This clinical picture, which he diagnosed as affecting every subject with varying intensity, has a number of other aspects in addition to the phenomenon of 'survivors' guilt'. But it is the feeling that one has unjustly escaped with one's life, that one did too little to save close relatives, which lies at the root of numerous psychological and physical symptoms from which survivors still suffer. In his studies, which were limited to Jewish victims, Niederland was able to show that Jews who spent only a short time in the camps – perhaps interned after *Kristallnacht* and released a few weeks later for immediate departure from the Reich – suffered from this syndrome as much as long-term prisoners did.[20] His explanation for this is that personality-altering influences already began with the discriminatory race laws, the ban on certain occupations, and the public branding of Jews – which is confirmed by Jean Améry's description of himself as having been 'a dead man on leave' from 1935 on (**Améry**, 1999: 86).[21] Jews who lived through the Third Reich in hiding were also exposed to a psychological strain which 'to some extent equalled that of the camps' (Niederland, 1980: 154).

It is true of all the survivors that they lived for a long time in the close proximity of death – an experience which left 'deep traces in the psyche' (Niederland, 1980: 232). Robert J. Lifton came to a similar conclusion in his study of the aftermath of Hiroshima; indeed the personality-altering effects of the experience of death were, in his view, so great that he defined them as characteristic of survivors *per se* (cited in Leiser, 1982: 80). As Jean Améry plausibly states in his essay on suicide, the familiarity with death acquired in these ways had effects which persisted in life after the camps.

Without wanting to offer an 'apology for self-murder', Améry draws on his own failed attempt in 1974 to set out the motives of the 'suicider' (to use his term) (Améry, 1986: 11). But he also has in mind the spectacular suicides of former concentration camp prisoners such as Tadeusz Borowski, Paul Celan and Peter Szondi, as well as many others who were not so well known. In an interview that he gave when *Hand an sich legen* was published, Améry described himself as having been suicidal since childhood. Yet he did not make a first attempt until he was tortured prior to internment in Auschwitz. In the camp, his predicament actually constituted a challenge to survive and warded off any thought of killing himself (cf. Schultz-Gerstein, 1978).

Améry – and in this he had the advantage over the great majority of his fellow-prisoners – was able to express himself articulately in autobiographical essays that revolved around the deformation of his psychological state. He describes his being a Jew *ex negativo* as being 'a Non-non-Jew' (**Améry**, 1999: 94). Towards the end of the 1960s, Améry broke with the German left-wing intelligentsia when he began to see their anti-Zionism as a cover for latent anti-Semitism (cf. Améry, 1971: 242–9; 1982b: 151–75), although, unlike his younger colleague Henryk M. Broder, he did not take this all the way and emigrate to Israel. (He only went there on a lecture trip, in 1976.) At a late date, Améry reflected on the 'murder of the mind' that had been inflicted on him, his exclusion from human society by the Nuremberg Laws, and his loss of confidence in the world as a result of torture (**Améry**, 1999: 82–101, 21–40). In his essay on suicide, however, it becomes clear that it was these very experiences which marked all his later thinking and contributed most to his sense of failure (for which he uses the French word *échec*). From then on, this *échec* dominated his life, which came to appear absurd and valueless – even 'unauthorized' (cf. Mayer, 1978). In 1966, not least under the influence of reading Frantz Fanon's defence of the Algerian Revolution, Améry still invoked the idea of regaining his dignity through the violence of revenge; in Auschwitz he had himself once struck a prisoner foreman in the face and luckily survived the consequences (**Améry**, 1999: 90f.) – an episode that long after filled him with satisfaction, although he often regretted not having done something more effective against his oppressors. Améry's call for retaliatory violence did not go undisputed among former concentration camp survivors. One of these, in the wake of Améry's suicide, was Primo Levi (who, like him, had done slave labour in the Buna factory operated by IG Farben within the framework of Auschwitz). In a partly self-protective attempt to escape 'the worst that he may already have felt inside himself' (Sebald, 1989), Levi countered Améry's call with a plea of his own for justice to be meted out to the guilty in proper courts of law (Levi, 1989: 109–11). What escapes Levi, however, is that in the late 1960s Améry resignedly gave up his wish for violence (cf. Améry, 1971: 221f; 1984). In camp or ghetto, Améry reflected, a Jew would have found himself completely alone in resisting violence; it would have meant certain death. Only by choosing to cause his own death, and by fixing the time himself, could he preserve some degree of sovereignty. This train of thought already anticipated the Améry of the essay on suicide, who is thus causally related to his self-understanding as a 'Non-non-Jew'. In any event, Améry's intellectualism was marked by a sense of failure and of the ultimate ineffectiveness of his resistance. With the help of words, he tried to achieve what he thought he had failed to do with his fist. The painter Lefeu, the protagonist of Améry's only novel, personifies this 'nay-saying'. He practises language as resistance: on the one hand, against the demolition of the house that contains his studio (and thus against eviction and a second homelessness – the first having been caused by the Nazis); on the other hand, against a success that he is unable to accept. 'Nay-saying', as Améry once called this self-refusal, 'is not so easy to express. It has to be lived' (Améry, 1982a: 108). But even Lefeu oscillates between resistance and resignation, neither carrying out his plan to set Paris alight as delayed compensation for his personal humiliation, nor in the end summoning the strength to commit suicide.

By 1971 at the latest, Améry seems to have been aware of the futility of his resistance through language, and there are already signs in his essays that he intended to turn his aggression against himself.[22] In 1973, when he added an explanatory afterword to his essay-novel *Lefeu* just before publication, he explicitly recognized the autobiographical features of the eponymous figure; more, 'the courage that the author did not possess was planted in the heart of his creation' (Améry, 1982a: 193). And yet the literary experiment showed that both the linguistic and the actual revolt were bound to fail because of the way the empirical world was constituted. This pessimism, which denied to individuals even power over their own lives, almost proved true for Améry. In 1974, perhaps affected by dismissive reviews of his only fictional work into which he had poured so much of himself (cf. Reich-Ranicki, 1974), he made an unsuccessful attempt at suicide. We know from Améry himself that, two years before his eventual suicide, he felt that *échec* was present within his success and led, even there, 'on a straight path to thoughts of suicide' (Améry, 1986: 146). This also sheds light on his fellow-writers Borowski and Celan, who saw a farewell to this world as the only way out of their mental suffering.[23] Their suicides are compelling evidence 'that even years of the most dedicated rational endeavour could do nothing against the deep marks' that death had left inside them (Sebald, 1989).

Former prisoners without literary ambitions also sometimes reflect in their reports on the process of coming to terms with their experience. Naturally, it is precisely from their written account that they hope to gain some psychical relief by giving a meaning to what they lived through. Religious believers are not the only ones among them who see some kind of eschatological significance; in some cases it is even contained in titles such as *Christus im Konzentrationslager*, by the Austrian priest Leonhard Steinwender, or *Teufel und Verdammte* (translated as *Devils and the Damned*), by the Social Democrat Benedikt Kautsky. Internment is often described as martyrdom, trial or penance, and the camp as purgatory or fate, although the use of 'shrine' for Dachau is rather exceptional (cf. **Lenz**, 1956: 396). Significantly, torture is especially prone to incorporation in a religious perspective. This, for example, is how Heinz Heger (a pseudonym) copes with the sight of a homosexual priest being violently mistreated:

> Suddenly the unimaginable happened, something that is still inexplicable to me and that I could only see as a miracle, the finger of God: From the overcast sky, a sudden ray of sunshine that illuminated the priest's blood-red face. Out of thousands of assembled prisoners, only him, and at the very moment when he was about to be beaten again.
> (**Heger**, 1980: 42f.)

The narrator is so taken by this scene, which evokes for him Jesus's baptism in the Jordan as well as the Passion, that he exaggerates the impact it had on his fellow-prisoners.

An interesting variation on the basic pattern is Ernst Wiechert's fusion of images of purgatory with the Teutonic Siegfried saga; his experiences in the camp, he writes, have both purified and 'toughened' him, made him 'invulnerable through the dragon's blood' (**Wiechert**, 1984: 150).

The ability of survivors to give a meaning to their time in the camps directly depended on whether they saw anything positive in it. More than on meaning, they therefore reflect on what kind of benefit, if any, the experience might have brought to their own life. One can gauge how important this was to them precisely from the intensity of their effort to uncover a positive side to it all. Most often, the period of internment is compared to a schooling in life, which made them catch up on things that formal education never offered. Thus, former prisoners repeatedly affirm that the situation in the camps could bring out a person's true character; Alfred Maleta even calls it 'an observation area for the study of human behaviour' (**Maleta**, 1981: 12). Many survivors claim that they got to know life by experiencing it at its harshest and would no longer be shattered by anything; that it had taught them self-discipline and detachment, or sharpened their feel for 'what is really important' in life.

What is described in the reports as a schooling in life is reminiscent of, but does not coincide with, what has been described elsewhere in this study as proto-political experience. This term of Peter Sloterdijk's always also has political action in mind, whereas the phenomena in question here are almost entirely limited to the personal domain.

Most of the concentration camp survivors were only much later, if ever, willing to speak of what happened to them there. Some understood, however, that a healing process could begin only if they consciously concerned themselves with the past – hence the interest in scientific analysis of the camp system, and the painful visits to particular sites. Alfred Haag even decided to make an active contribution to the Dachau memorial, although at first this cost him a real effort of will (cf. **Wenke**, 1980: 58f.). Hermann **Langbein** wrote not only a report on his internment in Dachau and Auschwitz (1982), but also several academic works on the camps (e.g. 1980a/b). Moreover, immediately after the liberation, he became heavily involved in the work of the International Auschwitz Committee and later acted as secretary of the 'Comité International des Camps'. Other survivors preferred a lower-profile form of mourning work; women in particular – for example, Ruth Elias and Grete Salus – found some fulfilment in the caring occupations. In recent years, many survivors have been making more direct attempts to come to terms with their experience, by reporting on it to groups of schoolchildren. In other cases, the decision to start a new life in Israel should not be seen as a mere escape reaction, since it often involves a conscious profession of Jewishness that was not present in the assimilationist diaspora in the years before the great persecution. After 1945, even Jews who did not emigrate to 'the land of their fathers' felt more closely associated with the community of Jews, if only, like Jean Améry, as being not non-Jewish.[24]

These latter ways of coming to terms with the concentration camps are independent of, and parallel to, attempts to achieve this through writing. But it cannot be emphasized enough that all these endeavours have been and still are in constant danger of failure – which in the end shows that no meaning given to an experience such as theirs can ever be guaranteed to last.

Notes

1. This period did, however, facilitate the rise of another genre which has become known as *Väterliteratur*, in which the children of former Nazi officials and fellow-travellers reflect about their fathers' past (typically in the wake of their death). See Briegleb (1992: 89–95).
2. Since the 1980s a new type of memoir, written by survivors who were interned as children or youngsters, has emerged. See the 'Epilogue'.
3. The record compiled by Helmut Peitsch, *Deutschlands Gedächtnis an seine dunkelste Zeit*, is limited to the first post-war accounts.
4. See *Encyclopedia Judaica*, vol. 5, Jerusalem: Keter Publishing House 1971, pp. 759ff.
5. H. G. Adler speaks of poetry in imprisonment as 'inner exile' (Adler, 1981: 18–28).
6. Reinhard Baumgart, 'Das Leben – Kein Traum? Vom Nutzen und Nachteil einer autobiographischen Literatur', in Herbert Heckmann (ed.), *Literatur aus dem Leben. Autobiographische Tendenzen in der deutschsprachigen Gegenwartsdichtung*, Munich/Vienna 1984, pp. 8–28; quoted in Mattenklott (1992: 171).

7. Alfred Schütz, *Der sinnhafte Aufbau der sozialen Welt. Eine Einleitung in die verstehende Soziologie*, Frankfurt/Main 1974.
8. On the way in which writing formally superimposes itself on memory, see Langer (1991).
9. Jurek Becker helped to make this phenomenon known in literature, through his novel *Jacob the Liar*.
10. For his film *Shoah*, Claude Lanzmann managed to find and interview the only two survivors from Chelmno (Lanzmann, 1985: vii).
11. Lanzmann's interviews with death camp survivors are therefore not representative for the Holocaust.
12. Arnold Gehlen, quoting Aristotle, understands experience as a function of memory (Gehlen, 1961: 27f.). Since completion of research for this book, interest in memory has increased.
13. Ruth Klüger was one of the few who had this experience, after her escape from a 'death march' (**Klüger**, 1992: 182–4).
14. See, for example, **Marum** (1988); **Matejka** (1983: 89–93).
15. The opinions of former prisoners are divided about the role of camp libraries in Nazi re-education (cf. Exenberger, 1992: 3f.).
16. Renata Laqueur names fourteen journals in her dissertation 'Writing in Defiance'.
17. According to Matejka, Karl Strobl was a Nazi even after 1945. However, his journal was attractive to internees because of the art pictures it contained.
18. Sebastian Winkler adds the names of Arnold Ulitz, Horst Wolfram Geißler, August Scholtis, Erich Landgrebe and Ernst Penzoldt (Winkler, 1986: 12f.). In some of these cases, however, it is doubtful whether the author should really be considered part of the internal emigration.
19. Consider, for example, the following:

    Well, I published my camp book over thirty years ago and I thought I'd worked the hell out of me. I'd had an analysis too, after the war. But in 1971, I had a kind of breakdown. I had symptoms identical to camp feelings: anxiety, fear, horror. One day I was crossing the road in Mill Hill and a tiny dog met me simultaneously from the other side. I went into panic. I didn't see a little pretty poodle I could have kicked all the way to the kerb. I saw a big dog of the kind they had in the camp, one of their horrible Alsatians, that was going to tear me in pieces. My heart was going like crazy even though I knew I was being ridiculous.

    ('Life after the Death Camps', *The Guardian*, 1 May 1989)
20. See, for example, the case of Dr U. (Niederland, 1980: 198–228).
21. This phrase had been used by other writers before Améry: for example, by Hans Sahl in his radio play in support of the American war effort in the 1940s, or by Austrian writer Milo Dor in 1952 as the title for the first novel in his trilogy (*Nichts als Erinnerung* followed in 1959, and *Die Weiße Stadt* in 1969). But the Marxist Eugen Leviné was perhaps the original source, in his famous trial speech in 1919 before his execution as head of the failed Bavarian Soviet Republic.
22. In 'Unmeisterliche Wanderjahre' he warns: 'If I don't know now I never will, for soon one who is no longer there will, for logically compelling reasons, no longer be able to know anything at all' (Améry, 1989: 30).

225

23. That this does not affect only former concentration camp prisoners, is shown by the suicide of the Swiss writer Hermann Burger, who also – in a reference to Améry – wrote a literary justification of his action beforehand (Burger, 1988).

24. See the collection of personal statements, *Mein Judentum* (1986).

6
Summary

The reports written by former concentration camp prisoners have previously been considered in literary studies, if at all, only as discrete objects. By traditional yardsticks, the literary value of most of them may be debatable, but within the autobiographical genre they hold a special place by virtue of their limited temporal span and their extremely unusual content. The present study has sought to demonstrate this through a detailed account of two, and selected quotation from the rest, of roughly 130 texts published in book form between 1934 and the late 1980s.

Given the special character of what the reports have to say, it was first necessary to clarify the prerequisites for the communication of the experience in question. Despite the psychological and social resistance they had to overcome, a surprisingly large (compared, say, with other pictorial or musical representations) number of witnesses without previous writing experience took up the pen over the years following their release.

It was shown, with reference to Fred Wander's *Der siebente Brunnen* and Albert Drach's *Unsentimentale Reise*, how two writers among the survivors do in fact take up existing genres such as the Hasidic tale or the travel novel, so that their personal experiences are presented within a familiar formal context and a certain tradition of reception, but at the same time also adapt these given elements to their own requirements. In most of the reports, where this adaptation is not as radical as one might expect, the conventional use of language threatens to blur the exceptional nature of the events. The struggle for adequate expression then often exhausts itself in awkward metaphors and undermines the cognitive achievement. This shortcoming, however, underlines not

227

only the linguistic and literary inexperience of most of the survivors, but also the crucial failure of language in the face of their unprecedented experiences. Flowery language may stem from a fear of having to remain silent. Whereas former internees often report the most horrific impressions with an almost astounding composure, they are critical of their own inability to cope with physical suffering. Ironical and self-ironical remarks on their part may best be seen, therefore, as an attempt to come to terms with experience through language.

As far as the personal experience of the authors is concerned, the telling of a story was bound up, both during and after the camp, with the hope that it would bring psychological relief. It is hence little surprise that the survivors' texts bear a certain resemblance to psychoanalytic records of conversations. After the liberation, however, the reports also came under a compulsion to bear witness; former victims wrote to give their voice to dead comrades, as a way of paying off their mortgage debt on survival. They accordingly stress the efforts they have made to be objective, in the belief that by keeping to the bare facts they can eliminate any subjective focus and best do justice to what they have lived through. This wish often fails, of course, because personal impressions can hardly be eliminated in the reporting of experience. For the reader, it is indeed the individual standpoint of the reports that conveys what things were like and makes it easier to grasp them.

Although the witnesses usually insist in a foreword that they have made every effort to be objective, they rarely, if ever, reflect upon the dichotomy of fictionality and non-fictionality in relation to their texts. Through a comparison between Bruno Apitz's fictionalization of personal experience in his best-selling *Naked among Wolves* and the survivors' reports of their personal experience, it is shown that the distinction lies not so much in the narrative methods *per se* as in the function they are allocated within the overall structure. In the novel these methods are subordinate to the aim of generating suspense through 'problematic style' (Staiger, 1983), whereas in most of the reports their effect is highly localized.

It is in their use of associations that the eye-witness reports are more akin to the fictional texts. For they too use set-piece references from literature or history to guide the reader's imagination, references which allow certain conclusions to be drawn about the author's socialization and reading habits. Precisely because only a tiny minority were professional writers, it is truly astonishing how many survivors produced written testimony about their period of internment in the camps. Not having the tricks of the trade, their texts afford a perfect example for the study of the rendering of personal experience in language – since what they display are more or less immediate reactions of individuals to their surrounding and nearby world. As in human experience in general, these reactions carry the stamp of remembered events in the past, although the exceptional character of what was happening in the camps naturally served to intensify the experience there.

The Holocaust did not create any writers. Indeed, in many cases it often blocked any attempt by survivors to come to terms with their experience by writing about it. The texts we have, though, despite all the resistances they had to overcome, give an unparalleled insight into the complexities of the narrativization of subjective experience.

Epilogue: the Holocaust seen through the eyes of children

Until recently survivors have employed traditional means for authentic representations of the Holocaust, but neither the dominant genre (the report) nor the choice of language has done justice to the radically new character of their remembered experience. Now, fifty or more years after the event, a new generation of memoirs has appeared in which survivors at the age of grandparenthood revisit their childhood experience of the concentration camps.[1] Meanwhile, a series of documentaries, Hollywood films (e.g., *Holocaust* or *Schindler's List*) and, of course, the camp reports themselves have imprinted themselves on many people's minds, helping to create a climate in which a book such as Daniel Goldhagen's *Hitler's Willing Executioners* (1996) could have the explosive impact that it did. It was not that Goldhagen adduced any new facts; rather, it was the way he expressed and interpreted them that caused the stir.

It may be argued that this is also true of some recent childhood-in-camp memoirs. Like the writers discussed in this book, the Viennese-born Ruth Klüger's *weiter leben* (1992) and Hungarian Imre Kertész's *Roman eines Schicksallosen* (1996) tell us the story of their own survival, but they do so in a way that forces the reader to look at the narrated events with new eyes. Perspective becomes a factor of the utmost importance, as the child's gaze allows us to see afresh that which we thought we already knew. In psychoanalytic theory the 'gaze' is associated with parental power, which the growing child internalizes but can never really meet.[2] Unlike the authoritarian gaze of the parent, the child's gaze is naive but accurate. The child's experience with adults in the camps does not invite internalization of the parental gaze.

When they remained together, children had to witness their parents' humiliation at the hands of their tormentors and their increasing regression to a childlike state (Bettelheim, 1979: 48–83). This could be a devastating experience, as Ruth Klüger remembers most painfully,[3] and even after their release it was often impossible to restore the children's confidence in an adult world felt to be powerless or alien. Since the camps had taught them that adults not only kill the under-aged but also threaten grown-ups, scepticism and mistrust came to overshadow the relationships into which they entered – as Kertész's voluntary self-incarceration shows in extreme form. Only when the lives of persecuted children were not in immediate danger did they identify with adults. Little Maciek in Louis Begley's *Wartime Lies*, for example, significantly identifies with the strong SS man rather than the tormented Jew. A vain battle with bedbugs

> provided, in addition to a temporary material improvement in our comfort, another war game … in this limited sphere, I could be a hunter and an aggressor, like SS units destroying partisans in the forest, very soon, rebellious Jews in the ghetto of Warsaw. The SS sometimes had to act in secret. So did we. Our landladies resented any mention of bedbugs on their premises. (**Begley**, 1992: 93–4)

Children and youngsters like Kertész were also impressed by the smart uniforms of the SS, and captivated by the position of power that they represented. The narrator in *Roman eines Schicksallosen* reports how relieved he was, on arriving at Auschwitz, to see the German soldiers: 'because they looked smart and clean, and were the only ones in this mess who seemed calm and firm' (**Kertész**, 1996: 91).[4] When he undergoes the infamous selection he feels immediate trust in the doctor, because of his pleasant appearance and likeable face (**Kertész**, 1996: 98). Claiming to be older than he actually is, the narrator is waved to the right. When he watches the doctor 'at work', he soon realizes the logic behind this exercise: the young, strong and able-bodied go to the right, while the older and frailer go to the left. The boy identifies with the selector to such an extent that he is annoyed when a man he does not regard as fit is sent to the right (**Kertész**, 1996: 100).

In their unprejudiced and uninformed attitude, children not only notice details that escape adults but interpret them in a way that makes them seem even more horrific. The child looks with the curiosity of the artist, with the burning eyes of the witness. Jehuda Bacon, for example, who was deported to Terezin at the age of 13 and transferred to Auschwitz a year later, writes: 'There I realized that – because I was a potential artist – I was seeing things very differently, perhaps more intensely. Even then I wanted to keep, I had to keep, everything before my eyes. This unconscious impulse: to keep, to remember. Why, I did not know' (Johr, 1997: 38). Often the child does not understand what he or she sees and, not yet being guided by adult logic, is able to interpret impressions more freely. The child's lack of understanding corresponds to the adult's inability to find words for common experiences in the camps. By emulating the child's situation, the adult narrator tries to overcome this predicament (Sokoloff, 1992: 15). In literary theory this limited insight of the child is known as a 'void' in the text, which serves as a pivotal point in the narration by triggering the productive imagination in the reader (cf. Iser, 1976: 228–45).

In addition to the problem of comprehension, there is the question of memory. It is a recognized fact that even adult survivors remember certain experiences better than others, and have forgotten some completely. Child protagonists not only witnessed the camps differently but also remember them differently. Thus, Kertész's narrator never departs from the perspective of the child, nor does he explain that with hindsight he knows better: '*Roman eines Schicksallosen* was not meant to contain a single sentence from beyond [the child's perception]. Only from the perspective of man's natural naiveté can it be told how Auschwitz was possible' (Radisch, 1997). Through this technique, Kertész draws his readers into the world of the novel and allows them no escape. It is only at the different level of the narrator's choice of incidents – some, like the selection at the ramp in Auschwitz, having archetypal status – that the greater insight of the adult becomes obvious. Here the child's perspective works both against and with the knowledge of the reader; the discrepancy between the two creates the charged atmosphere that gives the book its impact. We would not be so horrified at the boy's identification with the SS doctor if we did not already know what the selection entailed.

In *Roman eines Schicksallosen*, the narrator's abstention from qualifying the child's ideas, impressions and judgements thus becomes a literary stance, as further evidenced in the frequent use of such expressions as 'it was clear', 'of course' or 'I understood', which in semantic terms may be called 'supersigns'. Collectively, these constitute a meaning directly opposed to that which the narrator claims to attach to his experiences. The literariness of these supersigns becomes even more evident if we bear in mind that Kertész has translated into Hungarian the prose writings of the post-war Austrian writer Thomas Bernhard, one of whose hallmarks is recognized as the use of similar supersigns (cf. Kuhn, 1996). Kertész's consistent limitation of the narrator's point of view may thus be interpreted as a sign of literariness on his part.

Literariness was defined by the Russian Formalists as 'a function of the *differential* relations between one sort of discourse and another' (Eagleton, 1989: 5). It is the contrast of poetic language to practical language which makes for the status of a text as literature, and which involves what the Formalists called a technique of defamiliarization or estrangement (cf. Shklovsky, 1965: 3–24). In poetry, which Formalist analysis was originally designed to elucidate, defamiliarization makes familiar words look new, as it were, and thus noticeable. Similarly, a prose text is defined as an assemblage of devices that are seen by both author and reader against the background of a tradition of style and genre. Thus, for the reader, a genre arouses certain expectations. In everyday conversation these are usually fulfilled in order to permit the exchange of information. Literary discourse, on the other hand, frustrates these expectations, and the degree to which it does so has been taken as a measure of the literariness, and ultimately the quality, of a text. By analogy with the distinction between practical and poetic language in poetry, the Formalists distinguish between events and the reconstruction of events in prose: between the *fabula* and the *sujet*. 'The *sujet* creates a defamiliarizing effect on the *fabula*; the devices of the *sujet* are not designed as instruments for conveying the *fabula*, but are foregrounded at the expense of the *fabula*' (Jefferson, 1986: 31). This understanding also shapes the Formalists' attitude to reality: their preoccupation with literariness excludes mimesis; literature is taken to be non-referential; reality is one of the components of the work, not a referent (Jefferson, 1986: 26f.). This is obviously where the writers we have been considering differ in their texts. For them the creation of literariness is not an end in itself, but a means to cast fresh light on the suffering in the concentration camps.[5] Certain horrifying images, such as the piles of corpses filmed by Allied troops at the time of liberation, or the shoes, suitcases and other artefacts at the Auschwitz Museum, have lost some of their impact because we have grown used to them. Film-makers have noticed this saturation effect, and recent films about the camps make a point of avoiding such images.[6]

Defamiliarization in the Holocaust literature

Linked with the defamiliarizing quality of the child's perspective on the Holocaust is the presentation of questions hitherto deemed taboo. Violence, even that perpetrated by Jews, is now being presented for the first time, as are apathy and unwillingness to comprehend. The latent danger of slipping into a pornography of violence – of the kind present in John Sack's much-condemned journalistic account of Jewish revenge in *An Eye for an Eye* (1993) – is avoided, for instance, by Kertész's choice of narrative means and structure. Fifty years after liberation, Jewish guilt is also admitted by other survivors. Roman Frister, for example, who was a boy of about the same age as Kertész when he was deported, relates his survival as a success story, tainted only by the fact that he caused the death of a fellow-inmate by taking his cap after his own was stolen by a Kapo. (**Frister**, 1997). Whereas the child's perspective adopted by Kertész leaves no doubt as to who is to blame, even if his juvenile narrator seems to identify with his persecutors, Frister's traditional autobiographical approach invites the reader to absolve the narrator – which, in itself, implies an admission of guilt on his part. In other words, where Kertész presents, Frister argues and explains. And this makes for the different literary quality of the two books.

In Kertész, the simple-mindedness of the narrator's account of his camp experience causes the reader – perhaps for reasons of self-protection – to interpret it as ironic. Irony in *Roman eines Schicksallosen* is produced mainly through exaggeration, or through violation of the reader's expectations. The supersigns already mentioned are as much part of this mode of expression as is the narrator's frequent labelling of his perceptions as 'unimportant', when it always becomes clear in the end that they are important. To take another example, Kertész's use of the same adjective for totally different experiences serves to imply an equality between them. His deportation is judged 'curious', as is his first love just a few pages earlier. The youngster looks at all that happens to him with the same mood of detached wonderment. He looks at himself from without, so to speak, as he tries to understand; but he fails to put his isolated insights into relationship with one another and thus sees them only out of context. In this respect, Kertész is right to deny the ironic quality of his text. If the reader, like the narrator, agrees not to question the order of the concentration camp, passages such as the following can be read as non-ironic:

> So who actually benefits [from work in the camp]? – this, I remember, used to be the question asked by the 'expert'. I maintained that something was not right, that there was a mistake in the system, an omission, a failure. Any word, any sign, a flash of appreciation, just a spark once in a while – that would have helped me, at least. After all, if we think about it, what have we to blame ourselves for? And personal vanity still remains with us in captivity. Who, I thought, does not have a secret need for a little bit of kindness, for some understanding words to keep us going? (**Kertész**, 1996: 161)

The narrator does not question 'the system', but merely criticizes its shortcomings. He does not condemn the imposition of an inhuman workload in harsh weather, but complains about inadequate clothing as a 'source of discomfort' (*ibid*.: p. 184). Only once, when he says that he cannot be held responsible for his poor physical state, does he seem to attain some kind of insight (*ibid*.: p. 192).[7] Yet while the narrator thus identifies with the camp at the level of content, the mode of discourse tells a different story. A detached disagreement is expressed by interpolations such as the 'I thought' in the above example. The sentence structure, too, can sometimes relativize what has just been said:

> After a while, anyway, however slowly, reservedly and cautiously, I had to accept the fact that – so it seemed – such things were possible and thinkable; they might be more unfamiliar, and naturally more pleasant, but, if I thought about it, no more peculiar than all the other peculiarities which – it was a concentration camp, after all – were still possible and thinkable, this way as well as the other way around, of course. (**Kertész**, 1996: 228)

This single sentence alone contains at least four relativizing interpolations which not only emulate oral narration and the train of thought but signal that the reader should not take at face value everything that is being said. The lack of direct speech in Kertész's texts further supports this interpretation, since it is easier to incorporate such relativizing phrases into a report.

Ruth Klüger deploys yet another device when presenting herself as a child in Terezin, Auschwitz and Christianstadt (an auxiliary camp of Gross Rosen). Klüger, who is professor emeritus of German at the University of California at Irvine, discovered feminism in the 1960s, and it is with the eyes of a feminist that she views her childhood in the camps. This involves a critical assessment of her relationship with her mother, with whom she survived, and of the role of women in the Jewish religion ('I do not want to lay tables and light Shabbat candles, I want to say Kaddish' (**Klüger**, 1992: 23), as well as a controversial defence of the women among the camp orderlies.[8] Klüger does not rely on just one genre in her text, but amalgamates passages of report with her own poems and more essayistic sections. She, too, violates taboos – for example, when she criticizes her mother or denies the incomparability of Auschwitz. Her criticism is directed against a male-dominated Holocaust discourse.[9] What is relevant to our discussion is that Klüger, unlike Kertész, does not try to speak solely through the mind of the child but overlays the child's perspective with insights she has gained in adult life. Klüger, who has since the publication of her memoir established herself as a feminist critic,[10] managed to pick up the pieces after liberation and to lead a life seemingly untainted by her camp experience. Had it not been for a near-fatal road accident in Göttingen in November 1988, we would not have her account. For it was only during her slow recovery that she started writing about her childhood experiences.

All the devices discussed above violate our expectations as readers. When we dare imagine the fate of children in the camps, we anticipate sentimentality. When a child suffers, the reader sympathizes more readily. A tortured child mobilizes our instincts to protect, to care for, to save. It is thus easier to make a strong statement when showing the impact which the persecution of the Jews, or the experience of war and internment, had upon children. Steven Spielberg occasionally utilizes this characteristic in *Schindler's List*: at one point, for example, he picks out a little girl in a red coat from the grey mass of rounded-up Jews, so that the child's innocence makes the brutality of the Nazi regime not only more obvious but also more irrational. The emotive representation, however, detracts from the fact that the child's suffering is not intrinsically different from the adult's; indeed, it seems to suggest that the latter is somehow less unjustified. But where the child is presented as naively identifying with the persecutor, as in the example from Kertész's novel, the reader reacts with repulsion and feels irritated at the lack of opportunity for pity and sentimental identification. We should hardly be surprised, therefore, that the publication history of *Roman eines Schicksallosen* has been full of ups and downs. At first no Hungarian publisher would touch it, and it was only in 1975 – two years after completion – that it finally came out. Then another twenty years passed before its translation into German, when the book's sudden impact finally put Kertész's name on the literary map.[11]

If one thing unites these books on childhood in the camps, however, it is an absence of sentimentality. It is as if the authors could not afford self-pity, as if they needed to protect their psychological balance by spelling out even the most horrific experiences in ironic detachment, whether through detailed description or with the qualification of a theoretical framework. Thus, there may be personal as well as narratological reasons for the survivor-narrator to adopt a defamiliarizing mode of representation. A famous exception to this is Elie Wiesel's account in *Night* (1958), but he was one of the very few survivors who successfully turned their experience into an actual novel.

Imagined camp memoir

While even Wiesel employs the fictionalizing mode of narrative to produce an authentic account of his memories,[12] in 1995 a book appeared which was later unmasked as only posing as memoir. *Bruchstücke*, written by the Swiss Binjamin Wilkomirski, published by the renowned German publishing house Suhrkamp, hailed by survivors and Jewish organizations as one of the most intriguing camp memoirs to date, quickly translated into several languages (including English as *Fragments*), showered with literary prizes (from the *Jewish Quarterly*, among others)[13] was discovered in 1998 to be a fiction. Wilkomirski is accused of fabricating not only his very early childhood memories but even his Polish-Jewish identity. It is claimed that the book was written under the influence of psychotherapy specially developed to help child survivors,[14] and that its enthusiastic initial reception should be explained by this feature. In harrowing detail and with images that sometimes shock, Wilkomirski (re)constructs his early years through the estranging gaze of the child. But one example of his presentation of fiction as fact is an episode often quoted by reviewers in which the two- or three-year-old comes across a rat in a dead woman's body. The child – the narrator points out – knows that the belly of a pregnant woman swells. He has also heard that it begins to move just before the baby is born. When the boy witnesses this happening to an obviously dead woman, he is fascinated to see a rat eventually emerge. The childish mind cannot but conclude: 'I saw it, I saw it! the dead women are giving birth to rats!' (Wilkomirski, 1996: 86). He is horrified, but not so much at the event as at its implications. If what he has just seen is true, then mothers bear not only children but also the worst enemies of their offspring. (Wilkomirski relates how rats bit young children during the night, inflicting wounds which, in the circumstances of the camp, meant certain death.) Remembering the sight of his dying mother whom he had been able to visit a short time before, he wonders about his own identity: 'I touch my legs again and again. I undo the rags around my calves and feel the skin. Is it skin or do I actually have grey fur? Am I a rat or a human? I am a child – but am I a human child or a rat child, or can you be both at once?' (Wilkomirski, 1996: 86–7). Not for nothing does Wilkomirski temporarily abandon the child's perspective in the next passage: he needs to emphasize the authenticity of the horrific event by stressing its lasting effect on the adult narrator. When his own son was born, he claims, the unexpected sight of hair on the emerging head brought back the painful uncertainty about his own identity.

What Wilkomirski narrates here in this sensational fashion accords well – irrespective of its autobiographical authenticity – with the experience of alienation attested by many survivors. While psychologists describe this feeling as an internalization of the camp code – Viktor Frankl calls it the 'deformation which follows a sudden release of pressure' (**Frankl**, 1977: 146) – Jean

Améry interprets the 'deformation' as an experiential advantage that survivors have over ordinary people (Améry, 1980). Yet how is it possible that a certain Bruno Doessekker (Wilkomirski's former name) not only assumed the deformation caused by the camps to such an extent that it became his own 'real' identity, but, more important, that for over three years he could bluff even the informed public? In my view, this is due not only to guilt feelings among his readership but also to the narrative persuasiveness which the text displays despite a number of questionable details. The mode of experience of the small child, fragmentarily remembered and uncompromisingly narrated, once again moves the facts – so well known that they are easily disregarded – into a brightly illuminated field of attention. Although, as we now know, the text is not really autobiographical, it cannot be denied a literary authenticity. Wilkomirski, for whatever reason, broke the 'autobiographical pact' (Lejeune, 1975), yet the literariness of his book ensures that it will last.[15]

Wilkomirski's most striking narrative strategy, his thematic use of tenses, enables him to give the story a certain depth that makes it more convincing. Some of the nineteen short sections, all typified by their title, show the following pattern in the use of tenses: a short introduction in the imperfect sets the scene. Remarks such as 'I don't remember how it came about ... ' confirm the form of the memoir from the point of view of the narrating self, as does the following sentence in the present perfect (the tense mainly used in German for oral narration): 'My memory has only preserved the end of the journey and even that incompletely, confusing and in broken images, difficult to put in order, too many pieces are missing.' Without any warning, these remarks are then followed by present-tense narration of those fragments which have (supposedly) engraved themselves in Wilkomirski's memory. The scene unfolds in short and excited main clauses: by chance, and probably thanks to the child's small size, he survives the gassing in a van. The subsequent events are then again summarized in the imperfect. What is the point of switching in this way between the tenses? The imperfect, characteristically for a memoir, points to something that happened in the past. As to the present tense, the situation is less clear: the historical present does not seem to apply, since the narrator stresses the vagueness of his memory. Only the atmosphere is fresh in his mind – and also, we may assume, his emotional reaction to the event. Its surprisingly durative presentation, however, belongs to the realm of the imagination. The implication of the present tense for the (informed) reader can thus only be: 'This is how it could have happened' – which, of course, signifies fiction, as it does in certain modernist texts. However, Wilkomirski's deployment of the present tense does not fictionalize in the same way that Max Frisch's use of it does in his famous novel *Mein Name sei Gantenbein* (Petersen, 1993: 21–30). Wilkomirski, with his narrator, (re)constructs his own story out of the fragments of his (imagined) memory. Thus the present tense has not so much a temporal function in *Bruchstücke* as a constructive function: it facilitates the presentation. It creates the identity of 'Binjamin Wilkomirski'. In devising a quasi-autobiographical narrative situation and authenticating it through the skilful employment of narrative means, Wilkomirski assimilates his text to the concentration camp novel without exactly writing one himself. Predictably, neo-Nazis and deniers of the Holocaust were quick to utilize this text as proof of their own 'theories'. But the absolute singularity of Wilkomirski's case (it is hard to imagine its repetition, as he identifies with the first-person narrator to such an extent that he, no doubt, *believes* it was he himself who experienced what is being related) would seem to be strong evidence to the contrary. Rather, it is the narratological persuasiveness of the text which validates the use of the child's perspective in the authentic memoir.

Notes

1. On the role of grandparents in discourse about the Shoah, see *Spuren der Verfolgung. Seelische Auswirkungen des Holocaust auf die Opfer und ihre Kinder*, ed. by Gertrud Hardtmann (Gerlingen: Bleicher, 1992).
2. Laura Mulvey developed this idea from a feminist point of view in 'Visual pleasure and narrative cinema', in L. Mulvey, *Visual and Other Pleasures* (London: Macmillan, 1989), pp. 14–29. The term is actually borrowed from the theory of non-verbal communication: see, e.g., Michael Argyle, *Bodily Communication*, 2nd ed. (London: Routledge, 1988), pp. 161, 164.
3. See my essay ' "Ich wollte, es wäre ein Roman"; Ruth Klüger's feminist survival report', *2000* (forthcoming).
4. In this epilogue, all quotations referenced only to the German edition have been translated by myself [AR].
5. In contrast to Sokoloff, who mentions the defamiliarizing effect of the child's perspective only in passing (Sokoloff, 1992: 26, 35, 109), my point is that these

authors (all of whom relate personal experience) chose it precisely for that effect.

6. Consider, for example, Thomas Mitscherlich's *Reisen ins Leben* (1996) and Wilhelm Rösing's trilogy on Jewish exiles (*Ernst Federn*, 1992; *Hans Keilson*, 1996; *Thomas Geve*, 1997).

7. It is true that, soon after his arrival in Auschwitz, the narrator realized the extent of the mass killings and the deception employed to keep them running smoothly. (See Barbara Bauer, 'Jüdische Identitätsprobleme und ein Strukturgesetz der Holocaust-Memoiren. Ein Unterrichtsvorschlag für die Sekundarstufe II', *Der Deutschunterricht* 4/1997, pp. 5–19.) This insight remains isolated, however, and does not cause him to question his internment as such.

8. For a critique of Klüger's feminist stance, see Eva Lezzi, '*weiter leben*. Ein deutsches Buch einer Jüdin.', *Frauen in der Literaturwissenschaft: Rundbrief: Ethnizität*, No. 49 (December 1996), pp. 14–20.

9. See my 'Ich wollte, es wäre ein Roman'.

10. See, e.g., Ruth Klüger, *Frauen lesen anders: Essays* (Munich: Deutscher Taschenbuchverlag, 1996).

11. See ' "Das 20. Jahrhundert ist eine ständige Hinrichtungsmaschine": Imre Kertész im Gespräch mit Gerhard Moser', *Literatur und Kritik: Sprache und Verbrechen*, 313/314 (April 1997), pp. 44–9. In comparison, it took only four years for Frister's Hebrew novel to be published in German translation.

12. See the discussion of Bruno Apitz's *Nackt unter Wölfen*, in Chapter 4.

13. See Lappin (1999).

14. See Jörg Lau, 'Ein fast perfekter Schmerz. Die Affäre um Binjamin Wilkomirski zieht weite Kreise: Darf man Erinnerungen an den Holocaust erfinden?' *Die Zeit* 39, 17 September 1998; also Elitsur Bernstein/Binjamin Wilkomirski, 'Die Identitätsprobleme bei Überlebenden Kindern des Holocaust. Ein Konzept zur interdisziplinären Kooperation zwischen Therapeuten und Historiken', *Werkblatt. Zeitschrift für Psychoanalyse und Gesellschaftskritik* 39 (1997), pp. 45–57.

15. See my paper 'Memorialization and Authenticity: The case of Binjamin Wilkomirski', delivered at the conference *Memory of Catastrophe* (Southampton, April 2000).

Southampton
May 2000

Notes on the concentration camp authors

The varying length of these biographical notes reflects less the importance of the authors in question than the availability of information about them; sometimes it was not even possible to find the date of their birth or death. The internment and concentration camps to which each was deported are given in brackets after the name or the dates of the person's life.

Abraham, Max: (Oranienburg, Börgermoor, Lichtenburg)
Rabbi, arrested in 1934 in revenge for the alleged assassination of an SS man by another rabbi.

Adam, Walter: b. 1885 (1938–43 Dachau, Flossenbürg)
Austrian journalist; report written in April 1945.

Adelsberger, Lucie: (Auschwitz)
Jewish doctor; report written in 1946.

Adler, Hans G.: b. Prague, 1910, d. London, 1988 (Theresienstadt, Auschwitz)
Studied musicology and literature in Prague. Unsuccessful attempt to emigrate in 1938; married Gertrud Klepetar in 1941, was deported with her in 1942 to Theresienstadt. Transferred to Auschwitz, 1944. Freed in 1945 as sole surviving member of his family. Worked at the Jewish Museum in Prague, 1945–47; emigrated to Britain in 1947; married Bettina Gross. In addition to historical studies of Theresienstadt, he wrote fictional works on

the basis of his experience: e.g. *Panorama. Roman in zehn Bildern* (1968).

Aichinger, Ilse: b. Vienna, 1921
Father 'Aryan', mother Jewish. Survived Nazi period in Vienna. Studied medicine. Teaching assistant, later staff member at the Academy of Art and Design in Ulm. Married Günter Eich in 1953; has again lived in Vienna since 1989.

Altmann, Erich: (Auschwitz, Buchenwald, Oranienburg)
Jewish. Army volunteer in WWI. Arrested in France and deported to Auschwitz in November 1943; forced labour as fitter for Siemens; wrote report in Lyons, 1945.

Améry, Jean: born in Vienna, 1912, as Hanns Meier, d. Salzburg, 1978 (Auschwitz, Bergen-Belsen)
Childhood in Bad Ischl; literary and philosophical studies in Vienna, contacts with Vienna Circle, influenced by Moritz Schlick and Rudolf Carnap. Left Jewish community in 1933, rejoined in 1937. Escaped with wife to Antwerp in 1938–39, arrested in 1940 as 'enemy alien' and interned at Gurs, escaped from Gurs and returned to Brussels, arrested there in 1943 for distributing anti-SS leaflets, processed at Breendonk camp near Antwerp, tortured, sent to Auschwitz in January 1944 (No. 172364), clerk at IG Farben's Buna factory in Monowitz; January 1945 march to Gleiwitz II and Mittelbau (Buchenwald), and in April to Bergen-Belsen. Returned to Belgium after Liberation; essays on political and literary themes for Dutch and Swiss journals; later talks etc. for South German and West German Radio; in 1955 took pen name Jean Améry; in February 1964 met Helmut Heißenbüttel, who encouraged him to write autobiographical essays; in 1974 attempted suicide, in 1976 lecture trip to Israel, in 1978 suicide in Salzburg.

Andreas-Friedrich, Ruth: b. 1901, d. 1977
Training in social work, book trade. Worked as freelance journalist for women's magazines and books on 'applied psychology'. After the war, joint editor of first weekly edition of *sie*. Wartime journal, first published in USA as *Berlin Underground*, describes support and resistance work for the 'Emil' group between 1938 and 1945 in Berlin.

Antelme, Robert: (Buchenwald)
Arrested as French resistance fighter in 1944, deported to Gandersheim outcamp at Buchenwald.

Apitz, Bruno: b. 1900, d. 1979 (Buchenwald)
Punch cutter, Socialist working-class youth movement, arrested in 1917 for anti-war propaganda, again disciplined in 1919 for taking part in a strike. Joined KPD in 1927, began literary activity; member of League of Proletarian-Revolutionary Writers, 1930–33; briefly detained by Nazis in 1933, rearrested in 1934, imprisoned for 32 months in Waldheim, then eight years in Buchenwald. After 1945, *inter alia*, editor and manager of the Leipzig State Theatre, then film scriptwriter at DEFA. From 1955 freelance writer in Berlin.

Arthofer, Leopold: (Dachau)
Austrian priest, interned for writing articles hostile to Nazi regime.

Auernheimer, Raoul: b. Vienna, 1876, d. Oakland, California, 1948 (Dachau)
Son of a merchant, cousin of Theodor Herzl; studied law in Vienna; theatre and arts critic, editor of conservative *Neue Freie Presse* in Vienna, correspondent for *Baseler Zeitung*; deported to Dachau in 1938, released after intervention by Swiss writer Emil Ludwig, escaped to New York. Works include *Mondäne Silhouetten* (1910), *Das Kapital* (1923), *Casanova in Wien* (1924), *Die linke und die rechte Hand* (1927), *Wien. Bild und Schicksal* (1938).

Bakels, Floris: b. s'Gravenhage/The Hague, 1915 (Bergen-Belsen, Dachau)
Studied law in Leiden; 1938 Dr. juris, 1939–42 lawyer in Rotterdam, April 1942 arrested by security police, deported to Bergen-Belsen, liberated April 1945 in Dachau; 1946–80 worked in publishing; translated Winston Churchill's *The Second World War*; articles in journals, books; report based on notebooks kept in the camps.

Ballmann, Hans: (Dachau)
Political prisoner, arrested by Gestapo in 1935, accused of high treason, deported to Dachau in 1944.

Bartozewski, Wladyslaw: (Auschwitz)
Interned as member of Polish intelligentsia, seven months in
Auschwitz: September 1940 to April 1941. After release, member
of Polish Home Army and resistance movement in Warsaw; in
1963 honoured as a 'just man' by Yad Vashem for his help to
persecuted Jews; Polish Ambassador to Austria; honorary citizenship of Israel, 1992.

Beckert, Werner: (Buchenwald)
Report written in 1945.

Befford, Albert: (Buchenwald)
Survived the camp as librarian.

Begley, Louis: b. Poland 1933
Survived Nazi regime in hiding; 1952–58 studied law and lit-
erature at Harvard; lawyer since 1959; 1993 President of the
American PEN Center.

Begov, Lucie: b. Vienna (Auschwitz)
Born into academic/merchant Jewish family, educated in Vienna
and Budapest; early literary activity; escaped from Nazis to Dal-
matia; arrested and deported to Auschwitz-Birkenau; report
written in 1945–46.

Beimler, Hans: (Dachau)
Communist deputy in Reichstag and KPD leader in Southern
Bavaria; arrested in the 'hunt for Communists' following Nazi
takeover on 11 April 1933; escaped from Dachau after four
weeks.

Berke, Hans: (Buchenwald)
Austrian political prisoner.

Bettelheim, Bruno: b. Vienna, 1903, d. Maryland, USA, 1990
(Dachau, Buchenwald)
Austrian-Jewish psychologist; released from Buchenwald in 1939
after intervention by Eleanor Roosevelt; emigrated to USA; professor and child/youth therapist in Chicago. After his death, the
methods used in his work with children and the institutions he
founded came under heavy criticism.

Billinger, Karl (real name Paul Massig): b. 1920, d. 1979 Tübingen (Oranienburg)
Joined KPD in 1927, political prisoner, emigrated to USA in 1934, returned to Germany in 1937; worked for KPD, ordered to Moscow, broke with Party, interned in USSR. Allowed to leave in 1938, member of the Institute of Social Research from 1941.

Bleton, Pierre: b. France 1924 (Neue Bremm, Buchenwald, Porta, Dora)
Son of a bank manager, studied law and political science. Contacts with Resistance, arrested in 1943, deported to Germany in 1943 via Neue Bremm and Buchenwald to Porta Westfalica, and in 1945 to the Dora camp.

Bonhoeffer, Dietrich: b. 1901, d. 1945 (Flossenbürg)
Son of a psychiatrist, studied theology, 1930 lecturer in Berlin, 1934 dismissed for entering Confessional Church; leader of Preachers Seminar outlawed by the Nazis, contacts with churches abroad. In 1940 forbidden to teach, preach and publish; arrested in 1943 for 'undermining military strength', murdered in Flossenbürg on 9 April 1945.

Bornstein, Ernst Israel:
Member of Polish-German intelligentsia, interned at age of 19, wrote report in 1956 at his professor's suggestion.

Borowski, Tadeusz: b. Ukraine, 1922, d. 1951 (Auschwitz, Dachau)
From 1933 in Poland as building worker; student of Polish studies at Warsaw's underground university, arrested in February 1943, deported to Auschwitz. Liberated from Dachau, published verse in German after the war in Munich; 1946 editor in Warsaw, 1949–50 correspondent in Berlin, 1951 committed suicide.

Bredel, Willi: b. Hamburg 1902, d. 1964 (Hamburg-Fuhlsbüttel)
Joined KPD in 1919, sentenced to two years' imprisonment in 1923 for participation in October Revolt; interned again in 1929; after release in 1933 fled via Prague to Soviet Union; together with Brecht and Feuchtwanger edited *Das Wort* in Moscow (1936–39); returned to Germany in 1945; 1962 President of Academy of the Arts in East Berlin.

Bresler, Jakob: b. 1928 (Auschwitz)
Polish Jew, emigrated to USA after Liberation, film producer in Los Angeles.

Bruha, Antonia: b. Vienna, 1915 (Ravensbrück)
From 1934 member of the Revolutionary Socialists and a group of Vienna Czechs. Arrested October 1941, deported to Ravensbrück in 1942, liberated in 1945; report written soon after release, deposited at the Dokumentationsarchiv des österreichischen Widerstands in Vienna in 1979.

Buber-Neumann, Margarete: b. Potsdam, 1901, d. 1989 (GULAG, Ravensbrück)
Joined Community Youth League in 1921, KPD in 1926. Married Rafael Buber, divorced, second marriage to Heinz Neumann, a KPD leader who opposed Stalin in 1931 over policy in Germany; lived with him until his arrest in Moscow 1937; deported to Siberia 1938; handed over to Gestapo in 1940 along with 500 other prisoners as a result of Stalin–Hitler Pact. Interned in Ravensbrück, befriended Milena Jesenká (Kafka's friend) there; travelled widely in 1946–49, then a political publicist in Frankfurt-am-Main.

Buchmann, Erika: b. 1902 (Gotteszell, Lichtenburg, Ravensbrück)
Secretary. Interned in Gotteszell camp 1933–34, and again in 1939 in Ravensbrück via Lichtenburg; block elder; 1950 guest delegate to Third Congress of East German SED in 1950; 1952–56 member of KPD Secretariat; 1952–53 member of Baden-Württemberg constitutional assembly.

Carlebach, Emil: b. 1913 (Buchenwald)
Stalinist article in *Frankfurter Rundschau* witch-hunting Margarete Buber-Neumann; sentenced to a month's imprisonment for slander.

Castle-Stanford, Julian (born Julius Schloß):
1908 joined family firm Leonhard Tietz AG, Cologne; 1920 appointed board member; 1937 emigrated to Amsterdam; 1942–45 lived in hiding in the Netherlands.

De Martini, Emil: b. 1902 (Auschwitz)
Journalist, writer, socialist; emigrated 1933, interned after return
from 1940 to 1943; from 1945 freelance writer; report written in
1945.

Deutschkron, Inge: b. Finsterwalde near Cottbus, 1922
Daughter of SPD functionary and teacher, who emigrated to
England without family; racially persecuted. Later lived with
mother in hiding in Berlin; after war, secretary at the People's
Education Office in Berlin; from 1955 journalist in Western
Germany, 1958 correspondent (from 1960 main German corre-
spondent) for Israeli paper *Maariv*. In 1966 acquired Israeli
citizenship; editor at *Maariv* in Tel Aviv since 1972.

Dietmar, Udo: (Natzweiler, Buchenwald)
Deported from Cologne via Natzweiler to Buchenwald; first Kapo
assistant, then full Kapo; assigned to an outside detachment until
liberation in 1945.

Drach, Albert: b. Vienna, 1902, d. 1995 (Rives Altes)
Graduated in law in 1926, continued training at father's practice
in Vienna until Anschluss. Emigrated to France in 1938, interned,
then lived in hiding; resumed legal practice in Vienna in 1948;
writer, 1988 Büchner Prize, 1993 Grillparzer Prize.

Drexel, Joseph: b. Munich 1896, d. 1976 (Mauthausen)
Arrested in 1937 for association with Ernst Niekisch Resistance
Circle, sentenced to three and a half years in 1939 for 'preparing
to commit high treason', expelled from Bavaria at end of sentence;
arrested again after 20 July 1944, deported to Mauthausen; after
war, publicist, founder and joint proprietor of *Nürnberger
Nachrichten*; wrote report in 1945.

Edel, Peter: b. Berlin 1921 (Großbeeren, Auschwitz, Sachsenhausen, Mauthausen, Ebensee)
Mother German 'Aryan', father Jewish; grandson of Edmund Edel,
caricaturist and art critic; trained as painter and graphic designer;
interned in Auschwitz for leafleting; assigned to 'Bernhard Cor-
poration' (= special money-counterfeiting detachment in

Auschwitz); after liberation from Ebensee, spent two years in Bad Ischl and moved towards Communism as a reaction against antisemitism. Journalist for the *Weltbühne*; moved from West to East Berlin at height of Cold War; won Heinrich Heine Prize in 1961.

The account of his camp experiences in *Wenn es ans Leben geht* takes up three chapters (nearly whole of vol. 2) of his two-part autobiography. Had already dealt with the subject in the 1969 novel *Die Bilder des Zeugen Schattenmann*, filmed in 1972.

Edvardson, Cordelia: b. Munich 1929 (Theresienstadt, Auschwitz)
Writer. Until 1943 lived in Berlin with mother, Elisabeth Langgässer. At age of 14, deported to Theresienstadt and Auschwitz; after liberation emigrated to Sweden and worked as journalist; moved to Jerusalem during 1974 Yom Kippur War.

Eisenkraft, Clara: (Theresienstadt)
Converted Jew.

Elias, Ruth: b. Mährisch-Ostrau 1922 (Theresienstadt, Auschwitz, Taucha)
Denounced in 1942 and deported to Theresienstadt, where married first husband; 1943–44 Auschwitz; gives birth to baby, whom she kills so that they will not both be gassed; 1944–45 Taucha labour camp (outside Buchenwald); meets her second husband there; after liberation in 1945 returns to Czechoslovakia, in 1949 emigrates to Israel.

Engelmann, Bernt: b. Berlin 1921 (Flossenbürg, Hersbruck, Dachau)
Son of publisher. School-leaving Abitur in 1938, joined Luftwaffe, spent time in military hospital, studied in 1942 and worked at economic news agency; arrested 1944 as member of resistance group, deported to Flossenbürg, liberated in 1945 from Dachau; studies, from 1949 journalist (including 7 years at *Der Spiegel*). Since 1962 freelance writer, from 1977 to 1984 chairman of German Writers' Association (VS), from 1972 to 1984 member of presidium of PEN Centre in West Germany; resigned as VS

chairman in 1984 after stormy protests at his political leadership.

Fénelon, Fania (pseud.): b. 1922, d. Paris 1983 (Auschwitz, Bergen-Belsen)
Daughter of Jewish merchant. Music academy in Paris; arrested May 1943 by Gestapo as resistance fighter; deported January 1944 to Auschwitz; liberated 1945 from Bergen-Belsen; *chanson* singer in Paris; 1966 lecturer in East Berlin; later returned to France; wrote report in 1973–75, based on camp notebooks; filmed after a script by Arthur Miller.

Förmann, Jängi: (Gross-Rosen)

Frank, Anne: b. 1929, d. 1945 (Bergen-Belsen)
Daughter of Frankfurt merchant, escaped to Amsterdam, lived underground, denounced in August 1944, deported to Bergen-Belsen, where she died with mother and sister; father survived; kept diary in Dutch from age of 13.

Frankl, Viktor E.: b. 1905, d. 1997 (Auschwitz)
Studied medicine, deported to Auschwitz 1942; after liberation, Professor of Neurology and Psychiatry at Vienna University; founder of logotherapy; professor at various US universities; president of Austrian Doctors' Association for Psychotherapy; wrote report in 1945.

Freund, Julius: (Buchenwald)
Arrested in 1938 for political reasons, deported to Buchenwald, released in 1939; wrote report in 1939.

Friedenthal, Richard: b. Munich 1896, d. 1979 (internment camp, Isle of Man)
Son of university professor, youth in Berlin, studied history of literature, philosophy and art history; freelance writer until emigrated to England in 1938; editor and publisher; 1945–50 publisher and editor of *Neue Rundschau*; publishing director until 1955, then lived in Munich until his death. Publications: *Goethe, Luther, Karl Marx*.

Frister, Roman: b. Poland 1928
Survived several concentration camps in Poland; after the war worked as journalist until arrested by Communist government. In 1957 emigrated to Israel, worked for Ha'aretz, and in 1990 became director of Koteret training college for journalists in Tel Aviv.

Fritz, Mali: b. 1912, d. 1996 (Auschwitz-Birkenau, Ravens-brück)
Grew up in poor Jewish family in Vienna. Student, joined Communist Party, from 1935 politically active in England and France, arrested and interned in France in 1941. Escaped in mid-1942, denounced, sent to Vienna, nine months in prison, then in summer 1943 to Auschwitz, Ravensbrück, liberated in 1945, walked back to Austria.

Glas-Larsson, Margareta: b. Vienna 1911 (Theresienstadt, Auschwitz)
Gestapo prison in Prague-Karlsplatz, deported to Little Fortress at Theresienstadt, then to Auschwitz-Birkenau.

Goldschmidt, Arthur: (Theresienstadt)
Converted Jew.

Gollwitzer, Helmut: b. Pappenheim, Bavaria 1908 (Russian prison camp)
Studied theology and philosophy, 1932 vicar in Munich and castle preacher in Austria, responsibilities for new generation of Confessional Church theologians, doctorate in 1937, replaced Martin Niemöller in Berlin-Dahlem community after latter's arrest, lecturer at then-outlawed College of Confessional Church in Berlin, expelled from Berlin in 1940 and forbidden to speak in public, drafted into Wehrmacht, 1945–49 internment in Russia, 1950–57 Professor of Systematic Theology in Bonn, since then at Free University, Berlin.

Gostner, Erwin: (Dachau, Mauthausen, Gusen)
Son of South Tirolean parents in Innsbruck; father died in WWI in Russia; convinced Catholic, member of 'Reichsbund Hall' Catholic student fraternity; as member of political department of Tirol Security Office, had successes against 'illegal' National

Socialists; arrested in March 1938 by Tirolean SA members and deported to Dachau, then Mauthausen and Gusen; released at mother's instigation; drafted into Wehrmacht in December 1940, excused service at front as only son of war widow; after the war, again worked for Security Office but resigned after a year on health grounds; since then, private detective and journalist in Innsbruck; wrote report in 1945.

Grand, Anselm J.: (Dachau, Oranienburg, Sachsenhausen)
Austrian composer, painter and writer.

Graumann, Samuel: (Buchenwald, Auschwitz, Theresienstadt)
Viennese Jew. Lost wife and children in Holocaust; wrote report in 1947.

Gross, Karl Adolf: b. 1892, d. 1952 (Sachsenhausen, Dachau)
Studied philology and theology. Theologian, then publisher of Protestant literature, director of *Der Freie* publishing house. Arrested in 1939 for disseminating writings of Martin Niemöller and Otto Dibelius, held by Gestapo at Berlin-Alexanderplatz, then Sachsenhausen concentration camp, September 1940 Dachau, 1944 in office of Allach labour camp, which gave him the opportunity to keep a journal. Since 1946 editor of *Neubau* magazine and director of Neubau publishing house in Munich/Berlin.

Haag, Lina: b. 1907 (Gotteszell, Lichtenburg)
Daughter of working-class couple. Social worker, 1929–31 nanny in Argentina, 1933–37 in prisons and Gotteszell and Lichtenburg camps, from 1940 physiotherapist; in 1931 married KPD regional deputy Alfred Haag (b. 1904), and was able to free him from camp by personally approaching Heinrich Himmler; wrote report in 1940.

Hart, Kitty: b. 1927 as Kitty Felix in Biesko (Auschwitz)
Escaped with family in 1938, first to Lublin, then failed to get through to Russian-occupied sector of Poland; father separated from mother and daughter, who joined a Polish labour transport to the Reich with false papers. Denounced and deported to Auschwitz from 1942 to November 1943; liberated in 1945 from Salzwedel concentration camp. Emigrated to Britain in 1946,

trained as X-ray assistant, married *émigré* Ralph Hart, two sons. Now lives in Birmingham.

Heger, Heinz (pseud.): b. 1917 (Sachsenhausen, Flossenbürg) Student. Interned in 1939 as a homosexual.

Heilers, Margarete B.:
In 1934 married a Jew, but got divorced under pressure of Nazi racial laws. Husband deported to Theresienstadt and then via Auschwitz to Dachau, where he was murdered in January 1945.

Heilig, Bruno: b. Lower Austria 1888, d. Berlin 1968 (Dachau, Buchenwald, Isle of Man internment camp)
Studied law, soldier in WWI, 1920–23 foreign politics editor of Budapest daily *Pesti Napló*, and from 1920 wrote for the Berlin *Vossische Zeitung*. In 1928, expelled from Hungary because of his critical reporting. Worked in Berlin until 1931 at Ullstein Verlag, and then as foreign correspondent for the *Wiener Tag* and the *Prager Presse*. Returned to Vienna in 1933, where he wrote for the *Wiener Tag* until 1934. Until 1935 edited the Jewish paper *Die Stimme*, as well as writing for *Der Morgen*. Late 1937 became correspondent for the London *Jewish Chronicle*. In 1938 deported to Dachau, then Buchenwald, as part of purge of Austria's anti-Nazi intellectuals; released in 1939 after intervention by his wife. The *Jewish Chronicle* helped him to enter Britain and gave him initial financial support. Interned as an 'enemy alien' from July to September 1940 on the Isle of Man.

Heilig worked in Austrian Communist exile associations, such as Austria (of) Tomorrow and the Free Austrian Movement, and was a signatory of the 'Declaration of Austrian Associations in Great Britain'.

From June 1944 he wrote leaflets and other material for the psychological warfare operations of the Supreme Headquarters of Allied Expeditionary Forces (SHAEF). From the end of the war until summer 1946 worked for DANA news agency, and until April 1947 processed archive material for the Nuremberg trials. Then moved to Berlin, finally settling in the Eastern sector and joining the SED. In 1952 was forced for political reasons to leave the paper *Deutschlands Stimme* (on which he had been working as a main editor). Then worked until his death as a freelance writer and translator.

Herrmann, Simon Heinrich: (Bergen-Belsen)

Hildesheimer, Wolfgang: b. Hamburg 1916, d. Poschiavo/
Graubünden, Switzerland 1991
Childhood mainly in Hamburg and Berlin; in 1933 emigrated with
parents to England, and in December 1933 to Palestine; studied
carpentry in Jerusalem, trained in furniture and interior design;
travelled to England in 1937, staying for a time in Cornwall;
returned to Palestine in 1939; English teacher and later information officer at the Public Information Office of the British
government in Jerusalem; in 1946 a second stay in Cornwall;
1946–49 simultaneous translator at the war crimes trials in Nuremberg, and from 1948 editor of the complete trial records. First
works as a writer in 1950, first book in 1952; moved to Poschiavo
in 1957. Resumed work in 1960s as painter and graphic designer;
deliberately gave up production of primary literature in 1983.
Works include: *Tynset* (1965), *Masante* (1973), *Mozart* (1977),
Marbot (1981), *Mitteilungen an Max über den Stand der Dinge und
anderes* (1981), and *Das Ende der Fiktion* (1984).

Hiller, Kurt: b. Berlin 1885, d. Hamburg 1972 (Brandenburg,
Oranienburg)
In 1912 published expressionist anthology *Kondor*, in 1916–24
worked on *Das Ziel*. Collaborated with various periodicals, incl.
Weltbühne; in 1926–33 president of the Group of Revolutionary
Pacifists; interned in concentration camp 1933–34, then emi-
grated to Prague, London (1938) and finally back to West
Germany (1955).

Hilsenrath, Edgar: b. Leipzig 1922 (Mogilyov-Podolski ghetto)
Born into family of Jewish merchants. In 1938 escaped with
mother and younger brother to Romania, in 1941 deported to the
Mogilyov-Podolski ghetto. Emigrated to Israel in 1945 and to
USA in 1951. Now lives as freelance writer in Berlin.

Hindls, Arnold: (Theresienstadt)
Deported at beginning of 1940s from Brno to Theresienstadt, then
to the Piaski ghetto and via Sobibor to the Osowo labour camp;
wrote report after retirement.

Hinrichs, Klaus (real name August Wittfogel): b. Woltersdorf/ Hanover 1896, d. New York 1988 (Moorlager Papenburg)
Joined USPD in 1918 and its part-successor KPD two years later; studied in Leipzig, Berlin and Frankfurt-am-Main, published on bourgeois sciences and society, later on Sinology; in 1925 joined the Frankfurt School, from 1931 worked with *Die Linkskurve*. Interned in 1933 at the marshland camp in Papenburg, emigrated to England in 1934, then to USA. In 1939 finally broke with Communist Party because of his experiences in China; became a radical anti-communist.

Hochhäuser, Abraham: (various labour camps: Fünfeichen, Gross-Rosen, Buchenwald, Büsingen)
Denounced in 1934 and imprisoned for nine weeks. In 1936 escaped from Breslau to Free City of Danzig, and in 1938 to Poland. Sent in October 1940 on a transport out of Sosnowiec (from whose ghetto his family was deported in 1943 to Auschwitz) to work for German war industry at the Brande forced labour camp; transferred in winter 1941 to camps at Tarnowitz and Markstädt, in November 1943 to Fünfeichen, January 1945 to Gross-Rosen, March 1945 to Buchenwald and Büsingen, and April 1945 to Allach, from where he was liberated.

Hornung, Walter (real name Julius Zerfops): (Dachau)
Political prisoner.

Hurdes, Felix: b. Bruneck, South Tirol 1901, d. 1974 (Dachau, Mauthausen)
Studied law and political science in Vienna. 1936–38 member of Carinthian regional government, 1938–39 nine months in Dachau, 1939–44 legal adviser, late 1944 to end of war imprisoned by Gestapo in Vienna, then Mauthausen; 1945–51 General Secretary of Austrian People's Party; 1945–52 Education Minister, 1953–59 chairman of the National Assembly.

Jursa, Hermine: b. Vienna 1912 (two years in prison, then Ravensbrück)
Orphaned at early age; factory worker. From 1936 in Communist resistance, arrested in 1939, deported in 1941. Now lives in Vienna.

Kalischer, Ben-Zwi: (Sachsenhausen)
Persecuted for racial reasons.

Kalmár, Rudolf: b. 1900, d. 1974 (Dachau, Flossenbürg)
Until 1938 editor-in-chief of *Wiener Tag*; Austrian political prisoner, deported in 1938 to Dachau, 1939 Flossenbürg, then back to Dachau.

Katz, William: (Buchenwald)
Interned 1939 in Buchenwald, in aftermath of *Kristallnacht*. Subsequently emigrated to Australia.

Kautsky, Benedikt: b. Stuttgart 1894, d. Vienna 1960 (Buchenwald)
Son of Socialist theoretician Karl Kautsky. After WWI secretary to Austrian Socialist leader Otto Bauer, and until 1938 economic adviser to Vienna Chamber of Labour. Arrested in 1938 for anti-Nazi activity and on racial grounds, although these were ignored during his imprisonment; mother murdered in Auschwitz. Interned in Buchenwald until liberation. Member of Graz Chamber of Labour, and deputy director of Creditanstalt in Vienna. Played a major role in drafting Socialist Party programme in 1958.

Kertész, Imre: b. Budapest 1929 (Auschwitz, Buchenwald)
Deported to Auschwitz in 1944 and Buchenwald in 1945; after liberation returned to Budapest; translator of Nietzsche, Freud, Hofmannsthal, Canetti, Wittgenstein and Thomas Bernhard; other works: *Kaddisch für ein ungeborenes Kind* (1989), *Galeerentagebuch* (1992).

Kielar, Wieslaw: b. Przeworsk, Poland 1919 (Auschwitz)
Political prisoner, interned in Auschwitz in May 1940. After liberation, spent a year in Germany then returned to Poland. A freelance writer in Wroclaw.

Klieger, Bernhard: (Auschwitz)
Belgian journalist.

Klüger, Ruth: b. Vienna 1931 (Theresienstadt, Auschwitz, Christianstadt)
Deported with mother and grandmother to Theresienstadt (September 1942 to May 1944), then to Auschwitz (summer 1944), transferred to Christianstadt (a subsidiary camp of Gross-Rosen); escaped from death march in February 1945; after the war studied philosophy and history at University of Regensburg where she met Martin Walser; emigrated with her mother to USA in October 1947; 1947–50 Hunter College, New York; 1951 married a historian, had two sons; studied German language at Berkley, PhD in 1967; 1965–94 teaching jobs at various American universities; retired Professor of German Literature at University of California, Irvine; 1988–90 director of the Californian student centre at Göttingen; began to write her camp testimony while recovering from collision with a cyclist in Göttingen.

Kogon, Eugen: b. Munich 1903, d. 1988 (Buchenwald)
Attended Benedictine school, came under the influence of Othmar Spann in the 1920s. Arrested by the Nazis after the Austrian Anschluss; spent six years in the camps. From 1945 co-publisher of the *Frankfurter Hefte*, founder member of Christian Democratic Union; 1951–69 Professor of Politics at the Darmstadt Technical College. His sociological study *Der SS-Staat*, which already appeared in winter 1945, was based on a report that he wrote for the Allied 'Psychological Warfare Division'.

Kommleitner, Erwin: (Ennsland concentration camp)

König, Joel (real name Ezra Ben Gershôm): b. Würzburg 1922 (in hiding in Berlin)
Son of a rabbi. Escaped in 1943 via Hungary to Palestine. Studied biochemistry in Jerusalem. 1953–60 worked on scientific projects at various universities in Britain, USA and the Netherlands; since 1960 head of the biochemical laboratory at a children's hospital in Rotterdam. Camp report written in 1944–45, first published in 1967 with the title *Den Netzen entronnen* [Escaping the Nets]; filmed in 1979 as *David*, with Peter Lilienthal.

Kopp, Guido: (Dachau, Buchenwald)
Austrian political prisoner. Survived two years of the 'Bunker' in Dachau (1937–39); interned in Buchenwald from April 1940.

Krasovec, Marianne: b. 1911 (Ravensbrück, Eberswalde)
Born into a mining family in Styria. In domestic service from the age of 14. Arrested in August 1944 and deported for supporting the partisans in the Leoben region.

Kruk, Hermann: b. Ploz 1897, d. Klooga, Estonia 1944 (Vilna ghetto, Klooga concentration camp)
Son of a bookkeeper. Was 17 when his father died. Joined Communist Party of Poland in 1918, left in 1920, entered the 'General Jewish Workers' Bund of Lithuania, Poland and Russia'. 1920–39 cultural work in Warsaw; ran various libraries, including the 'Grosser Bibliothek'. September/October 1939 escaped to Vilna; September 1941 in Vilna ghetto, where he helped build the YIVO Library and Museum. Sketches of everyday life in the ghetto 1941–43; deported to Klooga 1943–44, murdered on 18 September 1944.

Kupfer-Koberwitz, Edgar: b. Koberwitz, Silesia 1906 (Dachau)
Journalist and travel guide; pacifist and conscientious objector; arrested in 1940 on the Brenner Pass for political reasons and interned in Dachau; after release, emigrated to USA.

Langbein, Hermann: b. Vienna 1912, d. Vienna 1995 (Dachau, Auschwitz, Neuengamme)
1938 member of International Brigades in Spain, then interned in French camps; deported in 1941 to Dachau, in 1942 to Auschwitz, where he was a leading member of the International Resistance Organization; from 1944 to end of war in Neuengamme. In 1958 broke with Austrian Communist Party over its support for Soviet intervention in Hungary; General Secretary of the International Auschwitz Committee, later Secretary of the 'Comité International des Camps'; lived in Vienna until his death. Wrote report between autumn 1947 and spring 1948.

Langhoff, Wolfgang: b. Berlin 1901, d. 1966 (Börgermoor, Lichtenburg)
Merchant's son. At 18 actor in Königsberg, Hamburg, Berlin, Düsseldorf; 1928 joined KPD, 1933 arrested; spent 13 months in prison and concentration camps; 1934 emigrated to Switzerland – performed at the Zurich Theatre; member of the Freies Deutschland movement. Returned to Germany in 1945; artistic director of

Düsseldorf municipal theatre until 1946, and until 1963 of the Deutsches Theater and the Kammerspiele Berlin; vice-president of the German Academy of Arts. Report first published in 1935 in Switzerland, 1945 in Germany; since printed in numerous editions and translations.

Laqueur, Renata: b. 1919 (Bergen-Belsen)
Daughter of a university professor and pharmacologist in the Netherlands; arrested with husband in November 1943, deported to Westerbork and in March 1944 to Bergen-Belsen. After liberation, emigrated to USA. Studied literature, wrote dissertation on concentration camp diaries, worked at a cancer research institute in New York. Journal published in three parts: March to December 1944; winter 1944–45 (written later); and train journey (written 1945–46).

Leeuwen, Evelien: b. 1928 (Bergen-Belsen)
Arrested in October 1942, released, then deported in April 1943 with mother via Vught to Westerbork, and in February 1944 to Bergen-Belsen. Lives in The Hague. Translator of German literature, especially Christa Wolf, Jurek Becker, Peter O. Chotjewitz.

Leibbrand, Robert: b. 1901, d. 1963 (Dachau, Buchenwald)
Son of a tram worker. Specialist cabinet-maker. Joined KPD in 1919, secretary of various districts from 1922, member of Central Committee, Politburo and Comintern Executive between 1923 and 1929; editor at the 'Verlag für Literatur und Politik' from 1930 to 1932. Arrested in February 1933 in Brunswick as strike leader, kept in preventive detention until 1935, then in Dachau until June 1939, rearrested in September 1939, sent to Buchenwald, where he was a member of the International Camp Committee. 1946–50 Communist fraction leader in Württemberg-Baden regional parliament; 1949–50 Bundestag deputy; resettled in GDR, where he was active as teacher in Party schools. From 1956 deputy head of the history department of the SED's Marxism-Leninism Institute.

Lenz, Johann Maria: b. 1902, d. 1985 (Dachau)
Austrian priest.

Levi, Primo: b. Turin 1919, d. Turin 1989 (Auschwitz)
Son of Jewish parents; doctorate in chemistry in 1941. In September 1943 escaped from German troops to Val d'Aosta, where he founded a partisan group affiliated to the 'Giustizia e Libertà' underground movement. Arrested in December 1943 and deported to Auschwitz. Liberated by the Russians in 1945, spent several more months as an internee in various camps in Belorussia and Ukraine before repatriation in October 1945. Chemist, then freelance writer in Turin. Committed suicide in 1989.

Lévy-Haas, Hanna: b. Sarajevo 1914 (Bergen-Belsen)
Studied Romance languages and literature in Belgrade and the Sorbonne; came in contact with Marxist circles; 1938–41 schoolteacher, then banned as a Jew; took part in partisan struggle in Montenegro; arrested by Gestapo in February 1944 and deported to Bergen-Belsen; returned to Yugoslavia in August 1945. Emigrated to Israel in late 1948, active in Communist Party and feminist movement.

Lingens-Reiner, Ella: b. Vienna 1908 with Serbian citizenship (Dachau, Auschwitz)
Studied law and medicine, involved in Social Democratic organizations. Arrested in 1942 in Vienna and deported in February 1943 to Auschwitz, 1944 to Dachau. After liberation, returned to Austria and retired in 1973 as assistant head of government department.

Loidl, Franz: b. 1905, d. 1987 (Ebensee concentration camp)

Lundholm, Anja: b. Düsseldorf 1918 (Ravensbrück)
Jewish mother. Active in Italian underground until arrest in 1944. Deported to Ravensbrück. After the war, translator and publicist. Since 1953 a Swedish citizen, living as a writer in Frankfurt-am-Main.

Maleta, Alfred: b. 1906, d. 1990 (Dachau, Flossenbürg)
Legal expert, leader of the Fatherland Front in Upper Austria. As such, arrested in 1938 and deported on the third and last Austrian transport to Dachau. After 1945 deputy in National Assembly and national representative of the Austrian Workers and Employees

Federation; 1962–70 chairman of the National Assembly, until 1975 deputy chairman.

Marcuse, Bruno: b. 1878 (Theresienstadt)
Deported in January 1944 to Theresienstadt.

Marum, Ludwig: b. Frankenthal 1882, d. 1934 (Kislau)
Son of a lower-middle-class Jewish merchants' family. Studied law and practised in Karlsruhe; SPD local politician; 1918–19 Justice Minister in the Baden government; 1928 elected to the Reichstag. Deported to Kislau in May 1933, and murdered there in March 1934.

Matejka, Viktor: b. Vienna 1901, d. Vienna 1993 (Dachau, Flossenbürg)
Doctorate in history in Vienna, cultural work in the People's College, active in the European peace movement. April 1938 deported on the first Austrian transport to Dachau, released in July 1944, in hiding in Vienna until the Liberation. 1945–49 Communist city councillor responsible for culture and popular education, involved in establishing the Vienna Cultural Fund. Made efforts to secure return of artists driven out of Austria. Lived in Vienna until his death.

Meier, Heinrich Christian: (Neuengamme)

Mendel, Hersch: b. Warsaw 1893, d. Israel 1968
Worker in Warsaw. Joined the Bund in 1911, self-taught especially in Social Democratic and Communist texts. Arrested in 1912 for leaflet distribution, sent to Pawiak prison; released in 1913. Travelled to Paris (1913), Russia (1917) and back to Warsaw (1919). Joined Communist Party in 1919, and its Revolutionary-Military Committee in 1920. Arrested in 1933 in Vienna, returned to Warsaw in 1936.

Müller, Charlotte: b. Berlin-Wedding 1901 (Ravensbrück)
Daughter of a committed Social Democrat. Apprenticeship in plumbing; later an office clerk. Joined Communist Party in 1928. Escaped in 1934 to Netherlands, arrested in Brussels in October 1940, deported to Ravensbrück in April 1942. After liberation,

returned to Berlin: magistrate's work in Wedding district, later on the central executive of Volkssolidarität and the Volkspolizei.

Müller, Filip: b. 1902? (Auschwitz, Mauthausen, Gusen)
Deported in 1942 from Slovakia to Auschwitz; transferred in January 1945 to Mauthausen, then to Gusen, where he was liberated.

Naor, Simha (née Stella Silberstein): b. Vienna 1899 (Auschwitz, Bergen-Belsen)
Studied art, chemistry and physiotherapy in Vienna. After the Anschluss, escaped through Italy to France, where she went into hiding during German occupation. Escaped, arrested by Gestapo, deported in 1944 to Auschwitz-Birkenau, transferred to Bergen-Belsen in January 1945. Emigrated to Palestine in 1946, private physiotherapy practice until 1967, then USA from 1967 to 1979, then to Haifa.

Neumann, Siegfried: b. Grandenz 1895 (Oranienburg)
1914–18 serviceman in war; then lawyer in Berlin. Emigrated in 1939, was living in Israel when his report came out in 1976.

Paepcke, Lotte:
Studied law, but prevented from finishing on 'race grounds'. Survived the Third Reich as 'Aryan-related' Jewess. A journalist after the war.

Pawlak, Zacheusz: (Majdanek)
Arrested by the Gestapo in 1941 for involvement in Resistance. Deported in January 1943 to Majdanek. Liberated in Bavaria in May 1945.

Pintus, Liesel: (Theresienstadt)

Poller, Walter: b. 1900 (Buchenwald)
Son of a moulder and later chief of police. Joined SPD youth organization and worked on the Party's *Kieler Arbeiterzeitung*. Called up during WWI. In 1919 chief editor in Hamm. Arrested in 1934 after denunciation for leaflet production. Imprisoned from 1935 to 1938; Buchenwald 1938–40. Released in 1940 at his son's

instigation. 1945 Political Secretary of the SPD regional organization in Hamburg; 1948 editor-in-chief of the *Westfälische
Rundschau* in Dortmund.

Riemer, Hermann: (Sachsenhausen, Natzweiler, Dachau)
Sculptor. Interned in various camps from 1940 to 1945.

Röder, Karl: b. Nuremberg 1911, d. 1987 (Dachau, Flossenbürg)
Metal craftsman; interned from 1933 to 1945. Produced the camp
gate in Dachau with the slogan '*Arbeit macht frei*'. After liberation,
worked in municipal offices of Viktor Matejka. Writer, later
managing director of Universal-Film, lived in Vienna until his
death.

Rohme, Reiner (real name August Ponschab): (Soviet prison
camp)
German diplomat; eight years in Soviet camp after 1945.

Rost, Nico: b. Groningen 1898, d. 1967 (Dachau)
Journalist, critic, essayist, translator, joined resistance movement
after German occupation of the Netherlands, arrested by Nazis,
interned in various camps, from 1944 to liberation in Dachau.

Rousset, David: (Buchenwald, Neuengamme)

Rovan, Joseph: b. Munich 1918 (Dachau)
Studied German language and literature, politics and law in
Vienna, Berlin and Paris. Emigrated to France in 1933, was
involved in the Resistance. Deported in 1944 from Compiègne to
Dachau. After 1945 political adviser to Minister Edmond Moche-
let, member of French High Commission in Germany, and of
French TV Programming Commission. Worked continually for *Le
Monde* and was a correspondent for Bavarian Radio and the
Mannheimer Morgen; 1968–86 Professor of German History and
Politics at the Sorbonne, chairman of the 'Bureau International de
Liaison et de Documentation' of the Society for German-French
Cooperation.

Rozanski, Zenon: (Auschwitz)
Survived the punishment battalion.

Sachs, Nelly: b. Berlin 1891, d. Stockholm 1970
Daughter of industrialist. From 1900 privately educated on health grounds, 1903–08 at Aubert ladies' college; from 1907 corresponded with Selma Lagerlöf, on whose recommendation she emigrated with her mother in 1940 to Sweden. In 1960 met Paul Celan in Paris; had a nervous breakdown after her return to Stockholm; in 1967 was made honorary citizen of the City of Berlin.

Salus, Grete: b. Böhmisch-Trübau (now Česká Třebová) 1910 (Theresienstadt, Auschwitz, Oederan)
Deported in 1942 with husband to Theresienstadt, and in 1944 to Auschwitz, where her husband, a doctor, was selected for gas chamber after helping a fellow-prisoner. Sent a few weeks later to Oederan labour camp, liberated in Theresienstadt; emigrated in 1949 to Israel, worked for 15 years as choreographer and physiotherapist.

Scheuer, Lisa: b. Böhmisch-Leipa (now Česká Lípa) (Theresienstadt, Auschwitz, Freiberg, Mauthausen)
Deported in January 1944 to Theresienstadt, sent 'voluntarily' to Auschwitz in September 1944, assigned from November 1944 to forced labour in Freiberg arms factory, 'evacuated' in February 1945, liberated in May from Mauthausen. Returned to Prague, left in 1968 after Warsaw Pact occupation, now lives in Cologne.

Scheurenberg, Klaus: b. 1925 (Theresienstadt)
Kept journal in Theresienstadt.

Schifko-Pugnartnik, Manfred: (Mauthausen, Dachau)
Political prisoner, deported in 1938, released in 1943.

Schmidt-Fels, Lucia: (Ravensbrück)
Worked as journalist after 1945; now lives in France. Report written in 1945, published 35 years later at friends' urging.

Schneeweiss, Josef: (Gurs, Dachau)
Doctor, fought in Spain, political prisoner, deported in 1942 to Dachau.

Scholten, Gerhard: b. Trautenau 1923 (Little Fortress at Theresienstadt, Auschwitz)
Son of Sudeten German industrialist; arrested in Prague in July 1944 'on racial grounds' and because of a letter to his father in the USA intercepted by the Gestapo. Deported to Theresienstadt, and in September 1944 to Auschwitz. After liberation, returned to Prague but was arrested again after someone denounced him as a former SS man; released after four months. Officer in UNRRA, escaped from Prague to Austria before Communist takeover; now lives in Vienna.

Schramm, Hanna: (Gurs)
Political prisoner.

Schupack, Joseph: b. 1923 (Majdanek, Auschwitz, Dora, Bergen-Belsen)
Deported in 1940 to Majdanek, then to Auschwitz; forced labour at Buna-Monowitz, 'evacuated' in January 1944, sent to work in Dora-Nordhausen on V-1 and V-2 rockets, liberated in April 1945 from Bergen-Belsen. Lost entire family in Holocaust. Now lives in Germany.

Schuschnigg, Kurt von: (Sachsenhausen)
Former Austrian prime minister, interned from March 1938 to October 1939; wrote report between summer 1938 and summer 1940.

Schweinburg, Erich: b. Vienna 1890, d. Vermont, USA 1959 (Dachau)
Son of an architect-builder; became lawyer, poet and fiction writer. Arrested in November 1938 on account of his writing and deported to Dachau; released in early 1939 after intervention by relatives and friends; emigrated to England, and in late August to USA, where he finally resumed legal practice. Report finished shortly before his death.

Schwerin, Alfred: (Dachau)
Deported in aftermath of *Kristallnacht*; escaped from Germany to Switzerland.

Seger, Gerhart: b. Leipzig 1896, d. New York 1967 (Oranienburg)
SPD Reichstag deputy; 1923–28 General Secretary of German Peace Movement; arrested in March 1933, deported to Oranienburg, escaped in December 1933 to Czechoslovakia; from March 1934 lecture trips to Britain (which helped him secure his wife's and daughter's release from Nazi clutches) and to the United States.

Selbmann, Fritz: b. 1900 (Sachsenhausen, Flossenbürg)
Political prisoner, deported in May 1940.

Semprún, Jorge: b. Madrid 1923 (Buchenwald)
Escaped in wake of Spanish Civil War to France, took part in Resistance, deported in 1943 to Buchenwald. Later writer, politician and, *inter alia*, Spanish minister of culture. Report written 16 years after liberation.

Senger, Valentin: b. Frankfurt-am-Main 1918

Sherman, Hilde: b. 1923 (Riga ghetto, Hamburg-Fuhlsbüttel)
Born into Orthodox Jewish family. Deported in 1941 to Riga, where his family was murdered. Transferred in 1944 to Hamburg-Fuhlsbüttel. Escaped in April 1945 to Sweden.

Siegelberg, Mark: (Dachau, Buchenwald)
Austrian Jew, arrested in 1938, escaped to Shanghai in 1939. Report written in 1939.

Spies, Gerty: b. Trier 1897, d. Munich 1997 (Theresienstadt)
Youth in Trier, deported in July 1942 to Theresienstadt. After liberation, returned to Munich and was active in social matters and literature.

Spritzer, Jenny: b. Vienna 1909? (Auschwitz)
Moved with family in 1910 from Vienna to Berlin; middle-class schooling, ladies' college, business school; shorthand typist. Married in 1931. Was in Rotterdam with husband until 1933, and they stayed in the Netherlands after Hitler's seizure of power in

Germany. Deported in 1940 to Auschwitz. Now lives in Switzerland.

Starke, Käthe: (Theresienstadt)
Survived the camp as librarian.

Steinbock, Johann: b. 1909 (Dachau)
Austrian churchman.

Steinwender, Leonhard: (Buchenwald, Dachau)
Austrian churchman and journalist; interned from November 1938 to November 1940.

Sternberg-Newman, Judith: b. Breslau 1920 (Auschwitz)
Deported in 1942 to Auschwitz, worked there as nurse; only survivor in her family; married Senek Newman in camp, emigrated to USA in 1947, obtained State Examination Registered Nurse's Certificate in 1948.

Stojka, Ceija: b. Kraubath, Styria 1933 (Auschwitz, Ravensbrück, Bergen-Belsen)
Born into a travelling Roma family. Deported in 1941 to Auschwitz. After return, was a travelling market stallholder in Vienna and surrounding area. Lives in Vienna.

Sturm, Hanna: b. Klingenbach, Burgenland 1891, d. 1984 (Lichtenburg, Ravensbrück)
Born into a family of poor Croatian artisans. Factory worker; from 1909 trade unionist, from 1933 active in Communist resistance; repeated imprisonment; arrested by Nazis in 1938 and interned in Lichtenburg until May 1939, then in Ravensbrück until liberation. After war, was key witness in several war crimes trials; survived assassination attempt in 1946.

Sydow, Rolf von: b. Wiesbaden 1924 (racially persecuted)
School-leaving Abitur in 1942, then war service; 1944–47 Canadian prisoner-of-war, subsequently actor and assistant director; 1961–72 independent director for TV, film and theatre; 1973–77 head of TV drama for Südwestfunk in Baden-Baden; 1977–79 head of TV drama and entertainment for Saarländischer Rundfunk in Saarbrücken, then independent director, author and producer.

ten Boom, Corrie: (Scheveningen, Vught, Ravensbrück)
Watchmaker in Haarlem, interned at an age over 50 for pro-Jewish activity based on her Christian beliefs, released in winter 1944, returned to the Netherlands.

Thälmann, Ernst: b. Hamburg 1886, d. Buchenwald 1944 (Gestapo prison, Buchenwald)
Son of a coachman. Joined USPD in 1918, elected to Hamburg City Parliament 1919, chairman of Hamburg KPD and city councillor 1921; unemployed because of political activity, survived bomb assassination attempt in 1922; deputy chairman of KPD 1924, elected to Reichstag from Hamburg, nominated as KPD candidate for presidential elections in 1925, chairman of KPD 1925–33. Arrested in Berlin in March 1933, held in various prisons, murdered in Buchenwald in 1944.

Utiz, Emil: (Theresienstadt)
Austrian psychologist.

Utsch, Bert: (Oranienburg, Sachsenhausen)
Author, screen-writer, librarian, committed Christian, political prisoner.

Vermehren, Isa: b. 1918 (Ravensbrück, Buchenwald, Dachau)
Her father was a lawyer, mother journalist at the *Berliner Tagblatt*. Cabaret performer in Werner Fink's Berliner Ensemble, opera singer, converted to Catholicism in 1938, did tours of the Front in WWII. From 1944 to 1945 was interned for family connections in the 'prominent persons block' in Ravensbrück, Buchenwald and Dachau. After 1945 trained as teacher of English and German. Studied theology in 1948, joined Order of the Sacred Heart of Jesus. From 1970 to 1983 teacher at a Catholic school in Hamburg.

Walletner, Hugo: (Flossenbürg)
Painter in Vienna.

Wandel, Fritz: (Dachau)
Political prisoner.

Wander, Fred: b. Vienna 1917 (Buchenwald, Auschwitz)
Son of a Jewish sales representative; escaped to France in 1938;

interned in 1939, deported to Auschwitz and Buchenwald. After war, a photographer and reporter in Vienna, freelance writer, moved to GDR in 1958 with his wife Maxie Wander. Since 1982 has lived again in Vienna.

Weglein, Resi: b. 1894, d. 1977 (Theresienstadt)
Daughter of a fashion and clothing manufacturer in Ulm; her two sons emigrated to England in 1938; deported with husband to Theresienstadt, where she survived as a nurse. Returned to Ulm in 1945.

Weinstock, Rolf: (Dachau, Gurs-Drancy, Auschwitz, Jawischowitz, Buchenwald)
Arrested and interned in 1938 in wake of *Kristallnacht*; released in 1939, rearrested in 1940.

Weiss, Peter: b. near Berlin 1916, d. Stockholm 1982.
Emigrated with parents in 1934 via Prague to London; moved in 1939 via Switzerland to Sweden; from 1945 a Swedish citizen. 1947–52 first phase of literary work (prose poems, prose and plays); 1952–60 success in experimental and documentary film-making; 1960 first work published in Germany; remained a resident of Stockholm until death. Works include: *Marat/Sade* (1964), *The Investigation* (1965), *Rapporte* (1968), *Rapporte 2* (1971), *Die Ästhetik des Widerstands* (1975–81), *Leavetaking* (1983).

Weiss-Rüthel, Arnold: b. 1899, d. 1949 (Sachsenhausen)
Studied theatre and musicology. Playwright until 1925, then freelance writer; 1934–37 editor of *Jugend* magazine. Arrested in 1939 for 'anti-state and anti-national attitudes' in his notebooks, deported in 1940 to Sachsenhausen, forced labour in clinker brickworks, released in February 1945 for army service. 1945–46 librarian, 1946–47 public plaintiff at Wasserburg denazification court, 1947 chief theatrical adviser at Radio Munich.

Wells, Leon W.: b. Eastern Galicia 1925 (Janowska Road camp in Lvov)
Interned in 1941, only survivor in his family. After war, engineering diploma at Munich Technical College, took US citizenship in 1953.

Wiechert, Ernst: b. 1887, d. 1950 (Buchenwald)
Son of a forester. Appointed graduate teacher in 1911; soldier in WWI, successful writer. Promoted by Nazis in early years after 1933; gave critical lectures in 1935 and 1937; arrested in 1938, two months in Buchenwald. Resettled in Switzerland, in 1947.

Wiesel, Elie: b. Sighet, Transylvania 1928 (Birkenau, Buchenwald, Auschwitz)
Deported in 1943 at age 15 from a Hasidic-Jewish environment, together with father, who died before liberation. Lost much of his family. After the war, lived and studied in Paris, then emigrated to USA in 1963. A journalist, he also teaches in New York and Boston, and at Yale. President of the Holocaust Memorial Council. Won Nobel Peace Prize in 1986.

Wiesenthal, Simon: b. Buczacz, Galicia 1908 (Mauthausen)
Studied architecture in Lwow (then Polish) and Prague; arrested in 1941, interned in a total of 12 camps. In 1947 opened a documentation centre in Linz (Austria) to collect testimony on the persecution of the Jews. In 1960 played a significant role in capture of Adolf Eichmann in Argentina; ran the Jewish Documentation Centre in Vienna. Simon Wiesenthal Center in Los Angeles named after him.

Wolff, Jeanette:
Jewish, Social Democrat; arrested for first time in 1933.

Zweig, Zacharias: (Buchenwald)
Lawyer. Forcibly resettled in 1941 in Krakow ghetto, deported in 1944 to Buchenwald; was able to smuggle his 3-year-old son into camp. After the war went to France, where the child received medical treatment; emigrated in 1949 to Israel, worked until 1956 for Jerusalem city council, afterwards in Tel Aviv.

Zywulska, Krystyna (pseud.): b. 1918 (Auschwitz-Birkenau)
Studied law in Warsaw until beginning of war, 1939–42 in Warsaw ghetto, escaped with false papers, worked in the resistance in the 'Aryan' part of the city, arrested in 1943 by the Gestapo, deported to Auschwitz. Has lived in West Germany since 1969.

Primary sources

Where a title has appeared in several editions, the date of first publication is given in round brackets immediately after the title, and the date of publication of the quoted edition at the end of the main entry; the date of the English edition (if any) refers to the text consulted by the translator and/or author.

Abraham, Max. *Juda verrecke. Ein Rabbiner im Konzentrationslager*. Teplitz-Schönau: Druck und Verlagsanstalt, 1934.

Adam, Walter. *Nacht über Deutschland. Erinnerungen an Dachau. Ein Beitrag zur Kulturgeschichte des Dritten Reiches. Aus dem literarischen Nachlaß von Walter Adam, Sektionschef, Oberst a.D. (Häftling Nr. 268)*. Vienna: Österreichischer Verlag, 1947.

Adelsberger, Lucie. *Auschwitz. Ein Tatsachenbericht. Das Vermächtnis der Opfer für uns Juden und für alle Menschen*. Berlin: Lettner, 1956; *Auschwitz: A Doctor's Story*. London: Robson Books, 1996.

Adler, H.G., Langbein, Hermann and Lingens-Reiner, Ella (eds). *Auschwitz. Zeugnisse und Berichte*. Frankfurt/Main: EVA, 1984.

Aichinger, Ilse. *Die größere Hoffnung* (1948). Frankfurt/Main: Fischer, 1986; *Herod's Children*, New York: Atheneum, 1963.

Aichinger, Ilse. 'Herodes' (1965) in *Ilse Aichinger, Meine Sprache und ich. Erzählungen*. Frankfurt/Main: Fischer, 1984.

Altmann, Erich. *Im Angesicht des Todes. Drei Jahre in deutschen Konzentrationslagern. Auschwitz, Buchenwald, Oranienburg*. Luxemburg: Luxemburgensia, 1947.

Améry, Jean. *Jenseits von Schuld und Sühne. Bewältigungsversuche eines Überwältigten* (1966). Stuttgart: Klett-Cotta, 1980; *At the Mind's Limits*. London: Granta Books, 1999.

Andreas-Friedrich, Ruth. *Der Schattenmann. Tagesbuchaufzeichnungen 1938–1945*, with an afterword by Jörg Drews (1986). Berlin, 1947; *Berlin Underground, 1938–1945*. New York: Henry Holt & Co., 1947.

Antelme, Robert. *L'Espèce humaine*. Paris: Gallimard, 1978.

Apitz, Bruno. *Nackt unter Wölfen. Roman* (1958). Frankfurt/Main: Röderberg, 1982; *Naked among Wolves*. Berlin: Seven Seas Publishers, 1960.

Arthofer, Leopold. *Als Priester im Konzentrationslager. Meine Erlebnisse in Dachau*. Graz/Vienna: Moser, 1947.

Auernheimer, Raoul. *Das Wirtshaus zur verlorenen Zeit. Erlebnisse und Bekenntnisse*. Vienna: Ullstein, 1948.

Bakels, Floris. *Nacht und Nebel. Der Bericht eines holländischen Christen aus deutschen Gefängnissen und Konzentrationslagern*. Frankfurt/Main: Fischer, 1977 (parts first published in Dutch); *Night and Fog: From the Diary of Floris B. Bakels*, trs. and adapted by Hermann Friedhoff. Cambridge: Lutterworth, 1993.

Ballmann, Hans. *Im KZ. Ein Tatsachenbericht aus dem Konzentrationslager*. Backnang: Praktikus, 1945.

Bartoszewski, Wladyslaw. *Herbst der Hoffnungen. Es lohnt sich, anständig zu sein*, ed. by Reinhold Lehmann. Freiburg/Basle/Vienna: Herder, 1984.

Bauman, Janina. *Winter in the Morning: A Young Girl's Life in the Warsaw Ghetto and Beyond*. London: Virago, 1986.

Becker, Jurek. *Jakob der Lügner*. Berlin/Weimar: Aufbau, 1969; *Jacob the Liar*. London: Picador, 1990.

Beckert, Werner. *Die Wahrheit über das Konzentrationslager Buchenwald*. Weimar: Verlag Antifaschistischen Schriftums, n.d. [1945].

Bednarz, Dieter and Lüders, Michael (eds). *Blick zurück ohne Haß. Juden aus Israel erinnern sich an Deutschland*, with an afterword by Helmut Gollwitzer. Cologne: Bund, 1981.

Befford, Albert. 'Ich war Bibliothekar im KL Buchenwald', in *Rappel*, Luxemburg, 1947 (in six parts).

Begley, Louis. *Wartime Lies* (1991). London: Picador, 1992.

Begov, Lucie. *Mit meinen Augen. Botschaft einer Auschwitz-Überlebenden*, with an afterword by Simon Wiesenthal. Gerlingen: Bleicher, 1983.

Beimler, Hans. *Im Mörderlager Dachau. Vier Wochen in den Händen der Braunen Banden*. Moscow-Leningrad: Foreign Languages Publishing House, 1933; *Four Weeks in the Hands of Hitler's Hell-Hounds. The Nazi Murder Camp of Dachau*. London: Modern Books, 1933.

Berger, Karin and Holzinger, Elisabeth *et al.* (eds). *Der Himmel ist blau. Kann sein. Frauen im Widerstand. Österreich 1938–1945*. Vienna: Promedia Druck, 1985.

Berger, Karin and Holzinger, Elisabeth *et al.* (eds). *Ich geb Dir einen Mantel, daß Du ihn noch in Freiheit tragen kannst. Widerstehen im KZ. Österreichische Frauen erzählen*. Vienna: Promedia Druck, 1987.

Berke, Hans. *Buchenwald. Eine Erinnerung an Mörder*. Salzburg: Ried-Verlag, 1946.

Bettelheim, Bruno. *The Informed Heart: The Human Condition in Modern Mass Society*. London: Thames & Hudson, 1961.

Billinger, Karl (real name Paul Massig). *Schutzhäftling Nr. 880. Aus einem deutschen Konzentrationslager. Roman* (Paris 1935). Munich: Rogner und Bernhard, 1978.

Bleton, Pierre. *Das Leben ist schön. Überlebensstrategien eines Häftlings im KZ Porta*, ed. Wiebke von Bernstorff *et al.*, with an essay by Reinhard Busch on the history of the outcamps at Porta Westphalia. Bielefeld: AJZ Verlag, 1987.

Bonhoeffer, Dietrich. *Widerstand und Ergebung. Briefe und Aufzeichnungen aus der Haft*, ed. Eberhard Bethge. Munich: Christian Kaiser Verlag, 1970; *Letters and Papers from Prison*, London: SCM, 1971.

Bornstein, Ernst Israel. *Die lange Nacht. Ein Bericht aus sieben Lagern*. Frankfurt/Main: EVA, 1967.

Borowski, Tadeusz. *Bei uns in Auschwitz. Erzählungen* (Polish 1959). Munich: Piper, 1983; *This Way for the Gas, Ladies and Gentlemen*. Harmondsworth: Penguin, 1976.

Bredel, Willi. *Die Prüfung. Roman aus einem Konzentrationslager*. London: Malik, 1935.

Bresler, J[akob]. *Du sollst nicht mehr Jakob heißen. Kindheit in Ghetto und KZ. Dokumentation einer Sprachlosigkeit*. Vienna: Orac, 1988.

Bruha, Antonia. *Ich war keine Heldin*. Vienna: Europa Verlag, 1984.

Buber-Neumann, Margarete. *Als Gefangene bei Stalin und Hitler, mit einem Kapitel 'Von Potsdam nach Moskau'. Zwei Bücher in einem Band*. Stuttgart: Seewald, 1968; *Under Two Dictators*. London: Victor Gollancz, 1949.

Buchmann, Erika. *Frauen im Konzentrationslager*. Stuttgart: Das Neue Wort, 1946.

Burger, Felix. *Juden in brauner Hölle. Augenzeugen berichten aus SA-Kasernen und Konzentrationslagern*. Prague: Die Abwehr, n.d.

Bürger, K. (ed.). *Aus Hitlers Konzentrationslagern*. Moscow-Leningrad: Foreign Languages Publishing House, 1934.

Carlebach, Emil. 'Der Untergang des Philosophen Hegel im KZ Buchenwald und seine Auferstehung'. *Das Magazin* 26/4, April 1979, pp. 24–7.

Castle-Stanford, Julian. *Tagebuch eines deutschen Juden im Untergrund*. Darmstadt: Darmstädter Blätter, 1980.

De Martini, Emil. *Vier Millionen Tote klagen an . . . ! Erlebnisse im Todeslager Auschwitz*. Munich-Obermenzing: Hans von Weber, 1948.

Deutschkron, Inge. *Ich trug den gelben Stern*. Cologne: Wissenschaft und Politik, 1978.

Dietmar, Udo. *Häftling . . . X . . . in der Hölle auf Erden!* Mainz: Rheinischer Volksverlag, 1946.

Drach, Albert. *'Z.Z.' Das ist die Zwischenzeit. Ein Protokoll*. Munich: Hanser, 1990.

Drach, Albert. *Unsentimentale Reise. Ein Bericht* (1966). Munich: Hanser, 1988; *Unsentimental Journey: A Report.* Riverside, CA: Ariadne Press, 1992.

Drach, Albert. *Das Beileid. Roman.* Graz: Droschl, 1993.

Drexel, Joseph. *Rückkehr unerwünscht. Joseph Drexels 'Reise nach Mauthausen' und der Widerstandkreis um Ernst Niekisch,* ed. Raimund Beyer. Stuttgart: DVA, 1978; 1980.

Edel, Peter. *Wenn es ans Leben geht. Meine Geschichte.* 2 vols. Frankfurt/Main: Röderberg, 1979.

Edvardson, Cordelia. *Gebranntes Kind sucht das Feuer. Roman.* (Swedish 1983). Munich: Hanser, 1986.

Eisenkraft, Clara. *Damals in Theresienstadt. Erlebnisse einer Judenchristin.* Wuppertal: Aussaal, 1977.

Elias, Ruth. *Die Hoffnung erhielt mich am Leben. Mein Weg von Theresienstadt und Auschwitz nach Israel.* Munich/Zurich: Piper, 1988; *Triumph of Hope: From Theresienstadt to Auschwitz to Israel.* New York/Chichester: John Wiley and Sons, 1998.

Engelmann, Bernt. *Bis alles in Scherben fällt. Wie wir die Nazizeit erlebten 1939–1945.* Cologne: Kiepenhauer und Witsch, 1983.

Fénelon, Fania (pseud.). *The Musicians of Auschwitz* (French orig. 1976). London: Joseph, 1977.

Förmann, Jängi. *KZ'ler: Aus deutschem KZ. Tatsachenberichte.* n.p./n.d.

Frank, Anne. *Anne Frank: The Diary of a Young Girl* (Dutch orig. 1947). London: Constellation Books, 1952.

Frank, Anne. *Tales from the House Behind.* London: Pan Books, 1962.

Frankl, Viktor E. *... trotzdem Ja zum Leben sagen. Ein Psychologe erlebt das Konzentrationslager,* with a preface by Hans Weigl. Munich: Deutsche Verlagsanstalt, 1977.

Freund, Julius. *O Buchenwald!,* with a preface by Franz Theodor Csokor (1943). Privately printed, 1945.

Friedenthal, Richard. *Die Welt in der Nußschale. Roman.* Munich: Piper, 1956.

Frister, Roman. *Die Mütze oder Der Preis des Lebens. Ein Lebensbericht.* Berlin: Siedler, 1997 (Hebrew original 1993).

Fritz, Mali. *Essig gegen den Durst. 565 Tage in Auschwitz-Birkenau.* Vienna: Verlag für Gesellschafskritik, 1986.

Fritz, Mali and Jursa, Hermine. *Es lebe das Leben. Tage nach Ravensbrück.* Vienna: Verlag für Gesellschafskritik, 1983.

Glas-Larsson, Margareta. *Ich will reden. Tragik und Banalität des Überlebens in Theresienstadt und Auschwitz,* ed. and commentary by Gerhard Botz, preface by Bundeskanzler Dr Bruno Kreisky. Vienna/Munich/New York: Molden, 1981.

Goldschmidt, Arthur. *Geschichte der evangelischen Gemeinde Theresienstadt 1942–1945*. Tübingen: Furche, 1948.

Gollwitzer, Helmut . . . *und führen wohin du nicht willst. Bericht einer Gefangenschaft* (1951). Gütersloh: Mohn, 1983.

Gostner, Erwin. *1000 Tage im KZ. Ein Erlebnisbericht aus den Konzentrationslagern Dachau, Mauthausen, Gusen* (1945). Innsbruck: Edition Löwenzahn, 1986.

Grand, Anselm J. *'Turm A ohne Neuigkeit!' Erleben und Bekenntnis eines Österreichers. Ein Komponist, Maler und Schriftsteller schildert das KZ*. Vienna/Leipzig: Ludwig Doblinger, 1945.

Graumann, Samuel. *Deportiert! Ein Wiener Jude berichtet*. Vienna: Stern, 1947.

Gross, Karl Adolf. *Fünf Minuten vor Zwölf. Des ersten Jahrtausends letzte Tage unter Herrenmenschen und Herdenmenschen. Dachauer Tagebücher des Häftlings Nr. 16921*. 2 vols, Munich: Neubau, n.d. [1946].

Gross, Karl Adolf. *Sterne in der Nacht. Lieder eines Ausgestoßenen*. Munich: Neubau, 1946.

Gross, Karl Adolf. *Zweitausend Tage Dachau. Erlebnisse eines Christenmenschen unter Herrenmenschen und Herdenmenschen. Berichte und Tagebücher des Häftlings Nr. 16921S*. Munich: Neubau, n.d.

Haag, Lina. *Eine Handvoll Staub*, with a preface by Oskar Maria Graf. Frankfurt/Main: Röderberg, 1985; *How Long the Night*. London: Victor Gollancz, 1948.

Hart, Kitty. *I Am Alive*. London/New York/Toronto: Abelard-Schumann, 1961.

Hart, Kitty. *Return to Auschwitz: The Remarkable Life of a Girl Who Survived the Holocaust*. New York: Atheneum, 1985.

Heger, Heinz (pseud.). *Die Männer mit dem Rosa Winkel. Der Bericht eines Homosexuellen über seine KZ-Haft von 1939–1945*. Hamburg: Merlin, 1972; *The Men with the Pink Triangle*. Boston: Alyson Publications, 1980.

Heilers, Margarete B. *Lebensration. Tagebuch einer Ehe 1933–1945*. Frankfurt/Main: Tende, 1985.

Heilig, Bruno. *Men Crucified*. London: Eyre and Spottiswoode, 1941.

Hermann, Simon Heinrich. *Austauschlager Bergen-Belsen (Geschichte eines Austauschtransportes)*. Tel Aviv: Irgun Olej Merkaz Europa, 1944.

Hiller, Kurt. 'Schutzhäftling 231'. *Neue Weltbühne*, 2/1934, 1/1935.

Hiller, Kurt. *Leben gegen die Zeit*. vol. 1: *Logos*. Reinbeck/Hamburg: Rowohlt, 1969.

Hiller, Kurt. *Leben gegen die Zeit*. vol. 2: *Eros*. Reinbeck/Hamburg: Rowohlt, 1973.

Hilsenrath, Edgar. *Nacht. Roman*. Cologne: Literarischer Verlag, 1978.

Hindls, Arnold. *Einer kehrte zurück. Bericht eines Deportierten*. Stuttgart: DVA, 1965 (= publication of the Leo Baeck Institute).

Hinrichs, Klaus (real name August Wittfogel). *Staatliches Konzentrations-lager VII. Eine 'Erziehungsanstalt' im Dritten Reich.* London: Malik, 1936.

Hochhäuser, Abraham. *Unter dem Gelben Stern. Ein Tatsachenbericht aus der Zeit von 1933 bis 1945.* Koblenz: Humanitas, 1948.

Hornung, Walter. *Dachau. Eine Chronik.* Zurich: Europa, 1936.

Hurdes, Felix. *Vater Unser. Gedanken aus dem Konzentrationslager.* Vienna: Herder, 1950.

Kalischer, Ben-Zwi. *Vom Konzentrationslager nach Palästina. Flucht durch die halbe Welt.* Tel Aviv: Edition Olympia, n.d. [1944].

Kalmár, Rudolf. *Zeit ohne Gnade.* Vienna: Schönburg, 1946 (reissued as *Die Wahrheit 1938–1945,* Edition Wien, 1988).

Katz, William. *Ein jüdisch-deutsches Leben 1904–1939–1978.* Tübingen: Katzmann, 1980.

Kautsky, Benedikt. *Teufel und Verdammte. Erfahrungen und Erkenntnisse aus sieben Jahren in deutschen Konzentrationslagern.* Zurich: Büchergilde Gutenberg, 1946; *Devils and the Damned: The Story of Nazi Concentration and Extermination Camps.* London: Brown, Watson, 1960.

Kertész, Imre. *Roman eines Schicksallosen.* Berlin: Rowohlt, 1996 (Hungarian original, 1975).

Kielar, Wieslaw. *Anus Mundi. Fünf Jahre Auschwitz.* Frankfurt/Main: S. Fischer, 1979 (orig. Polish).

Klemperer, Victor. *Tagebücher 1933–1945.* 2 vols. Berlin: Aufbau, 1995; *The Diaries of Victor Klemperer.* 2 vols. London: Weidenfeld & Nicolson, 1998, 1999.

Klieger, Bernhard. *Der Weg, den wir gingen. Reportage einer höllischen Reise,* with 10 drawings by Josette Cagnant and 7 official German documents on the 'final solution to the Jewish problem' in France. Brussels: Codac Juifs, 1960.

Klüger, Ruth. *Weiter leben.* Göttingen: Wallstein, 1992.

Köhler, Jochen. *Klettern in der Großstadt. Geschichten vom Überleben zwi-schen 1933–1945.* Berlin: Wagenbach, 1981.

Kommleitner, Erwin: *Todeslager Ennsland im Moor.* Privately published, Vienna, 1947.

König, Joel. *David. Aufzeichnungen eines Überlebenden.* Göttingen: Vanden-hoeck und Ruprecht, 1967 (originallly published as *Den Netzen entronnen*) (1983).

Kopp, Guido. *Ich aber habe leben müssen. Die Passion eines Menschen des 20. Jahrhunderts.* Salzburg: Ried-Verlag, 1946.

Kruk, Hermann. *Bibliothekar und Chronist im Ghetto Wilna.* Hanover: Laurentius, 1988.

Kupfer-Koberwitz, Edgar. 'Als Häftling in Dachau ... geschrieben von 1942 bis 1945 im Konzentrationslager Dachau', in *Aus Politik und Zeitge-*

schichte, Beilage zur Wochenzeitung 'Das Parlament', VII–IX/56, 15/2–7/3/1956 (offprints in four parts).

Kupfer-Koberwitz, Edgar. *Die Mächtigen und die Hilflosen. Als Häftling in Dachau.* vol. 1: *Wie es begann.* vol. 2: *Wie es endete.* Stuttgart: Vorwerk, 1960.

Das Lagerliederbuch. Lieder gesungen, gesammelt und geschrieben im Konzentrationslager Sachsenhausen, 1942.

Langbein, Hermann. *Die Stärkeren. Ein Bericht aus Auschwitz und anderen Konzentrationslagern.* Cologne: Bund, 1982 (first published in 1949 by Stern-Verlag, close to the Austrian CP).

Langhoff, Wolfgang. *Die Moorsoldaten.* Frankfurt/Main: Röderberg, 1986 (first published by Edition Aurora, 1935); *Rubber Truncheon: Being an Account of Thirteen Months Spent in a Concentration Camp.* London: Constable & Co., 1935.

Laqueur, Renata. *Bergen-Belsen Tagebuch 1944/45.* Hanover: Fackelträger Verlag, 1983 (originally published in Dutch, 1965).

Leeuwen, Evelien. *Späte Erinnerungen an ein jüdisches Mädchen. Autobiographische Erzählung.* Trier: Edition Trèves, 1984.

Leibbrand, Robert. *Buchenwald. Lieber sterben als verraten. Zur Geschichte der Deutschen Widerstandsbewegung*, with a preface by Wolfgang Langhoff, ed. by the Centrale Sanitaire Suisse in collaboration with the Freies Deutschland movement in Switzerland, October 1945.

Lenz, Johann Maria. *Christus in Dachau. Ein religiöses Volksbuch und ein kirchengeschichtliches Zeugnis.* Für Priester und Volk. Privately published, 1956.

Levi, Primo. *The Periodic Table.* London: Sphere Books, 1986 (Ital. orig. 1975).

Levi, Primo. *If This Is a Man.* London: Sphere Books, 1987a (Ital. orig. 1958).

Levi, Primo. *If Not Now, When?* London: Sphere Books, 1987b (Ital. orig. 1982).

Lévy-Hass, Hanna. *Vielleicht war das alles erst der Anfang. Tagebuch aus dem KZ Bergen-Belsen 1944–1945. Ein Gespräch mit Hanna Lévy-Hass 1978* (1946). Berlin: Rotbuch, 1979.

Lingens-Reiner, Ella. *Prisoners of Fear.* London: Victor Gollancz, 1948.

Lingens-Reiner, Ella. *Eine Frau im Konzentrationslager*, Vienna/Frankfurt/ Zurich: Europa Verlag, 1996.

Loidl, Franz. *Entweihte Heimat. KZ Ebensee.* Lunz: Muck, 1946.

Lundholm, Anja. *Das Höllentor. Bericht einer Überlebenden.* Reinbeck/ Hamburg: Rowohlt, 1988.

Maleta, Alfred. *Bewältigte Vergangenheit. Österreich 1932–1945.* Graz: Styria, 1981.

Marcuse, Bruno. *Erlebnisse im KZ Theresienstadt*. Ulm: Ebner n.d. [1946/47].

Marum, Ludwig. *Briefe aus dem Konzentrationslager Kislau*. Karlsruhe: Müller, 1988.

Matejka, Viktor. *Widerstand ist alles. Notizen eines Unorthodoxen*. Vienna: Löcker, 1983.

Matejka, Viktor. *Anregung ist alles. Das Buch Nr. 2*. Vienna: Löcker, 1991.

Matejka, Viktor. *Das Buch Nr. 3*. ed. Peter Huemer with a foreword by Johannes Mario Simmel. Vienna: Löcker, 1993.

Meier, Heinrich Christian. *So war es. Das Leben im KZ Neuengamme*. Hamburg: Phönix, 1948.

Mendel, Hersch. *Erinnerungen eines jüdischen Revolutionärs*, with a foreword by Isaac Deutscher. Berlin: Rotbuch, 1979 (Yiddish orig. 1959).

Migdal, Ulrike (ed.) *Und die Musik spielt dazu. Chansons und Satiren aus dem KZ Theresienstadt*. Munich: Piper, 1986.

Müller, Charlotte. *Die Klempnerkolonne in Ravensbrück. Erinnerungen des Häftlings Nr. 10787*. Berlin: Dietz, 1981.

Müller, Filip. *Auschwitz Inferno: The Testimony of a Sonderkommando*. Literary collaboration by Helmut Freitag. London/Henley: Routledge & Kegan Paul, 1979.

Naor, Simha. *Krankengymnastin in Auschwitz. Aufzeichnungen des Häftlings Nr. 80574*. Munich: Herder, 1986.

Neumann, Siegfried. 'Vom Kaiserhoch zur Austreibung. Aus den Aufzeichnungen eines jüdischen Rechtsanwalts 1933–1939', *Aus Politik und Zeitgeschichte, Beilage zur Wochenzeitung 'Das Parlament'*. vol. 45/76, 6 November 1976, pp. 3–32.

Paepcke, Lotte. *Ich wurde vergessen. Bericht einer Jüdin, die das Dritte Reich überlebte*. Freiburg: Herder, 1979 (originally published as *Unter fremdem Stern*. Frankfurter Hefte, 1952).

Pawlak, Zacheusz. *Ich habe überlebt . . . Ein Häftling berichtet über Majdanek*, with a foreword by Gerhard Mausz. Hamburg: Hoffmann and Campe, 1979 (Polish orig. 1969).

Pintus, Liesel. *Die Befreiung*. Typescript, 1947 (Wiener Library 171/K432).

Poller, Walter. *Arztschreiber in Buchenwald. Bericht des Häftlings 996 aus Block 39*. Hamburg: Phönix, 1946.

Riemer, Hermann. *Sturz ins Dunkel*. Munich: Funck, 1947.

Röder, Karl. *Nachtwache. 10 Jahre KZ Dachau und Flossenbürg*. Vienna/Cologne/Graz: Böhlau, 1985.

Rohme, Reiner. *Die Marionetten des Herrn. Erlebnisbericht aus sowjetischen Gefangenenlagern*. Zurich/Stuttgart: Eugen Rentsch, 1960.

Rost, Nico. *Goethe in Dachau*. Hamburg: Konkret Literatur, 1983 (Dutch orig. 1948).

Rousset, David. *The Other Kingdom*. New York: Reynal & Hitchcock, 1947.

Rovan, Joseph. *Geschichten aus Dachau*. Stuttgart: DVA, 1987 (French orig. 1987).

Rozanski, Zenon. *Mützen ab . . . Eine Reportage aus der Strafkompanie des KZ Auschwitz*. Hanover: 'Das andere Deutschland', 1948.

Sachs, Nelly. *In den Wohnungen des Todes*, Berlin: Aufbau, 1947.

Salus, Grete. *Niemand, nichts – ein Jude. Theresienstadt, Auschwitz, Oederan*. Darmstadt: Verlag Darmstädter Blätter, 1981 (first published 1958).

Scheuer, Lisa. *Vom Tode, der nicht stattfand. Theresienstadt, Auschwitz, Freiberg, Mauthausen. Eine Frau überlebt*. Reinbeck/Hamburg: Rowohlt, 1983.

Scheurenberg, Klaus. *Ich will leben. Ein autobiographischer Bericht*. Berlin: Oberbaum-Verlag, 1982.

Schifko-Pugnartnik, Manfred. *Leichenträger ans Tor. Bericht aus fünf Jahren Konzentrationslager*. Graz: Ulrich Moser, 1946.

Schmidt-Fels, Lucia. *Deportiert nach Ravensbrück. Bericht einer Zeugin 1943–1945*. Düsseldorf: Dehnen, 1981.

Schneeweiss, Josef. *Keine Führer. Keine Götter. Erinnerungen eines Arztes und Spanienkämpfers*. Vienna: Junius edition, 1986.

Scholten, Gerhard. *Zwischen allen Lagern. Leben in einer Zeit des Wahnsinns*. Munich: Universitas, 1988.

Schramm, Hanna. *Menschen in Gurs. Erinnerungen an ein französisches Internierungslager (1940–1941)*. Worms: Heintz, 1977.

Schupack, Joseph. *Tote Jahre. Eine jüdische Leidensgeschichte*. Tübingen: Katzmann, 1984; *The Dead Years*. New York: Holocaust Library, 1986.

Schuschnigg, Kurt von. *Ein Requiem in Rot-Weiss-Rot. Aufzeichnungen des Häftlings Dr. Austen*. Zurich: Amstutz Herdeg & Co., [1946?].

Schwartz-Bart, André. *The Last of the Just*. London: Secker & Warburg, 1961 (French orig. 1959).

Schweinburg, Erich. *Eine weite Reise*. Vienna: Löcker, 1988.

Schwerin, Alfred. *Erinnerungen. Von Dachau bis St. Chrischona*. Basle, 1944 [typescript].

Seger, Gerhart. *Oranienburg. Erster authentischer Bericht eines aus dem Konzentrationslager Geflüchteten*, with an introductory note by Heinrich Mann. Berlin: Guhl, 1979 (first published Karlsbad: Graphia, 1934).

Selbmann, Fritz. *Alternative – Bilanz – Credo. Versuch einer Selbstdarstellung*. Halle/Saale: Mitteldeutscher Verlag, 1969.

Semprún, Jorge. *The Long Voyage*. New York: Grove Press, 1964 (French orig. 1963).

Semprún, Jorge. *What a Beautiful Sunday!* London: Secker & Warburg, 1983 (French orig. 1980).

Semprún, Jorge. 'Das letzte Abenteuer', Gespräch mit Fritz J. Raddatz, *Die Zeit*, 48, 24 November 1989.

Semprún, Jorge. *L'Écriture ou la vie*. Paris: Gallimard, 1994; *Literature or Life*. New York: Penguin Books, 1997.

Senger, Valentin. *Kaiserhofstraße 12*. Darmstadt: Luchterhand, 1978.

Sherman, Hilde. *Zwischen Tag und Dunkel. Mädchenjahre im Ghetto*. Frankfurt/Berlin: Ullstein, 1984.

Siegelberg, Mark. *Schutzhaftjude 13877*. Shanghai: The American Press, n.d. [1939].

Solzhenitsyn, Alexander. *One Day in the Life of Ivan Denisovich*. London: Victor Gollancz, 1963 (Russian orig. 1962).

Spies, Gerty. *Drei Jahre Theresienstadt*. Munich: Kaiser, 1984.

Spritzer, Jenny. *Ich war Nr. 10291. Tatsachenbericht einer Schreiberin der politischen Abteilung aus dem Konzentrationslager Auschwitz*. Darmstadt: Darmstädter Blätter, 1980 (orig. published 1946).

Starke, Käthe. *Der Führer schenkt den Juden eine Stadt. Bilder – Impressionen – Reportagen – Dokumente*. Berlin: Hande und Spenersche Verlagsbuchhandlung, 1975.

Steinbock, Johann. *Das Ende von Dachau*. Salzburg: Österreichischer Kulturverlag, 1948.

Steinwender, Leonhard. *Christus im Konzentrationslager. Wege der Gnade und des Opfers*. Salzburg: Otto Müller, 1946.

Sternberg-Newman, Judith. *In the Hell of Auschwitz: Wartime Memoirs*. New York: Exposition Press, 1963.

Stojka, Ceija. *Wir leben im Verborgenen. Erinnerungen einer Roma-Zigeunerin*, ed. Karin Berger. Vienna: Picus, 1988.

Sturm, Hanna. *Die Lebensgeschichte einer Arbeiterin. Vom Burgenland nach Ravensbrück*. Vienna: Verlag für Gesellschaftskritik, 1982.

Sydow, Rolf von. *Angst zu atmen*. Frankfurt/Main: Ullstein, 1986.

ten Boom, Corrie. *A Prisoner And Yet*. London: Christian Literature Crusade, 1954. (First published as *Dennoch*. Wuppertal: Brockhaus, 1983).

Thälmann, Ernst. *Zwischen Erinnerung und Erwartung. Autobiographische Aufzeichnungen, geschrieben in faschistischer Haft*. Frankfurt/Main: Röderberg, 1977.

Utiz, Emil. *Psychologie des Lebens im Konzentrationslager Theresienstadt*. Vienna: Continental Edition Verlag Sexl, 1948.

Utsch, Bert. *Gestapo-Häftling 52478. Aus dem KZ Oranienburg-Sachsenhausen*, with a foreword by Bert Irving. Ottobeuern: privately published, n.d. [1945].

Vermehren, Isa. *Reise durch den letzten Akt. Ravensbrück, Buchenwald, Dachau. Eine Frau berichtet*. Reinbeck/Hamburg: Rowohlt, 1979 (orig. pub. Hamburg: Christian Wegner Verlag, 1946).

Walletner, Hugh. *Zebra. Ein Tatsachenbericht aus dem Konzentrationslager Flossenbürg.* Bad Ischl: privately published, n.d. [1945].

Wandel, Fritz. *Ein Weg durch die Hölle. Erlebnisbericht.* n.p., n.d. [1946].

Wander, Fred. *Der siebente Brunnen*, with an afterword by Christa Wolf. Darmstadt: Luchterhand, 1985 (orig. pub. 1970).

Wander, Fred. *Hotel Baalbek.* Frankfurt/Main: Fischer, 1994 (orig. pub. 1991).

Wander, Fred. *Das gute Leben. Erinnerungen.* Munich: Hansa, 1996.

Weglein, Resi. *Als Krankenschwester im KZ Theresienstadt. Erinnerungen einer Ulmer Jüdin*, ed. Silvester Lecher and Alfred Moos. Stuttgart: Silberburg, 1988.

Weinstock, Rolf. *Das wahre Gesicht Hitler-Deutschlands. Häftling Nr. 59000 erzählt von dem Schicksal der 10.000 Juden aus Baden, aus der Pfalz und aus dem Saargebiet in den Höllen von Dachau, Gurs-Drancy, Auschwitz, Jawischowitz, Buchenwald.* Singen: Volksverlag, 1948.

Weiss, Peter. *Fluchtpunkte. Roman.* Frankfurt/Main: Suhrkamp, 1965; *Leavetaking.* London: Calder & Boyars, 1966.

Weiss-Rüthel, Arnold. *Nacht und Nebel. Ein Sachsenhausen-Buch.* Berlin-Potsdam: VVN-Verlag, 1949.

Wells, Leon W. *The Janowska Road: An Account of the Author's Experiences in Lvov from 1941 to 1945.* (French orig. 1962). London: Jonathan Cape, 1966.

Wenke, Bettina. *Interviews mit Überlebenden. Verfolgung und Widerstand in Südwestdeutschland*, ed. by Landeszentrale für politische Bildung Baden-Württemberg. Stuttgart: Kurt Theiss, 1980.

Wiechert, Ernst. *Häftling Nr. 7188. Tagebuchnotizen und Briefe.* Munich: Desch, 1966.

Wiechert, Ernst. *Der Totenwald.* Frankfurt/Main: Ullstein, 1980 (1984) (orig. pub. Zurich: Rascher, 1946); *The Forest of the Dead: An Account of the Author's Experiences in Buchenwald.* London: Victor Gollancz, 1947.

Wiesel, Elie. *Night.* London: MacGibbon & Kee, 1960.

Wiesenthal, Simon. *KZ Mauthausen.* Linz/Vienna: Ibis, 1946.

Wolff, Jeanette. *Sadismus oder Wahnsinn. Erlebnisse in den deutschen Konzentrationslagern im Osten.* Dresden: Sachsenverlag, n.d.

Zweig, Zacharias. *'Mein Vater, was machst du hier . . . ?' Zwischen Buchenwald und Auschwitz. Der Bericht des Zacharias Zweig.* Frankfurt/Main: dipa-Verlag, 1987 (orig. in Polish).

Zywulska, Krystyna (pseud.). *Wo vorher Birken waren. Überlebensbericht einer jungen Frau aus Auschwitz-Birkenau.* Darmstadt: Darmstädter Blätter, 1980 (orig. in Polish).

Secondary sources

Adelsberger, Lucie. 'Psychologische Beobachtungen im Konzentrationslager Auschwitz', *Schweizerische Zeitschrift für Psychologie und ihre
Anwendungen*. Bern 6 (1947), pp. 124–31.

Adler, Hans G. *Theresienstadt 1941–1945. Das Antlitz einer Zwangsge-
meinschaft. Geschichte. Soziologie. Psychologie*. Tübingen: Mohr, 1960.

Adler, Hans G. *Der verwaltete Mensch*. Tübingen: Mohr, 1974.

Adler, Hans G. 'Dichtung in der Gefangenschaft als inneres Exil', in Bernt
Engelmann (ed.) *Literatur des Exil. Eine Dokumentation über die PEN-
Jahrestagung in Bremen vom 18. bis 20. September 1980*. Munich:
Goldmann, 1981, pp. 18–28.

Adorno, Theodor W. *Stichworte. Kritische Modelle 2*. Frankfurt/Main: Suhrkamp, 1980.

Adorno, Theodor W. *Noten zur Literatur*. Frankfurt/Main: Suhrkamp,
1981; *Notes to Literature*. vol. 1, New York: Columbia University Press,
1991; vol. 2, New York: Columbia University Press, 1992.

Adorno, Theodor W. *Negative Dialektik*. Frankfurt/Main: Suhrkamp, 1988;
Negative Dialectics. London: Routledge & Kegan Paul, 1990.

Adorno, Theodor W. *Ästhetische Theorie*. Frankfurt/Main: Suhrkamp,
1990; *Aesthetic Theory*. Minneapolis: University of Minnesota Press,
1997.

Albrecht, Richard. 'Antifaschistische Lektüren. Zu neuaufgelegten Exil-
Romanen von Konrad Meiz, Paul Westheim und Karl Billinger', in
Sammlung 2. Jahrbuch für anti-faschistische Literatur und Kunst. Frankfurt/
Main: Röderberg, 1979, pp. 229–35.

Albrecht, Richard. ' "Zirkus Konzentrazani" – eine Modellanalyse', *Diskussion Deutsch* 15 (1984), pp. 668–77.

Améry, Jean. *Unmeisterliche Wanderjahre. Aufsätze*. Stuttgart: Klett, 1971
(1989).

Améry, Jean. *Örtlichkeiten*, with an afterword by Manfred Francke. Stuttgart: Klett-Cotta, 1980.

Améry, Jean. *Lefeu oder Der Abbruch. Roman-Essay.* Stuttgart: Klett-Cotta, 1982 (cited in text as 1982a).

Améry, Jean. *Weiterleben – aber wie? Essays 1968–1978*, ed. Gisela Lidemann, Stuttgart: Klett-Cotta, 1982 (cited in text as 1982b).

Améry, Jean. *Radical Humanism: Selected Essays*, ed. and trans. by Sidney Rosenfeld and Stella P. Rosenfeld. Bloomington: Indiana University Press, 1984.

Améry, Jean. *Hand an sich legen. Diskurs über den Freitod.* Stuttgart: Klett-Cotta, 1986.

Anatomie des SS-Staates. vol. 2: Martin Broszat: *Konzentrationslager 1933–1945*; Hans-Adolf Jacobsen: *Kommissarbefehl*; Helmut Krausnick: *Judenverfolgung.* Munich: Deutscher Taschenbuchverlag, 1984; *The Anatomy of the SS State.* London: Collins, 1968.

Anderegg, Johannes. 'Das Fiktionale und das Ästhetische', in Dieter Heinrich and Wolfgang Iser (eds) *Funktionen des Fiktiven.* Munich: Fink, 1983, pp. 153–72.

Anders, Günther. *Kafka pro und contra. Die Prozeßunterlagen.* Munich: Beck, 1967; *Franz Kafka.* London: Bowes & Bowes, 1960.

Anders, Günther. *Besuch im Hades. Auschwitz und Breslau 1966. Nach 'Holocaust' 1979.* Munich: Beck'sche Verlagsbuchhandlung, 1985.

Andersch, Alfred. 'Anzeige einer Rückkehr des Geistes als Person', in idem, *Norden, Süden, rechts und links. Von Reisen und Büchern 1951–1971.* Zurich: Diogenes, 1972, pp. 27–243.

Apel, Karl-Otto. 'Szientistik, Hermeneutik, Ideologiekritik. Entwurf einer Wissenschaftslehre in erkenntnisanthropologischer Sicht', in Jürgen Habermas *et al.* (eds) *Theorie-Diskussion. Hermeneutik und Ideologiekritik.* Frankfurt/Main: Suhrkamp, 1980, pp. 7–44.

Arendt, Hannah. *Eichmann in Jerusalem: A Report on the Banality of Evil* (1964). Harmondsworth: Pelican, 1977.

Arendt, Hannah. *The Origins of Totalitarianism.* New York: Harcourt Brace Jovanovich, 1973; *Elemente und Ursprünge totaler Herrschaft.* vol. 1, *Antisemitismus.* Frankfurt/Main: Ullstein, 1980.

Argyle, Michael. *Bodily Communication.* 2nd edn. London: Routledge, 1988.

Arnold, Heinz Ludwig (ed.). *Jean Améry, Text + Kritik 99* (1988).

Arnold, Heinz Ludwig and Sinemus, Volker (eds). *Grundzüge der Literatur- und Sprachwissenschaft.* vol. 1, *Literaturwissenschaft.* Munich: Deutscher Taschenbuch Verlag, 1983.

Ash, Sholem. *One Destiny: An Epistle to the Christians.* New York: Putnam, 1945.

Atteslander, Peter. *Methoden der empirischen Sozialforschung.* Berlin/New York: de Gruyter, 1975.

Auerbach, Erich. *Mimesis: Dargestellte Wirklichkeit in der abendländischen*

Literatur. Berne/Munich: Francke 1971; *Mimesis: The Representation of Reality in Western Literature*. Princeton: Princeton University Press, 1968.

Aufmuth, Ulrich. *Zur Psychologie des Bergsteigens*. Frankfurt/Main: Fischer, 1989.

Auschwitz 1940–1945: Guidebook through the Museum. 1974; *Auschwitz. Geschichte und Wirklichkeit des Vernichtungslagers*. Reinbeck/Hamburg: Rowohlt, 1982.

Baigent, Michael, Leigh, Richard *et al. The Messianic Legacy*. London: Corgi Books, 1987.

Barth, Aron. *Der moderne Jude und die ewigen Fragen*. Jerusalem: Rubin Mass, 1983; *The Perennial Quest*. Jerusalem, 1984.

Bauche, Ulrich, Bundigam, Heinz *et al*. (eds) *Arbeit und Vernichtung. Das Konzentrationslager Neuengamme 1938–1945. Katalog zur ständigen Ausstellung im Dokumentationshaus der KZ-Gedenkstätte Neuengamme, Außenstelle des Museums für Hamburgische Geschichte*. Hamburg: VSA-Verlag, 1986.

Baumgart, Reinhard. *Literatur für Zeitgenossen. Essays*. Frankfurt/Main: Suhrkamp, 1966.

Baumgart, Reinhard. 'In die Moral entwischt? Der Weg des politischen Stückeschreibers Peter Weiss', *Text + Kritik 37: Peter Weiss*, ed. by Heinz Ludwig Arnold. Munich: 1982, pp. 47–57.

Baumgart, Reinhard. *Glücksgeist und Jammerseele. Über Leben und Schreiben, Vernunft und Literatur*. Munich: Hanser, 1986.

Beckmann, Jürgen. *Kognitive Dissonanz. Eine handlungstheoretische Perspektive*. Berlin/Heidelberg/New York: Springer, 1984.

Bendix, Reinhard. *Von Berlin nach Berkeley. Deutsch-jüdische Identitäten*. Frankfurt/Main: Suhrkamp, 1985.

Benjamin, Walter. 'Das Kunstwerk im Zeitalter seiner technischen Reproduzierbarkeit', in idem, *Illuminationen. Ausgewählte Schriften*. Frankfurt/Main: Suhrkamp, 1977, pp. 136–69; 'The work of art in the age of mechanical reproduction', in idem, *Illuminations*. New York: Schocken Books, 1968, pp. 217–52.

Benn, Gottfried. 'Probleme der Lyrik', in idem, *Gesammelte Werke in 4 Bänden*, ed. Dieter Wellershoff, vol. 1: *Essays. Reden. Vorträge*. Wiesbaden: Limes, 1959, pp. 494–532.

Berendsohn, Walter A. *Die humanistische Front. Einführung in die deutsche Emigranten-Literatur. Erster Teil: Von 1933 bis zum Kriegsausbruch 1939*. Zurich: Europa 1946.

Berenson, Bernhard. 'Sehen und wissen', *Die Neue Rundschau 1959*, pp. 54–77.

Berning, Cornelia. 'Die Sprache des Nationalsozialismus', *Zeitschrift für deutsche Wortforschung* 17 (1961), pp. 171–82.

Berning, Cornelia. *Vom 'Abstammungsnachweis' zum 'Zuchtwart'*. Berlin: de Gruyter, 1964.

Bettelheim, Bruno. 'The Holocaust: some reflections a generation later', *Encounter* 12 (1978a), pp. 7–19.

Bettelheim, Bruno. *The Uses of Enchantment: The Meaning and Importance of Fairy-Tales*. London: Thames & Hudson, 1978.

Bettelheim, Bruno. *Surviving and Other Essays*. London: Thames and Hudson, 1979.

Bettelheim, Bruno. *Erziehung zum Überleben. Zur Psychologie der Extremsituation*. Stuttgart: DVA, 1980.

Bichsel, Peter. *Der Leser. Das Erzählen. Frankfurter Poetik-Vorlesungen*. Darmstadt/Neuwied: Luchterhand, 1982.

Bierwisch, Manfred. 'Sprache und Gedächtnis. Eregnisse und Probleme', in idem (ed.) *Psychologische Effekte sprachlicher Strukturkomponenten*. Berlin: Akademieverlag, 1979.

Blankenagel, John C. 'Die Hauptmerkmale der deutschen Romantik' (1940), in Helmut Prang (ed.) *Begriffsbestimmung der Romantik*. Darmstadt: Wissenschaftliche Buchgesellschaft, 1968, pp. 324–36.

Bloch, Ernst. 'Die Frau im Dritten Reich', in idem, *Vom Hasard zur Katastrophe. Politische Aufsätze aus den Jahren 1934–1939*. Frankfurt/Main: Suhrkamp, 1972a, pp. 129–36.

Bloch, Ernst. 'Die Nazi und das Unsägliche', in idem, *Vom Hasard zur Katastrophe. Politische Aufsätze aus den Jahren 1934–1939*. Frankfurt/Main: Suhrkamp, 1972b, pp. 382–89.

Blumenberg, Hans. 'Licht als Metapher der Wahrheit. Im Vorfeld der philosophischen Begriffsbildung', *Studium Generale* 10/7 (1957), pp. 432–47.

Blumenberg, Hans. 'Wirklichkeit und Möglichkeit des Romans', in Hans Robert Jauss (ed.) *Nachahmung und Illusion. Kolloquium Gießen Juni 1963. Vorlagen und Verhandlungen*. Munich: Fink, 1969, pp. 9–27.

Blumenberg, Hans. *Arbeit am Mythos*. Frankfurt/Main: Suhrkamp, 1979; *Work on Myth*. Cambridge, MA: MIT Press, 1985.

Blumenthal, Nachman. 'Magical thinking among the Jews during the Nazi occupation', *Yad Vashem Studies* V (1963), pp. 221–36.

Boeschenstein, H[ermann]. 'Das Konzentrationslager in der deutschen Literatur. Einige Bemerkungen', in Jörg Thunecke (ed.) *Formen realistischer Erzählkunst. Festschrift für Charlotte Jolles*. Nottingham: Sherwood Press, 1976, pp. 66–78.

Bokser, Rabbi Ben Zion. *From the World of the Cabbalah: The Philosophy of Rabbi Judah Loew of Prague*. New York: Philosophical Library, 1954.

Bongartz, Dieter. 'Kindheit und Jugend im Faschismus. Zu neuen Büchern von Deutschkron, Finck, Koehn und von der Grün', in *Sammlung 2*.

Jahrbuch für antifaschistische Literatur und Kunst. Frankfurt/Main: Röderberg, 1979, pp. 235–41.

Bornscheuer, Lothar. *Topik. Zur Struktur der gesellschaftlichen Einbildungskraft*. Frankfurt/Main: Suhrkamp, 1976.

Braak, Ivo. *Poetik in Stichworten, Literaturwissenschaftliche Grundbegriffe. Eine Einführung*. Kiel: Hirt, 1974.

Braham, Randolf L. (ed.) *Perspectives on the Holocaust*. Boston/The Hague/London: Kluwer-Nijhoff, 1983.

Brand, Mathias. 'Stacheldrahtleben. Literatur und Konzentrationslager (bei Tadeusz Borowski, Bruno Apitz, Fred Wander und Jurek Becker)', in *Sammlung 2. Jahrbuch für antifaschistische Literatur und Kunst*. Frankfurt/Main: Röderberg, 1979, pp. 133–42.

Brandenburg, Rainer. 'Zwischen Morosität und Moral. Jean Améry im Spiegel der Kritik'. *Modern Austrian Literature* 23 (1990), pp. 69–84.

Brandt, Leon. *Menschen ohne Schatten. Juden zwischen Untergang und Untergrund 1938–1945*. Berlin: Oberbaum, 1984.

Brecht, Bertolt. 'Furcht und Elend des Dritten Reiches', in idem, *Gesammelte Werke 3: Stücke 3 Werkausgabe*. Frankfurt/Main: Suhrkamp, 1967, pp. 1073–193.

Breloer, Heinrich. *Mein Tagebuch. Geschichten vom Überleben. 1939–1947*. Cologne: Verlagsgesellschaft Schulfernsehen, 1984.

Brettschneider, Werner. *Zorn und Trauer. Aspekte deutscher Gegenwartsliteratur*. Berlin: Schmidt, 1981.

Briegleb, Klaus and Weigel, Sigrid (eds) *Gegenwartsliteratur seit 1968*. Munich/Vienna: Hanser, 1992.

Bringmann, Fritz. *Neuengamme. Berichte, Erinnerungen, Dokumente*, ed. by the Arbeitsgemeinschaft Neuengamme für die BRD e.V. Hamburg, Frankfurt/Main: Röderberg, 1981.

Brooks, Peter. 'Symbolization and meaning', in Robert Jay Lifton and Eric Olson (eds) *Explorations in Psychohistory: The Wellfleet Papers*. New York: Simon & Schuster, 1974, pp. 214–30.

Broszat, Martin. *Der Staat Hitlers. Grundlegung und Entwicklung seiner inneren Verfassung*. Munich: Deutscher Taschenbuchverlag, 1969 (1983); *The Hitler State: The Foundation and Development of the Internal Structure of the Third Reich*. London: Longman, 1981.

Broszat, Martin. 'Konzentrationslager 1933–1945', in *Anatomie des SS-Staates* [see separate entry]. vol. 2, Munich: Deutscher Taschenbuchverlag, 1984, pp. 11–132.

Buber, Martin. *Die chassidischen Bücher*. Hellerau: Hegner, 1928 (1984).

Buchenwald ein Konzentrationslager. Bericht der ehemaligen KZ-Häftlinge Emil Carlebach, Paul Grünewald, Hellmuth Röder, Willy Schmidt, Walter Vielhauer. Frankfurt/Main: Röderberg, 1986.

Bund proletarisch-revolutionärer Schriftsteller: 'Hirne hinter Stacheldraht.

Schicksale deutscher Schriftsteller in Konzentrationslagern' (1934), in Heinz Ludwig Arnold (ed.) *Deutsche Literatur im Exil 1933–1945*. vol. 1, *Dokumente*. Frankfurt/Main: Fischer Athenäum, 1974, pp. 9–28.

Burger, Hermann. *Tractatus logico-suicidalis. Über die Selbsttötung*. Frankfurt/Main: Fischer, 1988.

Burke, Kenneth. *The Philosophy of Literary Form: Studies in Symbolic Action*. New York: Vintage Books, 1941 (1957).

Busse, Günther. *Romantik – Personen – Motive – Werke*. Freiburg/Basle/ Vienna: Herder, 1982.

Cassirer, Ernst. *An Essay on Man: An Introduction to a Philosophy of Human Culture*. New Haven: Yale University Press, 1944.

Cernyak-Spatz, Susan E. *German Holocaust Literature*. New York/Berne/ Frankfurt: Lang, 1985.

Chagoll, Lydia. *Im Namen Hitlers. Kinder hinter Stacheldraht*. Frankfurt/ Main: Röderberg, 1979.

Chappell, Connery. *Island of Barbed Wire. The Remarkable Story of World War Two Internment on the Isle of Man*. London: Robert Hale, 1984.

Chodoff, Paul. 'The German concentration camp as a psychological stress', *Archives of General Psychiatry* 22 (1970), pp. 78–87.

Claessen, Dieter. *Instinkt, Psyche, Geltung. Zur Legitimation menschlichen Verhaltens. Eine soziologische Anthropologie*. Cologne/Opladen: West-deutscher Verlag, 1970.

Cohen, Arthur A. (ed.). *Arguments and Doctrines: A Reader of Jewish Thinking in the Aftermath of the Holocaust*. Philadelphia: The Jewish Publications Society of America, 1970.

Cohen, Elie A. *Human Behaviour in the Concentration Camp*. London: Jonathan Cape, 1954.

Constanza, Mary S. *The Living Witness: Art in the Concentration Camps and Ghettos*. New York: The Free Press, 1982.

Czollek, Walter. 'Begegnung mit der Vergangenheit', *Neue Deutsche Literatur* 12 (1971), pp. 156–8.

Danimann, Franz. *Flüsterwitze und Spottgedichte unterm Hakenkreuz*. Vienna: Böhlau, 1983.

Deak, Istvan. *Weimar Germany's Left-Wing Intellectuals: A Political History of the Weltbühne and Its Circle*. Berkeley, CA: University of Califormia Press, 1968.

DeKoven Ezrahi, Sidra. *By Words Alone: The Holocaust in Literature*. London/Chicago: University of Chicago Press, 1980.

Des Pres, Terence. *The Survivor: An Anatomy of Life in the Death Camps*. New York: Oxford University Press, 1976.

Dilworth, Ernest Mervin. *The Unsentimental Journey of Lawrence Sterne*. New York: King's Crown Press, 1948.

Döbert, Rainer and Nunner-Winkler, Gertrud. 'Konflikt- und Rückzugspotentiale in spätkapitalistischen Gesellschaften', *Zeitschrift für Soziologie* 2/4 (1973), pp. 301–25.

Dokumentationsarchiv des Osterreichischen Widerstandes. *Jahrbuch 1992*, ed. Siegwald Ganglmair, Vienna, 1992.

Dostoevsky, Fyodor. *The House of the Dead*. London: J.M. Dent & Sons, 1939; Dostojewskij, Fjodor. *Aufzeichnungen aus einem toten Hause*. Munich: Winkler, 1988.

Douglas, Mary. *Purity and Danger*. Harmondsworth: Pelican, 1970.

Dundes, Alan and Haunschild, Thomas. 'Kennt der Witz kein Tabu? Zynische Erzählformen als Versuch der Bewältigung nationalsozialistischer Verbrechen', *Zeitschrift für Volkskunde* 83 (1987), pp. 21–31.

Eagleton, Terry. *Literary Theory: An Introduction*. Oxford: Blackwell, 1989.

Edvardson, Cornelia. *Die Welt zusammenfügen*. Munich: Hanser, 1989.

Ehalt, Hubert Christian (ed.). *Geschichte von unten. Fragestellungen, Methoden und Projekte einer Geschichte des Alltags*. Vienna/Cologne/Graz: Böhlaus Nf., 1984.

Eliach, Yaffa. *Träume vom Überleben. Chassidische Geschichten des 20. Jahrhunderts*. Freiburg/Basle/Vienna: Herder, 1985.

Emmerich, Wolfgang. 'Die Literatur des antifaschistischen Widerstandes in Deutschland', in *Die deutsche Literatur im Dritten Reich*. Stuttgart: Reclam, 1976, pp. 427–58.

Engeler, Urs Paul. *Sprachwissenschaftliche Untersuchungen zur ironischen Rede*. Zurich 1980.

Engelmann, Bernt (ed.). *Literatur des Exils: Eine Dokumentation über die PEN-Jahrestagung in Bremen vom 18. bis 20. September 1980*. Munich: Goldmann, 1981.

Enzensberger, Hans Magnus. 'Europa in Trümmern. Ein Prospekt', *Die Zeit* 23, 1 June 1990.

Epstein, Helen. *Children of the Holocaust: Conversations with Sons and Daughters of Survivors*. New York: Putnam's Sons, 1979.

Esch, Saul. 'The dignity of the destroyed', *Judaism* 11/2 (1962), pp. 99–111.

Exenberger, Herbert. 'Viktor Matejka – Bibliothekar im KZ Dachau. Die vielen Freuden am Kleinen sind die kleinen Freuden', in *Laurentius. Von Menschen, Büchern und Bibliotheken, Lebensbilder I.* 2/1992, pp. 69–84.

Exilforschung. Ein Internationales Jahrbuch. vol. 4: *Das jüdische Exil und andere Themen*, ed. for the Gesellschaft für Exilforschung by Thomas Koebner, Wulf Köpke *et al.*, Munich: Text + Kritik, 1986.

Exner, Richard. 'Some reflections on Holocaust and post-Holocaust writing', *World Literature Today: Literary Quarterly of the University of Oklahoma* 60 (1986), pp. 402–6.

Fackenheim, Emil. *Jewish Return into History: Reflections in the Age of Auschwitz and a New Jerusalem.* New York: Schocken Books, 1978.

Fackenheim, Emil L. *Quest for Past and Future: Essays in Jewish Theology.* Bloomington: Indiana University Press, 1968.

Fein, Erich and Flanner, Karl. *Rot-Weiß-Rot in Buchenwald. Die österreichischen politischen Häftlinge im Konzentrationslager am Ettersberg bei Weimar 1938–1945.* Vienna/Zurich: Europa, 1987.

Felman, Shoshana and Laub, Dori. *Testimony: Crises of Witnessing in Literature, Psychoanalysis and History.* London: Routledge, 1992.

Festinger, Leon. *Theorie der kognitiven Dissonanz.* Ed. Martin Irle and Volker Möntemann, Berne/Stuttgart/Vienna: Huber, 1978.

Fetscher, Iring. *Wer hat Dornröschen wachgeküßt? Das Märchenverwirrbuch.* Hamburg: Claassen, 1973.

Feuchtwanger, Lion. 'Die Arbeitsprobleme des Schriftstellers im Exil', *Sinn und Form* 6 (1954), pp. 348–53.

Fischer, Wolfgang Georg. 'Zur Sprache der Emigranten', *Literatur und Kritik* 128 (1978), pp. 475–80.

Fleischmann, Lea. *Dies ist nicht mein Land. Eine Jüdin verläßt die Bundesrepublik,* with an afterword by Henryk M. Broder. Munich: Heyne, 1986.

Focke, Harald and Reimer, Uwe. *Alltag unterm Hakenkreuz.* vol. 1, *Wie die Nazis das Leben der Deutschen veränderten. Ein aufklärendes Lesebuch.* Reinbeck/Hamburg: Rowohlt, 1979.

Focke, Harald and Reimer, Uwe. *Alltag unterm Hakenkreuz.* vol. 2, *Alltag der Entrechteten. Wie die Nazis mit ihren Gegnern umgingen.* Reinbeck/Hamburg: Rowohlt, 1980.

Fogelmann, Eva and Savran, Bella. 'Brief group therapy with offspring of Holocaust survivors: leaders' reactions', *American Journal of Orthopsychology* 50/1 (1980), pp. 96–108.

Foley, Barbara. 'Fact, fiction, fascism: testimony and mimesis in Holocaust narratives', *Comparative Literature* 34 (1982), pp. 330–60.

Föster, Michael. 'Deutsche Theater spielen "Rosa Winkel" ', in *Sammlung 3. Jahrbuch für anti-faschistische Litertaur und Kunst.* Frankfurt/Main: Röderberg, 1980, pp. 231–5.

Foucault, Michel. 'What is an author?', in *The Foucault Reader,* ed. by Paul Rabino. Harmondsworth: Penguin, 1991, pp. 141–60.

Frankl, Viktor E. *Ärztliche Seelsorge.* Vienna: Franz Deuticke, 1946.

Frankl, Viktor E. 'Psychologie im Notstand. Psychotherapeutische Erfahrungen im Konzentrationslager', Hygiene 1 (1950/52), pp. 177–86.

Frankl, Viktor E. *The Doctor and the Soul.* Harmondsworth: Pelican, 1973.

Frankl, Viktor E. and Kreuzer, Franz. *Im Anfang war der Sinn. Von der Psychoanalyse zur Logotherapie. Ein Gespräch.* Vienna/Zurich: Piper, 1982 (reprinted 1986).

Frauen-KZ Ravensbrück. Autorenkollektiv, Leitung G. Zörner, ed. by Kommittee der antifaschistischen Widerstandskämpfer der Deutschen Demokratischen Republik. Frankfurt/Main: Röderberg, 1973.

Freud, Sigmund. *Abriß der Psychoanalyse. Das Unbehagen in der Kultur.* Frankfurt/Main: Fischer, 1953; *An Outline of Psychoanalysis.* London: Hogarth Press, 1949; 'Civilization and its discontents', in idem, *Civilization, Society and Religion.* Harmondsworth: Penguin, 1991, pp. 243–304.

Freud, Sigmund. 'Der Dichter und das Phantasieren', in idem, *Gesammelte Werke.* vol. 7, Frankfurt/Main: Fischer, 1972, pp. 213–23; 'Creative writers and day-dreaming', in idem, *Art and Literature.* Harmondsworth: Penguin, 1985, pp. 129–42.

Frye, Northrop. *Anatomy of Criticism: Four Essays.* Princeton, NJ: Princeton University Press, 1957.

Gabriel, Gottfried. *Fiktion und Wahrheit. Eine semantische Theorie der Literatur.* Stuttgart: Fromann-Holzberg, 1975a.

Gabriel, Gottfried. 'Fiktion, Wahrheit und Erkenntnis in literarischen Texten', *Der Deutschunterricht* 27/III (1975b), pp. 5–17.

Gadamer, Hans-Georg. *Wahrheit und Methode. Grundzüge einer philosophischen Hermeneutik.* Tübingen: Mohr, 1986; *Truth and Method.* London: Sheed & Ward Ltd., 1989.

Gebhardt, Jürgen. 'Symbolformen gesellschaftlicher Sinndeutung in der Krisenerfahrung', in Klaus Vondung (ed.), *Kriegserlebnisse. Der Erste Weltkrieg in der literarischen Gestaltung und symbolischen Deutung der Nationen.* Göttingen: Vandenhoeck und Ruprecht, 1980, pp. 41–61.

Gebhardt, Peter (ed.). *Literaturkritik und literarische Wertung.* Darmstadt: Wissenschaftliche Buchgesellschaft, 1980.

Gehlen, Arnold. 'Vom Wesen der Erfahrung' (1936), in idem, *Anthropologische Forschung.* Reinbeck/Hamburg: Rowohlt, 1961, pp. 26–43.

Gilbert, Martin. *The Holocaust: The Jewish Tragedy.* London: Collins, 1986.

Gilbert, Martin. *Atlas of the Holocaust.* London: Routledge, 1994.

Gilman, Sander L. (ed.). *NS-Literaturtheorie. Eine Dokumentation.* Frankfurt/Main: Athenäum, 1971.

Ginzberg, Louis. *Legends of the Jews.* ed. Jewish Publication Society of America, Philadelphia, 1967, vol. 4, pp. 128f., vol. 6, pp. 278–81.

Glaser, Hermann. *Spießerideologie. Von der Zerstörung des deutschen Geistes im 19. und 20. Jahrhundert und dem Aufstieg des Nationalsozialismus.* Frankfurt/Main: Ullstein, 1979.

Glinz, Hans. 'Fiktionale und nicht-fiktionale Texte', in *Textsorten und literarische Gattungen. Dokumentation des Germanistentages in Hamburg vom 1. bis 4. April 1979,* ed. by Vorstand der Vereinigung der deutschen Hochschulgermanisten. Berlin: Schmidt, 1983, esp. pp. 118–24.

Goffmann, Erving. *The Presentation of Self in Everyday Life*. Harmondsworth: Pelican, 1971.

Goldhagen, Daniel Jona. *Hitler's Willing Executioners: Ordinary Germans and the Holocaust*. New York: Alfred Knopf, 1996.

Grimm, Gunter E., Faulstich, Werner and Kuon, Peter (eds). *Apokalypse. Weltuntergangsvisionen in der Literatur des 20. Jahrhunderts*. Frankfurt/Main: Suhrkamp, 1986.

Grimm, Reinhold. 'Montierte Lyrik', in Heinz Otto Burger and Reinhold Grimm, *Evokation und Montage. Drei Beiträge zum Verständnis moderner deutscher Lyrik*. Göttingen: Sachse und Pohl, 1961, pp. 44–68.

Grimm, Reinhold and Hermand, Jost (eds). *Exil und Innere Emigration*. Third Wisconsin Workshop, Frankfurt/Main: Athenäum, 1972.

Grossmann, Frances G. 'Creativity as a means of coping with anxiety', *Arts in Psychotherapy* 8/3-4 (1981), pp. 185–92.

Habermas, Jürgen. *Theorie des kommunikativen Handelns*. vol. 1, *Handlungsrationalität und gesellschaftliche Rationalisierung*. Frankfurt/Main: Suhrkamp, 1981; *The Theory of Communicative Action*. vol. 1, *Reason and the Rationalization of Society*. Cambridge: Polity Press, 1991.

Habermas, Jürgen and Heinrich, Dieter *et al.* (eds). *Theorie-Diskussion: Hermeneutik und Ideologiekritik*. Frankfurt/Main: Suhrkamp, 1971.

Haft, Cynthia. *The Theme of Nazi Concentration Camps in French Literature*. The Hague: Nanton, 1973.

Halperin, Irving. *Messengers from the Dead: Literature of the Holocaust*. Philadelphia: The Westminster Press, n.d.

Hamburger, Käte. *Die Logik der Dichtung*. Stuttgart: Klett, 1957; *The Logic of Literature*, 2nd edn. Bloomington/London: Indiana University Press, 1973.

Hardtmann, Gertrud (ed.). *Spuren der Verfolgung. Seelische Auswirkungen des Holocaust auf die Opfer und ihre Kinder*. Gerlingen, Bleicher, 1992.

Härtling, Peter. *Der spanische Soldat oder Finden und Erfinden. Frankfurter Poetik-Vorlesungen*. Darmstadt/Neuwied: Luchterhand, 1984.

Hasan-Roken, Galit and Dunes, Alan (eds). *The Wandering Jew: Essays in the Interpretation of a Christian Legend*. Bloomington: Indiana University Press, 1986.

Hausjell, Fritz. *Österreichische Tageszeitungsjournalisten am Beginn der Zweiten Republik (1945–1947)*. Ph.D thesis, Salzburg, 1985.

Hegele, Wolfgang. 'Zum Problem des pathetischen Stils in der Dichtung des 20. Jahrhunderts', *Der Deutschunterricht* 15/3 (1963), pp. 83–97.

Heinemann, Marlene E. *Women Prose Writers of the Nazi Holocaust*. Ph.D thesis, Ann Arbor, MI, 1981].

Heubner, Christoph, Meyer, Alvin *et al. Lebenszeichen. Gesehen in Auschwitz*. Bornheim-Merten: Lamuv, 1979.

Heydecker, Joe, J. *Das Warschauer Ghetto. Foto-Dokumente eines deutschen*

Soldaten aus dem Jahr 1941, foreword by Heinrich Böll. Munich: Deutscher Taschenbuch Verlag, 1984; *The Warsaw Ghetto: A Photographic Record*. London: Tauris, 1990.

Hilberg, Raul. *Sonderzüge nach Auschwitz*. Mainz: Dumjahn, 1981.

Hilberg, Raul. *Die Vernichtung der europäischen Juden*, 3 vols. Frankfurt/Main: Fischer, 1990; *The Destruction of the European Jews*. New York: Holmes & Meier, 1985.

Hilberg, Raul. *Täter, Opfer, Zuschauer. Die Vernichtung der Juden 1933–1945*, 3 vols. Frankfurt/Main: Fischer, 1992; *Perpetrators, Victims, Bystanders: The Jewish Catastrophe 1933–1945*. New York: Aaron Asher, 1992.

Hildesheimer, Wolfgang, in Hans Jürgen Schultz (ed.) *Mein Judentum*. Stuttgart: Kreuz Verlag, 1978 (1986).

Hildesheimer, Wolfgang. 'The End of Fiction, Vortrag in drei Städten Irlands', in Wolfgang Hildesheimer, *Das Ende der Ficktion. Reden aus fünfundzwanzig Jahren*. Frankfurt/Main: Suhrkamp, 1984, pp. 103–22.

Hillmann, Heinz. *Alltagsphantasie und dichterische Phantasie. Versuch einer Produktionsästhetik*. Kronberg: Athenäum, 1977.

Hirschauer, Gerd. ' " … da ich ein gelernter Heimatsloser bin … " Über Jean Améry', *Allmende* 24–25 (1989), pp. 114–31.

Hocke, Gustav René. *Das europäische Tagebuch*. Wiesbaden: Limes, 1963.

Horbach, Michael. *So überlebten sie den Holocaust. Zeugnisse der Menschlichkeit 1933–1945*. Munich: Schneekluth, 1964 (1979).

Horkheimer, Max. *Zur Kritik der instrumentellen Vernunft. Aus den Vorträgen und Aufzeichnungen seit Kriegsende*, ed. Alfred Schmidt. Frankfurt/Main: Fischer, 1967 (1985); *Critique of Instrumental Reason*. New York: The Seabury Press, 1974.

Hormuth, Stefan and Stephan, Walter. 'Effects of viewing "Holocaust" on Germans and Americans: A first-world analysis', *Journal of Applied Social Psychology* 11/3 (1981), pp. 240–51.

Iltis, Rudolf (ed.). *Theresienstadt*. Vienna: Europa, 1968.

Ingendahl, Werner. 'Versuch einer energetischen Betrachtung des dichterischen Prozesses', *Wirkendes Wort* 20 (1970), pp. 73–85.

Ingendahl, Werner. *Der metaphorische Prozeß. Methodologie zu einer Erforschung und Systematisierung*. Düsseldorf: Pädagogischer Verlag Schwann, 1971.

Iser, Wolfgang. *Der Akt des Lesens. Theorie ästhetischer Wirkung*. Munich: Fink, 1976; *The Act of Reading: A Theory of Aesthetic Response*. London: Routledge & Kegan Paul, 1978.

Iser, Wolfgang. 'Akte des Fingierens. Oder: Was ist das Fiktive im fiktionalen Text?', in Dieter Heinrich and Wolfgang Iser (eds) *Funktionen des Fiktiven*. Munich: Fink, 1983, pp. 121–51.

Jäckel, Eberhard and Rohwer, Jürgen (eds). *Der Mord an den Juden im*

Zweiten Weltkrieg. Entschlußbildung und Verwirklichung. Stuttgart: DVA, 1985.

Jakobson, Roman. *Poetik. Ausgewählte Aufsätze 1921–1971*, ed. Elmar Holenstein and Tarcisius Schubert. Frankfurt/Main: Suhrkamp, 1979.

Jauss, Hans Robert. *Literaturgeschichte als Provokation*. Frankfurt/Main: Suhrkamp, 1974.

Jauss, Hans Robert. 'Über den Grund des Vergnügens am komischen Helden', in Wolfgang Preisendanz and Rainer Warning (eds) *Das Komische*. Munich: Fink, 1976, pp. 103–32.

Jauss, Hans Robert. 'Der Gebrauch der Fiktion in Formen der Anschauung und Darstellung der Geschichte', in Reinhard Koselleck, Heinrich Lutz *et al.* (eds) *Formen der Geschichtsschreibung*. Munich: Deutscher Taschenbuch Verlag, 1982, pp. 415–51.

Jefferson, Ann. 'Russian Formalism', in *Modern Literary Theory*, ed. by Ann Jefferson and David Robey, 2nd edn. London: Batsford, 1986.

Johr, Barbara. *Reisen ins Leben. Weiterleben nach einer Kindheit in Auschwitz: Mit einer Textliste zum gleichnamigen Film und Beiträgen von Susanne Benöhr und Thomas Mitscherlich*. Bremen: Donat, 1997.

Josephs, Zoë. *Survivors: Jewish Refugees in Birmingham 1933–1945*. Warley: Meridian Books, 1988.

Kahler, Erich. 'Die Verinnerung des Erzählens', *Die Neue Rundschau 1959*, pp. 1–54.

Kaiser, Wolfgang. *Das sprachliche Kunstwerk. Eine Einführung in die Literaturwissenschaft*. Berne: Francke, 1951.

Kallmeyer, Werner *et al*. *Lektürekolleg zur Textlinguistik*, vol. 1 *Einführung*. Königstein/Ts: Athenäum, 1974.

Kantorowicz, Alfred. *Die Geächteten der Republik. Alte und neue Aufsätze*, ed. Andreas W. Mytze. Berlin: Verlag europäische Ideen, 1977.

Katz, Steven T. *Post-Holocaust Dialogues: Critical Studies in Modern Jewish Thought*. New York/London: New York University Press, 1983.

Keilson, Hans. 'Wohin die Sprache nicht reicht', *Psyche* 38/10 (1984), pp. 915–26.

Kermode, Frank. *The Sense of an Ending: Studies in the Theory of Fiction*. New York: Oxford University Press, 1967.

Kielmansegg, Peter Graf. 'Abschied von Eugen Kogon', *Merkur* 469 (3/1988), pp. 250–7.

Klamper, Elisabeth. *Viktor Matejka. Beiträge zu einer Biographie*. Vienna, 1981 (typed diss.).

Klein, Judith. 'Am Rande des Nichts. Charlotte Delbos Trilogie *Auschwitz und danach*', *Die Zeit* 28, 23 November 1990.

Klemperer, Viktor. *Die unbewältigte Sprache. Aus dem Notizbuch eines Philologen 'LTI'*. Darmstadt: Metzler, 1946 (1966).

Klieber, Rupert. 'Religiosität in Extremsituationen. Am Beispiel Ausch-witz', Salzburg 1982 (master thesis).

Kloepfer, Rolf. *Poetik und Linguistik. Semiotische Instrumente*. Munich: Fink, 1975.

Klotz, Volker (ed.). *Zur Poetik des Romans*. Darmstadt: Wissenschaftliche Buchgesellschaft, 1965.

Klotz, Volker. *Abenteuerromane. Sue, Dumas, Ferry, Retcliff, May, Verne*. Munich/Vienna: Hanser, 1979.

Kluckhohn, Paul. *Das Ideengut der deutschen Romantik*. Tübingen: Nie-meyer, 1961.

Klüger, Ruth. *Frauen Lesen anders. Essays*. Munich: Deutscher Taschen-buchverlag, 1996.

Kochan, Lionel. *The Jew and His History*. London: Macmillan, 1977.

Kogon, Eugen (ed.). *Nationalsozialistische Massentötungen durch Giftgas. Eine Dokumentation*. Frankfurt/Main: S. Fischer, 1983; *Nazi Mass Murder: A Documentary History of the Use of Poison Gas*. New Haven/London: Yale University Press, 1993.

Kogon, Eugen. *Der SS Staat. Das System der deutschen Konzentrationslager*. Munich: Heyne, 1985; *The Theory and Practice of Hell: The Concentration Camps and the Theory Behind Them*. New York, 1950.

Kolb, Eberhard. *Bergen-Belsen. Geschichte des 'Aufenthaltslagers' 1943–1945*. Hanover: Verlag für Literatur und Zeitgeschehen, 1962.

Köller, Wilhelm. *Semiotik und Metaphern. Untersuchungen zur grammatischen Struktur und kommunikativen Funktion von Metaphern*. Stuttgart: Metz-lersche Verlagsbuchhandlung, 1975.

Kontroversen, alte und neue. Akten des VII. Internationalen Germanisten-Kongresses, Göttingen 1985, vol. 5, *Auseinandersetzungen um jiddische Sprache und Literatur. Jüdische Komponenten in der deutschen Literatur – die Assimilationskontroverse*. Tübingen: Niemeyer, 1986.

Koselleck, Reinhard. 'Geschichte, Geschichten und formale Zeitstruktu-ren', in Reinhard Koselleck and Wolf-Dieter Stempel (eds) *Geschichte – Ereignis und Erzählung*. Munich: Fink, 1973, pp. 211–22.

Koselleck, Reinhard. 'Sprachwandel und Ereignisgeschichte', *Merkur* 486 (8/1989), pp. 657–73.

Kröhle, Birgit. *Geschichte und Geschichten. Die literarische Verarbeitung von Auschwitz-Erlebnissen*. Bad Honnef: Bock und Herchen, 1989.

Kronsbein, Joachim. *Autobiographisches Erzählen. Die narrativen Strukturen der Autobiographie*. Munich: Minerva-Publikation, 1984.

Kuhn, Annette and Rothe, Valentine. *Frauen im deutschen Faschismus*, vol. 1, *Frauenpolitik im NS-Staat. Eine Quellensammlung mit fachwissenschaft-lichen und fachdidaktischen Kommentaren*. Düsseldorf: Pädagogischer Verlag Schwann, 1982.

Kuhn, Gudrun. '*Ein philosophisch-musikalisch geschulter Sänger.' Musikästhe-*

tische Überlegungen zur Prosa Thomas Bernhards. Würzburg: Königshausen und Neumann, 1996.

Kuhn, Hermann. *Bruch mit dem Kommunismus. Über autobiographische Schriften von Ex-Kommunisten im geteilten Deutschland*. Münster: Westphälisches Dampfboot, 1990.

Das kulturelle Leben im KL Auschwitz. Informationsbulletin. Comité International d'Auschwitz, 2 (167). Warsaw: February 1975.

Kwiet, Konrad and Eschwege, Helmut. *Selbstbehauptung und Widerstand. Deutsche Juden im Kampf um Existenz und Menschenwürde 1933–1945*. Hamburg: Christians, 1984.

Die Lage der Juden in Deutschland 1933. Das Schwarzbuch – Tatsachen und Dokumente, ed. Comité des Délégations Juives (Paris 1934). Frankfurt/ Berlin: Ullstein, 1983.

Lämmert, Eberhard. *Bauformen des Erzählens*. Stuttgart: Metzlersche Verlagsbuchhandlung, 1983.

Lämmert, Eberhard. ' "Geschichte ist ein Entwurf." Die neue Glaubwürdigkeit des Erzählens in der Geschichtsschreibung und im Roman', *The German Quarterly*, 1/63 (1990), pp. 5–18.

Lang, Berel (ed.). *Writing and the Holocaust*. New York/London: Holmes and Meier, 1988.

Lang, Jochen von (ed.). *Das Eichmann-Protokoll. Tonbandaufzeichnungen der Israelischen Verhöre*, with an afterword by Avner W. Less. Berlin: Severin und Siedler, 1982.

Langbein, Hermann. *Menschen in Auschwitz*. Frankfurt/Main: Ullstein, 1980 (cited in text as 1980a).

Langbein, Hermann. *. . . nicht wie Schafe zur Schlachtbank. Widerstand in den nationalsozialistischen Konzentrationslagern 1938–1945*. Frankfurt/Main: Fischer 1980 (cited in text as 1980b); *Against All Hope: Resistance in the Nazi Concentration Camps 1938–1945*. London: Constable, 1994.

Langen, August. 'Zur Lichtsymbolik der deutschen Romantik', in Hugo Kuhn and Kurt Schier (eds) *Märchen, Mythos, Dichtung. Festschrift zum 90. Geburtstag Friedrich von der Leyens am 19. August 1963*. Munich: Beck, 1963, pp. 447–85.

Langer, Lawrence. *The Holocaust and the Literary Imagination*. New Haven: Yale University Press, 1975.

Langer, Lawrence. *The Age of Atrocity: Death in Modern Literature*. Boston: Beacon Press, 1978.

Langer, Lawrence. *Versions of Survival: The Holocaust and the Human Spirit*. Albany, NY: State University of New York Press, 1982.

Langer, Lawrence. *Holocaust Testimonies: The Ruins of Memory*. New Haven: Yale University Press, 1991.

Lanzmann, Claude. *Shoah: An Oral History of the Holocaust. The Complete*

Text of the Film, with a foreword by Simone de Beauvoir. New York: Pantheon Books, 1985.

Lanzmann, Claude. 'Shoah as counter-myth', *The Jewish Quarterly* 33/1 (121) 1996, pp. 11–12.

Lappin, Elena. 'The man with two heads', *Granta*, 66 Summer 1999, pp. 7–65.

Laqueur, Walter. *Was niemand wissen wollte. Die Unterdrückung der Nachrichten über Hitlers 'Endlösung'*. Frankfurt/Berlin/Vienna: Ullstein, 1982; *The Terrible Secret: An Investigation into the Suppression of Information about Hitler's 'Final Solution'*. London: Weidenfeld & Nicolson, 1980.

Leibbrand, Robert. *Buchenwald. Lieber sterben als verraten. Zur Geschichte der deutschen Widerstandsbewegung*, ed. by Centrale Sanitaire Suisse in cooperation with the Freies Deutschland movement in Switzerland, with a preface by Wolfgang Langhoff. October 1945.

Leiser, Erwin. *Leben nach dem Überleben. Dem Holocaust entronnen – Begegnungen und Schicksale*. Königstein, Ts.: Athenäum, 1982.

Lejeune, Philippe. *Le pacte autobiographique*. Paris: Éditions du Seuil, 1975.

Lenz, Siegfried. 'Dankrede zur Verleihung des Literaturpreises der Heinz-Galiski-Stiftung am 16.4.1989 in Berlin', *Die Zeit* 19, 5 May 1989.

Levi, Primo. *The Drowned and the Saved*. London: Sphere Books, 1989.

Lifton, Robert Jay and Olson, Eric. *Living and Dying*. New York/Washington: Praeger, 1974.

Lixi-Purcell, Andreas (ed.). *Women of Exile: German-Jewish Autobiographies since 1933*. New York: Greenwood Press, 1988.

Loewy, Ernst. *Literatur unterm Hakenkreuz. Das Dritte Reich und seine Dichtung. Eine Dokumentation*. Frankfurt/Main: Fischer, 1983.

Loewy, Hanno and Schoenberner, Gerhard. *'Unser einziger Weg ist Arbeit.' Das Getto in Lódź 1940–1944. Eine Ausstellung des Jüdischen Museums Frankfurt am Main*. Vienna: Löcker, 1990.

Löffler, Sigrid. ' "Die Grundidee des Marxismus ist falsch." Der spanische Schriftsteller und Politiker Jorge Semprún über den langen Abschied vom Kommunismus, über Buchenwald und die Tücken der Erinnerung' (interview), *Profil* 5, 27 January 1992.

Lorenzer, Alfred. *Sprachzerstörung und Rekonstruktion. Vorarbeiten zu einer Metatheorie der Psychoanalyse*. Frankfurt/Main: Suhrkamp, 1973.

Löwith, Karl. *Gesammelte Abhandlungen. Zur kritik der geschichtlichen Existenz*. Stuttgart: Kohlhammer, 1960.

Lukács, Georg. 'Erzählen oder Beschreiben? Zur Diskussion über Naturalismus und Formalismus', in idem, *Werke*, vol. 4. Neuwied/Berlin: Luchterhand 1971a, pp. 197–242; 'Narrate or describe? A preliminary discussion of naturalism and formalism', in idem, *Writer and Critic and Other Essays*. London: Merlin Press, 1970, pp. 110–48.

Lukács, Georg. *Die Theorie des Romans. Ein geschichtsphilosophischer Versuch über die Formen der großen Epik*. Darmstadt/Neuwied: Luchterhand, 1971b; *The Theory of the Novel. A Historico-Philosophical Essay on the Forms of Great Epic Literature*. London: Merlin Press, 1971.

Lyons, John. *Structural Semantics: An Analysis of Part of the Vocabulary of Plato*. Oxford: Blackwell, 1972.

Macherey, Pierre. *A Theory of Literary Production*. London/New York: Routledge & Kegan Paul, 1978.

Manthey, Jürgen. 'Schwejk kommt ins KZ. Zur Neuausgabe der "Unsentimentalen Reise" des Büchnerpreisträgers Albert Drach', *Die Zeit* 22, 27 March 1988.

Marcuse, Herbert. *Eros and Civilization*. New York: Beacon Press, 1956.

Marcuse, Ludwig. *Mein 20. Jahrhundert. Auf dem Weg zu einer Autobiographie*. Zurich: Diogenes, 1975.

Marks, Erwin. 'Jüdische Bibliotheken in Berlin', *Zentralblatt für Bibliothekswesen* 192/8 (1988), pp. 345–9.

Marquard, Odo. 'Verspätete Moralistik. Bemerkungen zur Unvermeidlichkeit der Geisteswissenschaften', *Kursbuch* 91 (March 1988), pp. 13–18.

Märthesheimer, Peter and Frenzel, Ivo (eds). *Im Kreuzfeuer. Der Fernsehfilm 'Holocaust'. Eine Nation ist betroffen*. Frankfurt/Main: Fischer, 1979.

Maschmann, Melitta. *Fazit. Mein Weg in der Hitler-Jugend*, with an afterword by Helga Grebing. Stuttgart: DVA, 1963 (1981).

Mattenklott, Gundl. 'Literatur von unten – die andere Kultur', in Klaus Briegleb and Sigrid Weigel (eds) *Gegenwartsliteratur seit 1968*. Munich/Vienna: Hanser, 1992.

Matussek, Paul and Grigat, Rolf *et al.* *Die Konzentrationslagerhaft und ihre Folgen*. Berlin/New York: Springer, 1971.

Maurer, Karl. 'Für einen neuen Fiktionsbegriff. Betrachtungen zu den historischen Voraussetzungen der Verwendung lebensweltlicher Bauformen in modernen Erzähltexten', in *Erzählforschung*, Symposium ed. by Eberhard Lämmert. Stuttgart: Metzler, 1982, pp. 527–51.

Mausbach, Hans and Mausbach-Bromberger, Barbara. *Feinde des Lebens. NS-Verbrechen an Kindern*. Frankfurt/Main: Röderberg, 1979.

Mayer, Hans. 'Gedenkworte für Jean Améry, Berlin: Akademie der Künste, 29. Oktober 1978', in *Hermannstraße 14, Halbjahresschrift für Literatur*, special issue 1978: quoted in Karl Müller, 'NS-Hinterlassenschaften. Die österreichische Litertaur in ihrer Auseinandersetzung mit 'österreichischen Gewaltgeschichten', in Anton Pelinka and Erika Weinzierl (eds) *Das große Tabu. Österreichs Umgang mit seiner Vergangenheit*. Vienna: Edition S, Verlag der Österreichischen Staatsdruckerei, 1987, p. 91.

Memmi, Albert. *Portrait of a Jew*. London: Eyre & Spottiswoode, 1963.

Michelsen, Peter. *Laurence Sterne und der deutsche Roman des achtzehnten Jahrhunderts*. Habilitationsschrift, University of Göttingen, 1962.

Mintz, Alan. *Hurban: Responses to Catastrophe in Hebrew Literature*. New York: Columbia University Press, 1984.

Mitosz, Czestaw. *The Captive Mind*. Harmondsworth: Penguin, 1985.

Mitscherlich, Alexander and Mielke, Fred (eds). *Medizin ohne Menschlichkeit – Dokumente des Nürnberger Ärzteprozesses*. Frankfurt/Main: Fischer, 1978.

Mitscherlich, Alexander and Mitscherlich, Margarete. *Die Unfähigkeit zu trauern. Grundlagen kollektiven Verhaltens*. Munich: Piper, 1983.

Moll, Michael. *Lyrik in einer entmenschlichten Welt. Interpretationsversuche zu deutschsprachigen Gedichten aus nationalsozialistischen Gefängnissen, Ghettos und KZ's*. Frankfurt/Main: R.G. Fischer, 1988.

Mommsen, Hans. 'Die Realisierung des Utopischen. Die "Endlösung der Judenfrage" im "Dritten Reich"', *Geschichte und Gesellschaft* 9 (1983), pp. 381–420.

Moser, Jonny. *Die Judenverfolgung in Österreich 1938–1945*. Vienna/ Frankfurt/Zurich: Europa Verlag, 1966.

Mosler, Peter (ed.). *Schreiben nach Auschwitz*. Cologne: Bund, 1989.

Mozdzan, Jan J. *Der Postverkehr mit Konzentrations- und Gefangenenlagern im II. Weltkrieg. Ein Beitrag zur Lagergeschichte. Überarbeitete und aktualisierte Fassung des Vortrags auf der Tagung der Zeitgeschichtlichen Forschungsstelle Ingolstadt am 20. bis 21. November 1981*. Ingolstadt, 1982 (typed).

Müller-Münch, Ingrid. *Die Frauen von Majdanek. Vom zerstörten Leben der Opfer und der Mörderinnen*. Reinbeck/Hamburg: Rowohlt, 1983.

Mulvey, Laura. 'Visual pleasure and narrative cinema', in *Visual and Other Pleasures*. London: Macmillan, 1989.

Muschg, Adolf. *Literatur als Therapie? Ein Exkurs über das Heilsame und das Unheilbare. Frankfurter Vorlesungen*. Frankfurt/Main: Suhrkamp, 1981.

Neumann, Bernd. *Identität und Rollenzwang: Zur Theorie der Autobiographie*. Frankfurt/Main: Athenäum, 1970.

Niederland, William G. *Folgen der Verfolgung. Das Überlebenden-Syndrom. Seelenmord*. Frankfurt/Main: Suhrkamp, 1980.

Niemeyer, Doris. *Die intime Frau. Das Frauentagebuch – eine Überlebens- und Widerstandsform*. Frankfurt/Main: Materialis, 1986.

Nieraad, Jürgen. *'Bildgesegnet und Bildverflucht'. Forschungen zur sprachlichen Metaphorik*. Darmstadt: Wissenschaftliche Buchgesellschaft, 1977.

Olney, James. *Metaphors of Self: The Meaning of Autobiography*. Princeton, NJ: Princeton University Press, 1972.

Oschlies, Wolf. ' "Lagerszpracha". Soziolinguistische Bemerkungen zu KZ-Sprachkonventionen', *Muttersprache* 96 (1986), pp. 98–109.

Osterland, Martin. 'Lebensgeschichtliche Erfahrung und gesellschaftliches Bewußtsein', *Soziale Welt* 24 (1973), pp. 409–17.

Österreicher im Exil 1934 bis 1945. Protokolle des Internationalen Symposiums zur Erforschung des Österreichischen Exils von 1934 bis 1945, ed. by Dokumentationsarchiv des österreichischen Widerstands and Dokumentationsstelle für neuere österreichische Literatur. Vienna: ÖBV, 1977.

Ott, Karl August. 'Die wissenschaftlichen Ursprünge des Futurismus und Surrealismus', *Poetica* 2/3 (1968), pp. 371–98.

Otto, Stephan. 'Zum Desiderat einer Kritik der historischen Vernunft und zur Theorie der Autobiographie', *Studia Humanitatis. Ernesto Grassi zum 70. Geburtstag*, ed. Eginhard Hora and Eckehard Kessler. Munich: Fink, 1973, pp. 221–35.

Paepcke, Lotte. 'Sprache und Emigration', *Frankfurter Hefte* 18 (1963), pp. 185–92.

Parow, Eduard. *Die Dialektik des symbolischen Austauschs. Versuch einer kritischen Interaktionstheorie*. Frankfurt/Main: EVA, 1973.

Parsons, Talcott. *Social Structure and Personality*. New York: Free Press, 1964.

Pascal, Roy. *Design and Truth in Autobiography*. London: Routledge & Kegan Paul, 1960.

Patsch, Sylvia. *Österreichische Schriftsteller im Exil in Großbritannien. Ein Kapitel vergessener österreichischer Literatur. Romane, Autobiographie, Tatsachenberichte auf englisch und deutsch*. Vienna/Munich: Brandstätter, 1985.

Patzig, Günther. 'Die Sprache philosophisch befragt', *Die Deutsche Sprache im 20. Jahrhundert*. Göttingen: Vandenhoeck und Ruprecht, 1966, pp. 9–28.

Paucker, Arnold (ed.). *Die Juden im Nationalsozialistischen Deutschland: The Jews in Nazi Germany 1933–1945*. Tübingen: Mohr, 1986.

Paulsen, Wolfgang (ed.) *Das Nachleben der Romantik in der modernen deutschen Literatur. Die Vorträge des zweiten Kolloquiums in Amherst/Mass.* Heidelberg: Stiehm, 1969.

Peitsch, Helmut. *'Deutschlands Gedächtnis an seine dunkelste Zeit.' Zur Funktion der Autobiographik in den Westzonen Deutschlands und den Westsektoren von Berlin 1945 bis 1949*. Berlin: Edition Sigma Bohn, 1990.

Petersen, Jürgen H. *Erzählsysteme. Eine Poetik epischer Texte*. Stuttgart/Weimar: Metzler, 1993.

Pfeiffer, K. Ludwig. 'Apocalypse: it's now or never – Wie und zu welchem Ende geht die Welt so oft unter?', *Sprache im technischen Zeitalter* 81–84 (1982), pp. 181–96.

Picard, Hans Rudolf. *Autobiographie im zeitgenössischen Frankreich. Existentielle Reflexion und literarische Gestaltung*. Munich: Fink, 1978.

Pingel, Falk. *Häftlinge unter SS-Herrschaft. Widerstand, Selbstbehauptung und*

Vernichtung im Konzentrationslager. Hamburg: Hoffmann und Campe, 1978.

Plessen, Elisabeth. *Fakten und Erfindungen. Zeitgenössische Epik im Grenzbereich von* fiction *und* nonfiction. Frankfurt/Berlin/Vienna: Ullstein, 1981.

Poliakov, Léon, Delacampagne, Christian *et al. Über den Rassismus. Sechzehn Kapitel zur Anatomie, Geschichte und Deutung des Rassismus.* Frankfurt/Berlin: Ullstein, 1984.

Pollack, Martin. *Nach Galizien. Von Chassiden, Huzulen, Polen und Ruthenen. Eine imaginierte Reise durch die verschwundene Welt Ostgaliziens und der Bukowina.* Vienna: Edition Christian Brandstätter, 1984.

Possin, Hans-Joachim. *Reisen und Literatur. Das Thema des Reisens in der englischen Literatur des 18. Jahrhunderts.* Tübingen: Niemeyer, 1972.

Preisendanz, Wolfgang. 'Zum Vorrang des Komischen bei der Darstellung von Geschichtserfahrung in deutschen Romanen unserer Zeit', in Wolfgang Preisendanz and Rainer Warning (eds) *Das Komische.* Munich: Fink, 1976, pp. 153–64.

Raddatz, Fritz. ' "Brecht konnte mich nicht riechen." Ein ZEIT-Gespräch mit Günther Anders', *Die Zeit* 13, 22 March 1985.

Raddatz, Fritz. 'Das letzte Abenteuer. Ein ZEIT-Gespräch mit dem spanischen Schrifsteller und Kulturminister Jorge Semprún', *Die Zeit* 48, 24 November, 1989.

Radisch, Iris. 'Hiob von Ungarn', *Die Zeit* 13, 21 March 1997.

Reich-Ranicki, Marcel. *Deutsche Literatur in West und Ost. Prosa seit 1945.* Munich: Piper, 1966.

Reich-Ranicki, Marcel. 'Schrecklich ist die Verführung zum Roman', *Frankfurter Allgemeine Zeitung,* 1 June 1974.

Reich-Ranicki, Marcel. *Ohne Rabatt. Über Literatur aus der DDR.* Stuttgart: DVA, 1991.

Reißland, Eva. 'Bruno Apitz', in Autorenkollektiv, *Literatur der Deutschen Demokratischen Republik. Einzeldarstellungen.* vol. 1. Berlin: Volk und Wissen, 1976.

Renoldner, Klemens. ' "Ich sehe das so, nach all dem, was geschehen ist." Aus einem Gespräch mit Fred Wander', *SALZ* 11/42 (1985), pp. 5–6.

Renoldner, Klemens. 'Spät heim nach Wien. Der Schriftsteller Fred Wander wurde siebzig', *Die Presse,* 10–11 January 1987.

Richter, Kornelia. 'Bibliotheksarbeit im Ghetto Theresienstadt', *Zentralblatt für Bibliothekswesen* 102/3 (1988), pp. 97–103.

Riepl, Heidi and Stürzl, Isabelle. ' "Protokolle gegen sich selbst?" Interview mit Albert Drach', *SALZ* 16/64 (1991), pp. 36–9.

Riesman, David. *The Lonely Crowd: A Study of Changing American Characters.* New Haven: Yale University Press, 1958.

Robinson, Jacob. *The Holocaust and After. Sources and Literature in English.*

Yad Vashem Martyrs' and Heroes' Memorial Authority (Jerusalem)/ YIVO Institute for Jewish Research (New York) Joint Documentary Projects Bibliographical Series 12. Jerusalem: Israel University Press, 1973.

Rohr, Gesa. 'Die Rezeption der Exilliteratur nach 1945 in Deutschland', *Sprache in Wissenschaft und Unterricht* 1990, pp. 16–28.

Rosenfeld, Alvin H. *A Double Dying: Reflections on Holocaust Literature.* Bloomington/London: Indiana University Press, 1980.

Rosenfeld, Alvin H. and Greenberg, Irving (eds). *Confronting the Holocaust. The Impact of Elie Wiesel.* Bloomington/London: Indiana University Press, 1978.

Rosh, Lea and Jäckel, Eberhard. *'Der Tod ist ein Meister aus Deutschland.' Deportation und Ermordung der Juden. Kollaboration und Verweigerung in Europa.* Hamburg: Hoffmann und Campe, 1990.

Roskies, David G. *Against the Apocalypse: Responses to Catastrophe in Modern Jewish Culture.* Cambridge, MA: Harvard University Press, 1984.

Rossbacher, Karlheinz. 'Verfahrensweisen und Techniken im Gedicht', in Walter Weiss *et al. Gegenwartsliteratur. Zugänge zu ihrem Verständnis.* Stuttgart/Berlin/Cologne/Mainz: Kohlhammer, 1977, pp. 35–68.

Rossbacher, Karlheinz. *Heimatkunstbewegung und Heimatroman. Zu einer Literatursoziologie der Jahrhundertwende.* Stuttgart: Klett, 1975.

Rubenstein, Richard L. *After Auschwitz: Radical Theology and Contemporary Judaism.* New York: Collier/Macmillan, 1966.

Sack, John. *An Eye for an Eye.* New York: Basic Books, 1993.

Sahl, Hans. *'Und doch … '* Essays und Kritiken aus zwei Kontinenten, ed. Kalus Blanc. Frankfurt/Main: Luchterhand, 1991.

Sartre, Jean-Paul. *Anti-Semite and Jew.* New York: Schocken Books, 1948.

Saße, Günter. 'Faktizität und Fiktionalität. Literaturtheoretische Überlegungen am Beispiel des Dokumentartheaters', *Wirkendes Wort* 36 (I/1986), pp. 15–26.

Schlösser, Hermann. 'Subjektivität und Autobiographie', in Klaus Briegleb and Sigrid Weigel (eds) *Gegenwartsliteratur seit 1968.* Munich/Vienna: Hanser, 1992, pp. 404–23.

Schlüter, Hermann. *Grundkurs der Rhetorik.* Munich: dtv, 1974.

Schmidt, Siegfried J. *Sprache und Denken als sprachphilosophisches Problem von Locke bis Wittgenstein.* The Hague: Martinus Nijhoff, 1968.

Schnabel, Ernst. *Anne Frank. Spur eines Kindes.* Frankfurt/Main: Fischer, 1958 (1985).

Schnabel, Reimund. *Macht ohne Moral. Eine Dokumentation über die SS.* Frankfurt/Main: Röderberg, 1957.

Schneider, Wolfgang. *Kunst hinter Stacheldraht. Ein Beitrag zur Geschichte des antifaschistischen Widerstandskampfes.* Leipzig: VEB Seemann Verlag, 1976.

Schneider, Wolfgang (ed.). *Faschismus als soziale Bewegung. Deutschland und Italien im Vergleich.* Göttingen: Vandenhoeck und Ruprecht, 1983.

Scholem, Gershom. *Main Trends in Jewish Mysticism.* New York: Schocken Books, 1961.

Schulte-Sasse, Jochen. *Literarische Wertung.* Stuttgart: Metzlersche Verlagsbuchhandlung, 1976.

Schulte-Sasse, Jochen and Werner, Renate. *Einführung in die Literaturwissenschaft.* Munich: Fink, 1977 (1990).

Schultz, Jürgen (ed.). *Mein Judentum.* Stuttgart: Kreuz-Verlag, 1978.

Schultz-Gerstein, Christian. 'Améry: "Mein Tod soll meine Sache sein." ', interview, *Der Spiegel*, 30 October 1978.

Schwaberg, Günther. *Der Juwelier von Majdanek. Geschichte eines Konzentrationslagers.* Hamburg: Gruner + Jahr, 1981.

Schwaiger, Brigitte. *Eva Deutsch. Die Galizianerin.* Vienna/Hamburg: Zsolnay, 1982.

Schwarz-Gardos, Alice (ed.). *Heimat ist anderswo. Deutsche Schriftsteller in Israel. Erzählungen und Gedichte.* Freiburg/Br.: Herder, 1983.

Sebald, W.G. 'Überlebende als schreibende Subjekte. Jean Améry und Primo Levi. Ein Gedenken', *Frankfurter Rundschau*, 28 January 1989.

Seela, Torsten. 'Entstehung und Entwicklung von Büchereien in Konzentrationslagern', *Zentralblatt für Bibliothekswesen* 102/8 (1988), pp. 337–45 (cited in text as 1988a).

Seela, Torsten. 'Der Katalog der Häftlings-Bücherei des KZ Buchenwald', *Zentralblatt für Bibliothekswesen* 102/3 (1988), pp. 104–7 (cited in text as 1988b).

Seela, Torsten. *Bücher und Bibliotheken in nationalsozialistischen Konzentrationslagern. Das gedruckte Wort im antifaschistischen Widerstand der Häftlinge.* Munich: Saur, 1992.

Seghers, Anna. *Das siebte Kreuz. Roman.* Darmstadt/Neuwied: Luchterhand, 1962 (1988); *The Seventh Cross.* London: Hamish Hamilton, 1943.

Seidel, Sonja. *Kultur und Kunst im antifaschistischen Widerstand im Konzentrationslager Buchenwald.* Weimar-Buchenwald, 1983.

Seidman-Bilik, Dorothy. *Immigrant Survivors: Post-Holocaust Consciousness in Recent Jewish-American Fiction.* Middletown: Wesleyan University Press, 1981.

Serke, Jürgen. *Böhmische Dörfer. Wanderungen durch eine verlassene literarische Landschaft.* Vienna/Hamburg: Zsolnay, 1987.

Sève, Lucien. *Marxism and the Theory of Human Personality.* London: Lawrence & Wishart, 1975.

Seyfert, Michael. *Im Niemandsland. Deutsche Exilliteratur in britischer Internierung. Ein unbekanntes Kapitel der Kulturgeschichte des Zweiten Weltkriegs.* Berlin: Das Arsenal, 1984.

Shaked, Gershon. *Die Macht der Identität. Essays über jüdische Schriftsteller.* Königstein/Ts.: Athenäum Jüdischer Verlag, 1986.

Sherwin, Byron L. and Ament, Susan G. (eds). *Encountering the Holocaust. An Interdisciplinary Survey.* Chicago: Impact Press, 1979.

Shklovsky, Victor. 'Art as Technique', in *Russian Formalist Criticism: Four Essays*, trans. and with an introduction by Lee T. Lemon and Marion J. Reis. Lincoln: University of Nebraska Press, 1965.

Silbermann, Alphons. *Der ungeliebte Jude. Zur Soziologie des Antisemitismus.* Zurich: Edition Interform, 1981.

Silbermann, Alphons. *Sind wir Antisemiten? Ausmaß und Wirkung eines sozialen Vorurteils in der Bundesrepublik Deutschland.* Cologne: Wissenschaft und Politik, 1982.

Silbermann, Alphons. *Was ist jüdischer Geist: Zur Identität der Juden.* Zurich: Edition Interform, 1984.

Simon, Sam. *Handbook of the Mail in the Concentration Camp 1933–1945 and Related Material: A Postal History.* New York: Port Printed Products Corp., 1973.

Skreb, Zdenko. 'Zur Theorie der Antithese als Stilfigur', *Sprache im Technischen Zeitalter* 25 (1968), pp. 49–59.

Sloterdijk, Peter. *Literatur und Lebenserfahrung. Autobiographien der 20er Jahre.* Munich: Hanser, 1978.

Sloterdijk, Peter. *Euro-Taoismus.* Frankfurt/Main: Suhrkamp, 1987.

Sloterdijk, Peter. *Zur Welt kommen – Zur Sprache kommen. Frankfurter Vorlesungen.* Frankfurt/Main: Suhrkamp, 1988.

Sofsky, Wolfgang. *Die Ordnung des Terrors: Das Konzentrationslager.* Frankfurt/Main: S. Fischer, 1993; *The Order of Terror: The Concentration Camp.* Princeton, NJ: Princeton University Press, 1997.

Sokoloff, Naomi B. *Imagining the Child in Modern Jewish Fiction.* Baltimore and London, 1992.

Sontag, Susan. *Illness as Metaphor.* New York: Farrar, Straus & Giroux, 1978.

Sperber, Manès. *Churban oder Die unfaßbare Gewißheit. Essays.* Vienna: Europa Verlag, 1979 (1983).

Sperber, Manès. *Ein politisches Leben. Gespräche mit Leonhard Reinisch.* Stuttgart: DVA, 1984.

Sperber, Manès. 'Des Autobiographen verlorene Zeit', in idem, *Geteilte Einsamkeit. Der Autor und sein Leser.* Vienna/Munich/Zurich: Europa Verlag, 1985, pp. 57–64.

Spiel, Hilde. 'Das verlorene Werkzeug. Schriftsteller in zwei Sprachen', *Literatur und Kritik* VIII (1973), pp. 549–52.

Staiger, Emil. *Grundbegriffe der Politik.* Zurich: Artemis, 1983.

Stanzel, Franz. 'Die Erzählsituation und das epische Präteritum', in Franz Stanzel, 'Die typischen Erzählsituationen im Roman. Dargestellt an *Tom*

Jones, Moby Dick, The Ambassadors, Ulysses u.a.', *Wiener Beiträge zur englischen Philologie*, LXIII (1955), pp. 122–37; quoted from reprint in Volker Klotz (ed.) *Zur Poetik des Romans*. Darmstadt: Wissenschaftliche Büchergesellschaft, 1965, pp. 303–18.

Stanzel, Franz. 'Episches Präteritum, Erlebte Rede, Historisches Präsens', *Deutsche Vierteljahrschrift für Literaturwissenschaft und Geisteswissenschaft* 33 (1959), pp. 1–12; quoted from reprint in Volker Klotz (ed.) *Zur Poetik des Romans*. Darmstadt: Wissenschaftliche Büchergesellschaft, 1965, pp. 319–38.

Stanzel, Franz. *Narrative Situations in the Novel: Tom Jones, Moby Dick, The Ambassadors, Ulysses*. Bloomington: Indiana University Press, 1971.

Stanzel, Franz. *Typische Formen des Romans*. Göttingen; Vandenhoeck und Ruprecht, 1981.

Stanzel, Franz. *Theorie des Erzählens*. Göttingen: Vandenhoeck und Ruprecht, 1985; *A Theory of Narrative*, Cambridge: Cambridge University Press, 1984.

Stark, Gary D. 'Vom Nutzen und Nachteil der Literatur für die Geschichtswissenschaft. A Historian's View', *The German Quarterly* 63/1 (1990), pp. 19–31.

Steffen, Hans (ed.). *Die deutsche Romantik. Poetik, Formen, Motive*. Göttingen; Vandenhoeck und Ruprecht, 1967.

Steiner, George. *Language and Silence: Essays 1958–1966*. London: Faber & Faber, 1967.

Steiner, George. *In Bluebeard's Castle: Some Notes Towards the Redefinition of Culture*. London: Faber & Faber, 1971.

Steiner, George. 'Das lange Leben der Metaphorik. Ein Versuch über die "Shoah" ', *Akzente* 34/3 (1987), pp. 194–213.

Steinitz, Lucy and Szonyi, David (eds). *Living after the Holocaust: Reflections by the Post-War Generation in America*. New York: Bloch Publishing Company, 1975.

Stempel, Wolf-Dieter. 'Gibt es Textsorten?', in Elisabeth Gühlich and Wolfgang Raible (eds) *Textsorten. Differenzierungskriterien aus linguistischer Sicht*. Frankfurt/Main: Athenäum, 1972, pp. 172–83.

Stempel, Wolf-Dieter. 'Erzählung, Beschreibung und der historische Diskurs', in Reinhard Koselleck and Wolf-Dieter Stempel (eds) *Geschichte – Ereignis und Erzählung*. Munich: Fink, 1973, pp. 325–46.

Stempel, Wolf-Dieter. 'Ironie als Sprechhandlung', in Wolfgang Preisendanz and Rainer Warning (eds) *Das Komische*. Munich: Fink, 1976, pp. 205–36.

Stern, J.P. *Hitler, the Führer and the People*. London: Collins, 1975.

Sterne, Lawrence. *A Sentimental Journey through France and Italy by Mr. Yorick*, ed. and introd. by Jan Jack. London: Oxford University Press, 1968.

Stierle, Karlheinz. *Text als Handlung*. Munich: Fink, 1975.

Stoffer-Heibel, Cornelia. *Metaphernstudien. Versuch einer Typologie der Text- und Themafunktion der Metaphorik in der Lyrik Ingeborg Bachmanns, Peter Huchels und Hans Magnus Enzensbergers*. Stuttgart: Heinz, 1981.

Strauss, Herbert A. and Hoffmann, Christian (eds). *Juden und Judentum in der Literatur*. Munich: Deutscher Taschenbuch Verlag, 1985.

The Study of Judaism: Bibliographical Essays, New York: Anti-Defamation League of B'nai B'rith, 1972.

Subiotto, Arrigo. 'Dante and the Holocaust: the cases of Primo Levi and Peter Weiss', *New Comparison* 11 (Spring 1991), pp. 70–89.

Szeintuch, Yechiel. 'Einführung in die Forschung zur jiddischen und hebräischen Literatur in Posen und Litauen zur Zeit der nationalsozialistischen Herrschaft und das jüdische Verhalten im Holocaust', in *Beter und Rebellen. Aus 1000 Jahren Judentum in Polen*. Frankfurt/Main, 1983, pp. 329–54.

Szeintuch, Yechiel. 'The corpus of Yiddish and Hebrew literature from ghettos and concentration camps and its relevance for Holocaust studies', *Studies in Yiddish Literature and Folklore. Research Projects of the Institute of Jewish Studies*. Jerusalem: Hebrew University of Jerusalem 1986, pp. 186–207.

Theweleit, Klaus. *Männerphantasien*, vol. 1, *Frauen, Fluten, Körper, Geschichte*. Reinbeck: Rowohlt, 1980.

Thieberger, Frederick. *The Great Rabbi Loew of Prague: His Life and Work and the Legend of the Golem. With Extracts from his Writings and a Collection of the Old Legends*. London: Horovitz Publishing Company, 1955.

Thuswaldner, Anton. 'Nelly Sachs', in *Kritisches Lexikon der deutschsprachigen Gegegenwartsliteratur*, ed. Heinz Ludwig Arnold. Munich: edition text + kritik, n.d.

Timm, Friedrich. 'Zu den Fragen der antifaschistischen Literatur' (1937), in Heinz Ludwig Arnold (ed.) *Die Literatur im Exil 1933–1945*, vol. 1, *Dokumente*. Frankfurt/Main: Fischer Athenäum, 1974, pp. 148–56.

Timms, Edward. *Karl Kraus: Apocalyptic Satirist. Culture and Catastrophe in Habsburg Vienna*. New Haven/London: Yale University Press, 1986.

Todorov, Tzvetan. *Angesichts des Äußersten*. Munich: Fink, 1993.

Trampe, Wolfgang. 'Der siebente Brunnen', interview, *Sonntag*, 16 August 1971.

Ueding, Gert. *Rhetorik des Schreibens. Eine Einführung*. Frankfurt/Main: Athenäum, 1991.

Vogl, Joseph. *Ort der Gewalt. Kafkas literarische Ethik*. Munich: Fink, 1990.

Vogt, Jochen. 'Bauelemente erzählter Texte', in Heinz Ludwig Arnold and Volker Sinemus (eds) *Grundzüge der Literatur- und Sprachwissenschaft*, vol. 1, *Literaturwissenschaft*. Munich: Deutscher Taschenbuch Verlag, 1983, pp. 227–42.

Vondung, Klaus (ed.). *Kriegserlebnisse. Der Erste Weltkrieg in der literarischen Gestaltung und symbolischen Deutung der Nationen*. Göttingen: Vandenhoeck und Ruprecht, 1980a.

Vondung, Klaus. 'Propaganda oder Sinndeutung?', in idem, (ed.) *Kriegserlebnisse. Der Erste Weltkrieg in der literarischen Gestaltung und symbolischen Deutung der Nationen*. Göttingen: Vandenhoeck und Ruprecht, 1980b, pp. 11–40.

Vordtriede, Werner. 'Vorläufige Gedanken zu einer Typologie der Exilliteratur', *Akzente* 15 (1968), pp. 556–75.

Walser, Martin. 'Unser Auschwitz', in idem, *Heimatkunde. Aufsätze und Reden*. Frankfurt/Main: Suhrkamp, 1968, pp. 7–23.

Wander, Fred. 'Brief an Primo Levi', *Sammlung 5. Jahrbuch für antifaschistische Literatur und Kunst*. Frankfurt/Main: Röderberg, 1982, pp. 21–7.

Weber, Max. *Soziologische Grundbegriffe*. Tübingen: Mohr, 1984; *Basic Concepts in Sociology*. New York: The Citadel Press, 1964.

Wehnert, Jürgen. ' . . . *und ich das einzige lebende Wesen in dieser Wildnis*. Zur Innovation des Ich-Helden bei Karl May', in *Karl May. Text + Kritik Sonderband*, ed. Heinz Ludwig Arnold. Munich: edition Text + Kritik, 1987, pp. 5–38.

Weiler, Eugen. *Die Geistlichen in Dachau*. Mödling, 1971.

Weinreb, Friedrich. *Die Symbolik der Bibelsprache. Einführung in die Struktur des Hebräischen*. Berne: Origo, 1981.

Weinrich, Harald. *Tempus. Besprochene und erzählte Welt*. Stuttgart: Kohlhammer, 1964.

Weinrich, Harald. 'Semantik der Metapher', in Walter Koch (ed.) *Strukturmerkmale der Textanalyse*. Hildesheim/New York: Olms, 1972, pp. 269–83.

Weisgerber, Johann Leo. 'Grundformen sprachlicher Weltgestaltung', *Arbeitsgemeinschaft für Forschung des Landes Nordrhein Westfalen* No. 105. Cologne: Westdeutscher Verlag, 1963, pp. 1–56.

Weiss, Peter. *Die Ermittlung. Oratorium in 11 Gesängen*. Frankfurt/Main: Suhrkamp, 1965 (1986); *The Investigation: Oratorio in 11 Cantos*. London: Boyars, 1966.

Weiss, Peter. *Rapporte*. Frankfurt/Main: Suhrkamp, 1968.

Weiss, Walter. *Thomas Manns Kunst der sprachlichen und thematischen Integration*. Düsseldorf: Pädagogischer Verlag Schwann, 1964.

Weiss, Walter. 'Literatur', in Erika Weinzierl and Kurt Skalnik (eds) *Österreich. Die Zweite Republik*. vol. 2. Graz/Vienna/Cologne: Styria, 1972a, pp. 439–76, 642–7.

Weiss, Walter. 'Zur Thematisierung der Sprache in der Literatur der

Gegenwart', in *Festschrift für Hans Eggers zum 65. Geburtstag*, ed. Herbert Backes. Tübingen: Niemeyer, 1972b, pp. 669–93.

Weiss, Walter. 'Stilistik und Textlinguistik am Beispiel eines Textes von Robert Musil', in Alfred Schöne (ed.) *Kontroversen, alte und neue. Akten des VII. Internationalen Germanisten-Kongresses.* Göttingen, 1985, vol. 3, *Textlinguistik contra Stilistik? – Wortschatz und Wörterbuch – Grammatik oder pragmatische Organisation der Rede?* Tübingen: Niemeyer, 1986, pp. 103–12, 128–9.

Weiss-Laqueur, Renata. *Writing in Defiance: Concentration Camp Diaries in Dutch, French and German 1940–1945.* New York University, 1971 (typed diss.); published in German as Renata Laqueur, *Schreiben im KZ. Tagebücher 1940–1945.* Bremen: Donat, 1991.

Wellek, René. *Concepts of Criticism.* New Haven: Yale University Press, 1975.

Wellek, René and Warren, Austin. *Theory of Literature.* Harmondsworth: Penguin University Books, 1976.

White, Hayden. *Metahistory: The Historical Imagination in Nineteenth-Century Europe.* Baltimore/London: Johns Hopkins University Press, 1973.

White, Hayden. *Tropics of Discourse: Essays in Cultural Criticism.* Baltimore/London: Johns Hopkins University Press, 1978.

White, Hayden. *The Content of the Form: Narrative Discourse and Historical Representation.* Baltimore/London: Johns Hopkins University Press, 1987.

Wiesenthal, Simon. *Recht, nicht Rache. Erinnerungen.* Frankfurt/Berlin: Ullstein, 1988; *Justice not Vengeance.* London: Weidenfeld & Nicolson, 1989.

Wilkomirski, Binjamin. *Bruchstücke*: Suhrkamp, 1995; *Fragments: Memories of a Childhood.* London: Picador, 1996.

Wilpert, Gero von. *Sachwörterbuch der Literatur.* Stuttgart: Kröner, 1969.

Windaus-Walser, Karin. 'Gnade der weiblichen Geburt? Zum Umgang der Frauenforschung mit Nationalsozialismus und Antisemitismus', *Feministische Studien*, ed. Ute Gerhard, Juliane Jacobi-Dittrich *et al.*, No. 6 (11/1988, 1), pp. 102–15.

Winkler, Sebastian. 'Die Pickbücher – Unbekannte Dokumente aus dem Konzentrationslager Dachau', Schondorf 1986 (= typescript, History Faculty) [Dokumentationsarchiv des österreichischen Widerstands 25064].

Winterfeldt, Hans. 'Die Sprache im Konzentrationslager', *Muttersprache* 78 (1968), pp. 126–52.

Wolfberg, Stefan. 'Propaganda und Wirklichkeit. Der Nazi-Propagandafilm *Theresienstadt', Tribune* 30/119 (1991), pp. 43–5.

Young, James E. 'Interpreting literary testimony: a preface to rereading

Holocaust diaries and memoirs', *New Literary History. A Journal of Theory and Interpretation* 18/2 (1987); *Literacy, Popular Culture and Writing of History*, pp. 403–23 (cited in text as 1987a).

Young, James E. 'Modern Jewish culture' (review of David Roskies's *Against the Apocalypse*), *Contemporary Literature* XXVIII/2 (1987), pp. 278–83 (cited in text as 1987b).

Young, James E. *Writing and Rewriting the Holocaust: Narrative and the Consequence of Interpretation*. Bloomington/Indianapolis: Indiana University Press, 1988.

Zijderveld, Anton C. *Humor und Gesellschaft. Eine Soziologie des Humors und des Lachens*. Graz/Vienna/Cologne: Styria, 1976.

Zimmermann, Jörg. 'Ästhetische Erfahrung und die "Sprache der Natur". Zu einem Topos der ästhetischen Diskussion von der Aufklärung bis zur Romantik', in Jörg Zimmermann (ed.), *Sprache und Welterfahrung*. Munich: Fink, 1978.

Zimmermann, Michael. *Verfolgt, vertrieben, vernichtet. Die NS-Vernichtungspolitik gegen Sinti und Roma*. Essen: Klartext Verlag, 1989.

Zirker, Herbert. *George Moore. Realismus und autobiographische Fiktion. Versuch zur Form der Autobiographie*. Cologne/Graz: Böhlau, 1968.

Index of concentration camp authors